# Leni Riefenstahl

# Leni Riefenstahl
## A Life

JÜRGEN TRIMBORN

TRANSLATED FROM THE GERMAN BY EDNA McCOWN

I.B. TAURIS

LONDON · NEW YORK

Published in 2008 by I.B.Tauris & Co Ltd
6 Salem Road, London W2 4BU
175 Fifth Avenue, New York NY 10010
www.ibtauris.com

Published in the United States in 2007 by Faber and Faber, Inc.
Originally published in 2002 by Aufbau-Verlag GmbH, Germany,
as *Riefenstahl: Eine deutsche Karriere*

Copyright © 2002 by Jürgen Trimborn
Translation copyright © 2007 by Edna McCown

ISBN: 978 1 84511 644 6

A full CIP record for this book is available from the British Library

Printed and bound in Great Britain by TJ International, Padstow, Cornwall

# Contents

# PREFACE: APPROACHING A MYTH

LENI RIEFENSTAHL the dancer, executing elaborate moves, an enraptured expression on her face. Leni Riefenstahl the star of mountain films, barefoot and fearless, scaling a vertical summit. Leni Riefenstahl the director, self-confidently issuing orders to an army of cameramen. Leni Riefenstahl the careerist, on a film shoot, laughing, with Adolf Hitler at her side. Leni Riefenstahl the defendant, gesticulating wildly during a court case in the postwar period. Leni Riefenstahl the photographer, camera in hand, a tall Nuba warrior beside her. Leni Riefenstahl the icon, emerging from the Indian Ocean, the oldest deep-sea diver in the world. Leni Riefenstahl, advanced in years, at the opening of a retrospective in her honor in Rome, Tokyo, or Potsdam—the myth.

A number of disparate images push their way to the fore when considering the life of Leni Riefenstahl. The roles she played in her long life were extremely varied, and the images of her in the limelight—as dancer, actress, director, and photographer—contradictory.

Some think of Leni Riefenstahl as a brilliant filmmaker, others as an artist who, through the work she did for Hitler, made a pact with the devil. In the final years of her life she was increasingly perceived as the icon of her own aging vitality, as someone who should be granted the absolution that she and her apologists long had demanded out of respect for her advanced age. She made the headlines once again when in August 2002, in anticipation of her one hundredth birthday, she announced the presentation of a new film, thereby establishing the longest directing career in film history. No other director had ever enjoyed so much admiration and at the same time drawn so much criticism as this woman, whose international popularity remains as constant as ever.

Who was Leni Riefenstahl? The longer I involved myself with this question, the more strongly I became aware of the fact that Riefenstahl herself was the person least capable of contributing an answer to the riddle surrounding her. On the contrary, with the revamped and corrected version of her own story that she had held to consistently as of 1945, she had laid the cornerstone of this riddle, and via protective statements and injunctions did everything possible throughout her life to reinforce its validity. Even if she didn't completely succeed in this, even if critics and skeptics continually appeared on the scene to confront Riefenstahl with the truth, even if documents were presented long ago that contradict her version of things, the image that the artist created of her life and her career still plays an essential role in the discussion of Leni Riefenstahl's place in history. Her self-constructed past, scoured of all unpleasant allegations, recounted again and again across the decades, had long since become reality to her. Even today, Riefenstahl's critics treat as fact many of the myths and legends she created.

But it is not only Riefenstahl's self-portrait that hinders a true understanding of who she was. The rumors and speculation that circulate independently of her own statements, and that mark the emotional discussion of her work and life, also contribute to this. The fact that only a small number of people have actually seen the films she made during the Third Reich, which would galvanize opinions of them, allows Riefenstahl to remain an elusive subject.

Views of Riefenstahl, the last of Hitler's narrow circle to die, remain divided. Conducting a factual and balanced discussion with her was scarcely possible, given the strongly biased arguments about "the Führer's filmmaker" and the "power of her images" that dominated. The only thing that can be agreed upon is that although she is the most controversial director in the history of the cinema, she is also one of the most important film artists of the twentieth century. There exists as yet no final judgment on this, but increasingly Riefenstahl's life is being examined beyond the parameters of those judgments once so quickly arrived at. There is growing interest in finding out more about the person behind the tangled web of preconceived notions, anecdotes, and rumors.

In the beginning, my interest in Leni Riefenstahl was based on my fascination with her extraordinary life and an interest in her films, but also in the woman who made them. The rumors and gossip surrounding her made her even more interesting. Before I began viewing her films, which are difficult to gain access to, I read her memoirs, *Memoiren*. What I liked about her in the beginning was how candidly she admitted her former enthusiasm for Hitler, a rarity among Germans of her generation. That this was but a part of an extensive web of explanations with which she concealed the facts of her life was something I already sensed at that time. The more I occupied myself with Riefenstahl's life and career, the more questions I had for the woman who had created *Triumph des Willens* (*Triumph of the Will*) and *Olympia*.

Over the years I collected as much as possible of what had been published on Leni Riefenstahl and her films—books, articles, essays, and exhibition catalogs from all over the world. The more I read, the clearer it became to me how little actually was known about her. Two questions in particular captivated me and deepened my interest: What is true about the story of her life as she tells it and how different are the revisions she made in order to present a certain image of herself? And why, decades after the Second World War ended, is the German reaction to Leni Riefenstahl still so conflicted?

I soon became aware that the debates over Riefenstahl after 1945 were primarily fueled by German attitudes, by a struggle with a long-suppressed, unresolved past, rather than any difficulty finding a new, objective access to her.

Over the decades, it appears to me, every discussion of Riefenstahl has been limited either to automatically branding her persona non grata or unreflectively celebrating her as a great artist, a brilliant director not to be measured by normal human standards whose work must be considered from a more or less depoliticized standpoint. Both views have little to do with what Riefenstahl really stood for and what her life and work truly amounted to. As any serious approach to the person of Leni Riefenstahl was absent in the passionate discussion surrounding her, I made it my goal to start at zero, as it were, beyond the preconceptions, but also beyond Riefenstahl's own image of herself, and to approach her life as objectively as possible.

In May 1997, a few months before her ninety-fifth birthday, I met

Leni Riefenstahl for a lengthy conversation. At this point I had already spent six years of intensive labor on her life and work and had corresponded with her concerning my plan to write a biography. I knew that Riefenstahl rarely gave interviews and had never supported any book project about herself, and therefore was surprised when she expressed the wish to meet me. The director received me in her villa on Starnberger See, a lake in upper Bavaria, and I encountered a particularly friendly and seriously engaged conversation partner. This was a woman who even at an advanced age still possessed enormous charisma, who was full of plans and talked about her work with infectious enthusiasm without, however, ever losing sight of her own legend or her version of the past. I got the impression, after hours of concentrated talk, that Riefenstahl had long bought into her own myth. Only in brief moments did it seem that she was conscious of the contradictions between her life and her depiction of it, though she never addressed them. We talked about her films, her current projects, her travels, the positive reception of *Memoiren* in America, the retrospectives devoted to her abroad, and the Riefenstahl revival, which was slowly starting up in Europe and in Germany as well.

Surprisingly, it was Riefenstahl herself who repeatedly brought the conversation around to the controversial chapters of her life, to those points when she was attacked after the war ended, the redress of which even in old age appeared to be perhaps the most important thing in life to her. At that point, I hoped that Riefenstahl and I could agree on a possible approach to her life and the background of her extraordinary career. But I soon was to learn otherwise.

In the correspondence and phone calls that followed, it eventually became clear that I could not expect Riefenstahl to contribute to a balanced and objective account. Though she repeatedly stressed that she was interested only in the "whole truth,"[1] it became apparent that she wished to convey her own truth alone, though this truth had long since been refuted in part or, after extensive research, appeared improbable. It is true that I was provided with articles and other writings from Riefenstahl's private archives,[2] items that presented the artist in a positive light, but my hope that she would grant me access to documents that would reveal new aspects of her life and career proved futile.

She attempted to answer critical questions by referring me to

*Memoiren*,[3] "the final and definitive proof of her innocence,"[4] which in reality, however, is worthless as a historical document and can serve a biographer of Riefenstahl only as a guide and comparison.

Over the course of my decade of research on Riefenstahl, I had formed a completely different picture of her, and it became apparent that there was nothing to be gained by further collaboration. Discovering new information would be possible only by being independent of Riefenstahl in every way, by not being influenced by her or allowing her to determine my point of view. Otherwise, the result would be nothing more than hagiography.

But as I had no more access to Riefenstahl's private archives than did other authors and journalists, I had to fall back on other sources for answers to the many questions about her that exist. Unfortunately, in terms of many chapters of her life—her childhood and youth, for example—there is no dependable evidence other than her own statements that could verify her self-portrait. And difficulties have always arisen in the research of Riefenstahl's career during the Third Reich, not least because she discussed her plans and projects with Hitler in private, and therefore, in many cases, no documentation exists against which to evaluate her statements.

The literature on Leni Riefenstahl was, of course, a starting point for my research but seldom a source for answers to the questions that interested me. The nearly incomprehensible number of journalistic and scholarly publications—at this point, the director is the subject of more than one hundred dissertations alone, worldwide—largely quote one another and therefore add little new material to the discussion. There are also a number of books devoted to Riefenstahl's films[5] or to her career, but they rarely take a biographical approach.[6]

A look at the literature confirmed the necessity of reopening Riefenstahl's case. Sources both familiar and as yet unpublished contradict much of Riefenstahl's version of things, which, following rigorous research, calls in part for significant revision. Of course, the myth surrounding Hitler's filmmaker, including the picture that Riefenstahl herself tried to create of her life, is at least as revealing as the established facts, knotted into a ball that has remained untangled until now.

The more intensely I engaged myself with Riefenstahl, the more astonished I was that certain issues, which the director resolutely avoided in *Memoiren*, had never been raised. For instance, of Riefenstahl's anti-Semitism or of the reasons for her sojourn to the Polish front in September 1939. But I also wanted to raise again questions that ostensibly had been answered long ago, such as what her relationship to Hitler and Goebbels, as well as to other Nazi party functionaries, had been.

Until now, Riefenstahl has never been considered primarily a careerist. Until her death on September 8, 2003, she was concerned solely with her artistic obsessions, her fame and recognition, and her control over the public's image of her. But the main thrust of her life and creativity was to create a major career, for which she willingly sacrificed everything and for which, through her pact with Hitler, she ultimately had to pay a high price. And it is precisely here that I found the key to Riefenstahl's character. Through her friendship with Hitler, Leni Riefenstahl made her career, the peaks and valleys, the breaches and contradictions of which are not atypical of many Germans of the twentieth century.

# The Ascent

# 1

## BERLIN IN THE TIME OF THE KAISER

### CHILDHOOD AND YOUTH

WHEN KING WILHELM I OF PRUSSIA was proclaimed German kaiser in 1871, Berlin became a center of political power. With its three million inhabitants, the metropolis on the Spree became an economic, civic, and, in particular, social and cultural hub. At the turn of the century, Berlin possessed an expressly international flair, even if restrictive Wilhelmian policies repeatedly checked modern developments and avant-garde movements. But this had little effect on the fascination that the city held. Visitors, both German and foreign, strolled along the elegant Unter den Linden, past spectacularly ostentatious architecture and tributes in stone to the Hohenzollern rulers. They visited the well-stocked department stores, the opulent opera houses, the magnificent revue palaces, and Max Reinhardt's celebrated theaters, sampling the various worlds that Berlin nurtured in the *Gründerjahre*, the years of expansion in the early 1870s when it basked in the light of its newfound importance.

The policies established in the Berlin of the monarchy, the "fastest-moving city in the world," were to set the course the German Reich was to follow in the years to come. Kaiser Wilhelm II, known for his comic opera costumes and his exaggerated rhetoric, came up with the catchphrase, embraced by the aristocracy as well as the bourgeoisie, that Germany, too, needed a "place in the sun." The quest for colonies that followed, enthusiastically supported by a complacent Reichstag, was to find its premature end in the years of the First World War.

In turn-of-the-century Berlin, the economy flourished. The city was in the grip of a near euphoric period of development, and a large number of ambitious enterprises were established during the building boom. And sharing in the general optimism was Alfred Theodor Paul Riefenstahl, trained as a master fitter.

Born in Berlin on October 30, 1878, as the son of the journeyman locksmith Gustav Hermann Theodor Riefenstahl and his wife, Amalie, Alfred Riefenstahl grew up with two brothers and a sister. He abandoned the artisan milieu of his forefathers to become a salesman and make his way on his own. Shortly after receiving his master's certificate, he took over a prosperous installation business, which he ran with a combination of practical knowledge and commercial farsightedness. His daughter Leni later portrayed him as a large and powerful man with blond hair and blue eyes. Contemporary photographs reveal a well-dressed figure mindful of his appearance, who commanded respect and appeared proud of the social standing he had achieved on his own. Alfred Riefenstahl had a strong character, and insisted on staying in control and exerting his authority. He was full of life, temperamental, and inclined to violent outbursts if anyone stood in his way, whether in business or private. He seldom tolerated argument.

He married Bertha Ida Scherlach, born to German parents in Włocławek, Poland, on October 9, 1880. Her father, Karl Ludwig Ferdinand Scherlach, a carpenter from West Prussia (in *Memoiren*, Riefenstahl promoted him to an "architect"[1]), had found work in neighboring Poland and settled there. Together, he and his East Prussian wife, Ottilie, had eighteen children. Ottilie died giving birth to their eighteenth child, Bertha, and the thirty-eight-year-old widower suddenly found himself alone with his offspring. Shortly after the death of his wife, he married a woman who had been a governess in the Scherlach household and who would bear him three more children in the years that followed.

When Scherlach made the decision to move with his family to Berlin, he was too old to seek new employment. So it was the children, including Bertha, who supported the family. Bertha had completed her training as a seamstress and, as the youngest offspring of a large family well accustomed to working from a young age, quickly found a position in the country's capital. Even with her own earnings she was forced to lead a very modest life, as she had to support her out-of-work father and her young siblings.

When the respectable businessman Alfred Riefenstahl entered her life, her rise in society was assured. But with her wedding she had to bury the secret dream of her youth of becoming an actress. Bertha Scherlach met Alfred Riefenstahl, two years her senior, at a costume ball in 1900. It was not a long courtship; the two quickly realized they would stay together—not least because Bertha soon was expecting her first child. The wedding took place in Berlin on April 5, 1902.

The relationship between Alfred and Bertha Riefenstahl was a difficult one, but typical for the times. On one side was a husband who demanded total authority, and on the other a woman who was not only unprepared but also probably unable to challenge him. The rules of Wilhelmian society dictated that she subordinate herself to her husband's wishes, and the two adjusted to a petit-bourgeois life, in which the young family soon was firmly rooted.

The birth of Bertha Helene Amalie Riefenstahl was recorded at the Berlin Registry Office XIII on August 22, 1902. As was customary at the time, the birth took place at home, in a simple, modest apartment on Prinz-Eugen-Strasse in the working-class quarter of Wedding. From infancy on, she was called "Leni."

Leni Riefenstahl led a protected childhood, free of material cares. The family slowly worked its way up from a petit-bourgeois milieu to the middle class. Alfred Riefenstahl quickly prospered in the heating and ventilation systems firm that he opened on Kurfürstenstrasse, but this prosperity was based more on luck than on business acumen. His business expanded owing to the installation contracts resulting from the city's countless new construction projects and the renovation of older buildings. These increased the family's earnings and guaranteed a certain standard of living.

As he did from his wife, Alfred Riefenstahl expected discipline and absolute obedience from his daughter. He had been raised to rule his family with a firm hand and tolerate no disagreement, and he considered the example set by his father to be the ideal for his own family. He was as uncompromising at home as he was in business, routinely imposing his own habits on his wife and his child, which led to constant conflict. Riefenstahl flew into a rage at the least disturbance of his daily routine and could "stamp like an elephant if the button on his starched collar proved hard to undo."[2]

Leni secretly wished for a gentle, loving father, but when she attempted to break away from his cold and severe control, rebelling against her predetermined role as the obedient daughter, he reacted with outbursts of rage. Nor did he shrink from beating and humiliating his daughter and locking her in the house for the slightest infraction, or from punishing her with a silence that would last for weeks. "Once, when I was caught [stealing apples] and my father found out about it, he gave me a terrible whipping and locked me in a dark room for an entire day. And I suffered his sternness on other occasions as well."[3] The girl suffered from her father's coldness and spent her whole childhood trying to wrest from him some proof of his love, but again and again she encountered only harsh rejection or emotional distance.[4]

And yet her father quickly registered that Leni had inherited his own stubbornness and, as she grew older, was prepared to battle her father's authority. More and more often she made decisions without first asking her father's permission, which she tried to keep secret. For example, she kept from him the fact that she had registered at a gymnastics club and, later, at dancing school. The volatile relationship between father and daughter was always threatening to explode, and the most innocuous event could turn into a contest of wills: "It was often difficult to get along with him. He liked to play chess with me—but I always had to let him win. Once, when I beat him, he became so mad that he forbade me to go to a costume party I was so looking forward to."[5]

As mother and wife, Bertha Riefenstahl often found herself caught between two fronts in the arguments between her daughter and her husband. Though emotionally she usually sided with her daughter, she dared not go against her husband. As a rule, she tried to mediate between them, at the risk of finding herself trapped in the minefield of family quarrels as soon as she took one side or the other.

Nor did the birth in 1905 of a second child, named Heinz—the son Alfred Riefenstahl had so wished for—improve the atmosphere at home. Things relaxed only when the father was out of the house on business or enjoying himself with his friends. "Luckily, my father often went hunting, and only when he was gone could we all finally feel free at home."[6]

Leni, Heinz, and their mother established something resembling a secret society. When Riefenstahl was away, they all were happy to go about their activities without reservation, activities he didn't approve of or simply forbade. Leni quickly developed a very affectionate relationship with her brother, who was three years younger. For the whole of her life she felt closely connected to him, though with his essentially reticent and shy personality he was totally different from his quick-witted and audacious sister.

From the outside, the Riefenstahls epitomized a happy family. No one was privy to the tensions that went on behind the scenes in an effort to appear a promising young middle-class family. A photo from the period shows the two children in their Sunday sailor suits, a symbol at the time not only of pride in the kaiser's navy but also of belonging to "better society."

Alfred Riefenstahl's flourishing businesses required that the family demonstrate a certain standard of living. Leni Riefenstahl's childhood, therefore, was marked by frequent moves and changes of neighborhood, which always called for her to adapt to a new location. The family first moved from Wedding to Hermannplatz in Berlin-Neukölln, then to Yorckstrasse in Schöneberg and on to Wilmersdorf before temporarily settling southeast of the city, in 1921, in Rauchfangswerder in the Brandenburg March.

"IN MY YOUTH I WAS A HAPPY PERSON"

Even before moving to Rauchfangswerder, located on a peninsula of the Zeuthener See, the outdoors played an important role in the Riefenstahl family's life. In portraying her childhood, Leni Riefenstahl always stressed how important nature was to her. The well-to-do family soon bought a small weekend house in a little village that Riefenstahl calls Petz and which presumably is the town of Pätz, located on the Pätzer Vordersee near the small Brandenburg city of Bestensee. Fleeing the hectic pace of big-city life, the Riefenstahls spent nearly every weekend here, an hour by train from Berlin. Leni Riefenstahl, by her own account, grew into a true "child of nature, beneath trees and bushes, with plants and insects, watched over and protected."[7] Being outdoors in nature was essential to her.

The girl who became accustomed to life in the country from an early age welcomed the family's later move to Rauchfangswerder, even though the daily hour-and-a-half trip to Berlin was time-consuming and exhausting. The idyllic country surroundings appeared more important to her than the comforts of the city. The Riefenstahls' property included a large overgrown meadow that ran down to a lake bordered by old weeping willows, the branches of which dipped into the water. The family owned a rowboat and also made outings to the nearby forest and meadows. Their not always simple family life became noticeably more relaxed in this bucolic setting, and, far from his business concerns and the noise of the metropolis, even Alfred Riefenstahl, with his weekday moods and his tendency to angry outbursts, became calmer here. He would lie for hours on the shore of the lake or work in the small garden where the family grew fruits and vegetables for their table.

Leni Riefenstahl tried her whole life to recapture the idyllic experience of nature that she had known as a child. Being outdoors in harmony with nature provided an important and incomparable source of strength. Particularly important to the young girl was the privacy and time for herself she found there. She played with the neighborhood children, of course, climbing trees and organizing foot- and swimming races: "Nothing was too high for me or too steep or too dangerous."[8] But, at least as she presented it in retrospect, she continually withdrew to spend whole hours and days in her own dreamworld. Even in early childhood she needed to withdraw from her playmates as well as from her family from time to time, often to the little wooden hut that her father built for her as a refuge amid the huge sunflowers in the garden. There she could get away from the world and enjoy the leisure time that her parents uncritically granted her: "It was here that I could dream."[9]

Riefenstahl's harmonious transfiguration of her past runs like a thread through all of her versions of her life. Despite the considerable burdens imposed by her hot-tempered, authoritarian father, and though she was a child and youth during the First World War and the revolutionary unrest in Berlin that followed, Riefenstahl's descriptions of this time culminate in a portrait of an Eden removed from the historical moment. No passages in *Memoiren* address material want or the existential fears that were endemic, or one single confrontation with political events. Instead, there is the simple declaration, "In my youth I was a happy person."[10]

In 1908, Leni Riefenstahl was enrolled in school in Berlin-Neukölln. She impressed her teachers as an inquisitive and alert young girl who was very mature for her age. At school she could at least partially satisfy her wide-ranging thirst for knowledge. But her spontaneity and vitality did not always conform to the strict Prussian school system, which insisted on discipline and order. As a student she often was at odds with the curriculum, interrupting her teachers with countless pointed questions that went far beyond the teaching materials and earned her many a bad grade in deportment.

While in school she forged a characteristic that marked her entire life: when something captured her interest, she was not satisfied until she had completely sated her quest for knowledge about the subject. Following elementary school, she attended the Kollmorgen Lyceum, a girls' school from which she successfully graduated. In her favorite subjects, including gymnastics, drawing, and math, she was said to be at the top of her class.

The Germany she had been born into was changing dramatically. In 1914, when she had just turned twelve, the First World War broke out in Europe, the end of which would mark the fall of the German monarchy, followed by a period of political upheaval and the declaration of the Weimar Republic. Soldiers marched out of Berlin to war with smiles on their faces, fully convinced they would be victorious. Political discussion among all levels of society in the German empire heated up; countless patriotic pamphlets were published on the war, and even the country's pulpits generated militant and chauvinistic slogans.

The war was soon to have an enormous effect on everyday life. By 1916, the blockade enforced by the Allies had led to serious food shortages and rationing. Many people went hungry. In the final two winters of the war, schools were no longer heated. And 1917 brought frequent strikes by Berlin's workers, which affected everyone's lives.

The war ended in 1918 in a capitulation that Germans perceived as a humiliating national defeat. The kaiser abdicated and Germany became known as the Weimar Republic. During this period, a bloody civil war was waged in the streets of Berlin; constant protest marches by workers were met with the brutal countermeasures of the government of Friedrich Ebert.

The revolution shook the foundations of German society. The streets and squares of Berlin were filled with huge numbers of uprooted men and women, and the conditions of unrest, palpable everywhere, contributed to people's uncertainty. There were many who exploited this extreme disorientation, aggravating the political discontent. The notion that German troops had been "stabbed in the back," allegedly undefeated in the field but victims of "betrayal on the home front," found an ever greater audience. Inflation, which pushed many Germans of the lower classes to the brink of starvation, increased political instability in the young republic.

Leni Riefenstahl minimally perceived the effects of the unrest, the strikes, and the misery that was becoming more visible everywhere, but she turned away from it, saying it gave her "goose pimples." In *Memoiren* she writes, "The fact that the world war had ended, that we had lost it, that a revolution had taken place, that there was no longer a kaiser and king—all of this was something I experienced as if in a fog. The orbit of my consciousness was a tiny little world."[11]

In her adolescence Riefenstahl concentrated solely on realizing her own goals in the face of her father's opposition and on escaping his dictatorial grip. She discovered new interests, including poetry and painting. But she was shortly to discover a hobby that became her true passion: dance.

In 1918, at sixteen years old, Riefenstahl left the Kollmorgen Lyceum with a General Certificate of Education, Ordinary Level. She wasn't looking forward to her father's plan—first to send his daughter to a school of home economics and then to a boarding school, in order to pull her away from her dreams and back to reality. "The thought of going there was unbearable to me."[12] She instead talked her father into allowing her to attend courses at the State School of Commercial Art on Prinz-Albrecht-Strasse, which led her mother to hope that her daughter would become an important artist.

During her school years she had developed a special enthusiasm for gymnastics and sports. Long before physical training and sports were ideologically exploited in the 1920s (culminating in the Nazis elevating the body hardened by sports into the ideal of the "Aryan individual"), Leni Riefenstahl regularly engaged in athletics, with an enthusiasm she carried into old age. Here, for a change, she encountered no resistance from her sports-happy father, only full support. Alfred Riefenstahl revered F. L. Jahn, the father of gymnastics, a popular figure of the time (though intellectuals made fun of him). Leni joined the gymnastics club at school and discovered her great love of apparatus gymnastics. She never showed fear or allowed herself to be discouraged when she lost. Even the injuries she suffered from an unsuccessful dive from a fifteen-foot board or a fall from the rings, which resulted in a concussion, didn't discourage her from devoting herself to sports with ever greater enthusiasm. And there were always new opportunities for physical activity, including roller skating and ice skating.

Another major interest of Riefenstahl's youth was theater and, of course, film. Though it was important to her to be able to escape to the dreamworld where she felt special, she had always craved public recognition. As a child she had spent hours after school in Tiergarten, "where I drew the public with my roller-skating abilities, until the police showed up and I had to run off."[13] Once, while attending a private concert given by the pianist Ferruccio Busoni, her narcissism led her to perform a dance before the assembled audience, and she was delighted by the spontaneous applause and the words of encouragement from the musician. The more often she attended the theater, the opera, or the ballet with her parents, the stronger became her wish to stand in the spotlight herself.

Though Riefenstahl's parents supported, or at least looked kindly on, her interest in the arts and her growing enthusiasm for sports, proudly presenting their daughter when the occasion arose as a "wunderkind," they firmly rejected her desire to go onstage or into film. Yet the theater held a particular fascination for both parents. In his youth, Alfred Riefenstahl himself had been onstage as an amateur actor, and he was a great admirer of the beautiful Fritzi Massary, then a celebrated operetta star. "But to him, actors, and particularly actresses, were 'of a dubious character,' if not outright members of the 'demimonde.'"[14]

Leni Riefenstahl, however, was not to be discouraged by her parents' total disapproval of her new goal. In 1918, more out of curiosity than conviction, she secretly auditioned as a film extra. She had read an announcement in the daily *B.Z. am Mittag* that twenty female extras were needed for *Opium*, a film set in the dance milieu. Without informing her parents, she auditioned and managed to secure a part, but then she turned it down because she knew she would never get her father's permission to participate in the film.

Yet this audition was to have far-reaching consequences for Leni Riefenstahl's future. The aspirant extras had to present themselves at Helene Grimm-Reiter's Berlin School of Dance, and while she was waiting, Leni observed with growing excitement the school's students as they performed their ballet exercises. This experience, which she described, as she did all further turning points of her life, as a revelation, a "twist of fate," awakened her interest in dance: "I was overcome by an uncontrollable desire to join in."[15] She immediately inquired about the admission requirements and, without asking her parents for permission, registered for the beginner's course.

# 2

## FIRST CAREER STEPS

### RISE TO SOLO DANCER

LENI RIEFENSTAHL'S CHOICE OF DANCE was an obvious one. Dance offered a logical synthesis of her love of movement and physical training, and her strong drive for self-presentation and for an intense physical expression of her emotions, something she had already sought in sports. Dance allowed her to merge her athletic enthusiasm with her artistic interests and give new form to her creativity and need to express herself. The young Leni Riefenstahl was convinced that in dance she had found the ideal medium, and so it became her new passion, the realm of her first serious career goals.

Immediately following World War I, and not only in Germany, there was a strong interest in dance, which was viewed as a form of expression that suited the age. In the twenties, interpretive dance in particular went through a multifaceted phase of development as a liberating physical art and was received with great enthusiasm by the public. The German capital, featuring many guest performances by German and international dancers, was deemed the center of modern dance during these years. It was here that the avant-garde held its initial rehearsals, experimenting with new forms, schools, and content. A generation of young male and female dancers was making a name for itself, and Riefenstahl got it in her head to become one of them.

Now it was only a matter of convincing others of her abilities and talent. The first hurdle along the way was to win over her own family. Despite the rejection she anticipated, Riefenstahl soon confessed to her parents her choice of career. Her father—as previously, when her dream had been to become an actress—was less than pleased with his daughter's plans. Her mother was more accepting, but to Leni's annoyance she acceded, as she so often did, to her husband's wishes. But though they could dismiss their daughter's acting ambitions as a young girl's harmless infatuation, her parents soon recognized that this time Leni was determined to turn her dream into reality. The conflict of interest between the zealous daughter, who believed she had finally found her goal in life, and the father, who wanted her to join his firm, peaked in a renewed power struggle. After a long back-and-forth that was difficult for both sides, Leni emerged as victor.

But despite her enthusiasm, one problem stood in the way of a career in classical ballet—Riefenstahl was already relatively old to begin training as a dancer. Most dancers began their schooling as children, but she was seventeen, and thus a career as a ballerina was never a serious option. But this did nothing to discourage Leni or cause her to change her plans. She threw herself into her training in order to catch up with a course of study that other dancers her age had long since completed. She simply ignored the pessimistic predictions around her. As so often with situations encountered later in life, she put all of her trust in her own decisiveness and ambition, and was convinced that she would succeed. This early quality, which allowed her to trust herself even when the rest of the world doubted her, was to mark the course of her life.

Bertha Riefenstahl couldn't bring herself to oppose her daughter's fondest wish. She made it possible for Leni to take dance lessons behind her father's back, but despite her maneuvering her husband found out about it. This led not only to his usual outburst of temper but also to a serious domestic crisis and nearly to the breakup of the family itself. It was hard to dissuade him from immediately filing for divorce. He forgave his wife, who had been in league with his daughter, only after Leni promised to give up her dance plans once and for all.

This was one reason Leni Riefenstahl registered at the State School of Arts and Crafts a few months after receiving her school diploma. For her father's sake alone, she halfheartedly and for a brief time applied herself to the study of painting. But as before, her thoughts were only on dance.

Soon, however, she also had to leave the School of Arts and Crafts, as her distrustful father continued to insist that his unruly daughter spend a year at a girls' boarding school at the foot of the Harz Mountains, far from big-city Berlin, where she would finally come to her senses. Leni had no choice but to bow to her father's wishes. In the summer of 1919, she packed her bags and traveled to the Lohmann Boarding School near Quedlinburg.

When she was allowed to return to Berlin in the spring of 1920, she resorted to deception. She agreed to work at her father's firm as his private secretary, and in exchange, he would allow her to continue her dance lessons on the side. During the day she learned typewriting, stenography, and accounting, but evenings she continued with her dance instruction.

At the next student recital at Helene Grimm-Reiter's school, in February 1921, the nineteen-year-old made her official stage debut together with her fellow students; she also appeared as a soloist, performing a "minor waltz." She saved the program from this evening, on which her name appeared four times (once under Helene Riefenstahl and three times under Leni Riefenstahl), as if it were a trophy commemorating her first real triumph over paternal authority.[1] Following this she came to a decision: "I resolved to train hard for the next few years, to do nothing else but work and, above all, prove to my father that I could become a good dancer, and never cause him the shame he so feared."[2]

Though Alfred Riefenstahl was still not convinced that his daughter had talent, he nevertheless decided to finance a first-class education for her. And so, between the years of 1921 and 1923, Leni Riefenstahl was able to devote herself totally to her dance career. In the mornings the young student learned the rudiments of classical ballet, and in the afternoon she attended a school for interpretive dance.

It was the famous American dancer Isadora Duncan who, hemmed in by the pretentiousness of classical ballet, went in search of a new style of dance that was simple and unaffected. She began by standing barefoot in plain, flowing dress on a stage devoid of sets and usually bare, reducing the expressive form of dance to a minimum. Mary Wigman took up these ideas and made them popular in Germany. Following her attempts at classical ballet, Leni Riefenstahl found modern dance, which Wigman taught in her world-famous school in Dresden-Hellerau, liberating at first. In 1923, she registered for instruction by Wigman, who accepted the young dancer into her class. Riefenstahl danced with such famous figures as Vera Skoronel and Gret Palucca. But once her initial enthusiasm waned, Riefenstahl quickly found Wigman's style too abstract, too ascetic, and too severe. Her plan was to express her own fairy-tale, dreamlike visions in a totally new, unique, and largely individual style. Troubled by serious doubts about her own talent, she broke off her study with Wigman after a few months and returned to Berlin to continue her studies with Eugenie Eduardova and Jutta Klamt.

## A SOBERING EXPERIENCE

Even though her dance training and her growing preoccupation with her own choreography claimed the major part of her time, Riefenstahl could not ignore the fact that men played an important role in the lives of her female friends: "All of my friends had been involved in love affairs, some of them were engaged, and Alice, my best friend, was already married. I was the only one who still hadn't had one single experience with a man. Over time I found this to be a shortcoming and began toying with the idea of having an adventure."[3] Having triumphed over her father's authority in terms of her professional desires, she now consciously decided to take her love life into her own hands.

Her first sexual relationship with a man, therefore, was neither inadvertent nor a logical outcome of first love, but a fully conscious, calculated, premeditated event, even though it turned out differently than she had imagined.

In August 1923, Riefenstahl turned twenty-one and thus came of age. She left her parents' home and moved into a small apartment on Fasanenstrasse, close to Kurfürstendamm. Her father paid her rent at first, but within a few months, following several performance engagements, she became financially independent. For the first time in her life she could meet and go out with admirers, which her father had strictly forbidden until then. Alfred Riefenstahl considered twenties Berlin, with its sexual freedom, to be a depraved city, and he wanted to protect his daughter from its dangers. Up until that point he had jealously guarded her against any sexual experience. In their prudery, her parents had not discussed sex with their daughter at all, and she wisely kept her secret crushes to herself.

She could do little more than admire from afar the men who aroused her interest. She occasionally arranged secret rendezvous behind her father's back, as those with Paul Lasker-Schüler, for instance, the slightly older son of the poet Else Lasker-Schüler, but these were overshadowed by the fear of being discovered by her father. Under the circumstances, these meetings remained platonic. The Riefenstahl house rules were clear: "Physicality existed only in sports; sensuality and sexuality were taboo in an environment over which her father jealously presided."[4]

Young Leni, however, refused to be influenced by her father; she wanted to choose the man for her "first time" herself. In *Memoiren,* she reports a whole series of "ardent admirers" whose attentions flattered her but in whom she wasn't interested.

Wealthy Harry Sokal, who was to play an important role later in her life, was among those Leni Riefenstahl rejected as a lover. She first met the Innsbruck banker, four years older than she, during a summer vacation in 1923. He was working for the Austrian Credit Bank and she described him as a man with dark hair and aristocratic features.[5] Riefenstahl and her friend Hertha were on vacation together, first on the Bodensee and in the Allgäu region, and then on the Baltic Sea. It was there that Sokal first met her as she was going through her daily dance exercises on the strand, and he immediately fell madly in love with her. He was so impressed with the young woman that he spontaneously offered to rent her a ballroom in Innsbruck, so that she could make her first public appearance.[6] She turned down his proposal of marriage at the end of the vacation on the Baltic Sea, but this didn't discourage Sokal from continuing to pursue her.

For the next ten years, Sokal was a major factor in Riefenstahl's life. He was not only the long-suffering admirer but also one of her most important patrons, and he wholeheartedly supported her career. Sokal played a central role in the life of the ambitious young woman, from serving as her producer during her acting career in the 1920s to financing and coproducing her 1932 directorial debut, *Das blaue Licht* (*The Blue Light*). And privately he was never far from her side. From 1926 until he was forced to leave Germany because he was Jewish in 1933, Sokal lived side by side with Riefenstahl in a large duplex apartment on Berlin's Hindenburgstrasse.

It is an open question whether the relationship remained platonic for this entire period, whether Sokal's support was offered in pure friendship or perhaps with the thought that one day he would win over the freedom-loving Riefenstahl, or whether their relationship developed into a love affair, at least for a time. Riefenstahl herself emphatically denied this. The fact that the star of the Third Reich had had a Jewish lover would have made things highly uncomfortable for her, and this may have played a significant role in her denial. For his part, Sokal told the writer Glenn Infield that he and Riefenstahl had a sexual relationship that lasted until 1925.[7]

As for her "first time," however, Leni planned for it to take place before the end of her twenty-first year. In the fall of 1923, she chose the heartthrob Otto Froitzheim. Deputy police chief of Cologne and a champion tennis player, Froitzheim was the darling of Berlin society. Among his lovers was the film diva Pola Negri, star of Ernst Lubitsch's silent masterpiece *Madame DuBarry* (1919). Leni Riefenstahl had seen the bachelor, who was eighteen years older than she, at Berlin's Ice-Skating Club, a sports club at which she had taken tennis lessons two years before. She was introduced to Froitzheim at the home of the famous gossip columnist Bella Fromm and a short time later sent a message to him through a mutual acquaintance that she wanted to meet with him. Froitzheim had nothing against making one more conquest and he accepted immediately. On the day they were to meet, the young woman suddenly doubted her own courage: "I would have liked to run away."[8] But she couldn't back out of it. "What I then experienced was horrible. This was what love was supposed to be like? I felt nothing but pain and disappointment. How very far this was from what I had imagined and wished it to be, with my longing for tenderness . . . I simply endured it and hid my tears with a pillow."[9] After it was over, Froitzheim escorted her to the door, showering her with compliments and trying to slip her some money, in case an abortion eventually became necessary.

As a totally inexperienced young woman who had given herself over to romantic ideas based on the reports of her female friends, Riefenstahl must have been shocked by the way Froitzheim treated her. She tore up the money and ran out of the apartment. Days later she still looked back on the experience with anger and shame. In a long letter "about my love and my infinite disgust,"[10] she wrote to him how annoyed she was by their encounter. Her letter seems to have kindled Froitzheim's interest in the young woman, and he began to court her, which confused her even more. "I never wanted to see this man again, and now he was sending me flowers. Why didn't I immediately throw them out the window instead of pressing them to me? Why did I kiss the card? I locked myself in my room and cried, cried, cried."[11]

The fact that she accepted Froitzheim's advances may be ascribed to her inexperience and her profound irritation. Although not in love with him, she felt herself "mysteriously enamored of him."[12] And even though she was never able to feel anything for him after their first disillusioning encounter, they nevertheless announced their engagement six months later. Froitzheim's possessiveness soon alienated the young Riefenstahl, but she continued the relationship for two years. Only as she was setting out on her film career and met director Arnold Fanck did she break the engagement. Whereas Riefenstahl gave the reason for the separation as Froitzheim having betrayed her with another woman, her friend Bella Fromm surmised that Froitzheim ended the relationship because marriage to a dancer would have ruined his law-enforcement career.[13]

The disappointing episode with Froitzheim, which under the circumstances could scarcely be called "first love," confirmed Riefenstahl's decision, made early in her youth, not to lose her independence when it came to affairs of the heart. She resolved at quite a young age never to become the "slave of a man" but to determine for herself the direction her life was to take. Her parents' marriage, in which her mother was forced to subject herself unconditionally to her husband's wishes, worked as a deterrent and was the basis of her obvious need for freedom: "My wish for independence became ever stronger . . . When I saw how my mother often was treated by my father . . . I swore to myself that later in life I would never let go of the controls. I would decide things only according to my own will."[14]

Her parents' largely loveless marriage, founded only on her father's possessiveness, and her repugnant experience with Otto Froitzheim subsequently led Riefenstahl to insist even more strongly on her professional independence.

What above all was unusual for that time was that Riefenstahl's independence and autonomy in her work also carried over to her love life. In an age when it was traditional for women to be conquered by men, and a man being pursued by a woman highly proscribed, Riefenstahl operated with absolute self-confidence. She chose her partners, summarily rejecting those men who courted her but whom she found physically unattractive.

### DEBUT AS A DANCER

Alfred Riefenstahl had finally accepted his daughter's decision to become a dancer and, at her request, even agreed to finance her dance debut in Berlin and rent Blüthner Hall for the occasion. Her teachers strongly discouraged this—they considered a solo performance after only two years of serious study to be far too premature. They warned Leni against overextending herself, as her muscles had not yet developed the necessary elasticity. But Riefenstahl did not hesitate to at long last realize her dream of performing onstage. As so often in her life, she ignored the advice of those who presumably knew better and acted on her belief in herself alone. At this point the young dancer must have eagerly hoped that her first public appearance would bring her the kind of overnight success that every dance student yearns for.[15] The fact that in the same time period—the spring of 1923—Riefenstahl entered a beauty contest in which she placed second is more evidence of her great desire for the spotlight. She wanted people to applaud her, she wanted the attention, the immediate gratification: "I could hardly wait for the moment when I would stand on the stage."[16]

She didn't choose to adapt classical models for the stage or use work by other choreographers. Instead, she set off down a new path with her own choreography. She reinvented herself for the stage, separating herself from all that had come before her, which for an inexperienced dancer called for a great deal of self-confidence. "As significant as the influence of her teachers or other great dancers may have been, Riefenstahl was a figure of her own creation."[17] As such, she made her first public appearance in October 1923.

Several days before this appearance in Berlin's Blüthner Hall, her admirer Harry Sokal sponsored a "rehearsal evening" for her in Munich and also took care of all necessary advertising. So Leni Riefenstahl's first solo dance performance took place on October 23, in Munich's Tonhalle, the audience filling three-quarters of the small hall. In *Memoiren*, in which she carefully constructed the "legend of the perfect beginning for a brilliant talent,"[18] she writes of the unbounded enthusiasm with which the Munich public as well as the critics reacted to her.

But a look at the articles from the time gives a somewhat different view.[19] The Munich critics did acknowledge her talent but clearly emphasized that more basic training and development was called for. The critics' well-intended suggestions appear to confirm the warnings of Riefenstahl's teachers that her first public appearance was premature. The *Münchener Zeitung* wrote, "Leni Riefenstahl brings to the stage a number of major prerequisites for success: a very lovely appearance and an obviously unique temperament, which holds the audience's attention throughout. But [she] defeats . . . a higher artistry by remaining in the realm of the emotions; she lolls about, for example, at precisely the point at which she should be expressing pleasure in its most refined form. And her movements occasionally are unsuccessful for the same reason; her temperament threatens to lead her toward . . . the sensational. But if she could use her passion as the departure point of her art instead of its end expression, she could become something special yet. May her success not stand in her way."[20]

Nevertheless, three days later, on October 26, the program was repeated in Berlin before a near-capacity audience at Blüthner Hall. With her skeptical father and the rest of the family in attendance, the evening was a success of the kind no beginner had been granted in years. The newspapers reported the "prolonged applause of the house."[21] Riefenstahl herself had choreographed and compiled the program—consisting of ten dances that lasted a total of one and a half hours. Her mother designed and sewed the costumes, some of which had been conceived by her daughter. The entire evening was Riefenstahl's creation, and her success belonged to her alone. She was transported by the applause.

At the insistence of the audience, Riefenstahl performed encores of several of the dances, pushing herself to the point of physical exhaustion. Though she was carried along by the enthusiasm of the crowd, she danced that evening primarily for one person alone—her father. The evening at Blüthner Hall was the starting point of her notable, if brief, career as a solo dancer. Offers poured in from everywhere, and she accepted them all. "As if in a frenzy"[22] she made seventy appearances in the next eight months, always accompanied by her mother and by her pianist, Herbert Klamt. During this period she scheduled a performance almost every third day, and the time in between was spent in long nights on trains and endless practicing. As a result, she soon found herself at the point of total exhaustion.

For the extent of her dance career, which was to end six months later following a knee injury, she traveled through all of Germany and also to neighboring countries. Her tour took her from Berlin to Dresden and Munich and on to Frankfurt and Cologne, Breslau, Halle, and Zürich, where she danced at the city's Schauspielhaus and met the celebrated actor Alexander Moissi, before continuing on to Innsbruck and Prague. For each engagement she earned the considerable sum of 500 to 1,000 German gold marks.

The most important performances of her dance career took place in December 1923, in her hometown of Berlin. Max Reinhardt, who according to Riefenstahl had attended her debut at Blüthner Hall,[23] engaged the young dancer all Berlin was talking about for several solo evenings at his world-famous Deutsches Theater. To be hired by the internationally acclaimed god of the theater—though she didn't meet him personally during this period—was a major distinction for Riefenstahl. She admired Max Reinhardt, whenever possible attending his new productions at the Deutsches Theater or the adjoining Kammerspiele, and appearing on one of his stages enhanced her reputation.[24] She gave matinee performances in the Kammerspiele on December 16 and 20, 1923, accompanied by Hans Mahlke. On May 16, 1924, she again appeared, this time accompanied by Herbert Klamt, who served as musical director for the majority of her solo appearances.

Similar to the dances of her former teacher, Jutta Klamt,[25] Riefenstahl's creative works bore descriptive names that lent them a certain symbolism. Her repertoire included *Cradle Song* (Brahms), *Caucasian*

*Suite* (Mikhail Ippolitov-Ivanov), *Summer* (Antonín Dvořák), *Mazurka* (Benjamin Godard), and the *Valse Caprice* that pianist and composer Ferruccio Busoni created especially for her. Among her favorite dances were the *Three Dances of Eros—Fire, Devotion, Separation* (Chopin, Tchaikovsky, and Grieg), *Traumblüte* (with music by Chopin), a work by the name of *Das blaue Licht* ("The Blue Light"), *Die Unvollendete* (Schubert), and particularly *Studie nach einer Gavotte*, with music by Gluck and Brahms. Her evening programs always consisted of ten of these dances, performed in two acts.

In the flurry surrounding her success, Riefenstahl, who had never tended toward self-criticism, increasingly acknowledged only those reviews that were flattering and that celebrated her as a great artist. She shielded herself from negative comments, so it comes as no surprise that in retrospect she portrayed her dance career as one long triumph: "Everywhere I went I experienced the same success—which transcends words—with the public and in the press."[26]

By the time she published a brochure of revamped critical reviews, her career as a dancer had ended. In June 1924, during a return engagement at Prague's Konzertsaal Central, preceded shortly before by a performance at the Volksbühne in Chemnitz, she injured a knee during one of her leaps, forcing a cancellation of her planned tour. The resulting torn ligament, which later led to cartilage growths, required that Riefenstahl walk with a cane and made further appearances impossible. All of the doctors she desperately consulted in Germany, Switzerland, and the Netherlands advised rest and warned her to be patient. The fact that her body had revealed its limits and that she was faced with the frightening question of whether she would ever dance again was extremely painful to Riefenstahl at this point in her life, when she had received invitations to perform in Paris and London. The whirlwind success that had occurred virtually overnight was followed by sudden and total disillusionment. "It seemed to be my fate that the art of dance, which I had achieved through sheer obstinacy, was to completely define my life, today and for all the days to come. And then I suffered this fall."[27]

In retrospect, the question arises: What significance did Riefenstahl's short but astounding career have for interpretive dance of the 1920s? Though she was always treated as a potential successor of Wigman, of

Valeska Gert, and of Niddy Impekoven, she never seriously had to measure herself against them. Without doubt she was granted a special status within the dance world of her day, which made her unusual career possible in the first place. But she had no imitators. Leni Riefenstahl, the dancer, remained a unique phenomenon.

# 3

## STAR OF MOUNTAIN FILMS

### WORKING AS AN ACTRESS WITH ARNOLD FANCK

HAVING ATTENDED THE CINEMA for the first time at the age of ten, Riefenstahl belonged to the first generation to grow up with movie stars. Along with millions of others, in her youth she worshipped screen idols such as Henny Porten, Mary Pickford and Douglas Fairbanks, Charlie Chaplin, Rudolph Valentino, and Lillian Gish.

At first the movies were considered "theater for the little people," but this changed when stars of the stage began acting in movies. Albert Bassermann was one of Germany's leading stage actors, "king of the German mimes" and recipient of the Iffland Ring, which was awarded to Germany's greatest theater actors. When he agreed to act in films and accepted the starring role in *Der Andere* (*The Other*) in 1913, it gave the young film medium a considerable boost. Many theater stars followed his example and abandoned their former refusal to appear before the camera, among them Emil Jannings.

Film acting became popular with actors, not only because the movies offered greater, nationwide popularity, but also because a film engagement brought in larger fees and greatly increased the market value of the star. Film offered opportunities for professional advancement that the theater couldn't match. As the technology expanded, the public began to demand better cinematic aesthetics and subject matter. Audiences wanted good stories and thrilling films. Though masterworks such as Robert Wiene's *The Cabinet of Dr. Caligari* (1919) brought German film international acclaim, moviegoers wanted to be able to worship their favorite stars in films that were entertaining.

In big cities, going to the movies became a habit among the middle class. Particularly after the economic crisis wrought by inflation, people poured into the variety shows and revue palaces, seeking the dreamworld of the movies as a diversion from the cares and hardship of their sad and often unsatisfactory lives.

This new enthusiasm for the movies also gripped the young Riefenstahl: "Theater and film captivated me more and more, because the rigid bourgeois world was all I knew."[1] The desire to go into film, which she shared with so many girls her age, was not far-fetched in the Berlin of the 1920s, which was developing into the metropolis of German film. But Leni Riefenstahl didn't want to work in just any kind of film, she wanted to be part of the "mountain film" genre specific to Germany, which began its boom in the first half of the twenties. In this she definitely differed from other girls her age who also dreamed of a movie career. It wasn't the luxurious life of a diva that Riefenstahl was after. Instead, she wanted to establish herself in a genre that up until then was a male domain and in which she would appear not as a beautiful star but in a stronger role as an athlete and alpinist. This was an unusual decision, but the mountain film captured her total attention and enthusiasm. And as so often in Riefenstahl's life, the future of her career turned on a key incident, which she repeatedly related in slightly differing versions.

In the early summer of 1924, she was standing on the subway platform of Berlin's Nollendorfplatz station, when suddenly she glanced at a film poster dramatically portraying the skier and actor Hannes Schneider scaling a rock chimney. The first hugely popular mountain film, *Der Berg des Schicksals* (*Peak of Fate*), had debuted a short time before, in May 1924.[2] "As if in a trance" and "filled with new desire,"[3] Riefenstahl went to the theater on Nollendorfplatz to see the film that was to have a permanent influence on her career. Set in the Dolomites and based on the first ascent of the Guglia di Brenta, *Der Berg des Schicksals* was the first film to feature Luis Trenker, a former mountain guide from South Tirol who was to become one of the leading stars of the twenties and thirties. The young dancer was captivated by the breathtaking nature shots and the film's artistry and rhythm. Her childhood romance with nature came alive on the screen. She later described her feelings: "At first glance I was strangely mesmerized—mountains and clouds, alpine slopes and bare cliffs stream past, it's a view into a strange world. Who would have imagined that mountains were so beautiful! I knew them only from postcards—lifeless and rigid, and now they rose up before me in unimagined splendor."[4]

## THE DISCOVERER

Arnold Fanck, the director of the film, was a geologist who made a name for himself in the early 1920s with lengthy nature documentaries shot in alpine settings. His first film, *Das Wunder des Schneeschuhs* (Marvels of Ski), arrived in movie theaters in 1920 and introduced viewers to various skiing techniques. The films that followed, such as *Eine Fuchsjagd auf Skiern durchs Engadin* (Foxhunting on Skis in the Engadine) (1922) and *Im Kampf mit dem Berge* (In Battle with the Mountain) (1921), all took place in the Alps and represented a "mix of ski instruction and propaganda for mountain skiing."[5] Fanck invented the "mountain film," a highly successful genre in Germany in the twenties and thirties for which he is still known. Producers at first refused to finance Fanck's films, considering them to be "abysmally naïve." On top of this, the location shooting, dependent on the weather, often lasted for months and incurred huge expenses. Distribution companies rejected Fanck's films as well, not expecting them to be profitable. So the director at first was forced to screen his films in halls he rented himself.

Because the films were a total novelty, they soon proved an unexpected, huge success among the public. As opposed to the overwhelming majority of films created at the time, which as a rule were shot entirely in the studio to avoid costly exterior and nature shots, it was precisely the actual outdoor setting that made these films so popular. Newspaper and magazine reports of dangerous location shooting were at least as important to the success of the mountain films as their breathtaking imagery. From the very beginning there was speculation about whether certain scenes were actually shot under extreme outdoor conditions or in the studio. As the integrity of the images was the most important factor in selling the films, Fanck quickly responded to the "spiteful suspicions concerning authenticity"[6] and "ignominious slander,"[7] always emphasizing that all scenes were filmed outdoors, at times under great stress. The physical achievements of the actors were not the result of trick photography but had actually been shot amid great danger; every avalanche was real and not "a studio avalanche."[8]

But it was also their content that set the mountain films apart from other contemporary genres. In these films, nature is not one among many dramatic elements (or a decorative backdrop, as in the German Heimat films of the thirties and the fifties[9]). Rather, nature and the elements play a major role: they become aesthetic objects. Spectacular mountain formations, massive storm-battered glaciers, and picturesque snowscapes excited and fascinated audiences.

## THE PATH TO THE MOUNTAIN FILM

Still under the influence of her experience at the movies, Riefenstahl traveled to the Dolomites with Harry Sokal (in some of Riefenstahl's accounts Sokal is erroneously replaced by her brother, Heinz[10]). Her fascination with mountains was to remain with Riefenstahl throughout her life, and she loved the Dolomite landscape with a passion—the rugged mountain faces, the wildly romantic peaks, the ravines coursing with water: "I'm overjoyed to spot the first rock towers. I want to hail them as new friends, greet them as acquaintances. I am strangely convinced that from now on my life will be unthinkable without them, that they will take on a significance for me the duration of which I am only vaguely capable of imagining."[11]

It was at the exclusive Karersee Hotel, where Riefenstahl was staying, that *Der Berg des Schicksals* was screened for the summer guests. Following the show, Riefenstahl, dressed in white tulle, had Harry Sokal introduce her to the star of the film, Luis Trenker, who was in attendance. She confidently announced to him that she would be starring in the next Arnold Fanck film. It did not occur to her that she would end up with anything less than a starring role.

Trenker strongly advised Riefenstahl against contacting Fanck. He wasn't encouraging about her chances, as she could neither climb nor ski, nor was she familiar with the mountains. The actor could also anticipate that his star status would be challenged by a pretty young woman pushing her way into the exclusively masculine domain of the mountain films. From the beginning, Trenker considered Riefenstahl competition. But the budding actress never let others discourage her. "Had Trenker said to me a hundred times, summoning all of his male logic, that I had no chance of acting in a film by Dr. Fanck, it would not have made the least impression on me. That's how totally convinced I was that my wishes had not derived from impulse or accident. I would have obsessively pursued my goal."[12] She took her leave of Trenker with the words, "See you in the next film."[13]

On her return to Berlin late that summer, Riefenstahl immediately telephoned Fanck, who had no idea who the young dancer was. But he agreed to meet with her and arranged a date in a coffeehouse on Kurfürstendamm. Fanck was very reserved at the meeting, listening silently to the talkative young woman's plans, but he nevertheless noted her enthusiasm for the mountains and for his films. In a letter written to Trenker following this meeting, he described Riefenstahl as "the most beautiful woman in Europe," who "soon" would become "the most famous woman in Germany."[14] Not least because he was attracted to the beautiful young dancer, Fanck accepted her self-confident offer and gave Riefenstahl— who had never appeared before the camera in a major role—the lead in his next film, *Der heilige Berg* (*The Holy Mountain*).

Why Fanck, who at first appeared uninterested, had granted Riefenstahl this kind of opportunity is a question often asked but never answered. The truth differs from the romantic version of the story— uncontested to this day and understandable for tactical reasons—that both Riefenstahl and Fanck later told concerning the beginning of their working relationship. Jan-Christopher Horak, an expert on Fanck, points out that Riefenstahl's admirer Harry Sokal, who had provided critical funding to get her dance career started, financed 25 percent of the production costs of *Der heilige Berg*.[15]

For Riefenstahl's sake, Sokal had given up his career at the Austrian Credit Bank in Innsbruck and joined the film business. In 1925 he bought Arnold Fanck's Freiburg company, Berg- und Sportfilm (Mountain and Sports Films)—which was on the verge of bankruptcy—along with its print laboratory, in order to reorganize the company together with the German film company Ufa.[16] This initially risky and impractical step was to prove financially profitable in the end: under the successful collaboration between Fanck and Sokal, the mountain film gained in popularity and became a flourishing industry. In addition, Sokal's move to join Fanck boosted the career of his friend Leni Riefenstahl. It is likely that this tactic caused Fanck to hire the dancer as an actress and even, in the end, to list her name above Trenker's on the posters for the film. Riefenstahl's association with Fanck, at any rate, was not achieved through her own "unbridled desire"[17] and engagement, as she implied, but was forced through by the convincing financial "arguments" of Sokal, her well-intentioned patron.[18]

After 1933, once she was on the side of the new German rulers, her Jewish benefactor became a great embarrassment to her career. And so the true circumstances of her entry into films were subsequently removed from the legend of her life, and she tried to disguise Sokal's valuable support as a mere romantic gesture: "I had no doubt that, above all, he wanted to be near me."[19]

*Der heilige Berg* was a typical example of the constellation of Arnold Fanck's mountain epics: the male bonding of the mountain climbers triumphs over temporary temptation by a female. In a reference to her former career as a dancer, Riefenstahl plays Diotima, a ballet dancer whose life is entirely devoted to dance and to the mountains, and whose character in the film is the very personification of threatening femininity. The film begins with a close-up of Diotima and her "Dance to the Sea," for which Riefenstahl reworked one of her own choreographies, adapting it to the demands of the two-dimensional medium. As part of a tour that takes her to the mountains, Diotima dances on the stage of the Grand Hotel in Zermatt, where she captures the attention of two particular members of the audience. The two men, skiers and mountain climbers Vigo (Ernst Petersen) and an old friend of his (Luis Trenker), soon are competing for her affection, and the film develops into a tale of jealousy that ends in the deaths of both men in the mountains. Following a bitter struggle over the woman, they plunge into the abyss, after which Diotima leaves the Alps and returns, alone and broken, to the sea.

When the film opened in December 1926, opinions on the new actress differed wildly. On September 24, 1926, Vienna's *Wiener Neueste Nachrichten* reported: "Who had ever heard of Leni Riefenstahl before? Today, it is clear that she is one of the film world's greatest actresses, an artist who masters the full range of most subtle mimicry and is a blend of love and kindness, courage and resolve. She is beautiful and fiery. Her acting can be compared only with the incomparable Asta Nielsen. In a word, she is great." The *Berliner Morgenpost* of December 19, on the other hand, delivered a crushing review: "Leni Riefenstahl offered nothing in the way of acting. Nor did she look particularly good. Her jumping around is, in places, hard to bear."

But the great success the film enjoyed with critics and the public was the cornerstone of Leni Riefenstahl's career as an actress. The mountain film genre produced by Ufa entered its professional phase, and Arnold Fanck assigned her the lead in his next five films. From then on, her name was closely associated with the mountain film, which determined the roles she would play in the coming years. In Fanck's films, Riefenstahl usually embodied the superior and self-confident woman who can hold her own. She is the courageous mountain climber and alpinist who is capable of asserting herself in this narcissistic male world and also of proving herself in the most difficult and dangerous situations. Leni Riefenstahl was celebrated in the press as a new type of film actress, and it was for her that the term "sports actress" was coined.

Riefenstahl's private life during this time revolved around her intimate and happy relationship with Hans Schneeberger, a Tirolean who was Fanck's best cameraman. The men she had rejected or dropped up until then—Fanck, Sokal, and Trenker among them—simply had to accept it. Following the shooting of *Der grosse Sprung* (*The Big Jump*) (1927) and a vacation together in the Dolomites,[20] Riefenstahl and Schneeberger moved into a three-room apartment on Berlin's Hindenburgstrasse, as her small apartment on Fasanenstrasse was no longer grand enough. For the next two years, the couple was almost inseparable: "My attraction to him developed slowly, then intensified and finally was so strong that we couldn't bear to be apart. Though Schneeberger was seven years older than I, he liked to be told what to do. He was the passive partner, I the active one. Our life together was harmonious . . . We were happiest when we could be alone."[21]

The end of the relationship was painful for Riefenstahl. In 1929, Schneeberger met another woman while working on *Ungarische Rhapsodie* (*Hungarian Rhapsody*) and wrote to Riefenstahl telling her that he was leaving her. Leni Riefenstahl, who had thought that Schneeberger was the great love of her life, was deeply hurt and never denied the humiliation she felt: "Never again, I swore to myself, never again did I want to love a man so much."[22]

Riefenstahl withdrew into herself for five months, a period she called "the worst time of her life," after which followed a number of short-lived superficial affairs. It was always Riefenstahl who ended the liaison and it was characteristic of her to maintain a good relationship with each of the men in order to continue to work with them without complications. She interpreted the failure of her relationship with Schneeberger, which left her feeling deceived and betrayed, as a sign that she should forever hold to her decision never to be a "slave" to a man.

While it is true that Riefenstahl had no competition as a star of mountain films, producers were convinced that she had reached the peak of her acting abilities. No one believed she could succeed in other types of productions. As she could expect no new or more demanding roles from Fanck, she quickly recognized that in the long run the mountain film was a dead end for her and that she would have to find new outlets. Once again she was determined to prove herself to everyone.

Nevertheless, Riefenstahl made yet another mountain film with Arnold Fanck, *Die weisse Hölle vom Piz Palü* (*The White Hell of Pitz Palu*). But in this case she insisted that G. W. Pabst serve as codirector. Pabst's direction of the major scenes (the studio scenes in Berlin as well as the important mountain exteriors) was intended to counterbalance Fanck's weak direction of actors. Though the collaboration between the two directors was not without conflict, the results were worthwhile. Riefenstahl drew new inspiration from the work: "For the first time I felt that I was an actress too."[23]

Soon after the premiere of the first German feature-length sound film, *Melodie des Herzens* (*Melody of the Heart*), in March 1929, it became obvious to everyone in the film world that the talkie was the medium of the future and that silent films were finished. All of the preceding discussions concerning the threat to the aesthetic value that silent film had attained and that the "nerve-racking sound film" could not match were thrown overboard, along with the industry's initial skepticism and animosity toward sound. A look at the way Hollywood was beginning to corner the world market in sound films made it clear that joining this international development was imperative. Great advances were rapidly made in the technical revolution that brought sound to the film medium. Only one year later, 101 of 146 German features were sound films, while only two silent films were produced. In 1931, following the rush to build sound studios, more than five thousand movie theaters throughout Germany were equipped for sound.

The introduction of sound was the source of great insecurity among actors, many of whom worried whether their voices were suited to the microphone. Even renowned stars such as Emil Jannings and Conrad Veidt had to return to Germany from Hollywood because they couldn't master American English well enough. Leni Riefenstahl also had to deal with this issue. She practiced hard and trained her voice by recording the first automatic announcements made by the telephone company in Berlin. But despite the intense efforts of Herbert Kuchenbuch, her speech instructor, her Berlin accent and her pitch irritated many of the moviegoing public, who felt these qualities didn't belong to the world of the mountain film or to the image of the mythical female that audiences had assigned to the young actress. So it is not at all true that Riefenstahl "easily"[24] made the transition from silent to sound films; rather, her voice became a disadvantage that further limited her opportunities with other directors.

## ADVENTURES ON THE ETERNAL ICE

*SOS Eisberg* (*S.O.S. Iceberg*) was to be the final collaboration of Fanck and Riefenstahl. Other than its unusual location—it was set in Greenland—the film offered little that was new, differing from previous productions only in that this time cast and crew did not have to battle glaciers and avalanches, but icebergs and ice floes. Fanck's treasured mise-en-scène of natural forces was carried to the extreme in this film, perhaps the most ambitious project of his career. It soon became clear that the brittle icebergs were more dangerous and unpredictable than the glaciers they had dealt with previously. This survival story set on the eternal ice at extraordinary cost could be brought to the screen only due to the fact that it was produced by the German subsidiary of Universal Studios. An English-language version was created simultaneously for distribution in America and England, with Tay Garnett serving as codirector.

In *SOS Eisberg*, which was singularly lacking in action, Riefenstahl plays a fearless pilot who joins a search party looking for her missing husband. The film was supported by the Danish government, and shooting took place between June and November of 1932—polar summer in the Arctic. The film crew set out from the Hamburg harbor with all its equipment, including several polar expedition planes that had been disassembled and three polar bears from the Hamburg Zoo, which were needed for the shoot. During filming, everyone lived in a tent city near Umanak on the west coast of Greenland. Knud Rasmussen was chosen as adviser and technical chief of the production. Rasmussen was a popular Danish polar explorer and ethnologist, celebrated in the press of the time as the "king of the Eskimos." Despite his expert guidance during filming, members of the team were continually placed in dangerous situations that threatened their health. Riefenstahl in one scene leaped out of an airplane into an ice-cold sea, and also suffered unbearably painful gallstones and had to leave the team early.

Nevertheless, *SOS Eisberg*, which premiered on August 31, 1933, was a big hit. Audiences everywhere wanted to see the first movie to be filmed in the fascinating landscape of Greenland, and theaters were sold out days in advance. No one would have guessed that this was to be the last film Riefenstahl would star in for a long time to come.

## "LOFTY HUMANITY AND ETERNAL BLONDENESS"

The mountain films of Arnold Fanck, and also those of his students Trenker and Riefenstahl, were the subject of bitter debate in the early postwar years. In his book *From Caligari to Hitler*, the German film historian and theoretician Siegfried Kracauer posits that the mountain films exemplified by Fanck, with their overblown heroism and glorification of the German Alps as a supernatural force, were examples of prefascist ideas, a thesis that determined the reception of the genre for years to come. The book, written by Kracauer during the harrowing years of fascism and his own exile, was published in 1947 and looks back on German film production from 1918 to 1933. The author seeks to establish a direct relationship between the mountain cult of the 1920s and the Hitler cult of the Third Reich, employing the unconvincing argument, for example, that the cloud formations in Fanck's *Stürme über dem Montblanc* (*Avalanche*) are similar to those of Riefenstahl's propaganda film *Triumph des Willens*, and declaring that the mountain film emotionally helped prepare the way for fascism. The conflicts over the mountain film genre that led to the "case of Arnold Fanck" developed not least from Kracauer's theses.[25]

Fanck's students—Luis Trenker, with his "Blut und Boden" (blood and soil) films in the Third Reich, and Leni Riefenstahl, with her propaganda films—belonged to the elite of the film world during the fascist period, with their films praised as exemplary. This was reason enough to point to the direct connection between the mountain film's view of the world and National Socialism's presentations to the public.[26]

This is not merely a projection of the postwar period; Fanck's films were met with sharp critical debate at the time of their release. "The representation of nature arouses emotions similar to those aroused by pornography."[27] Whereas bourgeois and conservative camps celebrated the aesthetic brilliance of the films, awarding them the status of their own art form, critics on the left protested the films' ideological direction. "There's more insufferable bluster and devious, deceptive hot air here than at twenty Hitler rallies put together," complained a reviewer in *Der Montag Morgen*.[28] A reviewer for the *Weltbühne* called *Der heilige Berg* "blatant propaganda for a lofty humanity and eternal blondeness."[29]

In all of Fanck's films, individuals in the most extreme situations prevail because of their bodies, steeled by sports, and their incorruptible moral stance. Only "the best"—the healthiest, the strongest, and the sturdiest—can survive. The Darwinism underlying many of Fanck's films placed them in dangerous proximity to National Socialist propaganda, with its "selective breeding," "national hygiene," and "racial considerations." The "alpinist" becomes the "superman"; the city dweller can be cleansed only when "healed" by nature. This was the message of Fanck's films.

Thus, Arnold Fanck was not the apolitical filmmaker he presented himself to be after 1945. He admired Adolf Hitler and considered himself a staunch German nationalist. While it is true that he avoided political activity, in both 1914 and 1939 he enthusiastically supported Germany's war plans and goals. He was a deeply committed anti-Semite, even though he counted several Jews among his best friends. During the Third Reich he ingratiated himself with the country's new rulers and didn't hesitate to join the NSDAP (National Socialist German Workers Party) in order to further his career. Not by accident was Fanck counted among the avant-garde of the right quite early on. National Socialist film critics enthusiastically praised his films as ur-German and consciously placed them in positive opposition to mainstream American films.

The mountain films were grounded in a very definite sociopolitical, ideological setting. The period of their greatest popularity, around 1930, significantly coincided with the rise of National Socialism. The reactionary enthusiasm for alpinism, prevailed over by increasingly antidemocratic, nationalistic, and anti-Semitic provocateurs, led to the introduction of an "Aryan article" into the bylaws of the Alpine Association by 1924. In the context of this nationalistic elevation of alpinism, the films of Arnold Fanck were praised as a "profession of the faith of many Germans."[30] Siegfried Kracauer maintained, "The wave of pro-Nazi tendencies during the prefascist period could not have been better confirmed than through the proliferation and specific development of the mountain film."[31]

Despite such arguments, it would be an oversimplification to consider the mountain films exclusively as prefascist creations, as this does not take into consideration the complex roots of the genre, including the literature of Romanticism, the alpinist movement, and the nature cult of the early twentieth century. The fact that Fanck was a committed German Nationalist and that his students, Riefenstahl and Trenker, made their careers in the Third Reich, is still not proof that the mountain films helped pave the way for National Socialism. Rather, they came out of a time and a conceptual world in which one could stage and screen bombastic, heroic epics set in the German Alps without necessarily having to place oneself in proximity to National Socialist thought.

That the films were attacked at the time they were made for prefascist tendencies does not mean that these tendencies were the predominant, determining elements of the films. Plenty of leftist film critics felt there was something to be gained from the mountain films without finding it necessary to dwell on charges of fascism. Even if this is obstructed by today's view of the mountain film, which links the genre's aesthetic to that of Nazi cinema, the fact remains that the majority of moviegoers at the time devoured Fanck's alpine adventures as thrilling entertainment. More recent publications treat the mountain film genre in a more balanced way than those of preceding decades.[32]

# 4

## EMBARKING ON A NEW CAREER

### DIRECTORIAL DEBUT: *DAS BLAUE LICHT*

WHEN RIEFENSTAHL SET OUT to secure her place in film history, acting as producer, director, screenwriter, editor, and star of *Das blaue Licht* (*The Blue Light*), she represented an absolute exception. And with her directorial debut she became one of Germany's first woman film directors.

Riefenstahl had the opportunity to learn a great deal about the practical aspects of filmmaking on the set of Arnold Fanck's films. Not only was her mentor Fanck a passionate mountain climber, athlete, and nature enthusiast, but he was also a director who loved the technical aspect of film. His joy in experimentation never diminished and his innovations in camera and editing techniques became the new standard. Fanck's colleagues took an active interest in these experiments and trials. They perceived themselves to be cineaste explorers and enjoyed contributing their own ideas on how to accomplish ever more spectacular and remarkable takes. While working as an actress in this creative atmosphere, Riefenstahl learned about the roles of director, cinematographer, and technician. She soon discovered a new fascination: "Film is becoming a mission for me, a new area I am determined to fathom and that I want to understand everything about."[1]

She learned to use the camera, mastering different focal lengths and the effects of various color filters and lenses. Fanck discussed with her how to frame scenes and taught her the importance of avoiding the accepted, routine ways of seeing and to find new points of view. He even let her look over his shoulder in the cutting room, for the editing process was of major importance to his films. By the time he shot *Der heilige Berg*, which Fanck edited in his Freiburg studio, Riefenstahl assisted him on all of the montage work done on the film: "Day and night, at every free moment, I'm in the printing lab learning to develop and copy. I'm learning editing and how to assemble the many, many short scenes."[2] During this time, Riefenstahl began to grasp the possibilities and artistic potential that lay hidden in the cutting and editing of film, and how a film is composed using these processes—experience that shaped her later work. Fanck taught Riefenstahl in the same meticulous manner that he had taught Luis Trenker and many others on his staff. Nevertheless, she later tried to downplay his influence. As opposed to Trenker, who for the rest of his life referred to Fanck, not without pride, as his "master,"[3] Riefenstahl's version is that she merely "unconsciously picked up some things from him . . . Without learning from it, it was then forgotten."[4]

Exactly when Riefenstahl decided to become a director is a matter of dispute. In her 1933 book *Kampf in Schnee und Eis* (*Battle in Snow and Ice*), she reported that ever since working on her first Fanck project she had dreamed of directing her own films. Later, in *Memoiren*, she made it seem as if she had first felt this desire only shortly before she filmed *Das blaue Licht*, a desire she then energetically acted on—a version she obviously felt better suited her.[5] This is important in that her directorial debut was not the result of accident or, as she maintained, a makeshift decision based on the fact that she lacked the money to hire another director,[6] a claim repeated even today.[7] What drove her was her artistic will, "which has to be expressed, otherwise I cannot exist."[8]

The desire to direct took more concrete form as it became clear to her that with Fanck she would never find the fulfillment as an actress that she had hoped for. In the summer of 1930, after the shooting of *Stürme über dem Montblanc* was completed, she drew the line: "I've studied the camera, the lenses. I know about film stock and filters. I've edited film and know how to achieve new effects. Without wanting it, I've been pushed increasingly in this direction. I defend myself against it, because I'm an actress and don't want to feel divided. But I can no longer change the fact that I see everything as if through a camera lens. I want to shape the images myself . . . I have an ever-increasing desire to create them myself."[9]

She now wanted to use what she had learned from Fanck and expand it to
the full extent of her powers, to make a film according to her own aesthetic ideas, a film that would differ fundamentally from those of her
mentor.

If Arnold Fanck's first concern was to show audiences things they had
never seen before, much less ever experienced (scaling inaccessible glaciers, life above the clouds), Riefenstahl's aim was to create "beautiful
images" that would stand alone in their aesthetic brilliance. She was not
interested in documentary films, as Fanck preferred; her material was the
stuff of fairy tales. When at the beginning of the 1930s she decided that
the time had come to make her own films, she had no problem breaking
with her onetime benefactor.

While it is true that Leni Riefenstahl the actress and director "grew
up" with Fanck, she was never his "creation." From the beginning she
worked to create herself, to define herself independently and to seek her
own way. What she had done previously in dance she now wanted to do
in film, insofar as the medium allowed for "solos." As Fanck had always
cast her in the same roles—bold athletic comrade or chaste lover—and
other directors weren't hiring her for the more conventional studio productions, she began to write parts for herself: "I longed for good roles and
as I wasn't getting them, I wrote my own."[10]

In Fanck's films, Riefenstahl often found herself at the center of a love
triangle. As the two men battled over her character, she stood off to one
side, oddly passive, never an active or independent force who moved the
film in a new direction. Naturally it disturbed the self-centered Riefenstahl that she was only one attraction among others—the mountains, the
forces of nature, and her male colleagues. In addition, it was her opinion
that the spectacular nature footage didn't always have to be tied to realistic plotlines, if only because the range of true-to-life stories set at high
altitudes was limited. She wanted to combine the nature shots, which at
times verged on the fantastic, with action of an equally fantastic, fairy-tale
nature. But Fanck was not won over by Riefenstahl's ideas on the total
stylization of both content and image.[11]

So she rightfully perceived her work with Fanck as a dead end.
According to the film scholar Rainer Rother, when "compared with the
true stars of silent film at the end of the twenties, and with her German

competition, she had become an interesting phenomenon under his direction, but nothing more."[12] That was to change fundamentally with the first film she directed.

### "IMAGES CREATED FROM MY DREAMS"

A film cost money, a great deal of money. So Leni Riefenstahl first set out in search of producers and financiers, but most important, people who believed in and supported her. In doing so, she found herself in a new situation: her will and persistence alone were not enough. This time it was necessary to find fellow collaborators who were prepared to join her in this adventure. What was new to her was that she met with rejection, that there were those who dared to say no to her, who showed her the door with the words "Boring!" and "Unacceptable!" Even Fanck, to whom she first offered the project, wasn't convinced by the material and refused either to direct the film or to offer it to Ufa. So she decided to make a virtue of necessity and organize the production herself.

By this point, if not earlier, she must also have been aware that this plan held hidden advantages, as only in this way could she alone determine how to translate her ideas into film. A big studio would never have given a young woman the kind of artistic freedom that Riefenstahl had in mind. So she became determined to create a film that bore her mark alone, that corresponded to her artistic concepts. She used what she had learned from Fanck about filming and editing and what she had learned from G. W. Pabst about directing actors during her work on *Die weisse Hölle vom Piz Palü*. She perfected this knowledge in her very first film. "In this way," writes the biographer Claudia Lenssen, "*Das blaue Licht* became the work of an auteur in a manner that up until then had existed only in avant-garde films."[13]

It is unclear how Riefenstahl came upon the material on which *Das blaue Licht* was based. There are two different versions of the story, both of which derive from Riefenstahl herself. In 1932, at the time the film originated, the director told a newspaper interviewer that she happened to have heard the tale from farmers as she was hiking through South Tirol. She had been so taken by the story that she couldn't get the idea of turning it into a film out of her head.[14] But in *Memoiren*, which appeared decades later, she wrote that she had dreamed the story: "Out of my dreams came images. Out of the mist emerged the outline of a young girl who lived in the mountains, a creature of nature. I saw her climbing, saw her in moonlight, I felt how she was pursued and had stones thrown at her, how this girl then let go of the face of the rock and fell into the abyss. These images took hold of me, they multiplied, and one day I wrote it all down—an eighteen-page exposition."[15]

Impatient to realize her first film, she went ahead planning and filming it without having found backers, and financed the film with 45,000 reichsmarks out of her own pocket, in the firm belief that in time she would find investors. Even though she had free use of Arnold Fanck's and Hans Schneeberger's technical equipment, she had to come up with the money for expensive film stock as well as sufficient funds for a shooting schedule that could last for weeks, in addition to paying for a few expensive days in the studio. She sold her jewelry and mortgaged her apartment but was 50,000 reichsmarks short of her goal.

In early summer 1931, Riefenstahl founded her own production company, L. R. Studio-Film of Sokal-Film GmbH, as sole shareholder, and began making concrete plans. To hold down costs she decided to forgo as much as possible the use of an expensive studio and instead to film almost totally on location. Both cast and crew declared themselves willing to postpone payment until the film had launched successfully.

Hans Schneeberger, from whom Riefenstahl had been separated for two years, acted as cinematographer without pay and served as her major adviser during the planning stage and shooting. In Schneeberger, she had one of the best cameramen in Germany.[16] The scars of their painful separation apparently had healed, but Riefenstahl never said whether or not they ever talked about it. At any rate, their renewed collaboration went smoothly and was for Riefenstahl a great piece of good luck she never would have expected at the time the relationship fell apart two years earlier: "Despite the distress it had caused me . . . there was no residue of bitterness."[17]

Following a long search, Riefenstahl found her "Monte Cristallo," the mountain at the center of her story, in Crozzon di Brenta Mountain in the Dolomites. Filming was scheduled to take place from July to September 1931 in Foroglio in Tessin, in Sarentino, a village in the Sarn Valley of South Tirol, and at the nearby Runkelstein Castle, near Bozen.

As difficult as the search for locations was finding amateur actors, which Riefenstahl depended on, as there was not enough money to fill the cast with professionals only. "They are the most difficult to find, because it's certain faces in particular that I have in mind. We're having to look in remote mountain valleys, far from anywhere. And it will take a while to search through all of them. Most of the time I'm disappointed with the faces. They're not specific enough, not typical enough. I had something else in mind for my film."[18] Finally, in a village in the Sarn Valley, she found farmers who, after they got over their initial distrust, agreed to act in the film. After some awkwardness at the beginning, they soon were acting completely naturally in front of the camera.

Her relationship with the Sarn Valley farmers, who had never left their village and knew nothing of the modern world, developed so well that in the end she even was allowed to film them in their daily village life, including at a church service. So *Das blaue Licht* includes many authentic images of farmhouses, alpine huts, and village churches. In this way she could get around extravagant, costly sets, which was a novelty in feature films of the period and which, decades later, led Italian director Roberto Rossellini to celebrate Riefenstahl as the godmother of neorealism.

The film shoot was determined solely by Riefenstahl's aesthetic ideas: "We can work in great peace, without haste. No one is looking over our shoulders, pressuring us, no one from the industry has sent anyone to keep an eye on us. We're our own masters."[19] She attached great importance to the quality of the shots, for which she wanted a graphic and alienating effect, and to this end she experimented with various angles, focal lengths, and film stock. These experiments were so important to her that on many days only a few minutes of film actually were shot. Everything had to be perfect. The lighting conditions of all of the takes were exactly measured beforehand and the necessary film stock procured. The team was continually preparing sample shots, to check whether the lighting could be further improved.

When she couldn't get the desired effect with the standards then current in Germany, she tried new solutions: she had portrait lenses sent from Hollywood, because at that point the close-up was more technically perfected in America than in Germany. With these, she could shoot soft, flattering images that greatly differed from the hard, sharp contours of the close-ups in Fanck's films and that had the look of being shot through gauze. She had the German film company Agfa develop a new film stock (the so-called R stock), which she could use to film night shots—difficult to light in the mountains—during the day, with the help of certain light filters.

With all these special effects and experiments, she succeeded in achieving exactly the magical images she was after and that appeared necessary to the telling of her story. By not setting the mountain-climbing scenes during the day, but at night in fog, they no longer had the realistic, sports-film look of Fanck's work. Instead, her alienated visual vocabulary, more strongly influenced by painting than by photography, better suited the fairy-tale context of her plot.

This unreal quality was also emphasized through her noticeably sparse use of dialogue and sound: "They'll be used as a means of enhancement, of a sudden outburst of aggression and fear."[20] With *Das blaue Licht,* Riefenstahl had in mind a film like those of Charlie Chaplin, which at the beginning of the sound era still widely abjured speech and therefore were intended as universally understandable (and distributable).

When she sent the first master copies to Berlin, the plan she had believed in so strongly succeeded. Unsurprisingly, she found a financier in Harry Sokal, who had produced Fanck's past three films, *Die weisse Hölle vom Piz Palü, Stürme über dem Montblanc,* and *Der weisse Rausch* (*The White Frenzy*), and who was still in love with Riefenstahl. Sokal joined the project with an investment of 100,000 marks and even took over postproduction and distribution costs. Thus the final hurdle had been cleared and the future of the film secured.

While the film still had to be completed on an extremely tight budget, Sokal was already organizing a major premiere at Berlin's Ufa-Palast am Zoo, the city's most important venue.

In September 1931, after the scenes set in the crystal grotto were shot over the course of three days in the Berlin studio, Riefenstahl enthusiastically got to work in the editing room, which is where she would have preferred to stay indefinitely. But she was as dissatisfied with her first edited cut as was her coproducer and distributor, AAFA-Film. Arnold Fanck, who had moved to Berlin in the interim, was asked to take a look at the film and work with Riefenstahl on new options. Fanck, who had not believed in the project at first but who was now excited by the takes, took her original copy and cut it himself, turning it into a Fanck film—just the opposite of what Riefenstahl had intended. In view of the "mutilation" of her film, Riefenstahl suffered a nervous breakdown. Soon enough, however, what she at first took to be an act of revenge on Fanck's part she came to view as a positive experience. In editing the film again—presumably together with Fanck[21]—and translating Fanck's suggestions into her own visual language, she perfected her cut. She inserted more close-ups into scenes, in order to visually build up tension, and chose a new and slower rhythm. The music by Giuseppe Becce,[22] the grand old man of German film music, in whose orchestra Marlene Dietrich had played the violin in the 1920s, underscored Riefenstahl's fairy-tale imagery and completed the moody atmosphere of her directorial debut.

## AN "INTERNALLY SICK FILM"?

The film program for *Das blaue Licht*, its language markedly calling up the blood-and-soil ideology of the National Socialists, states: "*Das blaue Licht* is an ancient legend from the Dolomites, an allegory for the stunted, carnal drive of earthbound and stolid peasants toward the light of the mountains, which at the same time they superstitiously fear."[23] Riefenstahl plays Junta, an Italian-speaking Gypsy girl who lives far removed from the life of the (German-speaking) village and is the only person capable of reaching the mysterious blue light of Monte Cristallo, which emanates from an all but inaccessible crystal grotto. Clad in enhancing rags and radiating a mystical eroticism, Junta is the stranger, the scorned beggar woman, the wild child "hounded by the lust of men and the hatred of women."[24] In the form of Junta and the peasants, *Das blaue Licht* skillfully pits mystical beliefs against reason, with the film's sympathies definitely inclined toward the former.

The blue light, which the mountain emits only on the night of the full moon, is created by moonlight penetrating a cave, the walls of which are completely covered in mountain crystal. The young peasants, drawn to it as if by magic, climb the mountain in an effort to find out what causes it, only to plunge from the rocks to their deaths. Junta, however, is able to reach the crystal grotto with the sureness of the sleepwalker, and so the peasants blame her for the deaths of their sons. Vigo, a painter from Vienna (played by Mathias Wieman), arrives in the village one day and immediately falls in love with the mysterious Junta. He follows her and reveals to the peasants her secret path to the cave, in the hope that the villagers will no longer persecute Junta as a witch. But the peasants are greedy and plunder the crystal grotto, thus destroying the magic that had eluded them for years. The blue light, previously feared, is now an object of greed.

As the entire village celebrates its newfound wealth, Junta finds a broken-off splinter of crystal in the forest and figures out what has happened. She climbs up to the grotto, finds it empty, and, without the blue light to illuminate her path, plunges into the abyss. With the disappearance of the crystal—the disappearance of the mystical from the modern-day world—Junta's soul dies as well.

In her debut, Riefenstahl succeeded in elevating the realistic portrayal of nature so appreciated in Fanck's films, both visually and as a motif, to the realm of fairy-tale mysticism and the allegorical, and in doing so gave the genre a totally new direction. Many critics were fully aware of this. Just as she had met with immediate success as a dancer and as a star of mountain films, with her very first film as a director she made a name for herself. She brought the specialized knowledge gained in her previous careers to her work as director, introducing new approaches to filmmaking, which in turn underscored the independence of her artistic achievement. Her choreographic rhythm, which also marked her editing work, was combined with the technical knowledge she picked up while working on the mountain films. In the making of *Das blaue Licht*, this synthesis marked the specific style of her film language.

Riefenstahl was confronted with the same criticism of her film that Arnold Fanck had faced. But can *Das blaue Licht* truly be viewed as a pre-fascist film? It is true that the first film Riefenstahl directed—with its mystical glorification of the forces of nature and disdain for the modern—is pervaded by prefascist concepts, as were most of Fanck's films, but one can scarcely seriously conclude from this that Riefenstahl was pursuing a concrete political goal or even that she was a forerunner of a fascist aesthetic. It appears, rather, that *Das blaue Licht* strongly reflected her childhood fantasies and the romantic dreams she had held on to since her youth.

Nonetheless, the material chosen by Riefenstahl was associated with certain significant tendencies. The theme of the only film she directed before Hitler came to power is not as innocuous and disconnected from its time as Riefenstahl later insisted. Had that been so, the bitter debate that surrounded *Das blaue Licht* following its German premiere would not have developed.

When the film opened at the Ufa-Palast am Zoo on March 24, 1932, critical opinion was divided. In addition to near euphoric reviews, which celebrated *Das blaue Licht* as a "uniquely lyrical film" and "the best film of recent years,"[25] there were harsher verdicts: "The characters of the tale are sketchy, they're ambiguous and indistinct, they don't have enough of a profile or substance and therefore what they deliver in terms of action is uneven, neutered. The mountain maid and mountain madness are suspiciously related. Giuseppe Becce's music, which all but engulfs this innately sick film, cannot cure it. It is a failure."[26] Riefenstahl's enthusiasm for the mystic forces of nature on the one hand, and the damnation of "corrupt civilization" that ensued on the other, was repeatedly criticized. Many refused to consider *Das blaue Licht* art, rejecting it as styleless kitsch and tediously mystical. The remarkably harsh reviews soon led to the film being removed from distribution in Germany, and in many cities it was not screened at all.

Riefenstahl's debut had offered exactly the same message that her mentor Arnold Fanck had delivered in each of his films: nature would bring human beings into harmony with themselves and their surroundings. People yearned for "these types of absolute values: blood and soil, fatherland, bravery, loyalty, nature."[27]

Viewed in retrospect, it is precisely this pessimism concerning civilization, this antimodernism that so dangerously approaches Nazi thinking, that was to determine aesthetic guidelines in Germany after 1933. All of the modern and avant-garde movements that preceded 1933 were denigrated as "Jewish cultural Bolshevism" and as a sign of decline and "degeneration," to be replaced by the heroic transfiguration of the Teutonic past. Paintings of the Nazi era were inspired by the idealized subjects of the preindustrial period, which before 1933 had been ridiculed as "forest, field, and meadow painting."[28] Architecture championed small-scale housing developments in the "regional traditional style," while prominent Nazi officials preferred the alpine "Obersalzberg" style. The literature promoted by the Nazis boasted nationalistic themes of the "*Volk*." It was here that a "new race" was propagated, which—following the nature-centered mysticism of blood-and-soil ideology—was rooted in "native soil": those who worked the land were declared the source of the nation's strength, their way of life far superior to modern urban living. In the art of the Nazi period, tillers of the soil were the bulwark against the "intellectual," "un-German spirit," which, according to the Nazis, marked the culture of the Weimar Republic.

Significantly, in *Das blaue Licht* it was the scenes with the farmers of the Sarn Valley that impressed Hitler. According to him, every work of art had to reveal through its form and shape the national characteristics from which it derived and was created. Twelve years after the film's premiere he was still talking about these scenes. At a table conversation in Obersalzberg on March 13, 1944, two weeks before he met with Riefenstahl for the last time, he described her first directorial effort as exemplary: "Years ago—it was before the war—I drove past a Labor Service camp near Bergedorf. My car was surrounded by a large number of youths, all browned by the sun. I said to my traveling companions: 'Why don't our filmmakers come here to find people with the right characteristics? It must be possible in one or two years to turn a young man—who has to possess a certain aptitude, of course—into an actor, even if it's for only one role that no one else could fill at that moment. Riefenstahl does it the right way, she goes to the villages and picks out her actors herself.'"[29]

The way Riefenstahl portrayed and mysticized mountain life was seen by certain circles at the time as being specifically "German." Paul Ickes, a film critic and friend of Riefenstahl, who wrote the foreword to Riefenstahl's book *Kampf in Schnee und Eis*, confirmed that Riefenstahl agreed with this assessment: "It seems as if the German, due to his spiritual structure, is particularly qualified to experience the mountains not only as a tourist does, but as a spiritual encounter—and to shape this experience artistically, whether as literature or in some other form. Over the course of recent years I was often able to speak to Leni Riefenstahl about precisely this, and it was precisely in this question that I discerned over and over again her aversion to the 'industrial' views then current."[30]

Despite this view of Riefenstahl and her surroundings, and also despite the reviews that *Das blaue Licht* received, it should not be overlooked that many audiences of the time considered Riefenstahl's film simply entertainment, without taking in its political implications.

The recognition that Riefenstahl was denied in Germany was granted her abroad. After the film was screened as the German entry in the first Venice Biennale in 1932 and honored with the Silver Medallion, there was nothing standing in the way of her international breakthrough. Critics in England and France almost turned somersaults in their enthusiastic hymns of praise for the film and its creator. *Das blaue Licht* ran for many weeks in Paris and London, where it premiered at the Rialto theater on October 30, 1932, with Riefenstahl in attendance. The British press called it "one of the most beautiful films ever made."[31]

Two years later, in 1934, the film opened in the United States, where it received considerable notice in major cities and placed first on the National Board of Review's list of the most important films of 1934–35. Even Hollywood greats such as Charlie Chaplin and Douglas Fairbanks were impressed by the debut of Germany's young director, and Ethel Barrymore found the film "divinely beautiful."[32] Chaplin, in his social satire *Modern Times*, modeled the role played by his companion, Paulette Goddard, on the character of Junta, virtually in homage to *Das blaue Licht*.


A COLLEAGUE WHO WAS NOT ALWAYS WELCOME


In 1938, when *Das blaue Licht*, distributed by Degeto, was brought back to theaters following the success of the *Olympia* films, the name Béla Balázs had vanished from the opening credits, making the film *judenfrei*,[33] "Jew-free." At a time when all it took to ban a film made in the Weimar period was the presence of a Jewish actor or director,[34] Riefenstahl clearly had become greatly uncomfortable with the fact that Balázs, a Jew and Communist, was her collaborator in her directorial debut.

Béla Balázs (1884–1949) was a well-known avant-garde film critic and theoretician of German-Hungarian heritage, who had also distinguished himself as the screenwriter for the film of Brecht's *Dreigroschenoper* (*Three-penny Opera*). Riefenstahl hired him in 1931, and together they wrote the script for *Das blaue Licht*. In addition, he declared his willingness to direct those scenes in which Riefenstahl acted. While Riefenstahl devoted herself to the visuals, Balázs was entrusted with the dramaturgy of the film as well as with writing the dialogue.[35]

As Riefenstahl was primarily concerned with getting the Junta legend on film, the frame story of the original script most probably can be traced back to an idea by Balázs.[36] The framework leads from the time of the legend into the present: the villagers have turned Junta's story into a tourist attraction decades after the original events took place and are profiting from images of the young woman who lost her life. Their greed is a visualization of how "her sacrificial death" was transformed "into a profitable myth for tourists."[37]

According to Riefenstahl, Balázs was not compensated for cowriting the script with her.[38] As Balázs understandably demanded the money owed him once the film became a success,[39] it appears that he—as did all of the collaborators on *Das blaue Licht*—had not intended to work gratis but rather delayed his fee until the film began to show a profit. It is unlikely that Balázs was the only member of the film to postpone pay. There are no existing corresponding agreements on fees, and presumably they were made verbally.

Immediately after the film had completed shooting, Balázs left Germany to work as a lecturer at the Film School in Moscow. Following the Nazis' seizure of power, he could not return to Germany, due to his Jewish heritage and his Communist leanings, and he remained in Soviet exile. In the beginning, he was still on friendly terms with Riefenstahl. On February 21, 1932, six days before she heard Adolf Hitler speak for the first time, at the Berlin Sports Palace, Riefenstahl wrote to Balázs in Moscow, reporting on the extensive work still needed on the film and asking when he was coming back to Germany.[40] The affable tone of her letter is evidence that at that point she thoroughly expected Balázs to return.

When Balázs, in exile, later heard of the film's international success, he wrote to Riefenstahl from Moscow requesting payment of his fee, which as an emigrant he desperately needed.[41] Whereas during his final visit to Berlin at the beginning of 1933 she had counseled patience in the matter, Riefenstahl, with the Nazis backing her, now brought out the big guns. As Harry Sokal had emigrated in the meantime, taking with him the original negative of the film and, much to Riefenstahl's displeasure, showing it commercially without sharing the profits with the director, she refused to pay Balázs the money he was due.

Her unscrupulous treatment of Balázs, who had made a great contribution to her first directorial effort, as well as her circumvention of his demands, makes very clear how adept Riefenstahl was at exploiting the new political situation and how close she was to the Nazi regime. She went so far as to authorize Julius Streicher, editor of the Nazi smear sheet *Der Stürmer* and one of the most feared anti-Semites of the Third Reich, to instigate proceedings against "demands made upon me by the Jew Béla Balázs." The handwritten letter in which Riefenstahl gave Streicher full authority to represent her in this matter is on file at the Federal Archive in Berlin.[42]

Riefenstahl never commented on this letter or on her excessive reaction to the Balázs affair.[43] She limited herself instead to referring to the division of responsibilities at the time. After all, she maintained, it was Harry Sokal who was responsible for paying Balázs.[44] She had never had a quarrel with Balázs, she said, and after 1945 they were still in amicable contact. Regardless of Riefenstahl's behavior toward Balázs, his influence on the film was major, and it was not without justification that the 1932 premiere of *Das blaue Licht* was heralded as a "collaboration among Leni Riefenstahl, Béla Balázs, and Hans Schneeberger."

According to Riefenstahl, the original negative of the film was lost during the war. She edited a new version from footage that had not been used in the original and that concentrated solely on the legend of Junta, omitting the frame story. When this version of the film was screened in 1952, she was credited with "book, direction, and cinematography." Hans Schneeberger was credited for "photography" and Béla Balázs only for "collaboration on the script."

Only in a restored version of the film, created in 2001, did Schneeberger and Balázs receive equal credit as creators, as they had when the film first premiered in 1932.

# *Fame*

# 5

## "I WAS INFECTED"

### LENI RIEFENSTAHL AND ADOLF HITLER

THE HARSH CRITICISM of Riefenstahl's *Das blaue Licht* in 1932 deeply affected the artist, who strongly identified with her film. She perceived every negative review as a personal attack. Harry Sokal acknowledged that it was precisely this situation that made her receptive to Hitler's ideas. In an interview with *Der Spiegel* in 1976, he described Riefenstahl's fits of rage in the face of the criticism, which stemmed largely from Jewish film critics: "Riefenstahl blamed the Jewish critics for ruining her career. She said they were 'foreigners' who didn't understand her art, and that Hitler, were he to come to power, would no longer allow something like that."[1] It was under these circumstances, feeling misunderstood as an artist and placing the blame for this on the "Jewish critics" in Germany, that Riefenstahl came across Adolf Hitler and his ideological work, *Mein Kampf*. She appears to have seen in Hitler the man who, were he in power, would protect her from such attacks in the future.

That she was correct in this is shown by the recognition that *Das blaue Licht* later received in Nazi Germany. When the film returned to theaters in 1938—without the name Béla Balázs and therefore "Jew-free"—the Nazi press hailed it as a masterwork of German cinema, as "the most German of all films,"[2] and didn't neglect to mention that in 1932 the film had not enjoyed the success it deserved because of its rejection by Jewish critics. The film was part of the state's evidence of the alleged misjudgment of "Jewish criticism." In the Tobis Film Company's press file on the rerelease of the film is this quote: "Seldom has a film received such divided opinion at its premiere [at the end of March 1932], as did this one. As strongly and enduringly as the public celebrated its success, the press greeted it negatively, with the few Aryan exceptions among the critics. The Jewish press described it in a manner that can only be termed maliciously scathing. This method ensured that the film received limited distribution, so that only a relatively small percentage of the German public was able to see it."[3] This delayed gratification for Riefenstahl allowed her to disregard the original insult. The Jewish "foreigners" who had denied her talent as a director had, as a result of the Nazis' racial laws, for the most part emigrated.

After 1945, Leni Riefenstahl distanced herself from the fact that it had been Hitler's anti-Semitism that had caused her to turn toward the man who became dictator. On top of this, she transformed her first momentous meeting with Hitler into a "fateful encounter."[4] Decades later, Riefenstahl was still puzzling over whether this had been "accident or fate."[5] It was neither, for the meeting had come about at the express wish of Riefenstahl, similar to her first encounter with her mentor Arnold Fanck. She herself said that she acted out of an "inner compulsion."[6]

Up until this time, according to her, she had never been interested in politics, being completely consumed by her work, which often removed her from the boiling pot that was Berlin in the final years of the Weimar Republic. Nevertheless, on the evening of February 27, 1932, she attended a National Socialist rally at the Berlin Sports Palace at which Hitler was scheduled to speak.[7] She walked past kiosks and walls plastered with large posters bearing Hitler's image to reach the Sports Palace on Potsdamer Strasse, which was packed to the rafters with twenty-five thousand people. She took in the agitated atmosphere, the slogan-chanting crowd, and the rousing martial music that prepared the way for Hitler's arrival.

Hitler appeared shortly before 10:00 p.m. As usual, his entrance was accompanied by the sound of the "Badenweiler March." This was Hitler's first speech as a candidate for the office of Reich president. His candidacy, which pitted him against the aged president Paul von Hindenburg, had been announced by Joseph Goebbels five days earlier and lent the upcoming election a special volatility. Hindenburg, the symbol of German militarism, had been elected Reich president in 1925 despite resistance from the country's leftist parties. In the 1932 elections, however, he was able to count on the support of the left, which had joined with the democratic forces in an effort to prevent at all costs Hitler's ascendancy to the office.

Despite the great coalition that had formed against him, Hitler appeared sure of victory at the Sports Palace on the evening of February 27. He affirmed his determination to redress the "disgrace of the Versailles Treaty," criticized the "policy of appeasement" of former administrations, and denounced the reigning unemployment and deprivation, which were the massive problems of the Weimar Republic—all were themes on which he based his campaign.[8]

Leni Riefenstahl followed Hitler's speech as if in a trance. His gestures and the intensity of his language fascinated her, whereas she later declared the substance of what he had said to be second rate. She described the experience as an "apocalyptic vision" (for Leni Riefenstahl it could be nothing less): "It was as if the earth opened up before me—as if the hemisphere suddenly split down the middle and out of it erupted an enormous waterspout, so powerful that it touched the sky and shook the earth."[9] Hours later she still was so shaken and confused that she was unable even to hail a cab: "I had been infected, no doubt about it."[10]

She avidly read Hitler's *Mein Kampf*[11]—in which he laid out his program—intensely engaged herself with his theories, and followed the National Socialist election results in the various states of the Reich in the papers.

It is often speculated how a woman who declared herself to have been apolitical her whole life could suddenly exhibit a devotion to Hitler and his message. But she was not alone in her reaction. At the end of the Weimar Republic and the beginning of the Third Reich, there was an astonishingly rapid and broad change in mood across almost all of German society in favor of Hitler and his party. The effects of the worldwide economic depression, the high unemployment rate, and Germany's distressed social system as well as the political disorder caused by the constantly changing government—which no one trusted to pull the country out of its despair—drove people into Hitler's arms. Hitler knew how to exploit the signs of the looming collapse of the Weimar Republic to his own advantage. His message was directly suited to the mood of the time.

Millions of Germans were fascinated by the man who declared himself to be the future of Germany, and they were willing to follow him, placing the fate of their country in his hands.

Albert Speer, who was to become Hitler's architect and minister of armaments, was as receptive to the suggestive power of Hitler's speeches as were Magda Goebbels and Winifred Wagner. Speer said that the first time he heard Hitler, he became a "changed person."[12]

Hitler had already claimed the political stage for himself with the sensational successes enjoyed by the NSDAP in the Reichstag elections of 1930. One year earlier, party membership had doubled. Although President Hindenburg beat Hitler at the polls in April 1932 with a majority of the six million votes cast, the leader of the National Socialist party remained a major figure in the political battle. And he persisted in his aim of becoming Reich chancellor and doing away with democracy.

On May 18, 1932, three months after she heard Hitler speak at the Sports Palace, Riefenstahl contacted him directly, by means of a brief letter in which she requested a personal meeting. The original document has not survived, but Riefenstahl quotes it in *Memoiren*, claiming to be able to recall every word from memory. Even if the value of the version later committed to paper is highly questionable, the letter, addressed to the "Brown House," the party headquarters of the NSDAP in Munich, at the very least reveals how Riefenstahl chose to view this central turning point in her life:

Dear Herr Hitler,

A short time ago I attended a political meeting for the first time in my life. You were delivering a speech at the Sports Palace. I must admit that I was impressed by you and by the enthusiasm of your audience. My wish is to meet you personally. Unfortunately, I am leaving Germany in a few days for several months, to make a film in Greenland. Therefore, a meeting with you will scarcely be possible before my departure. Nor do I know whether this letter will ever reach you. An answer from you would be most appreciated. With kindest regards,

Yours,

Leni Riefenstahl[13]

Riefenstahl's letter sounds more like a young girl's fan letter to a film star than a mature woman and successful artist writing to a politician. According to her own representation of the facts, she always separated Hitler the person from Hitler the politician and symbol of power. The brilliant orator fascinated her, she maintained, but not what he said. Given that her first encounter with the man who later would become dictator was arranged at her own initiative, after 1945 she had little choice but to explain the original contact in this way. The fact that beyond this private meeting she was deeply engaged by Hitler's agenda and began to become occupied with his political future[14] reveals, however, that her interest was not at all limited to Hitler the individual.

Much to her surprise, Riefenstahl received an immediate reply from the Brown House. Hitler—who had always been a movie fan—had long been an admirer of the beautiful and celebrated director, beginning with her days as a mountain films actress. Ever since her debut in *Der heilige Berg* he had followed her career attentively. He called the "Dance to the Sea" the "most beautiful thing that I have ever encountered on film."[15]

Consequently, he was greatly pleased at the actress's wish to meet him. And so occurred, more quickly than Riefenstahl had imagined, a first historic meeting between the Führer of the National Socialist party and the young and ambitious artist. According to Riefenstahl, it took place on May 22 and 23, 1932, in Wilhelmshaven, one day before she set off to Greenland to shoot *SOS Eisberg*.

There are no photographs of that first meeting,[16] which was held in the smallest of circles. Because Riefenstahl spoke privately with Hitler for most of that first encounter, only her own account of the meeting survives—as was true of almost all of the meetings with Hitler that followed. The memoirs of Otto Dietrich, NSDAP press chief, confirm that the initial meeting took place on the North Sea. He recalls the meeting place as Horumersiel, not far from Wilhelmshaven, where Hitler frequently spent time before 1933. Dietrich himself was in the car that took Riefenstahl to Hitler, and he reported: "It was here that he made the acquaintance of Leni Riefenstahl, with whom for years to follow he felt a connection as artist and comrade."[17]

From their first meeting, an obvious and amiable accord existed between the young woman and the future dictator, who appeared in civilian clothing. As they walked along the shore of the North Sea, talking about Riefenstahl's experiences in film and her future plans, Hitler allegedly suddenly made the remarkable offer: "If we come to power, you must make my films."[18]

After she had said good-bye to Hitler, the still thoroughly flustered Riefenstahl was flown to Hamburg, in a plane reserved exclusively for her. There, together with the rest of the film crew, she boarded the ship that was to take them to their location in Greenland, but not without taking a copy of *Mein Kampf* and a portrait of Hitler along with her in her baggage.[19] She writes of this time, "Suddenly I was standing on the deck of the ship, watching the Hamburg harbor slowly disappear. All of us standing at the railing of the *Borodino* felt the same thing. What would Germany look like on our return five months hence?"[20]

Just how the relationship between the Führer and the director developed after this first meeting is difficult to reconstruct, as there are almost no independent accounts for the period before 1933. What is certain is that due to her contact with Hitler, Riefenstahl soon was admitted to the innermost circles of the Nazi movement. Thus, she closely experienced the party's efforts to take over the government. When she returned to Germany in September 1932, the situation had totally changed. The Weimar Republic was on the verge of collapse, and the Nazis were finally on their way to power. Ridiculed for years as thugs and beer hall agitators, they now moved confidently in the social milieu of the Reich's capital, where increasingly people were adjusting to what originally had been considered the plebeian National Socialist movement.

Back in Berlin, Riefenstahl immediately contacted Hitler and reported on her experiences in Greenland at a second private meeting. It was during this period, the late fall of 1932, when only Hitler's inner circle was aware of her meetings with the Führer, that she first met Joseph Goebbels, future minister of propaganda. She also got to know Hermann Göring, second in command in the NSDAP, with whom she shared a mutual acquaintance, Ernst Udet. Udet, a former air force comrade of Göring from the First World War, and Riefenstahl had worked together on many films.

During the fall and winter of 1932, Riefenstahl appeared more and more often at parties and official receptions as a guest of high Nazi officials. She also frequented the Hotel Kaiserhof, where Hitler often stayed and where he held negotiations with influential and powerful figures from the financial sphere, those who, in the end, paved his way to power.

After 1945, Leni Riefenstahl tried to make most of her meetings with Hitler and other party functionaries appear to be the result of "pure coincidence." But the fact that she met with Hitler and other party leaders immediately following her return from Greenland in September 1932 as well as directly after her return from location shooting in Switzerland in May 1933 can mean only that Riefenstahl sought out the company of the Nazi leadership. Months before the Nazis seized power, Riefenstahl was constantly in and out of their offices, and quickly rose to become one of the most dazzling personalities within top party circles. Contemporary witnesses and photographs confirm, as do her own statements, that from quite early on she belonged to the social life of the party that was striving for power.

In addition to official occasions—an invitation to a reception given by Göring, for example, who had been named president of the Reichstag in August 1932 and who on December 11 hosted a party in honor of Italian Minister of the Air Force Italo Balbo[21]—Riefenstahl often attended private get-togethers of the party's inner circle, as well as semiofficial or private meetings with Hitler and his confidants.

Just how intense these contacts were at the time is shown not only by the fact that Riefenstahl served as an adornment at official occasions and was accepted in private circles, but also that she was present in the NSDAP's hours of crisis. On November 6, 1932, the day of the Reichstag elections, Riefenstahl was among the few guests Magda Goebbels invited to gather in her apartment on Reichskanzlerplatz for the evening. As ever, Riefenstahl claimed to be clueless: "Why I was invited is a mystery to me."[22]

Compared with the elections held in July 1932, this time the NSDAP garnered only two million votes, adding up to a loss of thirty-four seats in the Reichstag. Many of the party's donors who had been generous up until then, such as Fritz Thyssen, immediately withdrew their support, plunging the party into a financial crisis.

One month later, Hitler himself was in crisis. A few weeks before he was named Reich chancellor, he felt his political future to be in grave danger and, according to Riefenstahl, it was she to whom he turned with his innermost fears. Whereas before he had believed the chancellorship to be within his grasp, suddenly he was facing the demise of his career. Because Hitler, supported by Göring and Goebbels, had demanded unlimited power, it had come to a break between him and his old comrade Gregor Strasser, who represented the more moderate left wing of the party. On December 8, 1932, Strasser resigned from all offices he held within the party and withdrew completely from political life. In June 1934, in an act of revenge, Hitler had him murdered in connection with the so-called Röhm Putsch. But in December 1932, the NSDAP was facing an ominous split in the party, even as it tried to present a unified front to the outside world.

Riefenstahl reports that the situation put Hitler in a mood of deep despair and hysteria: "His face was ashen, his hair was hanging down over his forehead, which was covered in sweat. Then he exploded, yelling, 'Those traitors, those cowards—and this right before our final victory— those fools—for thirteen years now we've been struggling, slaving away, giving our all—we've weathered terrible crises and now, right before we reach our goal, this treachery! . . . If the party falls apart, I'll put an end to my life.'"[23]

Despite several discrepancies in Riefenstahl's account—she places the meeting at Berlin's Hotel Kaiserhof, whereas Hitler spent the entire evening of December 8 at the Goebbels home—it appears credible. During the same period he also turned to his old benefactor Winifred Wagner in a similar manner. In a letter of December 1932, he wrote: "I've given up all hope. None of my dreams will ever be realized. After so many years of unending battles, my disappointment is all the greater. I hadn't lost courage all this time. I succeeded in saving everything, rebuilding everything, even after 1923, but now no hope remains. My opponents are too powerful. As soon as I am absolutely certain that all is lost, you know what I will do. I decided this long ago. I cannot bear a defeat. I'll keep my word and put an end to my life with a bullet. This time it's serious, because I simply see no way out."[24]

It is understandable that Hitler would confide in Winifred Wagner, who had accompanied and supported him on his path for more than ten years. But that he also revealed his fears and doubts in this difficult situation to a woman he had known for only seven months must mean that the friendship between Hitler and Riefenstahl already was very close, much closer, at any rate, than Riefenstahl later implied. Even if one were willing to accept Riefenstahl's assertion that this meeting, too, was pure coincidence, this doesn't alter the nature of the meeting. And if she hadn't been directly summoned by Hitler, but had met with him at the suggestion of someone in his circle, this only confirms the high position that she held within Hitler's entourage.[25]

The crisis within the NSDAP was resolved astonishingly quickly. No one joined Gregor Strasser and the party never came to a split that would have placed Hitler in a precarious position. On the contrary, in the period that followed, Hitler was besieged by declarations of loyalty from all over Germany. This was the final internal party conflict before Hitler was named Reich chancellor in January 1933.

When the Nazis came to power, Riefenstahl was in the Swiss spa of Davos, on an extended ski vacation during which she met her new lover, Walter Prager, a handsome and temperamental Swiss skier. The relationship lasted until early 1935, though as Riefenstahl described it, "It was not a passionate affair, but an affectionate liaison."[26]

Immediately following her return to Berlin in May 1933, she sent Hitler her congratulations, upon which she was invited to the Reich Chancellory. The later assertion in her memoirs that "he interested me far less after he became Reich chancellor than he had before he 'seized power'" is as barely credible as her statement that "after Hitler was in power I wanted nothing to do with him."[27] Quite the opposite—her private contact with Hitler and his paladins intensified in the period that followed. Riefenstahl was invited by the new leader to his private retreat at Berghof in Obersalzberg and to his private apartment in the Chancellory in Berlin. She reciprocated with invitations to Hitler to visit her in her studio and apartment on Hindenburgstrasse.

Though these visits took place late at night, Riefenstahl's neighbors did not fail to notice when Hitler privately called on Riefenstahl, considering the big and conspicuous Mercedes limousines that were parked outside her apartment.[28] Occasionally the procession of cars drew a crowd. To avoid notice, and because Hitler detested crowds at inopportune moments, he soon stopped visiting Riefenstahl at home. From that point

on they increasingly met at the Hotel Kaiserhof, at Hitler's private apart-
ments, at the Reich Chancellory, or at Obersalzberg. At joint visits to the
opera, film screenings, and official artist receptions in the Chancellory or
Ministry of Propaganda, Riefenstahl continued to be a welcome public
and private guest of the Nazi elite. She also was invited to outings and
picnics with the Führer, such as one on May 26, 1933, in Heiligendamm
on the Baltic Sea,[29] and to gatherings at the Goebbelses'.

From the very beginning, Goebbels, the new minister of propaganda,
had shown a great interest in film, and during this period Riefenstahl
accompanied him to the filmings of major productions.[30] Many of these
meetings are documented by photos as well as by Goebbels's diary
entries.

It is not known how many meetings took place at the time between
Riefenstahl and Hitler or other party functionaries. The relationship
between Riefenstahl and Hitler seemed closest in 1933, when she was
filming *Sieg des Glaubens* (*Victory of the Faith*) for him, but after this the
nature of their meetings became more professional than personal. Though
Hitler's schedule was increasingly tight once he was named Reich chancellor, he apparently always took time to meet with the young director.
At this point Riefenstahl was invited to dinner with Hitler several times
a week,[31] but his housekeeper stated that she always was sent home by
11:00 p.m., a fact that Riefenstahl herself confirmed.[32] Later, after 1934,
the frequent personal contact between the Führer and the filmmaker conspicuously waned, but they maintained a friendly relationship until their
final meeting, in March of 1944. They also regularly met at official and
semiofficial meetings until the outbreak of the war. In all probability,
Riefenstahl and Hitler rarely met after October 1939.

## HITLER AND WOMEN

Hitler was very conscious of his effect on women and used it to his advantage. In the early period of the Nazi movement, he had a number of influential patronesses and female supporters, who not only plied him with
money and gifts but also introduced him to society and to powerful
industrialists, so that he could establish important contacts. He enjoyed

a whole coterie of "maternal friends": Helene Bechstein, wife of the famous piano manufacturer; Elsa Bruckmann, wife of the publisher Hugo Bruckmann; Winifred Wagner, the head of the Bayreuth Festival; and the politically loyal Carin Göring, Hermann Göring's first wife, who was celebrated as the "heroine of early National Socialism" and who after her death became a cult figure of the regime.

But Hitler remained courteous and kind to these women only as long as they did not contradict him or attempt to talk politics with him. He did not appreciate interference in his policies and refused to engage in discussions about them. Thus it is difficult to assess if and to what degree Hitler and Riefenstahl spoke about politics during their private meetings.

Hitler nursed a real contempt for what he called "political women" and "females who talk politics": "It's bad when a woman begins to think about the issues of life. Ah, that's really when they can get on your nerves!"[33] He was quoted in 1942 as having rigorously asserted, "A female who mixes in political matters is anathema to me."[34] Herbert Döhring, Hitler's Obersalzberg caretaker, stated: "He never liked talking politics with women. Only rarely, and indirectly, when something important would come up . . . At table he deliberately steered all of his guests toward other topics and always kept the women at a distance from politics."[35] Women were tolerated in his private circle only as an audience to his often nonstop and exhausting monologues.

Riefenstahl's postwar statements to the effect that she had confronted Hitler with all the questions that many Germans later wished they had asked before 1945 therefore appear dubious. Nevertheless, in *Memoiren* she wrote that she had spoken openly to the dictator about his racism—"You're racially prejudiced. Had I been born an Indian or a Jew, you wouldn't even be speaking with me"[36]—and about the emigration of her friends.[37] It's more likely that the Führer was beyond criticism, as he was to all of those within his inner circle. Had Riefenstahl opposed Hitler's political views as she claims, it undoubtedly would have led to a break between them.

More likely than Riefenstahl's allegedly bold behavior is the fact that the rising young and ambitious director found her flirtation with power and the related temptation to collaborate with Hitler awe inspiring. In the

Third Reich, the Führer's favor meant everything, and other artists—sculptors Josef Thorak and Arno Breker, or Albert Speer, for example—were captivated by the wealth of possibilities presented to them, which they all willingly took advantage of. In keeping with her self-image, Riefenstahl did not "make common cause" with the Nazis after 1933 but merely fulfilled Hitler's personal wishes: it was for him that she made films, and they were meant to, and had to, please him. From this point of view, her relationship to the dictator was also the pivotal point of her life as a director.

The fact remains that Riefenstahl—who was unmarried until 1944—acted solely on her own behalf, was no one's "companion and mother," and did not suit the female ideal of National Socialist propaganda. But as she was known to be a protégé of and admired by Hitler, this did not prove an obstacle to the filmmaker becoming a figurehead for the Third Reich. After all, she could be presented as the "modern face" of the new Germany. On April 27, 1944, Joseph Goebbels noted: "Even though the Führer does not support the idea of women in public life, he nonetheless will make an exception in this or that case, so that we can point to this exception with people abroad. So it completely suits him that Frau Winifred Wagner leads the Bayreuth Festival and that Frau Riefenstahl is recognized as a filmmaker."

## RUMORS

There has always been much speculation about the personal relationship between Hitler and Riefenstahl. The connection between them was the source of great curiosity and envy at first, and then after 1945 of spite and schadenfreude.

At official occasions, the dictator was, of course, continually seen in the company of women, in particular Magda Goebbels and Emmy Göring, who were considered the "first ladies" of the Third Reich. Hitler made sure that it was primarily married women who numbered among his circle, in order to avoid rumors. No woman was allowed too near to him in public. According to the psychologist Manfred Koch-Hillebrecht, "When it was assumed that he was having a sexual relationship with an attractive woman, this in no way flattered Hitler's male pride. It was more likely to enrage him."[38]

But Riefenstahl, in addition to the British aristocrat Unity Valkyrie Mitford, who in 1938 advanced to the official position of the Führer's constant companion, was one of the few unmarried and attractive women frequently seen with Hitler. Even though many of their meetings were in truth work sessions during which they discussed Riefenstahl's party films and other projects, the public registered just how close the relationship between the filmmaker and the Führer was. At the beginning of the regime, Leni Riefenstahl, "obviously courting the favor of the man on the ascent,"[39] was repeatedly mentioned as a potential contender for Hitler's bride. The clandestine joke making the rounds at the time speaks volumes: "What would happen if Adolf and Leni got married? Then Germany would have two Führers." This played on Riefenstahl's self-confidence in the realm of power. As does the bon mot that Riefenstahl was not only under Hitler's control but also was "under" him.[40]

That Riefenstahl was lewdly referred to at the time as "the Reich's crevasse"[41] is a clear demonstration that rumors concerning intimate relations between Hitler and the filmmaker circulated widely, despite the high risk of making such jokes.

For the young and ambitious Riefenstahl, of course, it was a matter of great social prestige to be seen at Hitler's side and to be thrust into the center of Germany's political power through their personal acquaintance. Consequently, she did nothing to counter the rumors that roiled concerning her alleged intimate contact with Hitler. She was pleased by the speculations about her relations with those "at the top," which could only be of extreme benefit to her in the Third Reich. This impression is documented in the testimony given by Hitler's secretary, Christa Schroeder, to officers of the U.S. Army: "There is a category of women who do not refute such rumors. Leni Riefenstahl is that kind of woman; it was to her advantage."[42]

During the early years of the dictatorship, many within Nazi party circles found a relationship between Riefenstahl and Hitler not at all far-fetched. This is seen in Goebbels's attempts to make the two appear to be a couple. Goebbels was of the opinion that only a woman would be able "to connect Hitler with life."[43]

Together with his wife, Goebbels arranged for Hitler and Riefenstahl to spend an occasional evening together. Ernst Hanfstaengl, the foreign press chief, witnessed repeated efforts and reported on one such evening in 1932:

> Then the Goebbelses tried it with Leni Riefenstahl. She appeared one evening for dinner, a charming, pleasant creature who didn't have much difficulty talking Hitler and the rest of us as well into visiting her studio. Her home was decorated with a large number of mirrors and other clever furnishings, without being tasteless. As there was a grand piano, I knew just what to do, and the Goebbelses came over to lean on the instrument in order to give things a chance to follow their hoped-for course. Hitler thus was isolated and visibly embarrassed. I watched him study the books on the shelves as Leni Riefenstahl ran through her entire repertoire of feminine wiles. When the Goebbelses finally decided it was time to go, we left the two alone—once again ignoring all security measures. But our expectations regarding this nighttime tête-à-tête obviously were greatly exaggerated. A few days later, when by accident I found myself seated next to Fräulein Riefenstahl on a plane and asked her about Hitler, she responded with one of her famous shrugs. She must, however, have made an impression on Hitler, because in the Third Reich she enjoyed privileges with regard to her film work that understandably occasioned malicious talk and earned her many enemies.[44]

It can be assumed that Hitler restricted his close personal contact with the director after 1934 in order to squelch these rumors, among other reasons. But speculation concerning their connection never ceased—including abroad, where the press published sensationalist reports about their alleged relationship. When foreign papers published a crude photomontage showing Riefenstahl with a glass of champagne in her hand, seated on the lap of a half-clothed Hitler, the Führer reportedly was beside himself with anger.[45]

In actuality, there is no reason to think that Riefenstahl wasn't greatly fascinated by Hitler, perhaps beyond the limits that Hitler set on their friendship. There was a long period during which she tried to please Hitler, by largely renouncing makeup, for example, because Hitler didn't like it and became agitated when the women in his inner circle wore lipstick or cosmetics: "The German woman doesn't use makeup" was a widespread slogan of the Nazi era.

One reference point that supports a definite intimate relationship between the two is Riefenstahl's visit to Hitler's Munich apartment on December 25, 1934, which she records in *Memoiren*. Hitler lived at Prinzregentenplatz 16, in the fashionable Bogenhausen section of the city, in a nine-room apartment where he spent the Christmas holidays alone before traveling to Berghof to celebrate New Year's Eve. Hitler's manservant Karl-Wilhelm Krause corroborated that from 1934 to 1936, Hitler withdrew completely at Christmas, refusing even to have a Christmas tree. On Christmas Eve and the two holidays that followed (known as the first and second Christmas Days in Germany), he tolerated the presence of no one and had his meals and the newspapers left outside his door. He justified his behavior by saying that his mother had died right before Christmas in 1907, and he wanted the holiday to be an annual tribute to her memory.[46] If the visit that Riefenstahl mentioned actually took place, during which Hitler reputedly even showed her the room in which his niece, Geli Raubal, had committed suicide in 1931 and into which no one else was allowed, then Riefenstahl had the rare privilege of visiting the dictator at any time she wished.

The backing she received as well as the rumors circulating about her and Hitler secured for Riefenstahl an extremely comfortable and special status in the Third Reich. Her later attempt—perhaps to camouflage her interest in Hitler—to portray him as a lover thwarted by her own disinterest seems greatly implausible. She maintained that Hitler made advances, which she claims to have rejected, as early as their first meeting on the North Sea. And a scene she describes from one of their evening walks could have been lifted from the script of a melodramatic B-movie: "After a long silence he suddenly stopped, looked at me for a long time, then put his arms around me and pulled me to him. I was flustered, because this is not the way I wanted things to happen. He looked at me passionately. When he saw how unwilling I was, he immediately let go of me." He turned away from her, she wrote, raised his hands, and said imploringly, "I can't love a woman, not until my work is completed."[47] And years later, circa 1938, she still felt "that Hitler desired me as a woman."[48]

But according to statements made in 1948 by Anni Winter, Hitler's Munich housekeeper, Riefenstahl had confessed to her that Hitler was her great love but "hadn't wanted" her.[49] Wilhelm Schneider, another of Hitler's menservants, also recalled Riefenstahl's visits to Hitler: "Her eyes sparkled and she had a radiant expression that I'd never seen on a woman before."[50] Both Winter and Schneider rejected the idea of an affair between Riefenstahl and Hitler.

After the war, Christa Schroeder, Hitler's secretary, said in retrospect: "Hitler appears always to have stuck to: Everything was platonic! . . . including his relationships with the actresses and female artists he entertained in his apartment in the Chancellory in the first years of the Reich." His friendship with Riefenstahl was based solely on his "recognition of her work."[51]

Telegrams that Riefenstahl sent to Hitler, with their grateful and devoted tone, also are evidence of a friendship that was not truly intimate. After attending a speech by Hitler at the Reichstag, she wrote in an undated letter:

> My Führer—
> Completely thunderstruck by the hours I just spent in the Reichstag, and still completely under the spell of your magnificent speech, I am driven, as so often, to tell you how unutterably profoundly you are able to move people, to stir them. My admiration for you, my Führer, surpasses all else that I am capable of thinking and feeling.
> Devotedly yours,
> Leni Riefenstahl[52]

Despite how well they understood each other and despite the fact that their relationship could be termed warm, in the end there was always a certain distance between them. Hitler never addressed Riefenstahl in the intimate second-person "*du*" form, as he did Winifred Wagner, for example.

With few exceptions, Hitler had no deep connection to women, just as during his lifetime there was not one single person he opened up to completely. And Riefenstahl was not one of these exceptions. Early on she admitted that she was displeased by how impersonal their relationship was: "How strange, I thought, that for all his interest in my work, he never asked me one question of a personal nature. He never inquired about my family or my friends, never asked what I liked to read, what I thought about something or did or didn't like. He talked only about his own ideas. For that reason, despite the admiration and gratitude I often felt for him at the time, he remained deeply distant to me."[53]

In her absence, Hitler spoke of her as "Riefenstahl," evidence perhaps of his appreciation for her but definitely not of an erotic relationship.[54] But because the rumors of intimacy between them persisted, Riefenstahl, as the journalist and publisher Rudolf Augstein once put it, became "the bride of the Führer, but without the sex."[55] Taking into account what is known today, it can be assumed that Riefenstahl, despite her obvious closeness to Hitler, was never his lover. Like many women within the dictator's circle, she suffered from Hitler's disinterest. He didn't seem capable of true friendship or deep emotion. His biographers agree on his chronic lack of and trouble with relationships and depict how empty of people Hitler's life was. In retrospect, Albert Speer, who for more than ten years was one of Hitler's regular companions, often asked himself "if the man I served and whom I admired for many years was truly capable of feelings of friendship, gratitude, and loyalty."[56] The monotonous, empty, and distant qualities that marked all of Hitler's human relationships also, in the end, characterized his connection to Leni Riefenstahl.

Hitler maintained a personal as well as a political friendship with Winifred Wagner, but it appears that he saw Riefenstahl primarily as his "cinematographic comrade."[57] And conversely, Riefenstahl, once it became clear to her that the relationship would remain platonic, was interested in Hitler primarily as someone who promoted her work. For decades Riefenstahl denied that it could have come to anything more than friendship on her part: "I was not at all interested in Hitler as a man."[58] Not until forty-seven years after the end of the war did she admit to the British journalist Gitta Sereny, "In a certain sense I could happily say that I wasn't his type. He only liked 'little creatures.' He liked to talk to and appear in public with people like me. But I suppose that if he had wished, we would have become lovers; had he asked me it would have been unavoidable. I'm just extremely glad that he didn't ask."[59]

## THE FÜHRER AND HIS ARTISTS

As opposed to other artists who worked for him, the sculptors Arno Breker and Josef Thorak, for example, Adolf Hitler developed very special relationships with Leni Riefenstahl, his favorite director, and Albert Speer, his architect. Having felt his entire life like an artist manqué who had become a politician against his will, he claimed to recognize some part of himself in them.[60] Brigitte Hamann, the biographer of Hitler's early years, pointed out how significant Hitler's unfulfilled dream of becoming an artist was to the life of the future dictator. Even as Reich chancellor, he was involved in the planning of architectural projects carried out in his name, and also drew up designs for Wagner operas, which he then presented as proposals to his favorite stage designer, Benno von Arent.[61]

As chancellor, Hitler repeatedly sought out the company of artists, in whose presence he felt more comfortable than when he was in conversation with politicians and party comrades. He considered the Bavarian professor of architecture Paul Ludwig Troost, whom he greatly admired, to be his mentor. Immediately after Hitler came to power, Troost received a state commission to build the Haus der Deutschen Kunst (House of German Art), demonstrating that Germany's new ruler also saw himself as a patron of the arts. He enjoyed the role of supporting, through the "grace of the Führer," the careers of artists he valued. In Riefenstahl and Speer he encountered two people at the beginning of their careers whom he could shape as he wished and use to further his own fame and create a profile for his regime. Albert Speer, who built the backdrops for Hitler's mass gatherings of the German people, and Leni Riefenstahl, who captured these hypnotic events on film, came across Hitler at almost the same time—Riefenstahl a few months before his seizure of power, Speer a few months after. Within a very short time, the rising dictator succeeded in totally winning over both artists for his own purposes. He was able to offer the young architect and the ambitious filmmaker opportunities they would scarcely have dreamed of only a short time before.

Hitler recruited both, because he was enthusiastic about their work and appreciated them personally, but also because he valued their "practical understanding."[62] Interestingly, none of the artists whom Hitler supported embodied a bohemian lifestyle. Though in his youth, when he aspired to be an artist, Hitler had gone through phases of hard work[63] that alternated with those of a truly bohemian existence, his protégés all approached their art with great seriousness and absolute discipline. And it was precisely the director Leni Riefenstahl and the architect Albert Speer, with their great organizational gifts, who personified for Hitler the Third Reich's ideal of the hardworking artist, perhaps even the type of artist he mistook himself to be. They were to create the "face" of the National Socialist state, the backdrop for his regime. They were to work hard at this and be duly rewarded.

No price was too high, no demand too great in supporting Riefenstahl and Speer in the practice of their art. When Speer demanded huge sums for constructing his buildings during the war, he received them at Hitler's command. If Riefenstahl needed all available cameramen for her work, Hitler saw to it that his favored director got those she wanted, even if whole sections of the German film industry came to a standstill for this to happen. In the early years of the dictatorship, his relationship with each of them was very close.

For a long period, Riefenstahl and Speer enjoyed equal footing in Hitler's entourage. The Führer was aware that Speer, as the creator of his gigantic architectural fantasies, and Riefenstahl, with her films, were gaining worldwide recognition for his regime. At the 1937 World's Fair in Paris, when Speer and Riefenstahl each received the top award for their work, Hitler must have felt validated as a patron of the arts.

Only during the war did Hitler's relationship with Speer take on a new character. On the one hand, it grew closer. As Speer testified to the International Military Tribunal at Nuremberg: "If Hitler had any friends at all, then I was surely one of his closest friends."[64] On the other hand, their relationship increasingly shifted from the artistic sphere to the political. Hitler ceased to consider Speer an "artist removed from politics,"[65] as shown by the fact that in February 1942 he appointed him minister of armaments.

There were parallels not only in the way that Hitler received Speer and Riefenstahl but also in their behavior toward him. Both yielded to the lure of power and developed a near submissive bond to him.[66] Once confronted with the possibilities that Hitler's rise to power afforded them, they were willing to enter into any pact to attain their goals and over time were unable to view their patron's actions objectively. Both wanted major careers, to be able to carry out their artistic plans, and to achieve recognition and fame, which in the Third Reich soon took on megalomaniacal proportions. Just as Speer wanted to assure himself a place in art history with his architectural creations, Riefenstahl dreamed of making film history.

In advancing their own careers, both assertively used their powerful connection to the Führer if anyone tried to get in their way. Their close and friendly relationship with Hitler made it easy for them to put any rivals in their place. And they were infinitely grateful to Hitler for offering this protection. Riefenstahl's feelings were likely similar to those expressed by Speer: "I was twenty-six when I heard Hitler—whom I was not at all interested in up until then—speak for the first time; I was thirty when he lay the world at my feet."[67] Speer later acknowledged that even had he been aware of Hitler's true nature at the time, his role as Hitler's architect would have remained the same. Only a patron of such stature could assign the commissions architects such as Speer could only dream of: "I would have sold my soul, like Faust, for one major building project."[68]

Following her first personal encounter with Hitler, Riefenstahl also felt herself under his spell. Actually, Riefenstahl and Hitler, both egomaniacs, shared a number of similarities. Just as Hitler unconditionally pursued his political goals, Riefenstahl pursued her career with great ambition and total energy. She subordinated everything else in her life to it, including her own happiness. Just as Hitler believed in the "providence" that steered his fate, so Riefenstahl was convinced of her artistic "calling." Both were obsessed by an absolute faith in their own potential and their own iron will. They resembled each other in their efforts to fulfill themselves to the greatest possible degree and in their overblown and fanatic egocentricity.

Speer and Riefenstahl did exactly what Hitler expected of them: they supported him unconditionally and went at their work with great ambition. Hitler's relationship with both artists was marked by a mutual give-and-take: while it is true that Hitler advanced their careers and, in addition, made available to them a whole new standard of living, the dictator, in turn, profited from their work. Riefenstahl and Speer quickly rose to international prominence as figureheads of the Nazi regime and helped to erect the façade that diverted the rest of the world from Hitler's true plans and goals. Though their work had direct political relevance, both artists presented themselves as apolitical individuals after the fall of the regime that had so extraordinarily advanced their careers. They both maintained that even at the center of power they had not been interested in politics and had not comprehended what was going on around them.

Just as Riefenstahl maintained after 1945 that she had not been interested in Hitler's political aims, so Speer asserted, "I was never interested in politics; the arms buildup was merely an organizational challenge to me. Even at the height of my power I told Hitler that after the war I wanted to work as an architect again."[69] Despite all statements to the contrary, as Hitler's artists, Speer and Riefenstahl not only contributed to giving a respectable face to a regime that had no respect for humanity but also consciously benefited from the political constellation and Hitler's power in advancing their own careers.

# 6

## THE "FÜHRER'S FILMMAKER"

### ARTIST EXEMPLAR OF THE THIRD REICH

HITLER SEIZED POWER on January 30, 1933, and in March, against the wishes of his coalition partners and of Vice-Chancellor Franz von Papen, he named Joseph Goebbels minister of propaganda and public enlightenment. The ministry, which oversaw the entire cultural realm, including the film sphere, strictly controlled and steered public opinion. All cultural and journalistic institutions were soon "Aryanized" and subject to the policy of rigid coordination and conformity known as *Gleichschaltung* (literally, "consolidation"). The media were totally subordinated to and absorbed into the central propaganda apparatus. Opposition newspapers were banned and undesirable members of the cultural sector, those who up until then had supported the liberal spirit of the Weimar Republic, systematically removed. The first critical stage of these measures, aimed at the "recovery" of German culture, peaked with Goebbels's establishment of the Reichskulturkammer, the Reich Cultural Chamber, on November 15, 1933, and his concurrent appointment as its president.

Along with radio, the Nazis quickly acknowledged film as the most important medium in winning over the masses to National Socialism. But at this point it is unlikely that anyone could have anticipated just how total the indoctrination and control exercised over the German film industry would be.

The Nazis' seizure of power placed artists in the position of having to decide whether to remain in Germany and cooperate with the new rulers or leave their homeland and risk starting over abroad unknown and, on top of that, in a foreign tongue. Roughly two thousand actors, directors, authors, film composers, and cameramen, plus critics and film publicists, left the country.[1] Their places were eagerly filled by those in the film industry who unscrupulously exploited the emigrants' departure to boost their own careers or to secure their status. Many of them, such as Heinrich George and Emil Jannings, expressed their gratitude to the new despots by penning public tributes or issuing election appeals supporting them. Questioned on this after the war, most insisted that they had always seen themselves as apolitical artists. It seems none realized that the cinema was increasingly being incorporated into the propaganda machine as a political tool and used for ideological purposes. The only thing that counted was being cast in good roles and carrying out big-production projects. Leni Riefenstahl, too, recognized the opportunities for advancement she was suddenly being offered and did not hesitate to use them to her advantage. In this respect, Hitler's rise to power must have seemed to her the promise of a glorious future.

On March 28, 1933, Goebbels invited representatives and top decision makers of the German film industry to a meeting at the Hotel Kaiserhof. But neither the speech he delivered on the occasion nor his subsequent statements provided concrete details on his exact plans for German film. His ideas never went beyond assurances that film must be a "source of strength for every German" and align itself with the "needs of the nation," and that such a major means of mass influence should not be left to individuals.[2] He never developed a uniform National Socialist policy on film or a precise agenda on aesthetics or substance.

The first year of Nazi rule represented a transitional phase in moving toward the fundamental restructuring of the film industry. At this point it was primarily a matter of excluding "non-Aryan," Jewish colleagues and preventing their further participation in the business. In this, the industry even jumped ahead of state regulations. Ufa, for example, willingly fired Jewish employees even before this was ordered by Goebbels. The first propaganda films made by the Nazis—*Flüchtlinge (Refugees)*, *Hitlerjunge Quex* (*Hitler Youth Quex*), and *SA-Mann Brand (Storm Trooper Brand)*—arrived in theaters as early as 1933 and were designed to "turn those who had not yet been won over to the movement into committed National Socialists" and also to justify the brutal persecution of "enemies of the regime."

The "motion picture law" passed in February 1934 was a major step on the path to far-reaching state control. Goebbels used it to order an escalation of film censorship through Ministry of Propaganda officials, as well as to introduce "preventive censorship" designed to preclude films that "run counter to the spirit of the times" from even going into production. If a script wasn't approved by the ministry, the project was filed away. As film criticism also was placed under the control of the Ministry of Propaganda—until 1936, when it was done away with entirely and replaced by so-called art appreciation—there soon were no negative reviews either. Films particularly pleasing to the regime, on the other hand, were commended for "educating the *Volk*" or being "valuable to national policy."

In founding the Reichsfilmkammer, the Reich Film Chamber, in July 1933, Goebbels conclusively created an institution through which he could exercise control over who was hired in the film industry and who was not. Without exception, anyone involved in filmmaking had to register with the chamber, and only those who could prove Aryan heritage were accepted as members. On August 8, 1933, Riefenstahl, too, applied to the Reichsfilmkammer, and on October 2 filled out her application form.[3]

Parallel to structuring the mechanisms of state control, Goebbels pursued economic dominance over the film industry. This process was made easier by the fact that at the end of the Weimar Republic, countless production companies found themselves at the brink of financial ruin and liquidation, and production costs had rapidly increased with the introduction of sound. The Film Bank, established by the Nazis in June 1933 with the help of major German banks, became a significant instrument of further control. It could be used not only to improve the desperate financial situation of German film but also to exercise a strong influence over it. Eventually, all film production was taken over, an action initially carried out in secret, by buying up stock in film companies. By 1937, the transition from private film production to almost total state control had largely been realized. As of June 1941, private film production ceased to exist in Germany.[4]

Like Hitler, Goebbels had always taken a great interest in film. Consequently, he insisted on being involved in all stages of production and arbitrarily interfered in decision making. He selected material, approved screenplays, chose directors, intervened if he found salary demands too high, and even drew up lists of actors and directors he personally found worthy of promoting.

## WHAT SHOULD PROPAGANDA LOOK LIKE?

Surprisingly, there were fundamental differences between Hitler's and Goebbels's ideas on what effective propaganda should look like. The only thing they agreed on was the goal, as announced by Goebbels: "The essence of all propaganda is to win over people to an idea so intensely, so fundamentally, that in the end they capitulate to it, never to be separated from it again."[5] Whereas Goebbels, the skilled demagogue, preferred to influence people indirectly, concealing propaganda behind the mask of entertainment, Hitler favored more forceful methods. Like his chief ideologue, Alfred Rosenberg, the Führer believed that in order to be truly effective, propaganda should be identifiable as such. As he told the actress Toni van Eyck in 1933, "It's true, I want to use film, on the one hand, totally as a means of propaganda, but in such a way that every filmgoer knows: today I'm going to a political film. The same as if he goes to the sports hall. He doesn't want to hear a mix of politics and art. I despise it when politics is used as a pretext for art. Either art or politics!"[6]

Goebbels, on the other hand, aspired to a subliminal, "invisible propaganda," holding the view that propaganda is effective only when it is not recognized as such and is conveyed without a political lecture. He definitely wanted to steer Germans in a particular direction, but he didn't want them to realize the direction in which they were being steered. The message shouldn't be laid out in full view, and swastika banners and party songs were avoided on-screen. Nor did the officially prescribed "German greeting," the stiff-armed Nazi salute, appear in the films of the Nazi regime, at least not during the period when it was still thought they could be marketed abroad. The films created under Goebbels were to convey their messages as inconspicuously as possible, by presenting features for women and families that were compatible with National Socialism.

Immediately after the beginning of the war this concept was used to produce scores of film comedies and operettas meant to deflect the realities of war and the scarcities that Germans were suffering in their everyday lives.

Accordingly, the films of Leni Riefenstahl, which employed powerful images to glorify National Socialism, corresponded solely to Hitler's views on propaganda and had nothing to do with Goebbels's indirect tactics. But even though they ran counter to his understanding of propaganda, Goebbels was forced to admit that Riefenstahl's films were successful: "Even though he had a different understanding of 'good' propaganda, he most reluctantly had to confess that in this case a master had created her masterwork."[7]

### CAREER MOVES

Leni Riefenstahl began making films for the Führer in 1933, a career she could not have imagined one year before. Her cooperation with Hitler and the National Socialists was, in the end, based less on her fascination with their political program than on the opportunities that suddenly opened up to her in terms of artistic development. Of much greater importance to her than the "historical mission" of the Führer were her own career possibilities. The "new Germany" promulgated by the National Socialists would also make room for her, the insufficiently recognized artist.

After 1945, it became particularly important for Riefenstahl to mask this single-mindedness by referring to the fact that she was a "star" even before the advent of Hitler. She rejected any and all suspicions that from the beginning she owed her career to her involvement with the Nazi regime, suggesting first that she would have succeeded without Hitler, and second that even without his protection she was destined for an equally successful career. It is true that Riefenstahl was not an unknown quantity in 1933; *Das blaue Licht* had taken second prize at the Venice Biennale a few months before Hitler rose to power. Nevertheless, until she began her enthusiastic cooperation with Hitler, the artist remained an outsider in all that she did. While she had achieved astounding success as a dancer, an actress, and a director, there had been no early signs pointing to a great career.

All of that was to change in 1933, when she advanced from the second ranks to the center of the action. The professional ascent achieved by Leni Riefenstahl in the 1930s was no accident. Success may sometimes derive from accidents and luck, but going from film industry outsider to the world's best-known woman director in less than six years was the result of concrete planning, persistent and self-assured appearances, and the significant protection of the country's new rulers.

In Hitler, Riefenstahl had sought out the most influential patron possible. Whether Hitler actually attempted to strengthen Riefenstahl's position by offering her a post in the government is questionable at the very least. In the postwar period, Riefenstahl maintained that in May 1933, Hitler proposed that she, together with Joseph Goebbels, take over "the artistic direction of film production." But she allegedly refused the offer because she didn't feel she was in a position to manage such responsibility. On top of this, she envisioned her future as an actress and a director, not as a functionary. In any case, no documentation exists for this offer.

Because Leni Riefenstahl filmed by order of the Führer, she stood outside all of the structures that artists of the Third Reich had to adapt to. In the cultural sphere of Nazi Germany such a position, which allowed the artist to operate totally independently of Propaganda Minister Goebbels, was granted to only a few. In addition to Riefenstahl, there were Albert Speer, Heinrich Hoffmann, and Winifred Wagner. Speer, for example, as general building inspector for the Reich's capital city, was "subordinate [only] to Hitler, and responsible to no one else, neither to Lord Mayor [Julius] Lippert nor to Gauleiter Goebbels."[8] Hitler's personal photographer, Heinrich Hoffmann, was granted special status as well. This elevated him, as it did Riefenstahl, "above potential competitors and allowed him to hold his own against other powerful groups of the Third Reich, above all, the party apparatus and the Ministry of Propaganda, and to keep his work from being absorbed into the party's publishing house or the state propaganda apparatus, respectively."[9]

Comparable concessions were otherwise granted only to Hitler's close friend Winifred Wagner, whose Bayreuth Festival was spared interference from the Reich Theater Chamber by order of the Führer. "Bayreuth was the chief's affair and for this reason did not come under the authority of the Reich Cultural Chamber. Major artistic and organizational decisions were made only by the Führer himself, as evidenced by surviving festival documents."[10]

With this, Winifred Wagner also escaped Goebbels's control. Whereas Speer, Hoffmann, and Wagner all held membership in the NSDAP, Riefenstahl was the sole non–party member to benefit from such privileges. All of Hitler's artist protégés showed gratitude to the Führer for the unlimited trust he placed in them. Winifred Wagner, for example, turned the Bayreuth Festival into Hitler's own personal stage, and Leni Riefenstahl created a celluloid monument to the Führer with her *Triumph des Willens* (*Triumph of the Will*).

## THE ALLEGED MORTAL ENEMY

During the postwar years and into old age, Riefenstahl spoke with particular bitterness of Goebbels's animosity toward her, but no trace exists of the enmity the minister of propaganda allegedly displayed toward Hitler's filmmaker, at least from the early years of the dictatorship. Quite the contrary, Goebbels and Riefenstahl seem at first to have enjoyed a thoroughly relaxed and amicable relationship. The attractive actress had come to the attention of the future minister of propaganda quite early on. In December 1929, having seen *Die weisse Hölle vom Piz Palü*, he noted in his diary: "And the beautiful Leni Riefenstahl is in it. A magnificent child! Full of grace and charm." He came to know the actress personally in the winter of 1932. Later, Riefenstahl wanted to hear nothing of the active contact she had with Goebbels and his wife in the first months of the Third Reich, for this contradicts her version of the story.

Riefenstahl herself dates the beginning of her alleged enmity with Goebbels as early as December 1932, that is, in the period before the "seizure of power." Her reason for this was the advances that Goebbels persistently made toward her, which she angrily rejected. Thus the future propaganda minister became her "mortal enemy." At their first encounter, at Hotel Kaiserhof, he had "brazenly stared" at her in the elevator.[11]

And at their second meeting a day later, she again felt "this strange look" and experienced a "bad feeling" in his presence.[12] Soon thereafter his pursuit of her became intolerable. It seemed odd to her "that this man, who needed to muster all of his strength for the final phase of the struggle for power, threw himself into the hopeless attempt to win me over at any price."[13] Goebbels reputedly pestered her, telephoning several times a day. He arranged their first private meeting, in Riefenstahl's apartment, with the excuse that he wanted to talk to her about his political concerns. During one of these meetings the true reason for his advances toward her was revealed: "Then Goebbels lost control of himself, saying, 'You must become my lover, I need you—my life is unbearable without you! I've loved you for so long now!' He actually knelt down before me and even began to sob." She looked down in astonishment at the kneeling Goebbels. "But then, when he grabbed me by my ankles, it was just too much. I backed away from him and ordered him to leave my apartment. He turned pale as ashes . . . The future minister of propaganda never forgave me this humiliation."[14]

But his pursuit of her allegedly continued in the months that followed, into the summer of 1933, because her rejection supposedly excited him even more.[15]

Riefenstahl consistently stuck to this story after 1945, but how credible is this version? Reports of the propaganda minister's constant new love affairs are legion. In fact, it was the film branch that the "patron of German film" considered his personal "hunting ground." Countless actresses and minor film stars entered into an affair with the influential Goebbels, for it was he who could get them the much desired contract with Ufa or one of the other large production companies. While he and his wife, Magda, along with their six children, played the role of the model family,[16] behind the scenes he went from one amorous adventure to the next almost compulsively. In film circles he earned the nickname "the buck of Babelsberg." Outwardly—even during long-term affairs, with the young Czech actress Lida Baarova, for example—he was careful to uphold the image of concerned husband and father, but it was important to the notorious seducer that he be seen as a Casanova by the rumormongers.

It is not out of the question that Goebbels cast an eye on the beautiful Riefenstahl, who, with her dark hair and eyes, fit his ideal of feminine beauty. But it should be assumed that, given the friendly relationship between Hitler and Riefenstahl, Goebbels would have exhibited a certain reserve toward the director. After all, it was Goebbels and his wife who tried to fix Hitler up with Riefenstahl in the days before Hitler came to power. So it appears at least questionable that the Führer's loyal minister would really have dared to become his rival. On top of this, the self-possessed and power-conscious director didn't fit the type of woman Goebbels preferred, which for the most part was quite young. At any rate, Wilfried von Oven, who was Goebbels's adviser at the time and was in daily contact with the minister, came to the conclusion, "Not that he didn't try it with countless women, but with Riefenstahl? No. He knew all too well that this woman would cause him a great deal of trouble."[17]

Also contradicting Riefenstahl's version that she had rejected Goebbels as an admirer and that he "hated" her because of this humiliation is the fact that months after the reputed scene the two were on amiable and apparently even easygoing terms. In the summer of 1933, long past the point at which she supposedly incurred his enmity, they were still meeting privately.

In May 1933, a few days after the book-burning that Goebbels had initiated, Riefenstahl appeared with the two Goebbelses at the opera. During this period, Goebbels's remarks about Riefenstahl were generous and appreciative. On June 12, he noted in his diary: "She is the only one of all the stars who understands us." Such a statement doesn't substantiate a quarrel with Riefenstahl, which—according to the version of events in *Memoiren*—would have already taken place by this time.

If, then, a break between the director and the minister didn't occur before Hitler seized power, there must have been other reasons for the animosity between them that later existed. Their enmity was not the result of private disagreements but rather was based on Riefenstahl's role and behavior in the Third Reich. In September 1933 at the latest, there were conflicts during the shooting of *Sieg des Glaubens* in which the Ministry of Propaganda unavoidably became involved.[18] The fact that Riefenstahl was able to go over Goebbels's head and demand cameramen he had already assigned to other projects was something the egotistical minister never got over.

Their relationship, which had been entirely friendly in the beginning, during this time became a purely professional, official collaboration. That Goebbels boycotted her film projects, as the director maintained after 1945, was, at any rate, untrue. Goebbels's diaries confirm that he was always involved in Riefenstahl's plans at a very early stage and was in no way excluded from discussions between the Führer and his filmmaker on new projects.

Officially, the minister of propaganda treated Riefenstahl in a manner that corresponded to her rank as one of the leading directors of the Third Reich. Not only did he bestow prizes and awards on her, but he also invited her to all important events and occasions. For example, Riefenstahl appeared in April of 1935 as a "symbol of German film" and prominent guest at the International Film Conference. This event, long planned by Goebbels, took place at the Kroll Opera House in Berlin and was attended by representatives from thirty-eight countries. There is no doubt that Goebbels admired Riefenstahl as a filmmaker, but personally they had their differences, few of which, however, surfaced in public. Eyewitness accounts of such a rift, such as Goebbels publicly slighting Riefenstahl at a social gathering in July 1936,[19] are rare.

The guarantee of independence that Riefenstahl obtained from Hitler when she agreed to make her second party rally film rankled Goebbels enormously. Following *Triumph des Willens*, Hitler deprived Goebbels of any say in any film project Riefenstahl was involved in for the duration of the Third Reich. Whereas Goebbels could always take other artists to task and make them toe the regime's line, this wasn't the case in dealing with Riefenstahl. Her "proximity to the Führer" granted her an unusual power, which went beyond party and state. This was coupled with her access to an enormous amount of studio space, an expense that came out of Goebbels's budget. The greater her film successes, the more untouchable she became to him, inhibiting the exercise of his own power. The former Reich film director Fritz Hippler confirmed this: "In my opinion, there was a certain jealousy on the part of Goebbels, a certain envy that some personalities, here in the person of Riefenstahl, were appreciated by the Führer without his having played a part in it."[20]

In addition, Riefenstahl's direct access to Hitler and their friendly relationship must have pained Goebbels, as his own relationship with the

Führer was lacking precisely this familiarity. According to Traudl Junge, Hitler's secretary, "Hitler had great admiration for Goebbels, he valued him. But friendship wasn't a part of it. Hitler knew Goebbels's weaknesses, that he often used his position to make advances to actresses. And that did not at all correspond to Hitler's nature."[21] It must also have galled the propaganda minister that Riefenstahl used Hitler's fondness for her to put Goebbels in his place. In disagreements and disputes, she turned to Hitler with the "merciless skill of the ambitious career woman to get what she wants."[22] In competing for the favor of the Führer, it was always Riefenstahl who emerged victorious, having in Hitler a potent protector against whom Goebbels was powerless.

As Goebbels showed little understanding for the propagandistic significance of Riefenstahl's films, Hitler made decisions over his head. In his diaries, Goebbels describes Riefenstahl in turn as a "clever piece of work" (August 17, 1935), "deeply hysterical" (September 18, 1936), and a "courageous woman" (July 8, 1938). After a screening of completed sections of *Olympia*, he again changed his mind about her, following earlier disagreements: "Leni is capable of a great deal. I'm filled with enthusiasm. And Leni is very happy" (November 24, 1937). These words do not reflect a bitter animosity.

The fronts were clearly drawn from the time of *Triumph des Willens* at the latest, when Goebbels finally realized that there was nothing he could do against Riefenstahl, that he would never succeed in placing her under his supervision. In the future, when it came to Riefenstahl, he conspicuously restrained himself, as his diary entries show.

Despite the obvious facts, the fable of the "evil minister of propaganda" and the director he persecuted and boycotted stubbornly persisted, and is willingly circulated today.[23] In the end, Riefenstahl's version of the story fell on receptive ears because people were all too prepared to see in her the woman besieged by Goebbels, the love-crazed egomaniac. Her story was too good, too plausible, for anyone to question it closely.

# 7

## THE TRANSITION
## TO DOCUMENTARY FILMS

### THE PARTY RALLY FILM *SIEG DES GLAUBENS*

EARLY ON, Leni Riefenstahl rose to prominence as the Third Reich's consummate artist and, at the express wish of the Führer, accepted numerous commissions from the party and the state. With her party rally films, *Triumph des Willens* in particular, Leni Riefenstahl shaped the image of National Socialism as did no other film artist. Today there is no documentation of the Third Reich that does not include images from her films, which have come to embody fascist self-representation and number among the most exhibited works of film history. Between 1933 and 1945, the prestigious projects that Riefenstahl carried out in Hitler's name placed her at the top of the German film industry and of the social life of Nazi Germany.

Even before 1933, the annual party congress of the NSDAP was usually held in the ancient city of Nuremberg. The site of the Imperial Diet during the Middle Ages and safe depository of the crown jewels, Nuremberg was transformed by the Nazis into the "most German of all German cities." Hitler wanted to establish a connection to the city's ancient political significance and to use this historical association to legitimize his claim to rule Germany. In the year he seized power, Hitler declared Nuremberg the "city of the Reich's party congresses," and all party rallies were held there until the outbreak of World War II.

These increasingly pompous conventions were Hitler's most important means of publicly representing National Socialism. The party convention of 1933, attended by hundreds of thousands of party members from all over the Third Reich, took on particular significance, as it was the first time Hitler could greet his followers as head of state. And this was precisely what was to be appropriately staged and preserved on film, as a sign of the triumph and confirmation of the path he had chosen.

Films documenting the Nuremberg party rallies existed before 1933. The oldest surviving film dates from 1927, and another was made in 1929. They were, for the most part, unimaginative, cinematically mediocre reports and were rarely distributed or noticed outside the Nazi movement.[1]

But this was to change in 1933. Not only the party rally in Nuremberg but also the films of the rallies themselves were to play a central role in the self-presentation of the party and the regime. Hitler clearly understood the potential of film: millions of "comrades" who couldn't join the mass gathering in Nuremberg could take part through the films. Both within Germany and abroad, the party films were a demonstration of the Germans' enthusiastic support of him.

In addition to the fact that the NSDAP was now the ruling power in Germany, there was an extra detail that lent the party films new significance. The films from 1927 and 1929 were silent, made without the benefit of Hitler's major propaganda tool in winning votes—his speeches. The film of the 1933 party rally was the first to use sound and so could present Hitler's demagogic gift at length through its combination of sound and image.

In addition to the "marketing" of the 1933 rally in the media, the staging of party events in Nuremberg was perfected. Albert Speer, the regime's head designer, was granted a particularly important role in this context. In charge of the artistic and technical presentation of the party's mass outdoor rallies and marches, Speer developed their architectonic framework and stone backdrops and, like Riefenstahl, played a central role in the Nazi party's self-presentation.

In addition to the Congress Hall, in which the opening and closing speeches were held, two parade grounds alternated as the sites of individual events. Luitpold Field, an arena designed by Speer's predecessor, Paul Ludwig Troost, held 200,000 seats and was reserved exclusively for the SA and the SS. Zeppelin Field, with space for 340,000 people, hosted all other ritual gatherings of the party congresses. In 1933, it was still outfitted with provisional wooden stands, replaced in 1934 by a huge stand of limestone flanked by golden eagles and above which were mounted three immense swastika banners.

Both fields were of an imposing, overwhelming size. But soon even they did not meet Hitler's demands, and in 1934 he commissioned Speer to build another arena on the adjacent parade ground, which was designed to accommodate a half million people. Construction began in 1938 but was halted for good when the war began a year later.

Speer and Hitler's theatrical settings came alive each year during the annual performances of the propaganda plays of the party congresses, which were well calculated to achieve their outrageously emotional effect. Not only the power of the architecture but also the staging of events, with nothing left to chance, created an atmosphere and overall effect that were difficult to resist. With his taste for large stages and theatrical pageantry, Hitler organized overwhelming ritual ceremonies: "Every means, every theatrical trick was employed to escalate the air of excitement. The Nuremberg party rallies . . . were masterful examples of carefully orchestrated productions."[2]

Almost all of the party's rituals had already been developed by 1933, but they continued to be perfected during the Third Reich, so that eventually a specifically "National Socialist ceremonial style" was created, which always fell back on the same components: flags and banners, torchlight processions and parades, speeches and rituals, drum rolls and martial music, party anthems and the ever-recurring battle slogans and loyalty oaths.

When new effects were developed, they were immediately incorporated into the Nuremberg stagings. The most prominent example was Albert Speer's "light domes," used at all party rallies after 1936 but also at other events, such as the closing ceremonies of the Berlin Olympics.[3]

The organization of the party rallies, the establishment and performance of the rituals, the choice of the music and speakers all were "the boss's business," to which Hitler devoted himself with obvious enthusiasm. It was not, as is often inferred, Propaganda Minister Joseph Goebbels who was the organizer of the party rallies but Adolf Hitler himself. Hitler insisted that his productions be recorded on film in the most optimal way and suitably refined for the media.

## WHY RIEFENSTAHL?

After 1945, Riefenstahl consistently stressed how reluctantly she had made the films of the Nuremberg rallies. She boasted that she had turned down commissions suggested by Goebbels and Hitler for other party films before that, one on Horst Wessel, for example, who was made into a Nazi martyr.[4] Only when Hitler suggested that she make a film on the first Nuremberg rally to follow his seizure of power did she decide that this was an offer she could not turn down. Sources support the fact that the idea of filming the rallies did not originate at her suggestion but can be traced back to Hitler.

Her decision to accept the contract and make a documentary film for Hitler was not a given, as is evidenced by her application to the Reich Film Chamber, which reveals that at this time she still saw herself primarily as an actress[5] and not as a director. In applying to the film section on October 2, 1933, long after she had begun editing her first party rally film, she still listed her profession as "actress," not adding "director" to the form.[6] When it soon became clear that her documentaries would place her at the top of the German film industry, she followed this path with enthusiasm.

Even today, there is much confusion concerning her first film, *Sieg des Glaubens* (*Victory of Faith*), particularly regarding the actual conditions of her contract. At the end of the war, Riefenstahl maintained that she had received the contract for the film at the end of August 1933, only a few days before the Nuremberg rally began, because Goebbels had sabotaged Hitler's order to award her the contract and had not passed it on to her. In 1972 she added, "I [was] summoned to Hitler in the Chancellory—it was two days before the 1933 party rally—and he asked me how far along I was with the preparations for the party rally film. I was totally speechless, I had been told nothing of it, I didn't know anything about it at all. The Propaganda Ministry had said nothing to me about it; they had received the contract. And so Hitler told me that I had to go to Nuremberg and see if there was something I could still film there."[7]

Riefenstahl saw Hitler frequently during this period, which makes it improbable that the Führer had not spoken personally with her about the project. And her statement above belies the fact that on August 25,

1933, a week before the party rally began, it was announced in the press that Leni Riefenstahl had been assigned as director of the film, "at the express wish of the Führer," and was on her way to Nuremberg to prepare for the shoot, following "extensive discussions with party comrade Raether."[8]

Goebbels's diaries paint a different picture as well. On May 17, 1933, roughly four months before the party rally in September, he noted: "Afternoon: Leni Riefenstahl. She talks about her plans. I suggest to her that she make a Hitler film. She is enthusiastic." Further entries in Goebbels's diaries also mention the film project: ". . . discussed new film with Fräulein Riefenstahl" (June 12, 1933); "Riefenstahl has spoken with Hitler. She's now starting her film" (June 14, 1933); "Went through the film with Riefenstahl" (June 20, 1933). On July 19 he noted that he had received the script. Assuming that this project and the film of the party rally were one and the same,[9] Riefenstahl knew of the commission months before the Nuremberg rally took place and cooperated closely with Goebbels in its planning, which her version of the story refutes.

## INTRIGUES

The fact that the director's name was mentioned so late in the planning stage of the film can scarcely be used as evidence that Riefenstahl was awarded the commission at a late date. Rather, it implies certain differences and disagreements behind the scenes concerning the naming of Riefenstahl as director of *Sieg des Glaubens*.

In choosing Riefenstahl, Hitler brought to the project someone who had no experience in documentary filmmaking and who wasn't even a member of the National Socialist Party, which was not well received by many party members, especially the film functionaries. Many of them had waited years for the opportunity to make the films that Riefenstahl had now been assigned, and they reacted indignantly to her hiring.

Among Riefenstahl's major opponents was Arnold Raether, who prior to 1933 had already made a series of films for the NSDAP.[10] Once Hitler took power, Raether assumed that he would finally have the opportunity to prove his talent as a director outside of party circles. He publicly placed great emphasis on the "sanitizing of films, the careful selection of filmmakers and industry people, and a thorough reform of the entire film system,"[11] which shows that he foresaw a central role for himself in Nazi Germany's film production, a role he was not willing to allow Leni Riefenstahl to usurp.

Goebbels, unlike Hitler, at first had no doubts at all that the party's film section possessed the necessary artistic skills to continue making films of the party rallies. On May 11, 1933, he gave the Chief Film Section of the Reich Propaganda Administration of the NSDAP, under Arnold Raether, the monopoly on filming all party events. The fact that only a few days later he proposed the idea of making a "Hitler film" to Leni Riefenstahl shows that at this point he assumed that an equal cooperation between party filmmakers and an independent director appointed by him was possible.

But both parties were unhappy with this, which led to suspicion and animosity. Leni Riefenstahl felt that her artistic freedom was being compromised through the mandatory discussions with party filmmakers and insisted on total autonomy, which at this point she was refused. For his part, Arnold Raether assumed that Riefenstahl, as a non–party member, lacked the necessary ideological foundation for making a party documentary.

Party functionaries at first gave themselves over to the illusion that they could prevail over Hitler's and Goebbels's wishes. They tried to keep mention of Riefenstahl's connection to the film out of the press, or to assign her a merely advisory role and to promote Arnold Raether as the film's true creator.[12] Nor did they shrink from using slander to rid themselves of the competition.

Like all those who worked in film in Nazi Germany, Riefenstahl could be hired only after she provided indisputable proof of her Aryan heritage. Her opponents now tried to denounce her as a Jew. On August 28, 1933, right before the party congress convened in Nuremberg, the Ministry of Propaganda received a letter that repeated the rumor that Riefenstahl's mother was Jewish.[13] With this, probably instigated by Raether, it was hoped that Riefenstahl would be forced to withdraw from the prestigious film project at the last minute.

Rudolf Hess, also at Raether's instigation, immediately ordered an investigation into Riefenstahl's background. By September 6, the results were in, stating that "in the records of the Central Residents Registration Office, Riefenstahl was listed as belonging to the Protestant religion dating back to her great-grandparents on her father's side and to her grandparents on her mother's side, leaving no doubt at all as to her Aryan birthright."[14] Raether's plot against Riefenstahl had failed, but that didn't prevent rumors from continuing to circulate in the foreign press that Riefenstahl had Aryanized her family tree to hide the fact that her mother was of Jewish ancestry.[15]

Despite the dismissal of these suspicions, there were further vehement behind-the-scenes clashes concerning Riefenstahl's competence, in addition to other intrigues and rivalries. According to Riefenstahl, the conflicts went so far that there were those who believed her life to be in danger: "Some members of the SA even wanted to have me killed, Air Force General Ernst Udet told me. As a result, I was under the protection of the Secret Service for several months from 1933 to 1934."[16] The protective order reputedly was issued by Hermann Göring after he was secretly informed that there were circles within the SA that intended to have Riefenstahl killed. No evidence exists that Riefenstahl was under Gestapo protection or that her life truly was in danger at any point.

But after 1945, Albert Speer verified in his memoirs that there were indeed plots against Riefenstahl: "During preparations for the party congress I met with a woman who had impressed me since my student days: Leni Riefenstahl . . . She was commissioned by Hitler to film the party rallies. As the sole woman with an official capacity within the party administration, she often came up against the party organization, which initially came close to staging a revolt against her. As a self-assured woman who unapologetically ordered men around within this masculine world, she provoked the political leadership of a movement that was traditionally misogynist. All sorts of intrigues developed against her; she was defamed to Hess in an attempt to destroy her. After the first party film, however, which convinced those around Hitler who had doubted her talent, all of these attacks ceased."[17]

The fact that there is no mention of Arnold Raether's name in the opening credits of *Sieg des Glaubens* shows that after filming was completed it was Riefenstahl who emerged victorious in battle. She alone became known as the creator of the first party rally film. All of the plots against her had failed, not least due to the esteem in which the Führer held her. It was she who won the bitter struggle for Hitler's favor, and she who now plotted against her enemies.

Because of these internal disagreements, preparations for the filming of *Sieg des Glaubens* were brief. It remains unclear why, despite apparent earlier discussions with Goebbels and Hitler, Riefenstahl arrived in Nuremberg relatively late, at the end of August 1933, and began to film following only a brief introduction to the site and a bit of improvisation. But it is not improbable that, inexperienced in documentary filmmaking and counter to her own perfectionism, she simply underestimated the planning and the extent of the demanding preparations that were necessary.

Her crew, cameramen, and technicians also came almost exclusively from the sphere of feature films and had no previous documentary experience. The filming of the 1933 party rally was an adventure for them all. They embarked on it largely unprepared and succeeded only thanks to frequent improvisation. The organizational talent that Riefenstahl brought to the task, paired with her business skills, were her capital assets in the years to follow, qualities without which her later work on mammoth projects such as *Triumph des Willens* and *Olympia* would have proved impossible.

In comparison with her film projects to come, *Sieg des Glaubens* appears modest. Production costs ran to around 60,000 reichsmarks, of which 20,000 went to the director. The NSDAP financed the film in full and served as producer.[18] Filming took place from August 30 to September 3, 1933, at the Reich Party Congress of Victory in Nuremberg.


## NEW CHALLENGES

Documentary film was a young genre at the time, so Riefenstahl was able to expand and redefine its aesthetic and technical standards. Documentary films in Germany of the 1920s were largely left-oriented, emphasizing modernism and urban themes. Before Riefenstahl there were no right-leaning documentaries that were taken seriously. At the end of the twenties, the genre went through a massive politicization process, due to inflation and the worldwide economic crisis. In Europe, the United States, and the Soviet Union, documentaries attained new status as a useful tool of propaganda. The films of Soviet Realism, such as those by the filmmaker Dziga Wertow, and also the works of the documentary filmmaker John Grierson of Britain, increasingly devoted themselves to social themes and argued, at times persistently, for political change.

In Germany, too, filmmakers were seeking a new form for the documentary film, which now—once leftist films became impossible to make—was to correspond to the "new era" and serve the aims of the Nazi government. This did not mean a total break with tradition; rather, one applied the existing standards to one's own purposes. In making their documentary and cultural films, the Nazis utilized the innovative visual and sound techniques that had been discovered and established by the avant-garde of the 1920s.

The extent to which Riefenstahl followed and reflected the developments in documentary films inside and outside Germany before 1933 is not known. Even her effusive memoirs include no pertinent information on the subject, perhaps because she wished to characterize this turning point in her career as another moment for the myth of the self-created artist free of influential models. Regardless of how free Riefenstahl really was from conscious influences, it cannot be denied that with her first party rally film, she defined a new type of documentary.

One thing differentiated the films that Riefenstahl made for Hitler from what the documentary film sector had produced up until then: her striving for the highest degree of perfection and stylization of her subjects. The director established new standards, which far surpassed the purely reportorial film that had prevailed up until then. Her footage on the Nuremberg rally rose above the simple, purely informative documentation of events that the public was familiar with from the newsreels. Riefenstahl's works translated actual events into suggestive imagery. And it was at precisely this point where her ideas met with Hitler's, one of the reasons that he entrusted Riefenstahl with this task. Hitler was not interested in the dry reportorial style that the party's filmmakers would have created. He wanted an artistic film that would transport moviegoers, that targeted and overpowered the audience's emotions.

Riefenstahl achieved this through the use of particular effects. In interviews from the thirties she always listed the three essential elements of her films: First, the creative act of filming, which was to show subjects from as many different perspectives as possible. Striving for the highest number of "good pictures" conceivable was the most important component of her work. The second major element of her films was the edit, to which she applied a rhythmic sense that approached dance and for which she accepted only those takes that fully met her aesthetic demands. Anything that disturbed the balanced unity of the whole or the positive impression she wished to convey was shown no mercy at the editing table. The third element was music, which harmoniously merged with the images and was meant to underscore the film's message. By focusing on these three components, she declared the artistic elevation of reality her credo, and in so doing far exceeded pure documentation. Particularly in the editing process and its artistic articulation, she always aimed for certain emotional effects she wished her films to have on the public.

The Nazi press praised Riefenstahl's party films as ideal examples of an innovative and unrivaled form of documentary appropriate to the "new era." It never failed to emphasize the films' special characteristics and extraordinary qualities. There was talk of "heroic major reportage," of a "new aesthetic," of a "German camera style"[19] and "distinctive dramaturgy."[20] There was no doubt that Riefenstahl was the creator of a "totally new, monumental form of filmmaking," and one spoke matter-of-factly about the prototypical "Riefenstahl School."[21] Her films had the reputation of being a new and independent art form and, in the long run, were seen as "the German answer to Sergei Eisenstein,"[22] the genius of the Soviet revolutionary film. The magazine *Der deutsche Film,* which was published by the Reich Film Chamber and concerned itself with defining the position of film production in the Third Reich, extolled Riefenstahl's works as paradigms of "National Socialist film" and declared the director to be the leading figure of film production in the Third Reich. Her achievement, the magazine stated, was that the cinematic style she established took real occurrences and "translated them into rhythmic cinema, conveying political events as artistic experiences."[23]

———

Due to the brief period of preparation and also, presumably, to Riefenstahl's lack of experience in the genre, *Sieg des Glaubens* demonstrates only an early incarnation of the magazine's assessment of her work. "In retrospect, particularly in comparison with *Triumph des Willens*, filmed one year later, *Sieg des Glaubens* is not an integrated whole. One literally can see how the director is working to find 'her' style: she introduces dramaturgical innovations and unusual camera shots, but there are still traces of the reviled newsreel style."[24]

Riefenstahl had assembled a small team of only three cameramen and a few technicians, who gathered material for the film according to her instructions. In addition, all of the newsreel production companies in Germany (Ufa, Deulig, Tobis-Melo, Fox, and Paramount) covering the Nuremberg party rally independently of Riefenstahl's project made their films available to her. But what Riefenstahl had in mind was an artistic film that was to look completely different from all previous newsreels, and so she made little use of the others' material, as it did not, as a rule, meet her aesthetic ideals or her perfectionism. She rejected, for example, footage of participants who waved excitedly for the cameras—regular fare for the movie newsreels.

Despite behind-the-scenes disagreements, Riefenstahl's crew definitely enjoyed privileges that Riefenstahl later often neglected to mention. Head cameraman Sepp Allgeier, senior mountain film specialist and colleague of Arnold Fanck, was assigned a major role, becoming Riefenstahl's chief colleague on both *Sieg des Glaubens* and *Triumph des Willens*. With Allgeier as head photographer, Riefenstahl tried out many perspectives and techniques that were uncommon at the time.

Together they conceived the film's novel and dynamic tracking shots, whereas previously the camera had filmed the action from one single position. This gave audiences a totally new way of seeing, and almost none of the film critics of the time failed to mention the enormous mobility of the camera in Riefenstahl's films. Allgeier also increased the use of telephoto lenses, which he could employ at distances of up to thirty to forty-five yards.

Riefenstahl's most significant advantage was that she was permitted to film Hitler in close proximity, bringing the first close-ups of Hitler to the screen in order to show the Führer in a way never before seen. Walter

Frentz joined Riefenstahl's team at the suggestion of Albert Speer and later accompanied Hitler at every turn, thus becoming responsible for most of the newsreel footage of the dictator. Frentz succeeded not only in filming Hitler during official rally appearances, he also managed surreptitiously to shoot him in conversation with party leaders or watching the parades, which gave the public the impression of experiencing the "Führer in private." Until then, newsreels had filmed Hitler only from great distances and not always to his advantage. Riefenstahl's cameramen took care always to present the dictator in the best light.

Among the film's most important scenes was one that was repeated a year later in *Triumph des Willens*, in which Sepp Allgeier stood directly behind Hitler in a moving car, showing the triumphal ride through Nuremberg from the Führer's perspective. However, this was not, as previously assumed, Riefenstahl's idea but Hitler's. Hitler personally asked Allgeier to stand behind him and photograph the ride through Nuremberg, as the cameraman proudly reported in an article written after filming was completed.[25] This totally new type of take was a stroke of luck for Riefenstahl, of course, and she happily accepted the Führer's idea.

The director's achievement consisted in making the rally's boring and endless processionals, speeches, and rituals visually interesting to moviegoers. Through skillfully chosen transitions, she used montage to give events a fluid, almost choreographic rhythm.[26] She abolished any spoken commentary—an absolute novelty in documentary film and one that had a unique effect on contemporary audiences.

The images were accompanied only by original sounds captured during filming and by a film score by Herbert Windt, who was to become one of the most prominent film composers of the Third Reich. Windt enjoyed an intense collaboration with Riefenstahl in the period that followed, composing the music for *Triumph des Willens* and *Olympia*. He had distinguished himself as a composer of epic scores with *Morgenrot* in 1933, a feature that Ufa hoped would ingratiate the company with Germany's new rulers. For *Sieg des Glaubens* he wove music by Wagner, party anthems, and brisk marches into one continuous musical tapestry, which served to emphasize the rhythm of the images.

Riefenstahl's extravagant work method was already evident during the making of this first party film. Originally scheduled to be screened four weeks following the party rally, *Sieg des Glaubens* took three months to arrive in movie theaters. In the sixty-minute film the director did not present the Nuremberg rally chronologically but chose to re-create it for the screen.[27] She followed atmospheric scenes of the city's early morning awakening with footage of Hitler (arriving by plane and making his way through the city by car convoy) and shots of the opening ceremony, in which the Führer is feted by Rudolf Hess as the "guarantor of victory." In the central part of the film, Hitler greets, in Zeppelin Field and Luitpold Field, various formations of the party's organizations, party officials, Hitler Youth, and, finally, the SA and the SS, which both march in bearing their standards to great fanfare. In delivering his speeches, Hitler repeatedly turns to address party comrades. After an endless parade of the party's various associations through the streets of Nuremberg, the film reaches its apex and closes with the memorial to the "movement's fallen," one of the central rituals in party rally theatrics. The film ends to the tune of the "Horst Wessel Song," with swastika flags waving against a backdrop of dramatic cloud formations.

Much more than a recording of events, *Sieg des Glaubens* delivers the mood of the party rally. The Nazi press consistently pointed out that Riefenstahl's film was more than a documentary; it was the cinematic equivalent of the Nuremberg rally events.[28]

*Sieg des Glaubens* premiered on December 1, 1933, three months after the rally, at the Ufa-Palast am Zoo. It was a state ceremony, with Hitler and the entire leadership of the party as well as Nazi celebrities in attendance. In the preceding months the regime had revealed its true face and demonstrated what it held in store for its detractors. All opposition was suppressed, and those who supported it were hauled off to hastily constructed concentration camps. On April 1, the first boycott against Jewish businesses had taken place, to which the international press had reacted with indignation. On the day that *Sieg des Glaubens* premiered, the Law on Securing the Unity of Party and State was passed, which declared the NSDAP the "sole representative of the state's views." The "victory of the National Socialist revolution" was declared—and it was precisely this propaganda message that Riefenstahl's film delivered.

That evening, the Ufa-Palast was besieged and the jubilant crowds refused to disperse when Hitler entered the theater at 9:00 p.m., together with Joseph Goebbels, Ernst Röhm, and Rudolf Hess. As reported in the press the next day, the screening was repeatedly interrupted by clapping when Hitler appeared in close-up. When the film ended, the celebrity audience broke into wild applause, which continued long after Hitler had quietly left the theater by a side door. The uncontested star of the evening was Leni Riefenstahl, and a fanatic crowd outside the theater cheered for so long that she was finally forced to make an appearance.

The film, distributed through the state theaters of the NSDAP, began showings in all major German cities shortly thereafter. The press indicated that it was "obvious that every German man, every German woman, and every German child will see this film."[29] It was often coupled with *Blut und Boden*, the "educational film on settlement policies," and screened at reduced prices. On December 2, 1933, Goebbels decreed that no party events could be scheduled at the same time that Riefenstahl's film was being shown.

> To all local chapters of the NSDAP!
>
> The powerful film *Sieg des Glaubens* recently began its march through Germany. Only a few hundred thousand party comrades and SA and SS members had the privilege of attending the Reich party rally in Nuremberg. The film now delivers to the many millions of German national comrades the sounds and images of this great event. The local chapters of the NSDAP are therefore instructed not to schedule any other official events on the days this powerful film is screened in your area, in order to give party members and citizens the opportunity to make an emphatic statement in attending a screening of the Reich party rally film.[30]

Special classroom showings of the film were scheduled for members of the various school associations. According to actual theater estimates, roughly twenty million "national comrades" saw the film. With the help of special "sound film vehicles," it was shown in rural areas that didn't have their own movie theaters. Advertising for the film took a form possible only in a dictatorship. As was later the case with screenings of *Triumph des Willens* and *Olympia*, the façades, foyers, and screening rooms of theaters showing *Sieg des Glaubens* were festooned, even in the tiniest towns, with garlands, Nazi emblems, the national eagle, and swastika flags to demonstrate how special the event was.

The premieres in individual cities of the Reich were always attended by the local heads of the party, who missed no opportunity to expound in bombastic speeches on the ideals and goals of National Socialism. SA bands played brisk martial music outside the theaters and flag-bearing party organizations marched through the city to the screenings, alerting crowds of potential moviegoers to the event. It became common everywhere to stand and join in singing the "Horst Wessel Song," which ended every showing.

Riefenstahl's calculations had proved correct: her career prospects were excellent, and she knew to show her gratitude by publicly hitching her star to the Nazi regime. The director also made appearances abroad, where she was successfully promoted as the "messenger" of the "new Germany." In April 1934, she flew to England and spoke on her work in London, Cambridge, and Oxford before audiences that numbered in the hundreds and in the absence of any counterdemonstrations. The London papers greeted her as the "envoy of the good film," and the press in Nazi Germany rejoiced in the acknowledgment that "our Leni" was receiving abroad.[31]

### AN UNDESIRABLE FILM

Following this unprecedented press and public awareness campaign, *Sieg des Glaubens* disappeared from movie theaters and from the archives of the Third Reich. Almost all copies of the film, celebrated until then as a "masterwork of the nation," were destroyed in 1934, probably on direct order from Hitler.[32] Riefenstahl kept the original negative, but it, too, was lost at the end of the war. For decades it was assumed that no copies of the film existed, until it turned up in the Film Archive of the German Democratic Republic in the 1980s. It then quickly became apparent why the film had fallen from Hitler's graces only a few months after its great triumph.

In the first half of 1934, the political climate in Germany underwent yet another great change. At the party rally of 1933, Hitler was not yet the sole sovereign leader of the party that he would become a few months later. And it was precisely this that *Sieg des Glaubens* repeatedly underscored: for long stretches of the film it was clear that SA chief Ernst Röhm shared the party leadership with Hitler. But the so-called Röhm Putsch on June 30, 1934, disempowered the paramilitary organization. With the murder of Hitler's comrade and close friend Röhm, along with hundreds of other "deviators" from the ranks of the NSDAP, ordered by the dictator and carried out by the SS and the Gestapo, Hitler was a great deal closer to absolute power.

Hitler knew that he could attain absolute and incontestable leadership in Germany only with the accord of the Wehrmacht. But with the SA Röhm had created the world's largest private army and continually demanded that the Wehrmacht be dissolved in order to make the SA the "people's army." Thus, unless the party's own military organization was deprived of power, the conflict with the Wehrmacht was a given. In addition, it could not have been Hitler's intention that Röhm, in increasing the power of the SA, become the second most powerful man in the regime. For a long period both the SA and the Wehrmacht vied for Hitler's loyalty. Only after the dictator decided in favor of the latter and had his influential rival murdered was the path cleared for the Wehrmacht to become, from that time onward, the single most important armed force in Germany.

With this change in the political situation, Riefenstahl's party rally film had become unusable, for Röhm was not to survive on the movie screen either. The images from *Sieg des Glaubens* had to be erased from the minds of millions of "national comrades" and replaced by others.

After the SA was eliminated, a completely different image of the Führer emerged. If the people had seen both Hitler and Röhm as representing the party before, now there was only Hitler as omnipotent leader, or Führer. From that point forward he had no equals; everyone clearly was subordinate to him, an idea that was fundamental to Riefenstahl's second party film, *Triumph des Willens*.

Like Hitler, Riefenstahl also came to view *Sieg des Glaubens* as highly undesirable, though for completely different reasons. Due to its shortcomings—obvious when compared with *Triumph des Willens*, which appeared one year later—even decades later Riefenstahl was painfully embarrassed when the film was mentioned. She called *Sieg des Glaubens* "exposed stock," not a "real film."[33] In her memoirs, she speaks of "imperfect piecework" and a "modest film,"[34] thus herself establishing the myth of why the film failed. As long as the film was lost, many were willing to accept her opinion.

In truth, *Sieg des Glaubens* is marked by various technical failures: tracking shots that end in nothing, shaky camera work, many out-of-focus scenes, people running through the scene or blocking the camera. But it is not only the technical defects that are obvious; the party's organization of the rally was clearly less skillful in 1933 than it was one year later. Many of the scenes were unintentionally funny, which wasn't appropriate to the bathos the party intended: Göring staunchly marches right past Hitler's limousine as Hitler reaches out to shake his hand; Hitler receives a bouquet from a little girl and, though almost painfully touched, immediately and heedlessly hands the flowers to Hess; Röhm constantly fidgets with the belt of his SA uniform; Baldur von Schirach, who was in charge of the Hitler Youth, knocks Hitler's cap from the stage with his backside; messengers excitedly run back and forth across the picture as Hitler arrives at the party rally grounds. All of these are moments of irritation to the viewer, moments that later caused Riefenstahl to distance herself from the film, if only for aesthetic reasons. The faulty staging, magnified when projected onto the big screen, destroyed the intended solemnity of the occasion. No state could be formed based on this film or the party rally of 1933. Riefenstahl and Hitler kept practicing.

Riefenstahl's apologists didn't shy away from representing *Sieg des Glaubens* as an insignificant film that remained without influence or patronage. Charles Ford, who after 1945 worked zealously to rehabilitate Riefenstahl's reputation, falsely stated that the film had its premiere at Mozart Hall on Berlin's Nollendorfplatz, with no party leaders or prominent figures in attendance. It had been an "almost secret screening," he wrote, claiming Riefenstahl wasn't even present.[35] Following this "secret premiere," *Sieg des Glaubens* allegedly was never again shown in public. Hamilton Burden went even further: "It is not known whether the film with the title *Sieg des Glaubens* was ever shown in public . . . It is even possible that the film was never developed, as up until today not one single copy has been located."[36]

The truth, however, was different. The film was not as insignificant as presented. Despite its faults, it was a remarkable piece of propaganda, even though it lacked by far the qualities revealed in *Triumph des Willens* one year later. The film historian Martin Loiperdinger comes to the conclusion that "Leni Riefenstahl suppresses her unbridled artistic ambitions, on which Hitler could count, and presents as bare minimum what in fact was the birth of a new style of Nazi documentary film propaganda . . . The director's modesty, in terms of her first party rally film, is completely misplaced."[37]

# 8

## RIEFENSTAHL SHAPES THE FACE OF THE THIRD REICH

### *TRIUMPH DES WILLENS* AND *TAG DER FREIHEIT!*

BECAUSE RIEFENSTAHL HERSELF considered *Triumph des Willens* to be the perfect film, her masterpiece, she preferred to erase the memory of *Sieg des Glaubens*. After 1945 she attempted to remain silent about it, in part to be able to say that *Triumph des Willens* was the only film she made for Hitler. Interestingly, the second film, which made her internationally famous, was not made solely as a result of the disempowerment of the SA and the murder of Röhm; Hitler had commissioned it months before these events occurred. Well into old age, Riefenstahl maintained that only one party rally film was originally intended, with no initial plans for a second one.[1]

So why the plan for a second film at a time when no one could have foreseen the political changes that would necessitate it? In *Memoiren*, Riefenstahl describes a meeting with Hitler and Goebbels at the Reich Chancellory at the beginning of October 1933.[2] At this meeting she gave an extensive report on the experience of making *Sieg des Glaubens*, including the difficulties she experienced during shooting, and on the process through which she could take inadequate material and turn it into a good film in the cutting room. This report obviously convinced Hitler to give Riefenstahl another chance the following year and entrust her with a second party rally film.[3] Six months later, in April 1934—two months, that is, before the "Röhm Putsch"—he unofficially ordered Riefenstahl again to film in Nuremberg. At the same time, Hitler agreed that Ufa would distribute the film.[4]

As *Sieg des Glaubens* at first totally satisfied the aesthetic requirements of both Hitler and the party leadership, there is the possibility that it was Riefenstahl herself who proposed the second film. At the very least, the decision must have been made with her agreement. Presumably she saw that, provided with the necessary financing and total freedom, she would have a second chance to make the perfect party rally film that she hadn't been able to realize in 1933. It must have been clear to her that in doing so she would win Hitler's greatest appreciation.

This second rally film established itself as the most significant representative document of Hitler's rule, the film that was to bear witness to his triumph for all time. And indeed, *Triumph des Willens*—not least because Riefenstahl could draw upon the experience of *Sieg des Glaubens*—became the "memorial to the movement"[5] and the "spectacular portrait of the new Germany"[6] celebrated in the Nazi press. All the cinematic and organizational weaknesses of *Sieg des Glaubens* were now eliminated in order to perfect the characterization of Hitler as invincible, superhuman Führer. Not only did the theatrical event that was the 1934 Reich party rally go off without a hitch, the cinematic portrayal of the Nazis' fantasies of omnipotence were also perfected, thus delivering the ultimate homage to the dictator. After *Triumph des Willens*, no other film on Hitler was necessary, and none was commissioned. As the film historian Erwin Leiser writes, "Here, once and for all, he was shown as he wanted to be seen."[7]

No documentation on National Socialism today neglects to include images from *Triumph des Willens*, and no other film created a more profound visual impression of the movement. *Triumph des Willens* became the pivotal point of Riefenstahl's life history, establishing her position in the Third Reich and conferring upon her a near invincibility that would last for as long as the Nazi regime existed. And the fact that it was a woman who captured the male world of fascism on film created a sensation— at that time perhaps more so than it would today—that the ambitious director visibly enjoyed.

If her first party rally film barely differentiated itself from newsreel reports, there was no element of reportage in the film of 1934. Hitler's order to the director was clear in this respect: "Artistic creation of the Nuremberg party rally on film, that was the instruction the Führer gave me for the second time."[8]

## THE REICH PARTY RALLY OF UNITY AND STRENGTH

The NSDAP rally of 1934 lasted for an entire week, from September 3 to 10, longer than any previous rally. A half million party members and 200,000 guests traveled to Nuremberg. Together with the 350,000 residents of the city, Hitler had at his disposal roughly one million extras for his emotion-laden mass spectacle. The rally made an impact not only on followers of the Nazis but also on the foreign guests, diplomats, and representatives of the press, as journalist Bella Fromm noted in her diary: "The shameless and dishonest overstatement that dominates the celebration of the Nuremberg party rally, the boasting, the propaganda, are astonishing to those foreigners present. This mass meeting is strong and intoxicating poison. Not all of the foreigners are capable of keeping a clear head in the face of this overwhelming and showy spectacle . . . The Nuremberg party rally is a well-calculated, carefully rehearsed show, its psychological effect on the masses simply shocking. The few who were not hypnotized found the outbreaks of hysteria on the part of the women near repulsive."[9]

Above all, the Nazis wanted to demonstrate to the world Hitler's new position and authority. Whereas in the preceding year many people had considered National Socialism to be a temporary phenomenon, Nuremberg demonstrated that henceforth there was no alternative to Hitler. The message of the party rally—and of Riefenstahl's film as well—was the equating of Hitler with Germany. Hitler's deputy Rudolf Hess was the mouthpiece of this message during the opening and closing ceremonies: "You are Germany. When you act, the nation acts, when you make preparations, the nation prepares . . . Hitler is Germany, just as Germany is Hitler."

In a "people's survey" of August 19, 1934, an overwhelming majority of Germans, 38 million against 4.5 million, approved of Hitler's policies and his position of unlimited power. After the death of Hindenburg, the dictator had appointed himself Führer and Reich chancellor, signaling the extent of his power and popularity and positioning himself for the "Thousand-Year Reich." His enemies inside and outside the party had been either eliminated or rendered harmless. The murder of Röhm and the disempowerment of the SA, which resulted in the Wehrmacht's first participation in a party rally, led Hitler to call repeatedly for unity and unanimity within the movement.

This call to unanimity was underscored in new, quasi-religious rituals, which Riefenstahl captured on film. For example, amid gun salutes and to the tune of the "Horst Wessel Song," Hitler consecrated SA and SS banners—using the "blood flag of the movement," a flag soaked in the blood of those who had died in Hitler's attempted Beer Hall Putsch of 1923—by touching each and every one of them with the flag while gazing deeply into the eyes of each standard-bearer.

Given his new authority, the appearance of Adolf Hitler at the Reich Party Rally of Unity and Strength was distinctly more ostentatious this year. The historian William Shirer recorded his eyewitness impressions of the events in Nuremberg: "No wonder that Hitler appeared so self-satisfied at the party rally held on September 4. The next morning I observed how he strode down the middle aisle of the huge, flag-bedecked Luitpold Arena with the air of a victorious Caesar, as the band blared the 'Badenweiler March' and thirty thousand hands were raised in the 'Hitler greeting.'"[10]

Riefenstahl, as she had done in her feature film *Das blaue Licht*, wanted to stylize her second party rally film to the greatest possible degree, to "virtually shine a new light on those cherished days in our memory and the inexpressibly happy world they represented."[11] *Triumph des Willens* revels in an endless sea of flags, bombastic rituals, and rousing music. Two motifs dominate: on one side stands the Führer, on the other the party and the *Volk*, subordinates arranged before him in precisely ordered groups. The phrase "One *Volk*—One Reich—One Führer" is insistently placed at the center of the film. *Triumph des Willens* presents the image of a society in which obedience has replaced free will, in which identity is possible only in identifying with the Führer.

The film's importance as a historical document rests on its emphasis that Germans were more fascinated with the person of Hitler than attracted to his political ideas. *Triumph des Willens* replaces politics with aesthetics: instead of political discussion we see the image of the "tamed masses," shaped into and disciplined as marching columns and organized blocks. After her experiences of the preceding year, it was clear to Riefenstahl that she could edit the perfect film of her imagination only if she

had perfect takes at her disposal. In such takes a certain degree of stylization was inherent, which she then merely had to emphasize on the cutting table through montage. So she filmed every event of the party rally
from every possible angle, in order to be able to craft the film from the
whole. From the very beginning, she paid particular attention to presenting the Führer not in unobserved "private" moments as in the previous
film, but stylized into an impervious "deliverer of salvation" who ascended
above all others. Opposite him stood only the *Volk*, "in unified allegiance
to the Führer, and therefore to Germany."[12]

## NEW AUTHORITY

Riefenstahl officially received credit only as "artistic director" of *Sieg des
Glaubens*, but the NSDAP assigned her "overall artistic and organizational direction" of *Triumph des Willens*. Riefenstahl probably made this a
condition, in order to avoid the friction and questions about her expertise
that had arisen with the Chief Sector for Film in 1933. She now filmed
on direct "orders of the Führer," without having to answer to Goebbels
and the Ministry of Propaganda. From then on she was subject to orders
from no one but Hitler.

Riefenstahl now served as producer as well, and to this end changed
the name of her production company to Reich Party Rally Film. After
1945, she maintained, not least in order to be able to claim the rights to
*Triumph des Willens*, that she had made the film as an independent director and producer and it had had nothing to do with the party. This is contradicted, however, by the fact that on August 28, 1934, at a meeting of
Ufa's board of directors during which a distribution contract was negotiated, she appeared expressly as a "special agent of the Reich leadership of
the NSDAP."[13]

In terms of the film's financing, once again a different picture emerges
from the one Riefenstahl wished to convey. In the postwar period she held
fast to her statement that the second party rally film was financed without
funds from the party, that Ufa put up the money for the film in anticipation of box-office returns. This is implausible given the fact that the agreement with Ufa was signed only a few days before the second Nuremberg

rally began, by which time untold sums had been spent on the film's extensive preparations. In addition, the distribution contract that survives confirms that Ufa was not involved in the financing of the film:

> The board accepts the conclusion of a distribution agreement with Leni Riefenstahl as special agent of the Reich leadership of the NSDAP concerning the roughly twenty-four-hundred-meter film "Reich Party Rally 1934" for the German distribution area and of unrestricted monopoly, including double-8 film . . . Fräulein Riefenstahl is charged with the artistic and technical direction of the film according to the letter of April 19, 1934, issued by the Führer in the name of the Reich leadership of the NSDAP. According to this same letter, up to 300,000 reichsmarks shall be made available to Fräulein Riefenstahl. The Führer has declared himself in agreement that Ufa shall distribute the film.[14]

As Ufa established proof that it had not participated in the financing of the film and there is no evidence of other creditors, Riefenstahl's statement cannot reflect the truth.[15] The 300,000 reichsmarks for the production of *Triumph des Willens* must therefore have come from party sources.[16]

Before Riefenstahl went to Nuremberg in August 1934 to join her team, which had already begun preparations for the film, she recruited some of Germany's finest cameramen and technicians. She let everyone know that she was filming "at the order of the Führer" and didn't hesitate to use this privilege as a means of applying pressure. If cameramen she wished to hire resisted the engagement, she went to the authorities, charging a boycott of her "order from the Führer." She must have been aware that such a denunciation would seriously endanger those thus charged. On August 17, 1934, for example, she wrote to "party comrade" Karl Auen, of the Reich Film Group in the Ministry of Propaganda:

> As you may have heard, I once again am making a film, at the order of the Führer, of the 1934 Reich party rally. As I will need many crew members for the Nuremberg rally, I have asked the Film Group to provide me with names and addresses. Among these I found a Herr Schünemann. When my secretary telephoned Herr

Schünemann, Herr Schünemann said that he was already engaged, but [wanted to know] for which film he was being considered. My secretary answered that it was a film on the Reich party rally, at which point she was asked if it was the film Leni Riefenstahl was making. When this was affirmed, Herr Schünemann said, "Then I would not participate out of principle. It would be beneath my dignity." As I perceived his statement to be a disparagement of my work, which is being carried out at the order of the Führer, I consider it my duty to communicate this to you and leave it to you to take a position on this matter.[17]

Emil Schünemann believed that Riefenstahl's letter would create serious difficulties for him. In written statements of August 21 and 25, he stressed that he was very interested in working on the Reich party rally film and that this offer had been a great honor for him. He had refused only because, taking into consideration his thirty-year career, he did not wish to work under the artistic direction of a woman. Auen was satisfied with this explanation, and he communicated to Riefenstahl on August 27 that he did not consider this to be "duping" the Führer. But Riefenstahl again wrote to Auen, declaring that "that doesn't change the fact that this statement by Herr Schünemann is a boycott against the Führer . . . If the Führer doesn't consider it beneath his dignity to trust a woman with the artistic direction of this work, it is strange, in the very least, that Herr Schünemann considers it beneath his dignity to accept this. It would not be possible to carry out the orders of the Führer if other colleagues were to agree with Herr Schünemann's opinion."[18]

If Riefenstahl, as she later maintained, truly had made *Triumph des Willens* reluctantly and against her will, she undoubtedly would have had a greater understanding of Schünemann's refusal to be part of the project. The fact that, quite the contrary, she went back and, out of a sense of injured vanity, ruthlessly used her privileged position to force Schünemann to participate can be seen as evidence of a "first moral low-point" in her career, as Rainer Rother described it.[19] Riefenstahl wanted to set an example to prove her power—but was unsuccessful. In the end, Schünemann did not have to work for her. In Riefenstahl's *Memoiren* there is no mention of him.[20]

During the postwar period it was erroneously stated that the party rally of 1934 was staged solely for Riefenstahl's cameras.[21] This theory is refuted by the single fact that future party rallies were presented in an equally extravagant and even more pompous fashion.

To put the Nuremberg rally on film in the way that *Triumph des Willens* did represented an enormous logistical achievement and was possible only due to production conditions that never before had been applied to the making of a documentary film. It was not only in the streets of Nuremberg that, with the support of the town fathers, preparations were made exactly as the director felt necessary. On the rally grounds as well, workers constructed strategically placed "film towers" equipped with cameras, sound equipment, and huge spotlights. Tracks were laid down all around the podium that Hitler would speak from, in order to film the speeches while in motion and thus provide a totally new visual experience. The grounds were transformed into a huge, perfectly organized film studio. Albert Speer permitted Riefenstahl to install a small electric lift on one of the 120-foot flagpoles. From the lift, using a handheld camera, the monumental dimensions of the parade field could be filmed from a wholly new perspective.[22]

For *Triumph des Willens*, Riefenstahl's camera crew experimented with innovative techniques and perspectives. They practiced shooting on roller skates so they would be able to capture with a handheld camera motion shots that didn't shake. Special bicycles were built, similar to the old-fashioned penny-farthing models, and camera tracks were situated so that they could move through the mass formations on the rally grounds. The ultimate goal was to capture the most powerful footage possible, for only this would allow new and dynamic visual effects to be created later as montage.

A staff of roughly 170 worked under Riefenstahl's command, including 36 cameramen, 10 technical staff, 17 newsreel operators, 17 lighting crewmen, 9 aerial and 2 still photographers, 2 secretaries, and 26 drivers. The party contributed 4 general workers and 37 guards, recruited from the SS, the SA, and the military police, whose job it was to clear a path through the crowd for the film team.

During the shoot, Riefenstahl's cameramen had to "dress as SA men. This suggestion came from the chief of staff, so that crew wearing civilian clothing wouldn't disturb the official images."[23] Even Riefenstahl herself wore a kind of "fantasy uniform," a white coat with an armband that bore the word "film" in large Gothic letters. In costume, she strode together with her chief cameraman, Sepp Allgeier, through the streets of Nuremberg and the party grounds to calculate in advance how many cameras and operators would be needed for the individual events and the best locations to position them.

With Hitler's arrival in Nuremberg on September 4, 1934, the week-long shooting of the film could begin. Though Riefenstahl considered filming Hitler to be her chief activity, she, along with the Führer, was the star of the show and one of the rally's main attractions. According to the *Film-Kurier*, "There was always a chorus chanting, 'Leni, Leni!'—countless hands reaching out in the hope of a quick handshake."[24]

## THE MISTRESS OF CEREMONIES

In creating *Triumph des Willens*, Riefenstahl did not limit herself to the party's plans for staging the rally. She created it anew for the screen in the cutting room, thus becoming the event's true "mistress of ceremonies."[25] In this, Hitler gave her free rein and did not set a deadline for completing the film. Press notices at the end of September, stating that the film would be in theaters by December 1934, confirm that at first Riefenstahl scheduled only three, not six, months to edit the film.[26] The distribution agreement with Ufa provided that the film would be ready by mid-March 1935, in part so that it could be evaluated far in advance of the next party rally. Though Riefenstahl answered directly to Hitler, he seems to have exercised scant influence over the film.

One exception to this was the choice of the film's title, which, as in years past, was decided by Hitler based on a "Führer decree." Not only was *Sieg des Glaubens*, title of both the previous year's party rally and its film, Hitler's idea, he also had come up with the pompous *Eine Symphonie des Kampfwillens* (A Symphony of the Will to Fight) as the title for the short film on the first NSDAP party rally in 1927.

People believed that *Triumph des Willens* was the actual title of the 1934 rally. Riefenstahl played a significant role in this, repeatedly stating that "*Triumph des Willens* was what the party rally was called. It simply was the title of the party rally."[27] This statement is false, despite the fact that it was continually repeated until recently. The party rally of 1934 bore the official title Reich Party Rally of Unity and Strength. Hitler generated the title *Triumph des Willens* for Riefenstahl's film, which proves that he attributed a great importance to the film independent of the party rally.

After filming ended, Leni Riefenstahl withdrew with several of her crew and female assistants to the editing studios of the Geyer Works on Harzer Strasse in Berlin-Neukölln, where she occupied a building reserved solely for work on the Reich party rally film. In the anteroom hung "a picture from the 1934 Nuremberg party rally: the Führer!—an image that in its naturalness presented the Führer in a way never seen before."[28] Over the next months, Riefenstahl rarely left the cutting room. However, she maintained contact with her patron, visiting Hitler in Obersalzberg in the fall of 1934. She informed a reporter concerning the purpose of this visit: "The Führer wishes to receive reports on the progress of the work and, just as during the difficult filming period he discussed with me what was technically necessary in order to create the best possible footage, he now also contributes strongly to the work."[29]

The roughly three thousand meters of the final version of *Triumph des Willens* were chosen by Riefenstahl from approximately 128,000 meters of exposed film at her disposal. The initial viewing of this material alone took eighty-one hours. For six months she disappeared totally into her task, working every day, even Sundays, until three or four in the morning. Her postwar assertion, "It's true that I tried to get help on the project, but to no avail,"[30] can be relegated to the realm of fantasy.

She explained her procedure for editing *Triumph des Willens*: "The creative process demands that, based on the actual events in Nuremberg, one instinctively locate the one path that shapes the film in such a way that it overwhelmingly pulls those hearing and viewing it from one act to the next, from impression to impression. I'm looking for the inner drama of such a staging. It is there. And it will be conveyed to people as soon as the filmed material from Nuremberg is shaped, as soon as the speeches and words, mass images and head shots, marches and music, pictures of Nuremberg by night and morning, rise to a symphony that does justice to Nuremberg's significance."[31] The effect of the near choreographic, symphonic rhythm of Riefenstahl's edit was heightened by the music of Herbert Windt, composed and edited to precisely match the marching troops. It is the music that ties together the individual segments of the film and creates its transitions. Because the original music of the party rally could not be recorded due to technical reasons, it had to be performed again for Riefenstahl's film. When there were difficulties synchronizing image and music, Riefenstahl herself took the baton and directed the huge orchestra, as she was the only one who had every single cut of the film in her head.

During the time that Riefenstahl almost completely disappeared from view to edit her film, the daily papers and film publications repeatedly reported on the progress of her work or on visits that high party functionaries paid the director, in order to keep the public interested in the film. Everyone involved was aware that the long period between the events in Nuremberg and the premiere of the film was problematic. And yet for a long while, photographs of the director in her white smock at work at the editing table during a visit by Hitler or Goebbels, or by other party officials,[32] were the only images the public received of Riefenstahl or the film she was making. Finally, on February 1, 1935, *Film-Kurier* announced that the "party rally film was near completion. Only six hundred meters to go . . ." On March 9, it was publicized that the premiere of the film was set for March 28. Four days before the premiere, Hitler personally screened the film, which represented an absolute exception in the prewar period.[33] Riefenstahl freely admitted that she was gripped by "a terrible fear and heart palpitations" when Hitler showed up in the editing room afterward.[34] But her fears proved unfounded: not one single meter of film had to be reedited, nothing had to be changed, everything met with the full satisfaction of the dictator. Riefenstahl could now reap the fruits of her labor.

The press styled Riefenstahl's work on the film itself as the act of an iron, inflexible will. "A strength of will shapes *Triumph des Willens*."[35] Already the title of the film had become synonymous with Riefenstahl's obsession in artistic matters.

The two-hour film begins, as had the previous year's, with a prologue,

showing in feature-film-like sequences the city of Nuremberg as it awak-
ens and makes preparations for the party rally, until—to the music of
Wagner's *Meistersinger Overture* and the "Horst Wessel Song"—the silhou-
ette of the "Führer machine" emerges from the clouds.[36] Like a deus ex
machina, Hitler approaches the city from above. As was not the case with
*Sieg des Glaubens*, this time Hitler's first appearance is fittingly celebrated.
Also refined in comparison to the preceding year is the Führer's traditional journey by automobile—standing in an open Mercedes-Benz—
through the swastika-adorned streets of Nuremberg. Cinematic staging
replaced the spontaneous excitement and disorganized masses. The line
of cars drove extremely slowly, in order to avoid shaky camera takes. And
scenes were cut into the film that must have been discussed beforehand:
halfway along its route the procession of cars stops so that a woman holding a child in her arms can walk up to Hitler's car and present him with
flowers.

Riefenstahl achieved a special, evocative effect by employing the cross-
cut method rarely used in documentary films of the time. By combining
happy, enthusiastic, emotional faces from the crowd with close-ups of
Hitler, she constructed a virtual cult around the Führer. Riefenstahl's
montage has the effect of presenting Hitler, stylized as an almost erotic
object to his followers, in a quiet tête-à-tête with his *Volk*. In primarily
choosing the faces of women and young men for this cross-cutting technique, she stages this dialogue as an intimate relationship between an
enthusiastic *Volk* and the dictator, situated above all others, accepting the
love of his people as a given.

Riefenstahl once again used the technique of building suspense. Just
as it takes a while for the crowds to catch sight of Hitler for the first time,
it is a conspicuously long time—following a whole series of speeches
by various party members—before Riefenstahl first cuts to a speech by
Hitler. To avoid repetition, each of Hitler's speeches is presented differently; most are shot with moving cameras filming from a point lower
than the position of the Führer, so that the movie audience has the
impression of looking up at him.

Through stylized takes, but also through suggestive montage, Riefenstahl far outstrips what might have been a pure documentation of events.
The goal of her artistic creation was, as she herself formulated it, to "give

the image perhaps a stronger effect than it had in reality."[37] In an article published in 1941 titled "On the Essence and Creation of Documentary Films," she stressed that the documentary, as she understood it, was not a mere recording of external events but a "bringing to light"[38] of the ideal, of the true message of the respective event. With *Triumph des Willens*, she achieved just that.

This is particularly evident in the climax of the film, which is also its most famous scene, with the colossally staged ceremonial honoring of the dead in the Luitpold Arena. This ritual was highly dramatized and perfected over the preceding year, both organizationally and cinematically. To the subdued sound of a dirge, Hitler pays tribute to the "heroes of the movement," those who fell in the Hitler Putsch of 1923. The monument is located across the platform from which the dictator delivers his speech, and Hitler reaches it by way of a broad, granite-paved "Street of the Führer," to the left and right of which stand huge groups of SA and SS men in parade formation. Viktor Lutze, head of the SA, and Heinrich Himmler, head of the SS, follow behind him at a respectful distance. The scene leaves no doubt as to exactly who is the one and only Führer of the state and party.

In order to perfectly place this fundamental message in the picture, the party leadership also served as actors off the political stage. Some of the footage from the Congress Hall, where the opening and closing events of the party rally were held, needed to be reshot in order to document the major policy speeches of the Nazi leadership. Albert Speer, who was commissioned to construct the backdrop for the reshoot in Berlin in Europe's largest film studio, corroborated:

> I remember as well that shots of one of the ceremonial sessions of the party congress . . . were spoiled. Hitler, at the suggestion of Leni Riefenstahl, ordered the scenes to be repeated in the studio. In one of the largest film studios in Berlin-Johannistal, I reconstructed a segment of the Congress Hall along with the podium and the speaker's stand, lit by spotlights. The film crew was very busy—and in the background one could see Streicher, Rosenberg, and [Hans] Frank walking back and forth with their manuscripts, eagerly memorizing their parts. Hess arrived and was asked to be

the first to perform. He ceremoniously raised his hand, as he had before the crowd of thirty thousand at the party congress. With his own special brand of bathetic, earnest excitement he began turning precisely toward the spot where Hitler did not now stand, calling out, while standing at attention, "My Führer, I greet you in the name of the party congress. The congress resumes. The Führer speaks!" He was so persuasive that from that point on I was never completely convinced of the genuineness of his feelings. And the other three as well played their parts true to reality in the emptiness of the film studio, proving themselves to be talented actors. I was truly irritated; Frau Riefenstahl, on the other hand, found the staged takes better than the originals.[39]

If this scene actually played as Speer described, it supports the historian Klaus Kreimeier's point that "the party rallies' cult of dramatization could be reproduced effortlessly as staged scenes in a suitably large studio."[40] Riefenstahl disagreed with Speer's version, maintaining that a brief segment of a speech by Julius Streicher was filmed at the later date, but not speeches by Hess or other functionaries.[41] This restaging would have contradicted her self-image as a "passive chronicler of the events."

*Triumph des Willens* celebrated its world premiere on March 28, 1935, as part of an ostentatious and widely publicized gala event at Berlin's Ufa-Palast am Zoo. As had been the case with *Sieg des Glaubens*, neither cost nor effort was spared in presenting the new party rally film as the movie event of the year. The extraordinary amount spent on advertising (22,000 reichsmarks for the Berlin premiere alone) underscores the significance attached to Riefenstahl's film. To emphasize this, the façade of the movie theater in which the premiere took place was renovated at a cost of 8,000 reichsmarks. Albert Speer extended the upper façade by twelve feet, creating a towering forty-five-foot-high superstructure that was decorated with nineteen huge swastika flags, each thirty-six feet long. The main entrance was crowned by a free-floating gold Reich eagle almost fifteen feet high and twenty-seven feet wide, which was bathed in dazzling spotlights on the evening of the premiere.

After the screening, Hitler thanked Leni Riefenstahl before the assembled audience and presented the visibly moved director with a huge bouquet of flowers while gazing deeply into her eyes, an image captured on camera. At this moment, overcome by her success and the Führer's gratitude, Riefenstahl fainted, which she later explained as the result of overwork. Only three years after she had stood on the same stage to introduce her first film, *Das blaue Licht*, she now found herself at the peak of fame.

The Nazi press reacted to the film as expected. *Triumph des Willens* celebrated its premiere in seventy German movie houses simultaneously—this time, as opposed to the party rally film of the previous year, as part of Ufa's prestigious distribution system. All of the Reich's magazines published lengthy articles on the film. They celebrated it as a "symphony of the German will,"[42] a "national document,"[43] and an "exceptional event in an exceptional form."[44] On the day after the premier, the *Völkischer Beobachter* exulted, "The soul of National Socialism comes alive in this film!" Within a few days the film broke attendance records in many of Germany's movie theaters. Ufa theaters throughout the Reich reported their profits daily to the film magazines. In its first twenty days, more than one hundred thousand people in Berlin alone saw *Triumph des Willens*, making it at that early point the highest-attended film of the 1934–35 season. So that people would also perceive the film as a towering political and cultural event, measures were taken—as had been the case with *Sieg des Glaubens*—to present a trip to see the film as a major, near cultlike experience. Accordingly, Propaganda Minister Goebbels issued a nationwide ban on any supporting program being shown with the film.

In addition, great care was taken to see that *Triumph des Willens* encountered no competition. Amateur cinematographers had not been welcome on the party rally grounds. Had someone shot film nevertheless, he was forbidden to screen it, either publicly or semipublicly. In September 1934, it was declared, "It contradicts the ideas upon which the production of this unity film are based to screen moving pictures of the Reich party rally that were filmed by individuals. Therefore, all party organizations and administrative offices, including district and state film offices, and all individuals are forbidden to present screenings of footage taken during the party rally."[45]

In this way, *Triumph des Willens* remained, along with the officially approved newsreels, the only document of the Party Rally of Unity and Strength to shape the public's memory of this event.

For *Triumph des Willens*, Leni Riefenstahl was awarded the National Film Prize, which Goebbels presented to her on June 25, 1935, and a number of foreign prizes. Among them were the prize for best foreign documentary film at the 1935 International Film Festival in Venice and the 1937 Grand Prize of the Paris World's Fair, whose jury, including René Clair and Jacques Feyder, was headed by film pioneer Louis Lumière.

After 1945, Riefenstahl repeatedly attempted to use the Grand Prize of the World's Fair as evidence that *Triumph des Willens* had been seen not as a propaganda film but as pure documentary. She deliberately overlooked the fact that at its screening in France there had been a number of protests by French citizens (and also by American and British jury members) who, with respect to the film's function as propaganda, objected to Riefenstahl being honored. But the jury remained unmoved and stood by its decision; the prize honored Riefenstahl's extraordinary artistry, not her political views.[46] Leni Riefenstahl was overjoyed at receiving the prize. In spite of her support for Hitler, she had established a place for herself as a director on the international stage with this honor.

The film again played a special role after Austria was annexed by the German Reich. In March 1938, *Triumph des Willens*, previously banned by the Schuschnigg government, played to sold-out houses daily in Vienna and all other major Austrian cities. Vehicles equipped for sound film projection once again showed it in those provinces without movie theaters. In March 1939, it was widely screened directly following the occupation of Czechoslovakia in the Reich protectorates of Bohemia and Moravia. After the invasion of Poland in September 1939, a large number of copies were sent to the new Polish territory under German rule. In every case, *Triumph des Willens* was presented as a propaganda film that heralded Germany's strength and superiority.

## AN EMBARRASSING BOOK

At the film's premiere in March 1935, a book appeared under the title *Hinter den Kulissen des Reichsparteitagfilms* (Behind the Scenes of the Reich Party Rally Film). It was issued by the central publishing house of the

NSDAP in Munich, Franz Eher Verlag, which also published the party organ, the *Völkischer Beobachter*. In addition to a multitude of film stills, the roughly one-hundred-page book included photographs of the planning, preparation, and execution of the film. It also presented a diarylike report describing the shooting and editing of the film. There was great interest in the book and it sold very well. Leni Riefenstahl acted as the work's undisputed author. The press described it as "the work history of the Reich party rally film, authored by Leni Riefenstahl" and as "Leni Riefenstahl's words and pictures."[47] In the postwar period, however, the director disputed her authorship of the book. She maintained that Ernst Jaeger, editor in chief of *Film-Kurier*, had written the text and selected the pictures, and that she hadn't even seen the book before its publication: "I didn't write a word of it; I unfortunately didn't even get to read it, otherwise it would have been written in a different style."[48] After 1945, Riefenstahl always showed journalists a receipt for 1,000 reichsmarks that Ernst Jaeger had received for his work on the book.[49] This was meant to prove that she herself had had nothing to do with the publication. But in 1935, on her application to the Reichsschriftumskammer, the Nazi Chamber of Literature, Riefenstahl stated that *Hinter den Kulissen des Reichsparteitagfilms* was her own title.[50]

After 1945, this book became highly embarrassing to Riefenstahl, providing eloquent evidence that she approached her work with great enthusiasm and, in addition, had enjoyed a great many more opportunities than she had revealed. Her first-person narrative not only reports on the extensive preparatory work and filming of *Triumph des Willens*, but it also uses pretentious and hollow phrases to pay tribute to the "Führer," and praises the director to the skies. The book's photographs alone attest to this. In comparison to sixteen photos of Hitler, there are thirty-seven of Riefenstahl at work. The director, as she later did when making *Olympia*, engaged her own still photographer, who accompanied her during the shooting of the film every step of the way and took pictures of her in every situation, more than likely for the book that was already planned. In this respect, *Hinter den Kulissen des Reichsparteitagfilms* is, first and foremost, a memorial to Riefenstahl herself.

How likely is it that the director, famous for her perfectionism and her love of detail, would actually let someone else take over the work on this book? Early on she recognized how important skillful public relations were to her career. According to Rainer Rother, "Media relations remained one of her special talents; she recognized quite early on the significance of a good PR campaign and understood how to use it from that time forward."[51] As of 1928, she had regularly written reports on the shooting of Arnold Fanck's films, which then were published in various newspapers and magazines. In 1933, she published her first book, *Kampf in Schnee und Eis*. And she had been greatly involved in writing the press notices for *Das blaue Licht*. In addition to a series of lectures she delivered on the history of making *Triumph des Willens*, a book about the film would fit the picture, especially as it has the same tenor as her lectures and interviews. And she continued with this practice later: for the premiere of the Olympiad films she published a book titled *Schönheit im Olympischen Kampf* (*Beauty in Olympic Battle*), and after 1945 she penned extensive promotional reports on the Nuba for magazines and for her own books of photography. Writing about her work was, for her entire life, an important part of her public self. Is it plausible that she passed up the opportunity—precisely when it concerned the film that was to become the most important of her career—to write the text herself, or at the very least to edit it?

The foreword to *Hinter den Kulissen des Reichsparteitagfilms* was written by Hitler himself, and it was published in mid-March 1935 in the trade journal *Film-Kurier*: "This rare film allows a glimpse into a demonstration the extent of which remains unmatched, not to mention unsurpassed, today. It conveys at the same time an understanding for the work and the artistic achievement of Leni Riefenstahl in the making of the film *Triumph des Willens*. A unique and incomparable glorification of the strength and the beauty of our movement."[52]

The book also contains an introduction by Riefenstahl, one that must have caused her great discomfort later:

> Before this report in words and pictures leads the reader through the creation of a German film never before made in so generous a fashion, I would like to thank the Führer. It was at his wish that this work was undertaken and completed. I also would like to thank Dr. Goebbels, who supported the filming in every way possible. Franconian leader Streicher helped us through many diffi-

culties in Nuremberg. Special support for the totally innovative utilization of all technical means was provided courtesy of the city of Nuremberg. All of the resources we required, down to the street-cars and fire ladders, were placed at our disposal by Chief Burgo-master Liebel. With this book I would like to thank all of my colleagues. The work demanded something remarkable of them, and they achieved something remarkable.[53]

## PROPAGANDA AND COUNTERPROPAGANDA

While people in Germany were praising *Triumph des Willens* as the "great vision of the Führer," it was being used abroad to shape the image of Hitler's dictatorship. There were also those who attempted to turn it into counterpropaganda by revealing the empty pathos of Nazi ideology. The American director Frank Capra, for example, used images from Riefen-stahl's film in his own *Prelude to War* (1942). Capra used only the documentary material, skillfully weaving together seized German newsreels, images from *Triumph des Willens*, and cuts from American anti-Nazi films into a dramatic whole, which he then underlay with spoken commentary. Even today Capra's film is considered one of the best American propaganda films of the Second World War.

The attempt had already been made in America to illuminate the effectiveness of film propaganda using Riefenstahl's film. Luis Buñuel, the Spanish surrealist filmmaker, was commissioned to produce a short version of *Triumph des Willens* for this purpose.[54] New York's Museum of Modern Art was in possession of a copy of Riefenstahl's party rally film. Right after the war broke out, Iris Barry, the museum's film curator, talked Buñuel into joining a committee formed to open the eyes of those within the U.S. government who at the time did not believe in the effectiveness of film propaganda. Buñuel recalled this venture and the reactions that it evoked:

> I worked on it for two or three weeks in the cutting room. The films were horribly ideological, but fantastically made, impressive . . . It all went very well. The abridged films were shown as

examples to all possible types of people—senators, consulate people. René Clair and Charlie Chaplin saw them together and had totally opposite reactions. René Clair was horrified by the effectiveness of the films and said to me: "Don't show them to anyone, or we're lost!" Chaplin, on the other hand, laughed like a crazy man. He even fell off his chair laughing. Why? Was it because of *The Great Dictator*? I don't to this day understand it.[55]

In truth, *Triumph des Willens*, which produced the first close-ups of Hitler, provided the basic elements of Chaplin's brilliant Hitler parody, *The Great Dictator* (1940), certainly the most successful satire of Hitler and his dictatorship. It is said that Chaplin arrived at the final decision to make the film only after he had seen Buñuel's version of Riefenstahl's propaganda film. Chaplin saw the exaggerated staging of Riefenstahl's film and the theatrical, studied look of Hitler's gesturing, his rolling eyes, and the way his voice cracked as something laughable, something funny. Riefenstahl's film, which he watched over and over again while preparing *The Great Dictator*, allowed him to study Hitler's poses and behavior, which he parodied in his own film with great intelligence and subtlety.

But the influence of *Triumph des Willens* in the context of anti-Nazi propaganda involved a wider circle, extending to Great Britain, for example. It was here that an entire series of compilation films took Riefenstahl's images as their starting point, among them *The Curse of the Swastika* (1940), *Germany Calling* (1940), and *These Are the Men* (1943). In addition, Britain's Movie-Tone Newsreels produced the short film *Germany Calling (the Lambethwalk)*, which combined shots of marching Nazi troops from *Triumph des Willens* with the sounds of the hit song "Doing the Lambeth Walk."[56]

Images from *Triumph des Willens* continued to be used repeatedly after 1945 as well. The French director Alain Resnais inserted them into his 1955 film *Night and Fog*, which dealt with the genocide perpetrated by the Nazis. The antifascist films *The Life of Adolf Hitler* (1961) by Paul Rotha, *Ordinary Fascism* (1964) by Mikhail Romm, *Deutschland, erwache!* (1966) by Erwin Leiser, and *Hitler, A Career* (1977) by Joachim Fest and Christian Herrendörfer used Riefenstahl's images to document, with appropriate added commentary, the phenomenon of the mass hysteria of the time, as well as the manipulation and uniformization of the masses and their total fixation on the person of the Führer.

Even today, some viewers are moved by the force of Riefenstahl's images, which continue to convey their propagandistic effect. But to most, the pathos-drenched, swaggering dramatization of National Socialism is more alienating than impressive. Nevertheless, continuing emphasis on the "power of the image" fuels the myths of the film and its creator.

Leni Riefenstahl never distanced herself from *Triumph des Willens*. Even though she presented the film after 1945 as a "project imposed upon me," the propagandistic significance of which escaped her at the time, she was in the end too proud of it to undermine her own artistic achievement.

Through *Sieg des Glaubens* of 1933 and, especially, *Triumph des Willens* of 1935, Riefenstahl defined the image of National Socialism. These are the only films that both idealized the movement and attained a high degree of artistic merit. Riefenstahl's films visually document for all time just how the myth surrounding the figure of Hitler as dictator was celebrated and cultivated. Her pictures have long since become iconic images of the twentieth century and are essential when attempting to explain to younger generations what National Socialist rule, at least its official, representative side, looked like.

## MILITARY INTERMEZZO: THE SHORT FILM *TAG DER FREIHEIT!—UNSERE WEHRMACHT! NÜRNBERG 1935*

In late 1934 and early 1935, there had been vehement behind-the-scenes disputes concerning *Triumph des Willens*. These arguments were revealed only after the war, when Riefenstahl used them to explain why, following the party rallies of 1933 and 1934, she also filmed the 1935 Reich Party Rally of Freedom. The result was the twenty-eight-minute propaganda film *Tag der Freiheit!—Unsere Wehrmacht! Nürnberg 1935* (Day of Freedom!—Our Wehrmacht! Nuremberg 1935), which was devoted to only one item on the program of the third party rally to take place after the seizure of power: the presentation of Wehrmacht military manuevers on Zeppelin Field.[57]

When it became known internally that Leni Riefenstahl didn't want to include Wehrmacht exercises from the party rally of 1934 in *Triumph des Willens* because the filming of them didn't meet her standards of quality,[58] the Wehrmacht reacted with displeasure. It was, after all, the first year following the death of Hindenburg, at which the Wehrmacht had sworn its allegiance to Hitler, that it had participated in an NSDAP party rally. It had rained on the final day of the Party Rally of Unity and Strength, a day devoted to the Wehrmacht, and all the footage shot by Riefenstahl's team had been ruined. Only the film taken by the newsreel teams was usable. But Riefenstahl felt that inserting that into her film would represent a break in style, as it didn't fit her scheme to elevate the depicted events through stylization. They weren't "beautiful pictures": "they were gray and not utilizable for the film."[59]

Three months after the party rally, at the beginning of December 1935, General Walter von Reichenau paid an official visit to Riefenstahl's editing rooms to have the Wehrmacht segment screened for him. Reichenau found the footage thoroughly appropriate and didn't understand Riefenstahl's decision not to use it. As Riefenstahl wrote in her memoirs, she didn't realize at the time the serious consequences of her refusal: "I didn't know how significant it was that in 1934 the Wehrmacht was participating in a party rally for the first time."[60] Her naïveté is barely credible. After all, the preceding year, with *Sieg des Glaubens*, she had filmed a party rally in which the Wehrmacht had not yet taken part. In addition, she was familiar with Rudolf Hess's opening speech of 1934, which she herself had edited into *Triumph des Willens*. In it Hess expressly greeted the "representatives of the Wehrmacht, now under the command of the Führer."

Reichenau, at any rate, insisted that the Wehrmacht be given the proper respect in *Triumph des Willens*. Riefenstahl, however, stubbornly refused to grant this wish. Reichenau took his complaint directly to Hitler.

At Christmastime 1934, Riefenstahl met with Hitler in Rudolf Hess's apartment. Hitler suggested a compromise, which the director also didn't wish to accept. She apparently answered Hitler, stamping her foot, "I cannot do that."[61] When Hitler reacted with visible anger, she made the countersuggestion that at the party rally in Nuremberg of the coming year, she would make a short film on the Wehrmacht and so appease the generals, and Hitler is said to have agreed to this.

Despite this compromise, several takes of the Wehrmacht maneuvers of 1934 appear in *Triumph des Willens*. According to statements made by Riefenstahl after 1945 (obviously in order to continue to be able to maintain that Hitler had exercised no influence over her film), the two-minute sequence was not filmed by her but had been added after its premiere by Ufa, which held the national distribution rights to the film. Contradicting this is an article in *Film-Kurier* on March 29, 1935, which refers to the world premiere of *Triumph des Willens* and mentions "exercises by the cavalry." So the footage must have been included in Riefenstahl's original version. Apparently Riefenstahl acquiesced to the Führer's intervention after all and included the two-minute segment of the Wehrmacht exercises in *Triumph des Willens*. This short segment differs totally in quality from the rest of the film, its complete lack of style making it seem a foreign body. It remains unknown to what degree weaknesses in the organization of the maneuvers, in addition to the poor quality of the footage, contributed to the sequence being so noticeably brief. Apparently the exhibition maneuvers of 1934 were greatly disorganized, due partly to the lack of preparation time,[62] and little resembled the swaggering, arms-heavy Wehrmacht marches of the later party rallies. The Wehrmacht must have perceived Riefenstahl's artistic decision as a deliberate denigration and insult, particularly as she is said to have sensed "that the absence in the film of this badly equipped army, which only now is being built up, was planned by the party leadership."[63]

The disagreements concerning the presence of the Wehrmacht in Riefenstahl's party rally film should be viewed against the backdrop of the military rearmament the Nazis called for in mid-1934. As opposed to the Treaty of Versailles, which limited the German military forces to 100,000 members of the army and 15,000 marines, Germany's armed forces numbered 240,000 men by October 1934. After Hitler announced to his cabinet on February 26, 1935, that, in addition, he would establish an air force, the Luftwaffe, as the third branch of the military, he proclaimed to "the German *Volk*" on March 16 that he was reintroducing the mandatory draft. The Reich Party Rally of Freedom that took place in Nuremberg from September 10 to September 16, 1935, was intended, appropriately, to express Germany's "regained military freedom"—Riefenstahl assimilated this into her film.

Compared to the unspectacular footage of the Wehrmacht's military exercises found in *Triumph des Willens*, the short film *Tag der Freiheit!*, made one year later, delivered Riefenstahl's customary perfect images. Even though the shots of the military exercises had, by definition, a completely different character from the footage of other events from the same party rally, one could easily imagine them, from a qualitative point of view, as part of the action of *Triumph des Willens*.

There are conspicuous similarities in the dramatic action of both films. Actual occurrences—the individual party rally events in *Triumph des Willens* and the maneuvers of the various Wehrmacht divisions in *Tag der Freiheit!*—are preceded by prologues that revel in male-bonding fantasies. In these sequences, inspired by the theatrical editing techniques of Walter Ruttmann, the party rallies are stylized as recreational amusements. To brisk and spirited music—created for the Wehrmacht film by Peter Kreuder, well-known composer of operettas and popular songs and one of Joseph Goebbels's favorite composers—young men are shown preparing for their party rally appearance. In *Triumph des Willens*, Riefenstahl's cameras filmed scenes in the tent camps of individual party formations that approached the burlesque: one spies a group of Hitler Youth tussling and playing around; young men bathing, shaving, and grooming themselves; and others sitting down to meals in the mess tent. Beaming faces are everywhere. The easy camaraderie shown here stands in marked opposition to the uniformed and orderly human formations that assemble on the rally grounds shortly thereafter. The same type of morning scenes, depicting soldiers before they set off for their maneuvers, are included in *Tag der Freiheit!*

*Tag der Freiheit!—Unsere Wehrmacht!*, like Riefenstahl's first party rally film, *Sieg des Glaubens*, was long believed lost. Until the film reemerged in American and Soviet archives at the beginning of the 1970s, Riefenstahl avoided mentioning it whenever possible. When she did bring it up, she downplayed its significance, just as she had done with *Sieg des Glaubens*, mentioning the work's inferior formal qualities. When the film resurfaced, it quickly became apparent that the aesthetic quality of the images, in terms of style, was comparable to that of *Triumph des Willens*. So there must have been other reasons why the director, in retrospect, attempted to diminish the film's significance.

The scenes required to make the short film on the Wehrmacht were filmed in one or two days' time. What is not as well-known is that Riefenstahl was in Nuremberg for the entire duration of the party rally of 1935 as well, and shot footage of other rally events (roughly seventeen thousand meters of film), which again could have been financed only by the party. But in *Memoiren* the director stresses that in September 1935 she was in Nuremberg for only "two days."[64] Newspaper reports clearly refute this. *Film-Kurier* wrote on September 11, 1935: "A group of camera people entrusted with special assignments are once again working under Leni Riefenstahl's direction . . . The film that Leni Riefenstahl is shooting is partly supplementary footage for the Reich Party Rally Archive, which, as is widely known, is housed in the complex of the Geyer Works, where it is still in force. Particular attention, of course, is given to the speeches of the Führer." Two days later, the same publication stated, "The arrival of the Führer once again was a major object of the filming. The laying of the cornerstone at the Congress Hall, the Labor Service—in short, all phases of Nuremberg 1935—once again will be attended by 'the Riefenstahl film staff.'"

Riefenstahl's consistent silence when it came to this film must be viewed in the context of the character of the Reich Party Rally of Freedom. It was there, on September 15, 1935, that the Nuremberg Racial Laws were decreed, for which the German Reichstag was summoned to Nuremberg for a special session. The laws were designed to exclude Jews from all aspects of national, economic, and cultural life in Germany. All Germans of Jewish heritage were denied their citizenship. The Law for the Protection of German Blood and German Honor forbade so-called mixed marriages between Aryans and Jews, as well as the employment of German domestic help in Jewish households. These laws, Hitler explained, "carry a debt of gratitude to the movement, under whose emblem Germany has regained its freedom." If Riefenstahl, as *Film-Kurier* reported, attended "all phases of Nuremberg 1935," then her cameras also were there when the Nuremberg Racial Laws were announced.

It was not known until recently that at the time of the *Tag der Freiheit!* premiere, Leni Riefenstahl described her motive for making the film completely differently than she stated after 1945. In an article in *Filmwelt*, she wrote:

It was not our original intent to assemble into a separate film footage taken of our young army on parade. But we were carried by our enthusiasm, for we witnessed things and events we had not experienced for decades. Our young army stormed across the field, and with profound emotion we took in the sacred solemnity of this historical moment, as the Führer returned to his people the honor and freedom of bearing arms. Images of unimagined beauty, powerful and boldly proud, presented themselves to us and to our cameras. And so we merely filmed what was offered to our cameras. Within a few hours we had recorded seventeen thousand meters of film. We were delighted later on when we viewed the footage and regretted only that it could not be seen by all of the German *Volk*, as a true reflection of our inner, emotional strength. In the end, the plan evolved to turn this footage into a film, the likes of which had never before been seen.[65]

*Tag der Freiheit!* became a document of triumphant militarism in the initial stage of German rearmament. It is a militarism that is not yet directed against any specific enemy but instead represents a demonstration of a newly awakening military strength meant to contribute to the revitalization of German self-confidence. The inclusion of images of the enemy in documentary and feature films began only with the outbreak of the war in 1939, when films were needed to justify Germany's military aggression. Hitler arranged a celebration in the Reich Chancellory for the premiere of *Tag der Freiheit!* in December 1935, and Riefenstahl screened it for Benito Mussolini in Rome.[66] From the beginning, this film had a different significance: "Parallel to military rearmament, the National Socialist state from the mid-thirties on pursued in the cinema, as in all of its propaganda, a program of psychological mobilization and preparation for war. At first it was solely a matter of strengthening military readiness, popularizing the militarization and acclimating the population to the idea of armed struggle."[67]

# 9

## PERFECT BODIES

*OLYMPIA: FEST DER VÖLKER AND FEST DER SCHÖNHEIT*

DESPITE HER RESOLVE following the party rally films never again to work as a documentary filmmaker,[1] Leni Riefenstahl decided in the mid-thirties to take on *the* documentary film project that was being talked about around the world: the filming of the 1936 Olympic Games in Berlin. Though Luis Trenker, an equally privileged director of the Third Reich, had already been mentioned in connection with the project,[2] Riefenstahl in the end was awarded the assignment in September 1935. "For Leni Riefenstahl, the Games were the stuff of her dreams. What she now would portray was not monotonous mass processions or endless speeches. The passionate sportswoman now had a wealth of rich images and guaranteed suspense and drama to work with."[3]

The decision to hold the 1936 Olympic Games in Berlin had been made in 1931, sending a major signal following World War I that the world was prepared to recognize Germany again as a full member of the community of nations. Hitler, who had since risen to the position of Germany's Reich chancellor and Führer, was initially extremely opposed to the Olympics, as the international idea of the Games—to unite athletes of all nations and all races in peaceful sports competitions—could not be reconciled with the nationalist and racist ideas of National Socialism.

Nevertheless, the Nazi regime quickly realized that certain propagandistic gains could be achieved through the Games. The world, which continued to view developments in Germany with great skepticism, would be presented with a peace-loving, modern, and open country by means of the perfect staging of all the Olympic events. Hitler recognized that in hosting the Games he was dealing with "a onetime opportunity for us to bring in foreign currency and improve our standing abroad."[4] And he was right: the Reich invested one hundred million reichsmarks in the Games and took in a half billion. Once it was realized what was to be gained from the Olympics, everything possible was done to guarantee their smooth course. During this time, foreign policy provocations and negative headlines were intentionally avoided, and the Reich saw to it that the Berlin Olympics, even after they ended, would remain a positive memory in the minds of all those who participated.

Far in advance of the Games, everything objectionable that Germans long since had grown accustomed to disappeared from the scene. The anti-Semitic smear sheet *Der Stürmer* was sold only under the counter. Signs such as "Jews not wanted" and "We don't sell to Jews" were removed. International guests were to receive the impression that reports of anti-Semitism in Hitler's Germany were false.

Saul Friedländer wrote, "Visitors who came to Germany for the Olympic Games found a Reich that appeared strong, orderly, and happy. The American liberal journal *The Nation* reported on August 1, 1936, 'One doesn't see Jewish heads being bashed in or even given a sound thrashing . . . People smile, are friendly, and sing with enthusiasm in beer gardens. Food and lodging are good, cheap, and plentiful, and no one is swindled by greedy hoteliers or merchants. Everything is terribly clean and the visitor enjoys it all.'"[5] That all of this was merely a "beautiful illusion," a temporary measure, was transparent. Many Jews at the time spoke ironically of their patron saint, "St. Olympiad." By February 11, 1936, Victor Klemperer, as brilliant an observer as he was precise, prophesied that the easing of anti-Semitic hate campaigns, which he termed "off-season for Jews," was merely a passing phase and should not fool people: "At the moment, as the Olympic Games are taking place here, everything is being hushed up. Afterward they'll retake the hostages, the German Jews."[6]

Klemperer was correct. Once the athletes and international guests had departed, the signs reading "Forbidden to Jews" appeared again on park benches and shop doors. The waiters at Café Kranzler hauled out the silver tray with the engraving "Your presence is not desired" so once again Jewish guests could be escorted out of the establishment without fanfare.

The idea of recording the Games on film originated not with the Nazis but with the International Olympic Committee. Films of the Olympic Games had been made previously, and in 1932 the IOC directed that all Games be documented on film, a responsibility assigned to every host country. Before Riefenstahl's *Olympia*, these documentaries were conceived of primarily as sports instruction, to be used solely for informational value, and were for the large part quite dull.

Based on what we know today, Hitler commissioned Riefenstahl to film the Olympics in August 1935, shortly before her thirty-third birthday. Even before the official appointment, she told Propaganda Minister Goebbels of her plans. On August 17 he noted in his diary: "Frl. Riefenstahl reports on preparations for her *Olympia* film. She's a clever one!" It was an open secret at the time that Riefenstahl had been given the assignment by the Nazi regime. The director herself alternately mentioned the "commission from the Führer" and, as in a Tobis press announcement around 1936, a commission from Minister Goebbels.[7] Reports of this in papers both inside Germany and abroad went unchallenged at the time,[8] whereas in the postwar period Riefenstahl maintained that she had received the commission from Carl Diem, head of the German IOC, independently of the Nazi government.[9] In order to disguise the fact that the Nazi regime was providing preliminary financing for the film, the National Socialist press declared Riefenstahl its independent producer. As the National Socialists did not want to be accused of political partisanship and realized that the film's propagandistic value lay in the fact that it could be shown internationally as an objective image of a peace-loving and open Germany, great care was taken to keep the financial arrangements and origin of the commission from the public.

Today, however, based on indisputable sources, there is no doubt that the Reich initially financed *Olympia*, just as the NSDAP had prefunded the party rally films, even though Riefenstahl later insisted that she alone had privately financed the film.

Riefenstahl's version—that she provided early funding for the film independently of the regime by selling the distribution rights to Tobis—was refuted once the distribution contract with Tobis was located. The agreement was concluded in December 1936, months, that is, after the Games had ended, at a point when the extensive preparations and costly filming had already devoured untold sums of money. And it had not been with Tobis but with the Ministry of Propaganda that Riefenstahl had signed a contract one year before, a fact that Joseph Goebbels noted in his diary entry of October 13, 1935: "Contract with Leni Riefenstahl concerning Olympics film approved. Otherwise, my position on everything accepted. I'm very happy about this." On November 7 he added: "Frl. Riefenstahl gets her contract for the Olympics film. A matter of 1.5 million. She is very pleased."

The money for the project, which totaled more than 2.8 million reichsmarks, including all synchronized versions and additional short films, was paid to Riefenstahl in four installments, according to an October 1935 agreement with the Ministry of Propaganda.[10] The majority of that sum was used in preparing for the film and for production costs. Riefenstahl herself was awarded 250,000 reichsmarks as director and producer. Once it became clear that the film would be an international success, Riefenstahl's fee was raised to an exorbitant 400,000 reichsmarks. This represented the highest salary in the National Socialist film industry.

Also unique in the film history of the Third Reich is the concession to Riefenstahl that officials of the regime would exert no influence concerning the film's content, despite the fact that the Reich had fully funded it. At Hitler's order, Leni Riefenstahl, as had been the case with *Triumph des Willens*, was given sole artistic and organizational authority over *Olympia*. No one, not even Minister of Propaganda Goebbels, could interfere in the project or issue orders to her.

## STANDARDS OF SPORTS REPORTING

Essential to the concept of *Olympia* was the idea of transforming the Olympic Games into an epic film that would speak through its artistry to those people uninterested in sports as well as to sports fans. Riefenstahl was not interested in mere reportage; once again she wanted to document the event in an artistic fashion.

No expense was spared toward this end: when filming began, Riefenstahl had a team numbering roughly 130 at her disposal. In addition, the newsreel reporters, also under Riefenstahl's command, were to turn over their footage to Riefenstahl at the end of the Games. Together with the camera operators, lighting crew, drivers and couriers, plus those whose job it was to view each day's takes, Riefenstahl's staff came to more than three hundred people.

Even while she was working on the script, Riefenstahl began technical preparations for the shoot. Extensive experimentation with new film materials was demanded at this early stage, for no previous documentary had ever been forced to keep shooting outdoors after dark and under all conceivable weather conditions. By the end of the complex preliminary preparations, the crew had to be technically equipped to handle any eventuality, whether this meant shooting a regatta in the pouring rain or a pole-vaulting competition that continued into the night.

At the Olympic stadium, workers constructed towers and dug ditches for the cameras, to make breathtaking panoramic views and unique angles possible. Kite balloons and zeppelins (among them the legendary *Hindenburg*) were ordered for aerial shots, and tracks and catapults were constructed for tracking shots. The entire Olympic arena was turned into a perfectly functioning "film stadium."

Based on her experience, Riefenstahl was aware of the difficulties involved in creating a gripping artistic documentary of an actual event over which the director has no influence. So the goal of the meticulous planning phase was to be able to film as many high-quality takes as possible of the 136 Olympic competitions.

The many technical innovations permitted the filming of individual sports as they had never before been seen. In many respects Riefenstahl created images that were totally new and unique, and she established standards for modern sports reportage that remain valid today. No matter how one judges *Olympia* in terms of the historical background or its political dimension, the film can incontestably be regarded as an aesthetic milestone in film history.

The use of handheld and double-8 cameras, including those made by Siemens, enabled more flexible filming than was possible with the larger, ungainly cameras that were in general use at the time. By means of specially constructed camera tracks, roadways, and catapult rail systems, Riefenstahl was able to film track and swim competitions with a moving camera for the first time and so get close to the competing athletes. A portable steel tower facilitated a bird's-eye view of individual sports, providing fresh impressions of the filmed disciplines. A specially designed catapult camera was assembled for track events. It moved alongside the runners, enabling a realistic view of the sport to be filmed, something that was impossible with a stationary camera. A smaller kite balloon affixed with a camera delivered long shots of the entire stadium or the whole of the sailing regatta.

Riefenstahl employed experts for particular and special tasks, such as Kurt Neubert of the Fanck school, who was hired to shoot the high jump and high dive events in slow motion. For footage of high divers, filmed by Hans Ertl, the director had an underwater camera installed, and these first underwater shots in sports photography included each diver's entrance into the water.

The film's prologue reaches back to ancient Greece, showing scantily clad athletes with near-perfect bodies performing classical sports in the open, with remarkable freedom. Idealized by Riefenstahl's film techniques, these athletes are transformed into mythical archetypes who are beyond time and who move to increasingly rousing music. In order to portray the athletes not as modern competitors but as prototypes of health, strength, and vigor, the competitors chosen by Riefenstahl were filmed nonstop in alienating slow motion, so that their flowing and almost choreographic movements could be edited to the rhythm of Herbert Windt's music, which added to the mystical effect of the prologue.

In Part One of the film, *Fest der Völker* (*Festival of the Nations*), the director devotes herself to track-and-field events (including running, discus and hammer throwing, and the high jump) and then, to build suspense, chooses the marathon as the dramatic high point and conclusion. Her film of this sport provides a revealing example of Riefenstahl's work method. For this sequence she could draw not only from footage her cameramen had taken of the marathon but also from film that had been shot on the training field, which provided close-ups that would not have been possible during the competitions. When she combined the two in the cutting room, she was able, with the support of the music, to suggest the inner state of the runners, their extraordinary exertion, and also their will to win.

Riefenstahl attempted to work out the respective characteristics of each Olympic sport just as she had with the marathon and to emphasize them through montage. Some of the disciplines called for sequences similar to those in feature films, in which the individual sports are appropriately dramatized and repeatedly intercut with shots of tense or cheering faces among the stadium crowds. For the first time in her documentary film career, Riefenstahl used commentary, part of which was created especially for the film and part of which was taken from the original comments of the stadium announcers and radio commentators, most of whom spoke in the pithy, often near-military style typical of the time.

But whenever she was after a purely visual image, she relinquished all commentary. While at the end of the second *Olympia* film, *Fest der Schönheit* (*Festival of Beauty*), the spectators at the women's high dive get to hear the names of the participating athletes, the men's high dive that follows—the high point of the second film—concentrates only on the spectacular images, conveyed through unique editing techniques that represent diverse perspectives filmed at different speeds. The editing permits viewers to see the divers from near a bird's-eye view as they spring from the board and turn weightlessly in the air before finally plunging into the water.

## "THIS WOMAN WAS MY ENEMY!"

Among the most important crew members to work on *Olympia* was Willy Zielke, who had joined Riefenstahl's team the year before for the filming of the short film on the Wehrmacht, *Tag der Freiheit!* The director, who in her memoirs never failed to mention Zielke without adding the attribute "brilliant," was accustomed to choosing the appropriate experts for each of her projects, and she had no difficulty engaging them due to her privileged position. To her, Zielke seemed particularly qualified to participate in making the Wehrmacht film.

The contract Riefenstahl arranged with Zielke specified that he would be solely responsible not only for shooting the prologue to *Olympia* but also for the film's montage sequences.[11] Zielke, who first had to agree on the script with Riefenstahl, was to produce two final versions of the prologue: his own and one that adhered to the concepts of Leni Riefenstahl. One of these versions, unaltered, was then to introduce the first part of the *Olympia* film.

After the war, Zielke surmised that Riefenstahl had engaged him primarily because she found it too awkward to attach her name to the prologue, in which she included incredibly liberal nudity. In case the censors objected to the film, she could point to Zielke without incurring any damage to her own reputation.[12]

Disagreements quickly arose between the sensitive Zielke and the domineering Riefenstahl, in which Zielke was in the weaker position. It was a matter not only of artistic differences but also of private differences: Zielke was hopelessly in love with his boss, as Riefenstahl's colleague Hans Ertl confirmed.[13] She, however, didn't share Zielke's feelings and treated him rudely. In filming the prologue at the Kurische Nehrung, for which Zielke was contractually responsible (and for which he already had filmed independently in Greece), she took the controls out of his hands in late summer 1936 and directed it herself. In January 1937, as Zielke delivered both edited versions as per his contract, she reworked the prologue once more according to her own ideas, in the end using Zielke's version only as raw material.

The codirector, humiliated and rejected, suffered a nervous breakdown a month later and was taken to a sanitarium. All told, he spent seven years in various institutions and, according to his own declaration, was forcibly sterilized.[14]

Riefenstahl's involvement in any way with Zielke's forced hospitalization cannot be proved. But Zielke's later wife, Ilse, made statements that from the time of his release, "Frau Riefenstahl had the exclusive right" to make decisions concerning Zielke, and that the couple wasn't allowed to travel in the last days of the war without her approval: "If we had dared travel without her permission she would have had the means and the power to have us both locked up."[15]

In *Memoiren*, Riefenstahl defended herself against Zielke's insinuations.

She had not forced him out of the way or had anything to do with his hospitalization: "What I later heard about him depressed me greatly . . . Zielke is said to have maintained that I had him delivered to the asylum in Haar, and even arranged to have him castrated. A few of my coworkers who are still alive can confirm what I have said about him here."[16] But Riefenstahl does not talk about why Zielke thought these things in the first place.

The director, Zielke surmised, wanted to get him out of the way so that she could use his film for her prologue without having to share her success with him: "Because she was excessively vain and pathologically ambitious, she wanted to shine all on her own, to be admired and considered the incomparable star of the German film industry. That's why it didn't suit her to share credit on this film with someone named Zielke."[17]

Even if Zielke's suspicions against his one-time boss cannot be verified, a series of other cases from Riefenstahl's career in the Third Reich offers parallels. After Béla Balázs, whose name she had used to draw attention to her own in May 1932, was forced to emigrate from Germany, she removed him from the opening credits of *Das blaue Licht* and declared their collaboration as her work alone. Also revealing in this context is the way the name of Walter Ruttmann, who was originally slated to shoot the prologue to *Triumph des Willens*, suddenly disappeared from the credits of a film that was then celebrated for originating from a "uniform artistic will." In both instances, men who could have challenged the fame she claimed exclusively for herself were forced into the background so that she alone could stand in the spotlight. In these cases Riefenstahl acted just as unscrupulously as she had with the cameraman Emil Schünemann, who attempted to oppose her and whom she denounced to the authorities. When it came to her career plans, Leni Riefenstahl repeatedly demonstrated that she was not prepared for compromises or to tolerate anyone at her side.

However one judges Riefenstahl's actions in the matter of Zielke, today the images that Willy Zielke filmed for Riefenstahl's *Olympia* are known worldwide as Riefenstahl's own, an obvious falsehood she herself did not refute. When the film first opened in 1938 it was considered the work of Leni Riefenstahl alone, and the cinematographers were considered merely to have carried out the preliminary shooting on the brilliant director's film. Only in the 1937 picture book *Schönheit im Olympischen Kampf* (*Beauty in Olympic Battle*), published before the premiere of *Olympia*, does one find the statement that "Willy Zielke is responsible for the shots of the temple, statuary, and nudes."[18] But in the 1940s, when Zielke was confronted with images from his prologue in the international press, he realized that Riefenstahl was being treated as the author and that his name appeared nowhere.[19] Riefenstahl held staunchly to this practice after the war as well, which was not difficult; almost no one today is interested in the background history of *Olympia*.[20] When a gallery in Berlin offered images from *Olympia* for sale in May 2000, among them were images by Willy Zielke—autographed by Leni Riefenstahl.


## THE DISPUTE AT THE OLYMPIC STADIUM

Riefenstahl seemed obsessed with her pursuit of the best images possible. Foreign press reports of 1936 paint a vivid portrait of her overbearing conduct. Fighting for the best filming positions within the Olympic stadium, she didn't shrink from bitter arguments with judges and IOC functionaries, and continually disregarded regulations with the comment that she was filming under orders of the highest authority, that is, the Führer. It was said that newsreel operators working for other companies were constantly blocked by Riefenstahl's crew in the battle for the best camera positions.[21] They were viewed merely as workmen, whereas Riefenstahl's team was creating art and therefore entitled to claim the best camera positions for themselves.

Curt Riess wrote of the shooting of the film: "It was totally unimportant to her whether her coworkers were disturbing others or standing in their way or making the sports people nervous. It was totally unimportant to her whether her camera crew or the cranes she had erected obstructed a view of the big shots on the officials' stand. It was totally unimportant to her if the cameramen who dug themselves into the track influenced the outcome of the race, or if others, working with flashbulbs, spooked the horses. She wanted to get as many of the best possible shots in the can as she could."[22]

In retrospect, Hans Ertl, at the time one of Riefenstahl's closest colleagues, confirmed the impression that the director was interested not least in creating an image of herself and used the Olympics as the occasion to appear almost daily before an international public in the company of Hitler. "She was merely an observer in making the *Olympia* film. She only presented herself. The public took quick note of that and then they began yelling, 'Leni . . . Leni, show yourself!' And then she appeared. 'Boo, old cow, old cow!' they cried from the stands. They understood exactly that she was showing off . . . She always—even during the most riveting competitions—was running around from one camera team to the next, gesticulating wildly, as if she were giving some important direction. Had she sat down on the stage, our work would have been much more productive than it was with her eternal running around."[23] Bella Fromm, who observed the Games, came to the same conclusion as Ertl: "She tries to give the impression of tireless competence and in this way to underscore her importance. In the meantime, her assistants go quietly and efficiently about their work, which Leni merely gives her blessing to. Now and then she takes her seat next to her Führer, a frozen smile on her face like that of a cover girl, her head bathed in a halo of importance."[24]

The already tense relationship between Riefenstahl and Goebbels worsened appreciably during the work on *Olympia*. The independence that Riefenstahl enjoyed in her work due to Hitler's personal orders, which meant that she eluded Goebbels's grasp, added fuel to the fire. As early as the opening ceremonies the minister and the director were yelling at each other on the stadium stage. Riefenstahl wasn't willing to relinquish camera positions that Goebbels felt would disturb the guests of honor; Riefenstahl believed them to be necessary (and indeed, the placement of a large sound camera was needed to film close-ups of Hitler's opening speech).

Goebbels recorded in a diary entry of August 6, 1936, "Afternoon. Stadium. Running and jumping events. We aren't getting much. I give Riefenstahl, who is behaving indescribably, a dressing down. A hysterical woman. Simply not a man!" Entries that follow continue his furious attacks on Riefenstahl, whom he calls "wild" and unsuited for such a major task.

After the Olympic Games had concluded, their considerable differences went so far, according to comments made by Riefenstahl, that Goebbels issued a decree to the press forbidding it to publish any further reports on her in the context of the Olympics film. This absence must have been particularly noticeable, as before and during the Games readers were treated to daily glowing reports on the progress of the filming. Though Goebbels's decree no longer exists, a look at the film press of the time confirms that for several months there really was no mention of Riefenstahl. Reports on the director and the ongoing progress on the film began reappearing in mid-1937.

The crux of the battle between Riefenstahl and Goebbels was the enormously long editing time—two years—that the director demanded. Goebbels wanted to evaluate the film as soon as possible after the closing of the Games, but Riefenstahl successfully gained Hitler's backing: "And if you need ten years, the important thing is that it become a work of art."[25] Financial difficulties added another burden to her relationship with Goebbels: despite generous initial calculations, the director ran over budget and had to apply for additional funds in order to finish the film. Goebbels suspected that she was squandering money; at the beginning of October 1936, he ordered a cash audit to be carried out by Ministry of Propaganda officials. At first, Riefenstahl refused to agree to this: "Fräulein Riefenstahl resisted this with all means possible, repeatedly emphasizing that she alone must allot funds quite independently and would allow no one else to interfere. And she brought up the Führer."[26]

Attempts by Riefenstahl to win Goebbels over to her side failed. On November 6, 1936, he noted: "Frl. Riefenstahl is behaving hysterically. One cannot work with these wild women. Now she wants a half million more for her film and to turn it into two films. Something stinks to high heaven in her shop. I remain cool right down to my core. She cries. That's a woman's ultimate weapon. But it has no effect on me. She ought to work and keep things in order."

After four months of arguments between director and minister, Riefenstahl saw no other way to prevail over Goebbels than to go to Hitler personally. She took her problems with the minister of propaganda to him in December 1936, presenting her case by saying that under such financial conditions she could not summon the creative energy necessary to produce a cinematic work of art with the material at hand. Her intervention had the desired and expected effect. Hitler not only approved the additional 500,000 reichsmarks, but above and beyond this assured her that she would have no future disturbances to her work from the Ministry of Propaganda. With Hitler as her trump card, Riefenstahl once again succeeded in demonstrating her independence from Goebbels. From then on she could continue her work on *Olympia* as planned.

By removing the influence of Goebbels and the Propaganda Ministry over Riefenstahl's project and placing it under Rudolf Hess at NSDAP headquarters, which also paid a portion of the funds she was to receive, Hitler once again made clear that Leni Riefenstahl answered to him alone, and that no one else in the Third Reich had the right to interfere in her work. Though the behind-the-scenes battle had been settled by "order of the Führer," matters had to be smoothed over in public as well, as the foreign press was reporting on the obvious differences between the prominent filmmaker and the minister of propaganda at the Olympic Games. One example was a July 1937 article in *Paris Soir* that poked fun at their petty jealousies. As Goebbels had noted in a diary entry of June 16, 1937, measures had to be taken against the "joint insults to Leni Riefenstahl and myself." After the foreign press circulated that Goebbels had slapped Riefenstahl in public, and spread the rumor that the discovery of her Jewish heritage had caused the director to flee Germany and hide in Switzerland,[27] Hitler ordered a joint meeting at Riefenstahl's villa in Dahlem, at which Goebbels was to present her with a large bouquet of roses. Hitler's personal photographer, Heinrich Hoffmann, recorded the event.

Riefenstahl later asserted how uncomfortable she was with this staged photo shoot: "I can't say I was pleased by the idea of being photographed in the garden with Dr. Goebbels, but I understood Hitler's considerations."[28] The minister of propaganda's comment on the photo shoot in a diary entry of July 1, 1937, reads somewhat differently: "With Führer at Leni Riefenstahl's for lunch. She's built a very nice house. We have a long chat. She is so emotional."

The photos of this "arranged reconciliation" were launched in the press to show that the reports of apparent discord had no basis in fact. Goebbels was also forced to end the press ban that he had previously issued against Riefenstahl.

"Riefenstahl's work method of choosing from extravagantly lavish quantities of material"[29] reached a new high with *Olympia*. In November 1936, she began work on editing the film, with four hundred thousand meters of film at her disposal (roughly equivalent to 250 hours of running time). It took four months to view it, in order to edit it down to a two-part film totaling six thousand meters. The editing process took eighteen months, during which time she completely disappeared from public view.

Riefenstahl's labor was made easier by a perfectly worked-out system of organization. The film rolls delivered by each camera operator were scrupulously recorded and the various footage (of the training sessions, for example, or film that was shot during or at the periphery of the competitions) was color coded, in order to make it easy to locate. Each cameraman was assigned a number before work on the film began, in addition to which every single take was tagged with a note on cameraman, subject, and lighting. Every day a complete accounting of all film materials was made, organized according to the individual camera operators and subject of each film, so that Riefenstahl would have no problem locating particular film rolls and subjects.

Despite the lengthy editing period, interest in Riefenstahl's *Olympia* film had not waned in the least. To the contrary, interest was in fact sustained by newspaper reports written by Ernst Jaeger, press chief of Olympia-Film. The public waited excitedly for the result of Riefenstahl's work, now that it was expected in movie theaters after two years of production time. And then there was the directive, issued as early as May 1936, that allowed only Riefenstahl to screen any film made of the Olympic Games in Germany. The sole exception to this was the newsreels.

The director herself contributed to the public's excitement concerning the completion of the film. She ordered her Olympia-Film colleagues to produce a documentary on the film under the title *Rund um die Olympischen Spiele* (All Around the Olympic Games), which was to give a foretaste, so to speak, of the larger film. When the documentary was shown at the 1937 World's Fair in Paris, an international jury awarded it the Grand Prize.

Even after *Olympia* had opened worldwide, Riefenstahl's "analysis" of the Berlin Olympics did not end. At the suggestion of Arnold Fanck she had announced early on that her Olympia-Film wished to produce short instructional films on sports[30] in addition to the major films on the Olympic Games. The footage of Olympic competitions that had not been used, particularly that which depicted the preparations made for the Games, became the basis for a sports film archive founded by Riefenstahl and devoted to documenting all types of sports on film. Short instructional films were made using one portion of the material, each dealing with one type of sport or sports theme.

Of the roughly twenty films planned, only nine were produced between 1939 and 1943 and released commercially. There was interest in them not only among those who specialized in sports; the films also were shown in place of the short cultural films that traditionally ran before each feature film presentation. As a rule, the films—all but one of which have been considered lost since 1945—were three hundred eighty meters in length.

The first films were devoted to track-and-field events: *Der Wurf im Sport* (The Shot Put in Sports) (1939), *Kraft und Schwung* (Strength and Momentum) (1940), *Laufen* (Running) (1940), and *Der Sprung* (The Jump) (1940). In order to demonstrate how the individual disciplines could be ideally practiced, they juxtaposed, with the help of spoken commentary, positive and negative examples of each sport. Following these came *Oster-Skitour in Tirol* (Easter Ski Tour in the Tirol) (1939), *Bergbauern* (Mountain Farmers) (1940), *Wildwasser* (White Water) (1942), *Schwimmen und Springen* (Swimming and Diving) (1942), and, finally, the only surviving film, *Höchstes Glück der Erde auf dem Rücken der Pferde* (Earthly Joy on Horseback) (1943). Riefenstahl's colleagues were given credit for the films, with Riefenstahl listed only as producer. Serving as directors were the Lantschner brothers, Guzzi and Otto, who had served as cameramen on *Olympia*, as well as Joachim Bartsch.

## WORLD PREMIERE ON THE FÜHRER'S BIRTHDAY

At Riefenstahl's suggestion, the world premiere of *Olympia* was set for April 20, 1938, a day familiar to every German: the Führer's birthday. In her memoirs, Riefenstahl presented her version of how the date was decided on: apparently Tobis wanted to release the film in the fall, due to the Anschluss of Austria. As she was on a short recuperative holiday in the Tirol when Hitler marched into Austria, Riefenstahl went to Innsbruck, where she met with Hitler at the Tiroler Hof hotel. There she pleaded with him not to delay the release of the film until the fall, and together they agreed on April 20 as the new date for the premiere.[31] This version, a prime example of Riefenstahl's biased accounts of historical events, is false.

The historian Anna Maria Sigmund correctly pointed out that Hitler was not in Innsbruck in March 1938, and therefore the Innsbruck meeting could not have taken place.[32] In fact, Hitler crossed the German-Austrian border at Braunau, the city of his birth, and continued on through Linz to Vienna, where, on the Heldenplatz in front of Vienna's Hofburg, he proclaimed the "entry" of his native land into the German Reich. From Vienna he returned by plane to Munich, without ever going to the western part of Austria or to the Tirol.

But Sigmund overlooked the fact that Hitler returned to Austria a short time later, to speak—due to the pending elections, in which he hoped to be confirmed as "Führer of Greater Germany"—in a number of cities, Innsbruck among them. The meeting with Riefenstahl must have taken place during this period, in the first week in April.[33] When Riefenstahl met with Hitler at the beginning of April, the press had long since announced the date of the *Olympia* premiere as being in April, not on the Führer's birthday, but on the 19th.[34] Their discussion, therefore, would simply have concerned Riefenstahl delaying the screening by getting the date changed one day to the more prestigious date. After her meeting with Hitler, which by necessity took place between April 1 and April 9, the Reich Chancellory informed the Ministry of Propaganda that *Olympia* would premiere on the Führer's birthday. A short time later, on April 11, *Film-Kurier* ran the cover headline "*Olympia* Film Begins on the Führer's Birthday." Riefenstahl's meeting with Hitler in Innsbruck accomplished the desired effect and secured the director another unusual privilege.

Whether Riefenstahl actually traveled to Austria to talk Hitler into changing the date of the premiere or simply wanted to experience for herself the enthusiasm with which her Führer was greeted in his homeland can no longer be ascertained. A great number of prominent members of the "old Reich" traveled to Austria with Hitler on his election tour, as Albert Speer, who was there, confirmed.[35] In a hastily arranged referendum set for April 10, 1938, the annexation of Austria was to be presented to the world as an act of that nation's right of self-determination. A large number of public statements from prominent Germans appeared in the German press before the election, among them several from members of the film industry. Emil Jannings and Gustav Ucicky, for example, appealed to the public to cast a "yes for Hitler" and publicly swore their loyalty to the Führer. Leni Riefenstahl also spoke out, and her passionate election appeal in support of Hitler laid to rest once and for all the myth of the apolitical artist:

> Once, years ago, the Führer said that if artists knew what great tasks were in store for them in a better Germany, they would join the movement with even greater enthusiasm. Today every artist knows what also is clear to every comrade: reality is providing you with more than your fantasy ever allowed you to dream of. A Greater Germany has become a reality; we have seen it grow from year to year with increasing confidence and deep regard. The creator of Greater Germany is at the same time its most artistic member.
>
> With a warm heart we greet our Austrian brothers in the Reich. New and vital strength flows through them to Germany, strengthening as well Germany's artistic desires and struggles.
>
> The greatness of the German days of destiny during which the Führer liberated his homeland was like a miracle to us all. In recent years we have often heard the voice of the Führer urging us: "Begin." Artists often have answered the call, joining millions of their countrymen in acknowledging the Führer and what he has done for Germany's freedom, honor, and greatness. The election on April 10 will be a unanimous declaration of loyalty to our Führer, Adolf Hitler.[36]

In the plebiscite on April 10, Hitler, as expected, was confirmed as Führer and Reich chancellor, in the "old Reich" with 99.08 percent of the vote and in the "Ostmark," or Austria, with 99.75 percent. So Riefenstahl's *Olympia* opened in the new "Greater Germany." Though the dictator, according to Riefenstahl, "didn't show the slightest interest in my film,"[37] at Hitler's express wish the premiere became the most extravagant opening in all of the Third Reich. Once again, the façade of the Ufa-Palast was transformed for the world premiere of one of Riefenstahl's films, and many high-ranking guests of honor were invited. As usual, the Nazi press was highly enthusiastic about the new film, but the international press outdid itself in its praise of *Olympia* as well. Masses of Germans streamed into the theaters. After the premiere, during which both parts of the film were shown back-to-back, German movie theaters showed only the first part, *Fest der Völker*, planning to follow it four weeks later with *Fest der Schönheit*. Due to popular demand, however, this soon was changed to two weeks.

Box office success was followed by numerous awards. Not surprisingly and almost inevitably, it was declared the best film of the year for 1937–38. On May 1, 1938, shortly after its Berlin premiere, Minister of Propaganda Goebbels once again presented Riefenstahl with the state's highest film award, the German Film Prize, at a grand celebration held during a special session of the Reich Chamber of Culture, with Hitler in attendance.

On the occasion of the award presentation, both the domestic and foreign press again praised the director's remarkable industry and great idealism as well as her artistic and technical skills necessary to the production of such a monumental work. During this period the acknowledgment of Riefenstahl's creative achievements was almost universal. The international press spoke of an epochal masterpiece, one that splendidly re-created the atmosphere of the Olympic Games of two years before. As opposed to the postwar reception of the film, the foreign papers also mentioned the film's international character and called it a "masterpiece,"[38] "a work of art of the highest order,"[39] one "of the most excellent sports films ever made,"[40] and "the most beautiful love song that film has ever offered to sports."[41] At the time of *Olympia*'s arrival on-screen, Riefenstahl must have felt that the world lay at her feet.

She spent the following months traveling through Europe as "Germany's ambassador of honor," publicizing her film and personally attending its premiere in various countries (nineteen foreign capitals in all). Because Riefenstahl represented Nazi Germany with this European tour, thus contributing to the regime's prestige, Goebbels willingly agreed to an additional monthly compensation of 5,000 reichsmarks, to be paid from May 1938 to February 1939, as well as to a one-time "clothing allowance" of 25,000 reichsmarks. In addition, Tobis "most generously covered the entire cost of the tour."[42]

Riefenstahl was celebrated internationally as a star director. Due to her popularity, *Olympia* proved a box office success around the world, a phenomenon unheard of until then, earning more than all other German films of 1938 put together. This despite the fact that Riefenstahl refused the demands of the film's French distributor to edit out footage of Hitler, responding that Hitler had been a part of the Olympic Games of 1936.[43] In the excitement of her success, she was little disturbed by the fact that demonstrators in Paris and Brussels had protested the film by singing the *"Internationale."*

## RIEFENSTAHL IN AMERICA

Soon after, however, Riefenstahl's euphoria ended abruptly. In the second half of October 1938, she set off on a private trip to the United States, accompanied by her secretary, Miss Höchst, and her press agent, Ernst Jaeger. Once there, at the invitation of the Metro-Goldwyn-Mayer studios, she was to promote *Olympia* and sign the necessary distribution contracts.

At the beginning of November, a major reception in honor of Riefenstahl was to be held in New York. On November 4, after more than two weeks aboard the ship *Europa*, Riefenstahl, probably the world's most famous director, arrived in America and was greeted by roughly 160 reporters, photographers, and cameramen. New York society also exhibited great interest in the guest from Nazi Germany. Riefenstahl was known as the woman who belonged to Hitler's inner circle, and the American press referred to her as "Hitler's delegate in a skirt" and the "woman behind the dictator."[44] She received an enthusiastic welcome, marked by a curiosity that didn't stop short of asking whether she was Hitler's lover. Recently discovered newsreels of her arrival in New York show a coquette who smiles for the cameras and lowers her eyes as she protests that she is not the Führer's paramour, clearly flattered by the fact that this was considered a possibility.

But on November 9, this pleasant mood changed abruptly. Following the murder of the German diplomat Ernst vom Rath by a young Jew named Herschel Grynszpan in Paris, the NSDAP ordered the destruction of Jewish synagogues in Germany and the plundering of Jewish businesses, leading to the murder of almost one hundred German Jews. Kristallnacht, or "night of the broken glass," which Nazi propaganda organs reported as a "protest of the people," caused shock the world over.

As the most prominent representative of the Third Reich in the United States at the time, Riefenstahl was confronted with questions regarding the anti-Semitic attacks. When she arrived in Hollywood, the streets were plastered with posters saying, "There's no place for Leni Riefenstahl here."

One after the other, her scheduled appointments with producers and directors and her visits to the various film studios to study the facilities were canceled. Statements by German emigrants, who in 1933 had been forced to abandon their film careers in Germany and flee their homeland (among them Paul Kohner, producer of *SOS Eisberg*),[45] as well as appeals by two antifascist organizations, the Anti-Nazi League and the Motion Picture Artists Committee, led to a widespread boycott of the German director that few in the industry dared to ignore.[46]

Walt Disney, who was friendly with the Nazis, received Riefenstahl despite the general boycott and, as planned, opened the doors of his animation studio to her. Disney, along with the industrialist Henry Ford, was a great admirer of National Socialist Germany and regularly participated in meetings of the American Nazi party, later financially supporting anti-interventionist attempts to keep America from taking action in Europe. Max Roach, comedy czar and Chaplin's discoverer, and the famous director King Vidor, as well as Metro-Goldwyn-Mayer, known for its good business relationship with Nazi Germany, all kept their meetings with Riefenstahl. Even the eventual accusations that the company supported Nazis at home and abroad didn't deter MGM from continuing its successful business dealings with the Third Reich. In fact, until the outbreak of the war, Germany was the most important foreign market for the American film industry.

Following her triumphant tour of Europe, now confronted with Hollywood's hostility and rejection, Riefenstahl refused to recognize this as the logical consequence of her involvement with the despised Nazi regime. In an egotistical twisting of the facts, she perceived the boycott as a personal affront, as she had always insisted that her films were free of National Socialist tendencies and rigorously rejected any assumptions concerning propagandistic undertones in her work. In the climate of that period, all negotiations were doomed to fail, and *Olympia* was not distributed to American movie theaters.

However, worldwide, only Great Britain joined the *Olympia* boycott. In many other countries, the film ran with great success until the war started and was celebrated as a "memorial to sports"[47] and a "document of peace,"[48] expressly "free of any political tendencies."[49] But this changed fundamentally in the postwar era. Today Riefenstahl's film is seen as exemplifying the use of sports for purposes of national propaganda. Even if one grants the work its great film-historical significance and pays tribute to its visual aesthetic, the propagandistic effect nevertheless takes center stage in the discussion, in which the once remarkably positive criticism directed at the film is gladly ignored.[50]

It should be noted, however, that even before *Olympia*, Riefenstahl had expressed admiration for the physique steeled by sports, which, given her own wide and varied participation, she considered an ideal. Her view of the Olympic athletes was marked by a basic fascination with the beauty and perfection of the human body, and far surpassed the limited racial concepts of National Socialism. In *Olympia*, Riefenstahl portrays the bodies of those athletes who were "inferior," to use the terminology of Nazi racial ideology, in exactly in the same way that she does the bodies of "Aryan" German athletes.

This contradicts the later assumption that Riefenstahl's film made value judgments based on Nazi ideology. In addition, Riefenstahl successfully opposed Goebbels's demands that victories by athletes of color and of "foreign races" be downplayed against the successes of "Aryan" athletes by granting them little or no recognition. For example, broad coverage of the victories of Jesse Owens, who with four gold medals and two world records was the great star of the Games, did not suit National Socialist ideology.

Yet the film cannot be considered politically harmless. Even if *Olym-*

*pia* was primarily viewed at the time as "supranational," a precondition for its being thought of as having international significance, the film had eminent political meaning for Nazi propaganda. Though the director cannot be held responsible for the fact that the Berlin Olympics shone a false and distorted light on National Socialist Germany, she must have been aware that her film enhanced the prestige of the Third Reich. Quite consciously, she had portrayed Hitler and other party bosses of the NSDAP as humanitarians as well as passionately keen observers of the Olympic Games. After 1945, she was rightfully criticized for consciously participating in this masquerade and for deliberately depicting the Nazi rulers as harmless.

When the film was reintroduced to German theaters in 1958, the Office for Voluntary Self-Control of the Film Industry (FSK) requested that Riefenstahl cut the film's first part by nine minutes and second part by one minute. A close-up of Hitler in the prologue, the major part of his opening speech, the shots of prominent Nazis in attendance, several takes with swastika flags, and two German victory tributes were cut in Part One, and in Part Two, footage of Reich sports leader Hans von Tschammer und Osten was removed. Riefenstahl's attempts to receive a rating from the Film Assessment Board in Wiesbaden failed, despite support from Olympic functionaries. After it was rereleased, there was scarcely a German movie theater that would show the 1938 film. In 1972, an attempt was made to screen *Olympia*, with Riefenstahl in attendance, at Berlin's Ufa-Palast, but massive protests and the anticipation of demonstrations forced its cancellation. A copy of the film was later sold to a film foundation, the Stiftung Deutsche Kinemathek. But Leni Riefenstahl made it a condition of the sale that all screenings be approved by her in writing, in order to control the circumstances under which the film would be shown.

# 10

## PRIVILEGES OF A STATE ARTIST

THE THREE PARTY FILMS and the Olympics film had brought
Riefenstahl not only fame and recognition but money as well. Her relationship with Hitler had catapulted her career into spheres she could not
have dreamed of. The high fees that she commanded for her work as a
director allowed her to lead the life of an aristocrat in the Third Reich.
She had a grand villa built for herself on a forty-four-thousand-square-
foot lot at Heydenstrasse 30 in Berlin-Dahlem, right next to the Grunewald forest.[1]

Rumors persisted that the villa was a gift from Hitler,[2] but they could
never be proved. In *Memoiren*, Riefenstahl did not state how the villa was
financed, but it is entirely possible that she paid for it with her own fees.
Construction was completed in the summer of 1937, and a short time
later the director moved into her new home. The house, with its white-
washed façade and idyllic setting at the forest's edge (yet only ten minutes from Kurfürstendamm), was compatible with the taste of the times,
in particular the taste of Adolf Hitler. A contemporary newspaper description provides an impression: "The house could be located somewhere in
Tirol; with its ivy-framed windows and plain and lovely façade, it leaves
the metropolis far behind. If one closes one's eyes, one can dream of the
mountains, of great distances and vastness."[3]

A huge living room with fireplace and adjoining winter garden com-
prised the main part of the ground floor. As in Hitler's Berghof in Obersalzberg, an adjacent projection room allowed films to be screened in the

living room, transforming it into a home theater. When the Führer or other important guests visited, Riefenstahl hired Hans Kubisch as her projectionist. Following the screenings, guests could sit around the fireplace for quiet conversations, while Hitler's entourage waited in the rustic cellar bar. In addition to the generously apportioned living area, there was a large, bright entrance hall, a kitchen and dining room, a study, and a darkroom. Riefenstahl's private quarters were located upstairs. The garage in which a silver Mercedes sports car was kept was separate from the house, and located behind it were additional quarters, with bedrooms and living rooms for guests and staff. Behind the house, large terraces led to the garden, where under a wooden pergola Riefenstahl took tea and ate apple strudel with Hitler.[4]

The furnishings were also clearly reminiscent of the "Obersalzberg style." The spacious living room with its heavy ceiling beams, costly furniture, and old engravings on the walls barely differentiated itself from that of Berghof. Riefenstahl's study, with its furnishings chiefly of light wood, was also obviously modeled on the Führer's. It was no accident that Hitler, as well as Julius Streicher, gauleiter of Nuremberg, felt very much at home when he visited Riefenstahl.[5]

The living conditions of Riefenstahl's parents also improved dramatically during the Third Reich. Her father's installation business, which had nearly closed at the end of the Weimar Republic, now was prospering. The fact that Alfred Riefenstahl had joined the NSDAP in April 1933[6] soon boosted his business. The major contracts no longer came from India, where the firm had installed an air conditioner in the palace of a maharaja. Through Albert Speer's intervention, the company received very profitable state contracts during the war, assisting, for example, in the building of prisoner-of-war camps in Dreilinden and southern Russia.[7] By 1943, the firm, headed by Riefenstahl's brother, Heinz, employed more than two hundred workers, many of them forced laborers from German-occupied areas.[8]

Riefenstahl's parents, who once had been forced to give up their house on Zeuthener See for financial reasons, lived during this period in the exquisite neighborhood of Berlin-Wilmersdorf, at Prager Strasse 6. There was an uproar whenever their daughter arrived in her chauffer-driven BMW convertible and disembarked "like a queen" to visit her parents.[9]

PENTHESILEA: THE ARTISTIC DREAM OF A LIFETIME

True to Riefenstahl's character, she did not rest on her laurels following the overwhelming successes of *Triumph des Willens* and *Olympia* but immediately sought out new projects. On her return from the United States in the summer of 1939, she revisited the idea of switching from documentary to feature films. The desire to put her own ideas on celluloid, as she had in her directorial debut, *Das blaue Licht*, was as much the motivation for her new feature film project as was the wish finally to return to the screen as an actress for the first time since 1932. And so she began plans and preparations for filming Heinrich von Kleist's tragic play *Penthesilea*.[10]

It was to be an extravagant and extremely costly project, the financing of which was personally guaranteed by Hitler. On June 21, 1939, Joseph Goebbels noted in his diary: "[Hitler] wants to finance Leni Riefenstahl's 'Penthesilea' film himself." That Hitler wished to finance a feature film and not, as with the party rally and Olympics films, a propaganda documentary to benefit the regime is further indication of Riefenstahl's unique position in the Third Reich. Certainly this support was offered as "reward" for Riefenstahl's documentary work, for when she accepted the commission to make *Triumph des Willens* he had assured her that "after this Reich party rally film, you can make all the films you wish."[11]

Hitler's financing of the film would have meant that she could produce "Penthesilea" completely independently of backers, studios, and, once again, the Ministry of Propaganda. A document discovered in the spring of 2003 proves that Hitler and Riefenstahl's mutual plans go back to a time when the director was still editing *Olympia*. At Christmastime 1937, Riefenstahl presented Hitler with a deluxe edition of Kleist's drama, which she personally inscribed to him. Affirming to Hitler that for years it had been her "passionate wish" to film the work and to play Penthesilea, she added, "And for this film as well, you, my Führer, shall be the driving force that once again allows me the creativity to turn this, too, into the supreme work I dream it shall be. Your loyal and devoted, Leni Riefenstahl."[12] The expansive plans for the film reveal that the project exceeded all bounds of Riefenstahl's obsessive perfectionism and that the director's flights of fancy would have overshadowed all other feature films of the period. Money was no object. The gigantic temple and palace sets that Riefenstahl wanted constructed for the film would have swallowed untold sums all on their own.

Filming the story of the eccentric queen of the Amazons was something Riefenstahl always represented, even in retrospect, as the dream project of those years, indeed, perhaps of her lifetime. "Penthesilea" indeed appears to be the great and, in the end, unrealizable dream of her career. The film would have been her crowning achievement. In 1939, when she began work on the project, she admitted, "I considered all the artistic challenges that I had to resolve to be stages leading to 'Penthesilea.'"[13] Leni Riefenstahl had first read Kleist's tragedy, which takes place on the battlefields of Troy, in 1926, at the age of twenty-four, and from that point on viewed the play as her life's theme: "Reading this play was the greatest thing I had experienced."[14]

Despite the financing of the project by the regime, she was listed as the film's producer, and in March 1939 she registered "Penthesilea" in the title register of the Reich Film Chamber as number 1087. The governor general of Libya, Marshal Italo Balbo, a close confidant of Mussolini whom Riefenstahl had known since 1932, had already issued her a film permit. In addition, he also agreed to provide her with one thousand stallions and an equal number of Libyan horsemen for the filming planned for the desert.

Riefenstahl's preliminary work was done partly in her villa in Dahlem and then, in the summer of 1939, primarily in Kampen, on the island of Sylt. There she rented a small thatch-roofed house for herself, her mother, and her secretary. It was here that she not only wrote the sceenplay,[15] but also, for the role of Penthesilea, learned to ride bareback and backward as well as to leap onto a galloping horse. In addition, she took speech training in order to school her voice. Every day, with great discipline, she did athletic exercises that she called her "Amazon gymnastics": "My figure, too, was to resemble that of an Amazon. I had to train hard for that. Every morning a sports instructor would arrive to put me through the necessary exercises."[16]

Despite the extravagant preparations, Riefenstahl broke off the project immediately at the outbreak of the war, apparently because she hadn't yet received the film permit she was expecting from the Ministry of Propaganda and such a costly film was suddenly no longer conceivable. Undoubtedly it was true that in view of the war such "major projects" were no longer approved, unless, like the films Veit Harlan later made, they promoted the war and rallied the country to the cause. What is strange, however, is how curtly Riefenstahl later described the failure of her pet project: "In the middle of work on 'Penthesilea,' the war broke out. And then I was supposed to make films that came from the Ministry of Propaganda, that were 'essential to the war effort.'"[17] No further complaints, no words of regret on the foundering of the project that lay so near her heart. It may be assumed, however, that it was Riefenstahl herself who, in the face of war, no longer felt the desire to stage large-scale battle scenes for "Penthesilea" and so tabled the project. The great artistic dream of Riefenstahl's life fell victim to the war unleashed by the man who so persistently had advanced her career.

## RIEFENSTAHL'S FILM STUDIO

Plans to create a studio for Riefenstahl must also be viewed in light of the "Penthesilea" project.[18] In the spring of 1939, even before Hitler decided in June of the same year to finance the filming of "Penthesilea," there had been preliminary talks on constructing an opulent Riefenstahl Film Studio in Berlin, "at the wish of the Führer."[19] As part of the plan to turn Berlin into the world capital of "Germania," Hitler and Speer proposed a complex to include a print lab and studios that would accommodate the more elaborate sets anticipated for Riefenstahl's future films. With this, the director, whose company was one of the last private production companies in a sea of state concerns, finally would become totally self-sufficient.

After the nationalization of the film industry in June 1941, Riefenstahl's firm, despite the fact that it was supported and financed by the regime, was one of the last semi-independent production companies. The great disadvantage, which during the war years led to increasing tensions, was that though Riefenstahl worked independently, she was forced to depend on the production studios of the major firms of Ufa, Terra, or Tobis.

As Riefenstahl's laborious work method always required much more time at these studios to complete a project than initially planned, such tensions were inevitable, as other film projects were often blocked because of her. This led to difficult circumstances, especially in view of the limited funding available during the war, a period when far fewer films were being made than actually were needed. Had the director already had her own complex at this point as planned, with studios and open areas where she could have constructed the huge temple sets or staged the entire battle of Troy for the "Penthesilea" project, the conflicts with the other production companies could have been avoided. And she would have been able to do all of her own postproduction work there as well.

The film complex was to be financed completely by the Nazi regime and was expressly referred to as a "construction project of the party."[20] The initiative probably originated with Hitler himself. In March 1939, following her alleged conversation with the Führer in Obersalzberg the month before, Riefenstahl lay claim to a forty-thousand-square-foot piece of property, valued at 400,000 reichsmarks, for her complex.

In the course of further planning, the project took on even more lavish proportions. The first blueprints were submitted in August 1939 and showed—in addition to the studio and a print lab, each with its own buildings—facilities for editing and synchronization and a screening room. Also planned were a kitchen complete with a small bar, a gymnastics hall, and a climate-controlled cellar for the film archive, plus a teahouse. For her office Riefenstahl envisioned a panoramic window that could be lowered, like the one Hitler had had constructed for his private sanctuary in Obersalzberg. The complex now called for two hundred thousand square feet of land, valued at a cost of nearly 2,000,000 reichsmarks.[21]

Even though Albert Speer's Office of the Inspector General of Building worked on the project well into 1942, its realization was postponed to the distant future. And before the cornerstone could be laid, the Third Reich was already in ruins. As was the career of Leni Riefenstahl.

# *The Fall*

# 11

## A SECRET FILM PROJECT

### SEPTEMBER 1939 AT THE POLISH FRONT

RIEFENSTAHL'S STAY at the Polish front in September 1939, follow-ing "the trail of the Führer," is a dark and unexplored chapter in the director's life. Knowledge of the visit first emerged in the early postwar years, when photographs were published that showed Riefenstahl as a witness to a massacre. The true reason for her journey to the front has never until now been investigated, even if the question of what Riefen-stahl had seen in the small Polish town of Końskie (which, in any case, was more than she later was prepared to admit) was repeatedly asked and answered.[1]

Though Riefenstahl met with Hitler twice in August, two weeks before war broke out, she claimed to have found out about the imminent events only on August 30, 1939. Just as she was setting out on a mountain-climbing expedition to the Dolomites, she received a phone call from her sound technician, Hermann Storr, with whom she was involved at the time.[2] "A world collapsed for me . . . War—a terrible, an incomprehen-sible thought."[3] Whether this version of things, as reported in *Memoiren*, is true, whether she actually knew nothing, can no longer be ascertained. What can be established, however, is that she was not telling the truth about her two meetings with Hitler that took place in August 1939.

In mid-August, according to Riefenstahl, she met with Albert Speer in his Berlin studio on Pariser Platz, where he showed her the huge and then still secret model for rebuilding Berlin, at which point Hitler showed up unexpectedly.[4] Again according to Riefenstahl, her second meeting with Hitler took place on August 20 at the Reich Chancellory, where Hitler was watching Soviet newsreels.[5] Joseph Goebbels confirms this in his diary on March 15, 1940: "The Führer saw Stalin on film and liked him right away. That was the true beginning of the German-Russian coalition." The film screening, as well as the meeting with Speer and Hitler, did not take place in Berlin, however, but in Obersalzberg, where it can be confirmed that Hitler was staying until only a few days before war broke out. It was there, on August 21, that he was handed a telegram from Stalin, in which Stalin signaled his willingness to cooperate. Albert Speer substantiates that: "After this a film was screened for us that showed the Red Army parading before Stalin."[6] By that evening Hitler was already certain of his success with Moscow: "Hitler slapped his knee with delight. Champagne was served."[7] On August 23, in Moscow, the Russo-German Nonaggression Pact was signed, clearing the way for the Second World War.[8] Only on August 24 did Hitler fly back to Berlin from Obersalzberg. Riefenstahl, meanwhile, apparently traveled on to Bolzano, whence, according to her memoirs, she intended to set out on a climb on August 30.[9]

Riefenstahl's version, which locates the meeting in Berlin, supports her assertion that she met with the Führer only "by accident." This is not credible, of course, if the meetings took place at Hitler's private refuge in Obersalzberg, where she dined with the regime's power elite as they were making plans to attack Poland. Her distance from the regime, which she maintains in her version of events, obviously did not exist even a few days before the war.

In the early morning of September 1, Riefenstahl rushed back to Berlin to attend a special session of the Reichstag at the Kroll Opera House, where, along with other dignitaries, such as Magda Goebbels and Heinrich Hoffmann, she witnessed Hitler utter the famous words: "Tonight for the first time, regular troops from Poland fired on our territory. We have been returning fire since five forty-five a.m., and from now on every bomb will be answered with a bomb."

After listening to Hitler's speech, Riefenstahl, according to her own account, tried to assemble her own unit of war reporters. Subsequently, she depicted herself not as an active participant but as a woman persuaded to make the decisions she did: "I thought about how I could make myself useful in a war. At first I considered training as a nurse. But then several of my colleagues urged me to organize a film group, in order to report on the war from the front."[10]

Again, according to statements that have not been closely analyzed, she drew up a report on her intentions along with a list of colleagues and took it to the Reich Chancellory. There she read her plan to a "high-ranking officer of the Wehrmacht." The Wehrmacht approved it a mere twenty-four hours later.[11] Hitler is not mentioned in Riefenstahl's version of the story. With the permission of the Wehrmacht in her hands, she and her team accompanied an army major to Grunewald, where he showed them how to use gas masks and pistols. She then procured uniforms for herself and her crew, as no one was allowed at the front in civilian clothing. Once that was accomplished, she and her small film team set off for Poland. They left Berlin early on the morning of September 10, one week after Hitler departed for the front in his special train, and they traveled through Breslau and Oppeln to Końskie and the fighting at the front.

## WAR

"Case White," the code name for the attack on Poland, took place on September 1. The perfect coordination between army and Luftwaffe led to astoundingly rapid success, which soon formed the basis of the myth of the German blitzkrieg. Poland was attacked without any preceding declaration of war, and the Polish air force was destroyed by German bombers within forty-eight hours, before it could even mount a defense. The Polish army, which had quickly fallen into chaos, was effectively defeated within one week. In the second phase of the war, which began on September 9, it was a matter of tightening the noose around the encircled and disorganized Polish units and conquering the Polish capital of Warsaw. The Tenth Army was to carry out this task by approaching the city from the south under the leadership of General von Reichenau.

On September 10 (by September 8 according to her own account), Leni Riefenstahl traveled with her film unit directly to the main area of battle of this second phase of the war. After a major battle in the vicinity of Radom on September 9, in which seven Polish divisions were defeated and sixty thousand prisoners of war taken, Gerd von Rundstedt and Erich von Manstein, commander in chief and chief of the general staff of Army Group South, respectively, moved their headquarters from Oppeln to Lubliniec.

It was here, directly across the German-Polish border, that Riefenstahl and her film unit appeared on the afternoon of September 10,[12] where she was considered a somewhat burdensome visitor. In his 1996 memoir *Verlorene Siege* (Lost Victories), Erich von Manstein, to whom the excited Riefenstahl spoke first, presented himself as having been taken aback even then at Riefenstahl's "original visit"[13] to Lubliniec. He was also astonished at her "sensational outfit," which looked to him like a costume: "Incidentally, she looked very nice and jaunty, like an elegant partisan whose costume might have been purchased at the Rue de Rivoli in Paris. Her beautiful hair was like a flaming mane, enveloping an interesting face with close-set eyes. She was wearing a type of tunic, breeches, and tall boots of soft leather. A pistol hung from the leather belt around her waist. Her battle costume was completed in the Bavarian style by a knife stuck in her boot. The staff, I must admit, was a bit perplexed by this unusual figure."[14] Photos taken during this time support his depiction of Riefenstahl's appearance.

Erich von Manstein was one of the few superior officers of the Wehrmacht who weren't followers of the Nazi regime, and he was considered to be rather critical and bristly. In 1934, he had registered an official protest against the Wehrmacht's introduction of the "Aryan paragraph" limiting membership to Aryans only. It is not surprising that Manstein didn't greet Riefenstahl with open arms, given that she was a passionate admirer and friend of Hitler. He urgently advised her not to get any closer to the front. But the director was obviously determined to do so, and Manstein acquiesced and saw to it that the film unit left that very same day[15] for the front lines at Końskie.

Why Riefenstahl felt it was so urgent to get to Końskie was unclear for a very long time. Interestingly, on September 8 Hitler had altered the direction of his special train, switching from a northern route to one in the south that led into the battle area of the Tenth Army, precisely where Riefenstahl was headed with her film unit. Riefenstahl apparently followed Hitler to Końskie.

Located northwest of Kielce, the small city of Końskie was located just across the German-Polish border and had been occupied by German troops five days before. The battle continued to rage not far away, where a large number of panzer and motor divisions as well as three hundred thousand soldiers were deployed. After Hitler was flown back to his special train, Riefenstahl remained with her film unit in Końskie, while her colleague Guzzi Lantschner traveled to the front lines on September 11 to film the war.

Before the director and her team left the city, however, they witnessed, on September 12,[16] one of the first war crimes of the Second World War carried out against the Jewish population. On September 10, the day Riefenstahl arrived in Końskie, German Police General Roettig and four German soldiers were killed by Polish partisans. As in later incidents at other locations, the partisan battle in Końskie was exploited as a welcome opportunity to brutalize the Jewish population.

Wehrmacht soldiers rounded up local Jews at the town marketplace, where they were forced to dig graves for the dead German soldiers with their bare hands, while being beaten and kicked by the soldiers guarding them. When the Jews, who must have feared that the graves were intended for themselves, became more and more agitated, Flak Officer Bruno Kleinmichl fired a shot, which only increased the panic. At this, Wehrmacht soldiers fired randomly into the crowd, killing nineteen Polish Jews and leaving many others badly injured.[17]

We know that Riefenstahl witnessed this massacre because of a photo showing her standing in the midst of a group of German soldiers, a horrified look on her face. When this photo circled the globe in the late forties and the story of Riefenstahl's journey to the front surfaced, she denied having been an eyewitness to the outrage, maintaining instead that she had been protesting against German soldiers kicking Polish civilians: "That made me angry. I screamed at them: 'Didn't you hear what the officer told you? And you call yourselves German soldiers?' The angry men then turned against me in a threatening manner. One of them screamed, 'Hit her in the mouth, get that woman out of here!' Another of them cried: 'Shoot the woman down,' and pointed his weapon at me. I was looking at the soldiers in horror. It was at this moment that I was photographed."[18] At the same moment, she claimed, she heard shots coming from somewhere else. Only later did she receive word of the massacre, of which she had seen nothing. Even though after 1945 Riefenstahl's coworkers verified this version of things, it can be indisputably refuted today.

Even her own statements in the matter are contradictory. She directly connects her allegations of being threatened by German soldiers with the scene taking place at the marketplace in Końskie, the site of the massacre. Therefore, she could not have heard shots coming from a distance. And the photograph, too, refutes Riefenstahl's statements. In addition to Riefenstahl, it shows soldiers who also have horrified expressions on their faces and who are looking in the same direction as the director. The men are closely crowded around Riefenstahl. If other soldiers really were pointing their guns at her, those standing close by would have moved away, or at least shown some sort of reaction.

At the end of the 1990s, the photo album of a German army private surfaced in Poland. The private had been in Końskie at the time and had documented the event with his own camera. This material proved conclusively that Riefenstahl really was an eyewitness to the shootings.[19] The album shows the exact course of events that day. The first photograph in the series is captioned "Leni Riefenstahl with her film crew" and shows the director, dressed in her "uniform" and in the company of several of her unit, crossing a street in Końskie. The next picture, captioned "our Führer in Końskie," reveals the true reason for Riefenstahl's visit to the town. The third photo shows "four comrades on patrol, attacked by Jews and assassinated on the night of September 12." "The Jews have to dig the graves of the fallen comrades" is written under the next picture, which is followed by the decisive shot: "Leni Riefenstahl faints at the sight of the dead Jews." It shows the horrified filmmaker, surrounded by soldiers who have turned toward her.

Riefenstahl's reaction is undeniable, as is the fact that she protested against the brutality of the soldiers. Immediately following the incident, the still rattled director spoke about it with General Reichenau and reported what she had seen. Though Reichenau was a fervent National Socialist and an anti-Semite, who later in the war against the Soviet Union called on his soldiers to carry out "necessary punishment of the Jewish subhumans,"[20] Riefenstahl noted that he "was shocked and filled with disgust, as we all were. He said that never before had such shameful behavior taken place in the German army, and that the guilty parties would be court-martialed."[21] At Riefenstahl's intervention, the officer responsible for firing the first shot was actually brought before a court-martial immediately called by Reichenau, stripped of his rank, and sentenced to two years in prison for homicide and wrongful employment of a weapon, all of which was verified by Erich von Manstein.[22]

This satisfied Riefenstahl at the time, but she later closed her eyes to the fact that the officer—as all Wehrmacht officers who participated in anti-Semitic atrocities—was pardoned by Hitler in a general decree issued on October 4, 1939, and therefore never really held responsible. Abuses such as those that occurred in Końskie were retroactively declared retaliatory measures and dismissed as trifling. Today it is accepted that the incident in Końskie was a cold-blooded war crime, one of the first of its kind during World War II.

It is understandable that the director wanted to avoid at all cost having her name connected to such shameful acts. But there can be no doubt today that she witnessed a great deal more in Końskie than she later admitted: "I did not see one dead person in Poland, not one soldier, not one civilian."[23] Were this true, then Leni Riefenstahl would be the only person to have spent any length of time in a war zone without being confronted with death.

After the incidents in Końskie, according to Riefenstahl's version, which remained uncontested until now, she ceased her activities as a wartime film reporter and wanted to return as quickly as possible to Berlin, while her unit continued their work at the front. She didn't record in her memoirs what she did in the south of Poland during the period from September 13 to 19, other than the fact that she was waiting for an opportunity to leave the combat area. Together with a Tobis cameraman named Kluth (Riefenstahl erroneously calls him Knuth), she boarded a military plane that took her, under heavy artillery fire, to Danzig, "the most exciting flight of my life." The plane broke down on landing and she was forced to wait in Danzig, as there was no connecting flight to Berlin. Purely by "accident" Hitler arrived in the city at the same time, September 19:

"Suddenly word spread that Hitler was expected. After his arrival he hosted a lunch at the Kasino Hotel, to which I was invited."[24]

The Führer had left Berlin on September 3 in his armored "special train," which he used as his mobile "Führer headquarters" during the first three weeks of the war and jokingly referred to as the "hotel of the racing Reich chancellor."[25] In the first two weeks of the war, the train was sidetracked at various locations, from which Hitler then took a plane or his car convoy to the front in order to be able to follow the Wehrmacht maneuvers as closely as possible. He arrived in Danzig on September 19 and until September 25 resided at the luxurious Kasino Hotel in the nearby spa of Zoppott, where he coordinated further operations.

In Danzig, according to Riefenstahl, she spoke to the Führer about the events in Końskie while seated at his left at a meal he hosted on September 19 and to which he invited a number of guests of honor. He assured her that the guilty parties would be tried by court-martial. In *Memoiren* she declared herself satisfied with his reaction. That it was Hitler himself who a short time later pardoned all of the soldiers sentenced by court-martial did not appear to be of interest to her.

Just as in Końskie, it was unlikely that her meeting with Hitler in Danzig was a coincidence. Rather, it gave her the opportunity to film the Führer's triumphant entry into the city. It may also be surmised that Riefenstahl remained in Hitler's company after September 19. Supporting this is the fact that Riefenstahl herself reported nothing about how she returned to Berlin from Danzig. This becomes even more telling when one considers the great detail she used to describe her efforts to leave Końskie. This gap in her presentation of events suggests that Riefenstahl remained in Zoppott until Hitler's departure and then left Poland on Hitler's special train, arriving in Berlin on September 26. At least there is evidence that Riefenstahl spent a few days in Berlin at the end of September, precisely at the time the Führer was also staying in the Reich capital.[26]

Only a few days after Riefenstahl returned to Berlin, she again departed for Poland: "After my return from Danzig the radio reported on the occupation of Warsaw. Through Ernst Udet, who in the interim had become head of the Technical Office of the Luftwaffe, I had the opportunity to take a military plane to Warsaw, where I wanted to meet up with my unit."[27] But there is no further evidence of how she actually got to Poland, whether with Udet or as part of Hitler's entourage. According to her own statements, however, she was in the demolished Polish capital on October 5, on the occasion of a massive two-hour parade of victorious German troops before Hitler, which he attended in the company of Generals Walter von Brauchitsch, Johannes Blaskowitz, and Reichenau. Four days earlier, the last Polish forces had capitulated on the Hela Peninsula near Gdingen. Riefenstahl and her cameramen, who were also in Warsaw, wanted to capture on film what became the only parade of its kind attended by Hitler in a conquered land during World War II. "Sepp Allgeier and the Lantschner brothers filmed it. I stood next to Allgeier, close to Hitler, and experienced how the troops marching by stared at him as if hypnotized."[28]

## HITLER'S SECRET COMMISSION

The exact circumstances of Riefenstahl's stay in Poland remained unclear for a long time, as did the reasons why she traveled to the war zone in September 1939 to film. In particular, it was long unknown who actually ordered her to film at the front.[29] Riefenstahl's account that she received a commission from the Wehrmacht at her own initiative appears least credible, even though her version has been accepted without question until now. All of the films that Riefenstahl made during the Third Reich (even her feature films, which carried no direct propagandistic message for the regime) were realized on direct "orders of the Führer," a privilege the director guarded jealously. If she actually filmed in September 1939 at the orders of the Wehrmacht, this would have been the only one of her projects not directly initiated and supported by Hitler.

Also implausible is her account of approaching the Wehrmacht on her own initiative to raise the issue of creating a film unit. At the time that Riefenstahl left for Poland—one week after the war began—any number of propaganda companies, each with its own film and story reporters, were already long since at the front. These companies had not spontaneously formed at the beginning of the war; their work had been prepared well in advance.

In 1936, the Ministry of Propaganda, together with the leadership of the Wehrmacht, had established a propaganda unit, which in case of mobilization could quickly position war reporters and propaganda troops. As of that time, the cameramen, photographers, and journalists chosen for this task regularly accompanied the Wehrmacht on maneuvers, to practice that particular type of filming. Over time they were increasingly organized in military fashion and issued a special uniform. After the Sudeten crisis in 1938, the teams again were systematically expanded and finally were assigned the military designation of Propaganda Company. Though they were part of the army, organizationally speaking, they received their orders from the Ministry of Propaganda. Members received special courses of instruction but were also trained by the military.

On September 1, when the war machine was set in motion, the six propaganda units assembled long before the outbreak of war were sent to the front under the command of General Hasso von Wedel, in order to establish the "bond between the front and the homeland" through images and words. Each individual army of the Wehrmacht, but also units of the Luftwaffe and marines, was assigned a propaganda company, which followed directly behind the advancing troops. The Tenth Army as well, which Riefenstahl and her film troop called on, already had a propaganda company in tow, filming the fighting.

Riefenstahl, therefore, did not assemble yet another propaganda company in addition to those of the Wehrmacht, as she suggested after the war. Rather, she established an independent "special film troop," as it was called in a secret document.[30] The composition of her team alone reveals that this special film troop could have had nothing to do with the Wehrmacht. The Agreement on the Execution of Propaganda in Wartime, concluded in the winter of 1938–39 between the Ministry of Propaganda and the Wehrmacht leadership, stipulated that every propaganda company consist of both professional personnel and military personnel. Civilian propaganda troops were used by the Ministry of Propaganda only in areas either already occupied or no longer being fought for. Riefenstahl's film troop, however, except for the drivers, consisted exclusively of professional personnel, namely, the director and her colleagues. Against regulations, which stated that every propaganda company must be led by an officer of the Wehrmacht, the "Special Film Troop Riefenstahl" was headed by Chief SS Hauptsturmführer Stolze, from the Ministry of Propaganda.[31] This constituted an absolute exception.

A long undiscovered document from the Ministry of Propaganda, stamped "secret" and dated September 10, 1939, establishes that Riefenstahl filmed at the front on direct orders from Hitler. The document, which deals solely with the Special Film Troop Riefenstahl, states: "On September 5, 1939, Major Kratzer of the general staff of the OKW [Oberkommando der Wehrmacht, Supreme Command of the Wehrmacht] delivered an order from the Führer according to which a 'Special Film Troop Riefenstahl' was to be established within the framework of the Ministry of Propaganda's office of operations. In accordance with long-distance telephone instructions from the OKW (Captain Behle of the general staff) of September 9, 1939, at 6:45 p.m., this film troop is to set off for Oppeln on September 10 at 7:00 a.m. The troop will report there to Army Group South."[32]

The Propaganda Ministry document, issued without any connection to the propaganda companies and their work, lists seven regulations defining the responsibilities of the Special Film Troop Riefenstahl. The ministry ordered two six-seater Wanderer motor vehicles, plus drivers, which arrived from the Auto-Union in Chemnitz, along with a BMW motorcycle with sidecar and driver, to quickly transport the exposed rolls of film to the nearest airport. All of the vehicles were fully tanked and the troop was issued gas identification cards good for seven hundred liters of benzene.

SS Hauptsturmführer Stolze, who commanded the troop by order of the ministry, was responsible for "pending personnel and material costs," which were to be carried by the Ministry of Propaganda "until the final determination of the cost-incurring party."[33] Also revealing is the document's final clause: "The film material is to be sent by the fastest means possible to the Reich Ministry for Enlightenment and Propaganda, Berlin W 8, Mauerstrasse 45/Courier Office, Office G."[34] The document, which solely concerns Riefenstahl's action at the front, is signed by Leopold Gutterer, undersecretary in Goebbels's ministry. It incontestably proves not only that Riefenstahl went to the front on Hitler's instructions but also that her cooperation with the Ministry of Propaganda once again proceeded without resistance.

In her memoirs, Riefenstahl was silent not only about the fact that it was Hitler who issued her orders; there was also no mention of Goebbels's ministry in connection with her mission at the front. The Wehrmacht, which Riefenstahl claims gave the orders, was initially not even indirectly involved with the Riefenstahl troop, as the cited document substantiates. The Supreme Command of the Wehrmacht's office accountable for war propaganda was not even notified of the formation of the Special Film Troop Riefenstahl until September 13, 1939, long after the unit had begun filming in Poland.[35]

Before the backdrop of silence surrounding Hitler's patronage, it also is clear that the director flew to Danzig following the incident at Końskie not only so that she and her cameraman could film Hitler's march into the city but also, presumably, to speak personally to her patron about the future of the film troop and the films it was planning.

Even if Riefenstahl went to the front under direct order from Hitler, it remains unclear in the end whom this action can be traced back to, as only Riefenstahl herself could have provided this information. What remains is the question of why a Special Film Troop Riefenstahl was established at all, if the filmed documentation of the war for the movie newsreels was being provided by the propaganda companies of the Wehrmacht. In acknowledgment of the fact that the formation of the special troop can be traced back to an order from Hitler, it can be deduced that the troop's goals were a good deal more far-reaching and that the material Riefenstahl's camera crew was to film could not have been purely for the newsreels, as the director repeatedly asserted after 1945. Neither the Ministry of Propaganda document quoted above nor the Wehrmacht files give information on Riefenstahl's true mission. But it is striking that the talk always is expressly of a "special film troop" or of the "Film Troop Riefenstahl" and never of an additional propaganda company. In addition, the documentation is almost exclusively about the Wehrmacht propaganda, making separate mention of the work of the Film Troop Riefenstahl.[36] This too, points to the fact that Leni Riefenstahl was working on an essentially much more prestigious project, one that most certainly was beyond the influence of the propaganda machine for which the Ministry of Propaganda and Wehrmacht leaders were responsible.

In any case, it is not credible that the most famous woman director in the world, Hitler's privileged and status-conscious filmmaker, who was at the height of her career and had made the regime's most important documentary films, would suddenly have made herself available for simple newsreels, especially as she had always dismissed them for their lack of artistic value. Rather, in view of her reputation, her self-image as an artist, and her power- and career-conscious appearances, it can be assumed that Riefenstahl was working at the front on a film project that was planned but never realized. One that, independently of the newsreels, would bring to movie screens a comprehensive and artistic film on the Poland campaign, perhaps, or the Führer at the front. The fact that the director enlisted her best cameramen, the Lantschner brothers, Walter Traut, and Sepp Allgeier; her best sound technician, Hermann Storr; and her best photographer, Rolf Lantin, for this mission supports the fact that something bigger than mere newsreels was planned.

Also supporting this assumption is knowledge of other documentary films that already had been made under direct orders from Hitler. For example, though the newsreels had captured his triumphant march into Austria in 1938, he gave personal instructions that Ufa was to create a documentary film of this major event, for which huge sums of money were made available. Thus it's logical to assume that he also wanted a representative film made of the Poland campaign, the glorious outcome of which was a point of reference for every member of the Third Reich leadership. And it goes almost without saying that the regime's most prominent documentary filmmaker would receive this commission.

Further confirmation is provided by the fact that in September 1939, when Riefenstahl was in the war zone, she always stopped at precisely those places where Hitler also was staying, which she concealed (in the case of Końskie) or presented as pure coincidence (in the case of Danzig). But clearly it was not a case of coincidence, as by that time she had already spoken with Manstein about "following the trail of the Führer" to Poland. And Riefenstahl followed this trail precisely, right up to the end of the Poland campaign.

Pictures of the Führer at the front were near ubiquitous at the time. The newsreels showed them, as did all of the newspapers and illustrated magazines, which ran special editions. Nazi propaganda constantly broadcast the image of the omnipresent commander at the front, ceaselessly on the move and always concerned about the welfare of his soldiers—a "soldier among soldiers" who somehow always found the time to be photographed in dynamic poses, poised for victory. The goal of the press campaign was to closely connect the military victories in Poland with the person of Hitler: "The propaganda explained Hitler's participation in the Poland campaign as the paradigm of his powerful sense of responsibility; he himself became the shining example of the heroism required of every German."[37]

To present Hitler as a brilliant commander and to prepare the Poland campaign as propaganda, Hitler's personal photographer, Reich photojournalist Heinrich Hoffmann, was sent to Poland "on the trail of the Führer" in addition to Special Film Troop Riefenstahl. After the outbreak of the war, Hoffmann, at Hitler's request, produced one book of pictures after another for as long as Germany was victorious. In 1939, he published *Hitler in Polen*, which in a short time sold more than three hundred thousand copies, followed by *Die Soldaten des Führers* (The Führer's Soldiers) in two parts: *Der Polenfeldzug 1939* (The Poland Campaign 1939), and *Der Kampf im Westen* (The Battle in the West). *Hitler im Westen* (Hitler in the West), which appeared in 1940, was the most successful of the photography books, with more than six hundred thousand copies in print. Just as Hoffmann, independent of the other photojournalists of the propaganda companies, was responsible for the idealized image of the Führer at the front, Riefenstahl was obviously responsible for bringing to movie screens the special "Führer experience."

It is possible not only that Riefenstahl was to film a large-scale documentary on the Poland campaign but that the footage was to serve other purposes as well. Rarely taken into account is the fact that Riefenstahl, as of the time of *Triumph des Willens* at the latest, was working on a "Film Archive of National Socialism." Referred to in the press of the time as the "Archive of the Reich Party Rally," Riefenstahl's camera crew had also filmed all events of the 1935 Nuremberg rally for such a purpose.[38] The reason the film was shot has never been explained. Surprisingly, the question of the significance of such an archive has never before been raised. But the fact that Riefenstahl, following her trend-setting propaganda film, was apparently commissioned to film additional Nazi party events gives rise to the conjecture that at some later date Hitler planned a film along the lines of *Triumph des Willens* that would cover all the major stations of his reign that followed.

Supporting this thesis is the fact that Hitler spoke concretely with Riefenstahl during the war, in the spring of 1941, about how one could preserve such a film for all time: "Please get in contact with the Kaiser Wilhelm Institute in Berlin and discuss this problem with the excellent scientists and researchers there. I could imagine a film material made of the finest metal, which neither time nor atmospheric conditions could alter and which would survive for centuries."[39] With the "final victory" and the establishment of the "greater German Reich" that Hitler planned as the completion of his life's work, he doubtlessly would have also felt it necessary to create a monument to himself on film, just as he wished Albert Speer to construct the magnificent capital city of "Germania" as testimony to his power.

If Hitler planned and commissioned a film on the war, the question remains why Riefenstahl didn't create it, particularly after she and her Special Film Troop had filmed all the major stages of the Poland campaign for a solid month. In the end, only the director herself could have answered this question. But it can be speculated that she would have sought to distance herself from such plans, as they would have destroyed the myth of the apolitical artist she had so painstakingly created.

It can be proved that Riefenstahl was busy with her film project until the end of September,[40] and her trip to Warsaw to film the military review was clearly connected to this project. So the decision not to make the film could have been arrived at only with the end of the Poland campaign. It is not known whether the decision came from her or from Hitler. It is conceivable, however, given what Riefenstahl had witnessed at the front, that after viewing the film her camera team had shot she no longer believed herself capable of editing from the material a propaganda film that would have equaled the positive message of the documentaries she had made for the regime thus far. Perhaps before leaving for Poland she had harbored illusions about the big adventure she was embarking upon, then after the massacre in Końskie she knew that the war consisted not merely of Hitler's visits to the soldiers at the front, of meetings convened over map tables and of parades of victorious troops, but that it also had cruel and inhuman aspects that had burned themselves deeply into her memory.

After the planned war film was shelved,[41] Fritz Hippler, appointed head of the film department of the Ministry of Propaganda in September

1939, was instructed to assemble a film from the material taken by the propaganda companies, designed to present the entire Poland campaign in the right light and to pay tribute to the "lightning victory" of the Wehrmacht and the triumph of the Führer. Hans Bertram had already created *Feuertaufe* (Baptism by Fire), a film devoted solely to the air war in Poland, from footage taken by the propaganda companies of the Luftwaffe. As *Feuertaufe* included images of destruction and showed the true and brutal side of the war, it was widely rejected by German moviegoers. In contrast, Fritz Hippler's compilation film *Feldzug in Polen* (Campaign in Poland) was designed to present the war as a great adventure and represent the Poland campaign in far greater detail than those events that had been singled out for the newsreels. The film was a quasi-ersatz, makeshift solution that was substituting for something else, made more obvious by the fact that the twenty-nine-year-old Hippler, who held the rank of SS Obersturmbannführer, had not once been to Poland in September 1939. During this period, together with Goebbels, he was supervising the editing of the newsreels, a task he had assumed responsibility for at the beginning of 1939. He also was occupied with other routine duties in Berlin,[42] and during this time he accompanied a camera crew to the front in France in 1940 in order to oversee the filming of *Sieg im Westen* (*Victory in the West*) (1940).[43] That he wasn't entrusted with a similar task during the invasion of Poland is evidence that the film he ended up making was originally planned for another director. Riefenstahl rather hesitantly admits that such a project was planned and that she was to have been the director: "In the midst of work on 'Penthesilea,' the war broke out. And I was supposed to make films assigned by the Ministry of Propaganda that were 'vital to the war effort.'"[44] As her name is not connected to any other films "vital to the war effort," she must have been referring to the film on the Poland campaign.

Footage taken by Riefenstahl's film troop was clearly included in the compilation film *Feldzug in Polen*; mentioned in the credits are Sepp Allgeier and Guzzi Lantschner of the Special Film Troop Riefenstahl. Significantly, in addition to the cameramen working on Hippler's film, two participants in the film had worked primarily with Riefenstahl in the past. The music in *Feldzug in Polen* was composed by none other than Herbert Windt, and animation specialist Svend Noldan, who worked on *Olympia*, shot the footage of the maps used to elucidate the abstract maneuvers of the German advance.

But it is not only the personnel connections that are striking here. In creating the look of the film, Fritz Hippler was strongly influenced by Riefenstahl's principles of montage and composition: "Just as in Leni Riefenstahl's party rally film, events here were modeled on the slogan 'the Führer and his followers': Hitler in the midst of his generals as they bend over the maps table is the center of the action; marching troops, rolling panzers, and nose-diving Stukas are the anonymous instruments of the all-powerful will of the Führer; animated sequences abstracted them further, by representing them as arrows advancing across the map of Europe."[45]

Even though there are definite similarities to Riefenstahl's style, *Feldzug in Polen* did not in the least approach the degree of stylization that distinguishes her films, and the footage apparently taken by the Special Film Troop Riefenstahl did not differ qualitatively from the footage of the Wehrmacht's propaganda companies. Even Leni Riefenstahl could not have edited a film from this material that would have risen above a purely newsreel character. And this, too, could be sufficient reason for the perfectionist director to distance herself from the project.

In the end, what became of the footage taken by the director's Special Film Troop is not known. At the end of the war, the Ministry of Propaganda was in possession of more than five million meters of film negatives from the various fronts, of which only a portion (three hundred thousand meters) was used for the newsreels. In late April 1945, these negatives were reputedly to be removed from the limestone quarries in Rüdersdorf, where they had been stored, and taken by ship across the Elbe to Schleswig-Holstein. But the endeavor failed—the ship was hit by strafer aircraft and sank. The films of the Poland campaign, including those taken by the Special Film Troop Riefenstahl, which in all probability were among those negatives, did not survive the war.

## THE "CLARIFICATION"

The decision to break off filming in a Poland under siege was not made after the massacre in Końskie, as Riefenstahl asserted all of her life. Almost everyone who has dealt with this aspect of Riefenstahl's biography was prepared to accept her version of events, according to which Końskie was a cathartic experience for her.[46] In her memoirs, Riefenstahl claimed that she had quit her duties as a war reporter directly after the events in Końskie: "I was so affected by this experience that I asked the general to permit me to stop my film reportage. He was totally understanding. I wanted to return to Berlin as soon as possible."[47] However, the fact that she traveled from Lubliniec not to Berlin but to Danzig by plane, where she and her cameramen enjoyed a lengthy stay and where Hitler had set up headquarters, proves, as does her presence at the military review in Warsaw, that Riefenstahl was busy filming in besieged Poland long after the events in Końskie. And a newly discovered document also attests to the fact that further work by her film troop was discussed with her in a meeting in Berlin on September 29.[48]

The only consequence of Riefenstahl's Końskie experience on September 12 was that she turned over filming at the front to her camera crew in order to be able to move among Hitler's entourage in occupied Poland from that period on. But her statements on this point have remained unchallenged. Even the film scholar Rainer Rother, who dealt thoroughly with the events in Końskie, absolves her in this matter: "That she 'quit her service' speaks for her to a certain extent in this case," and her behavior "offers little cause for criticism."[49]

But reality, as represented above, appears to be different from what Riefenstahl claimed it to be. It is true that she was at the front for only a brief period and, having witnessed the massacre, left the area immediately. But this obviously did not cause her to distance herself from Hitler; the event seemed to have no far-reaching consequences for her.

In the face of Hitler's war, she was prepared to hitch herself to the Nazis' totalitarian propaganda apparatus, an act that sheds light on the deeply political character of her career in the Third Reich. It is totally credible that she went to Poland with a certain naïveté and at first created illusions for herself about the reality of war. Like millions of other Germans, she believed the headlines that made light of a "walk to Poland."

On September 5, days before Riefenstahl and her crew set out for the front, it was announced in Berlin that the enemy was as good as defeated. Krakow had already fallen and the Polish government had fled Warsaw. In her memoirs she admits, remembering bullets piercing her tent close to the front, "I had never imagined it would be so dangerous."[50]

After she witnessed the Końskie massacre, if not before, she knew that the war was different from the way that Goebbels was presenting it. It is to her great credit that she did not simply look the other way but instead raised objections and protested, something that rarely happened at the time.

And yet what she had seen did not lessen her belief in the "historic mission" of the Führer. Her enthusiasm for his military goals did not wane despite their criminal consequences. Nine months after the events in Końskie, she sent Hitler a telegram on the occasion of German troops marching into Paris: "With indescribable joy, deep emotion, and filled with profound gratitude, we share with you, my Führer, your and Germany's greatest victory, the entry of German troops into Paris. Surpassing all other powers of the human imagination, you are accomplishing deeds without equal in the history of mankind. How shall we be able to thank you? Offering my congratulations does far too little to convey to you the emotions that I am feeling."[51] Riefenstahl's role in the war became a topic of discussion in Germany immediately after the conflict ended and played a central role in the fourth and final denazification proceedings against her. On April 19, 1952, two days before the proceedings at the Berlin denazification tribunal, the magazine *Revue* published an article titled "Leni Riefenstahl Remains Silent About It" that included for the first time the photos showing her horrified expression in Końskie and the statement of a witness who testified that Riefenstahl had been an eyewitness to the massacre. This article was intended to prevent her from receiving yet another mild sentence and to force Riefenstahl to admit her moral complicity for the first time.

The article, which caused international outrage, came to the conclusion that

> her creative abilities are not subject to debate here. There would
> be little to say about Leni Riefenstahl if, seven years after the Nazi
> Reich was buried, she had displayed a different attitude after

1945. But after 1945, continually stating that she had not been a member of the party, she attempted to give the impression that she had known nothing of the monstrous atrocities and crimes of the National Socialist regime. In reality, Leni Riefenstahl is one of the few German women who not only knew of the terrible crimes under which Germany's reputation throughout the world suffers even today, and for which countless innocent soldiers today continue to be held responsible, but who witnessed them with her own eyes. Based on the object lesson that caused Leni Riefenstahl to fall into a faint in Konsky [*sic*] (Poland) on September 5, 1939, she was obligated to condemn the crimes of the Third Reich and to disassociate herself from them. Such an admission would have made a new start much easier for her.[52]

Riefenstahl successfully protested to the Berlin tribunal that the article contained libelous assertions that were untrue. She had never witnessed such a crime, she said. "Neither I nor any of my colleagues saw anything."[53] Based on statements by her crew from the Special Film Troop Riefenstahl, but also on those by high-ranking officers of the Wehrmacht, she was believed and was able to keep up her version of the story.[54] The memoirs of Erich von Manstein, which state the opposite view, had not yet been published, nor had the photographs that today clearly prove that Riefenstahl was an eyewitness to the events in Końskie. At the time, she spoke of the protest she had lodged with Reichenau and convinced the court that she had come to an immediate decision to quit her post. Because no one questioned her on the true purpose of her visit to the front, the sentence of the Berlin tribunal was surprisingly mild: "exonerated."[55]

1. Riefenstahl performing her daily morning exercises, circa 1924

2. Portrait of Leni Riefenstahl, Ateliers Balázs, Berlin, circa 1924

3. Left to right: Hans Schneeberger, Leni Riefenstahl, Richard Angst, Sepp Allgeier, and Arnold Fanck

4. Dancing on-screen: Leni Riefenstahl in *Der heilige Berg*, 1926

5. Leni Riefenstahl practicing climbing barefoot in the Dolomites, 1927, for the unfinished film "Die schwarze Katze"

6. Cover-girl star

7. New Year's Eve party, 1927: Leni with other German film luminaries. Left to right: (top) Lilian Harvey, Christa Tordy; (standing) Max Hansen, Willy Fritsch, Wilhelm Bendow; (seated) Leni Riefenstahl, Camilla Horn, Olga Tschechowa

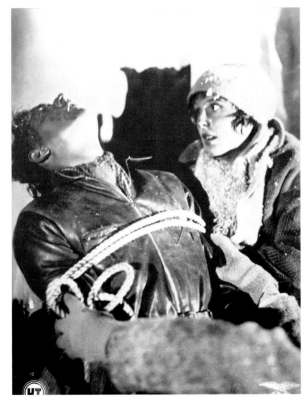

8. Ernst Petersen and Leni Riefenstahl in *Die weisse Hölle vom Piz Palü*, 1929

9. Leni Riefenstahl balances above a chasm for a scene from *Stürme über dem Montblanc*, August 1930.

10. BELOW: With Sepp Rist in *Stürme über dem Montblanc*, 1930

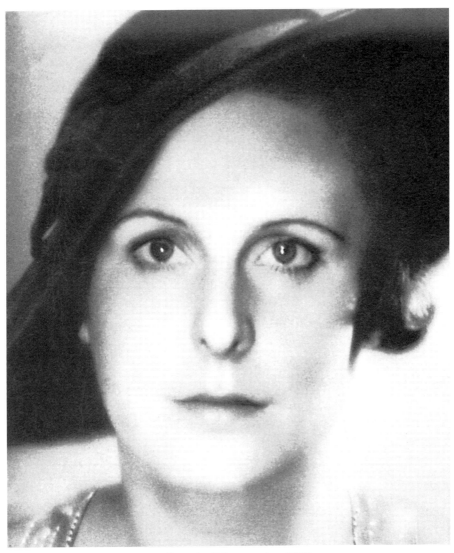

11. Portrait of the star, circa 1930

12. A scene from the ski comedy *Der weisse Rausch*, 1931

13. During the filming of *SOS Eisberg* in Greenland, 1932

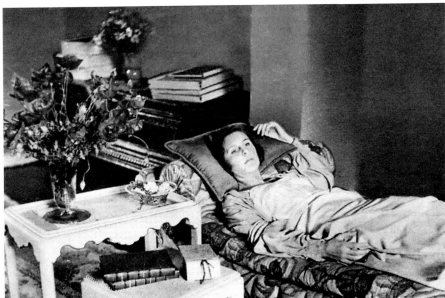

14, 15. Leni Riefenstahl in the parlor of her apartment at 97 Hindenburgstrasse in Berlin, and during her midday rest, 1932

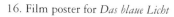
16. Film poster for *Das blaue Licht*

17. In a box at the opera, October 1933. Left to right: (seated) Leni Riefenstahl, Magda Goebbels, Italian Ambassador Vittorio Cerutti; (standing) Friedrich Christian, prince of Schaumburg-Lippe; unidentified man; Joseph Goebbels

18. Collage advertising *Sieg des Glaubens*: Hitler and SA commander Ernst Röhm

19. Leni Riefenstahl directs the Führer: filming *Triumph des Willens*, Nuremberg, 1934

20. Adolf Hitler and Leni Riefenstahl prepare for the filming of *Triumph des Willens*, 1934.

21. With cameraman Sepp Allgeier, 1934

22. ABOVE: On the best of terms: Leni Riefenstahl and Adolf Hitler on the sidelines during the filming of *Triumph des Willens*, 1934

23. On the Nazi Party rally grounds in Nuremberg, 1934

24. With Julius Streicher at the Nuremberg premiere of *Triumph des Willens*, April 1935

25. A housewarming party with the Führer at Riefenstahl's Dahlem villa, summer 1937

26. Leni Riefenstahl and her cameraman Walter Frentz, shooting at the Olympic Stadium in Berlin, 1936

27. Guests at Riefenstahl's home, summer 1937. Left to right: sister-in-law Ilse Riefenstahl, Frau Dr. Ebersberg, mother Bertha Riefenstahl, Joseph Goebbels, brother Heinz Riefenstahl, Leni Riefenstahl, Adolf Hitler

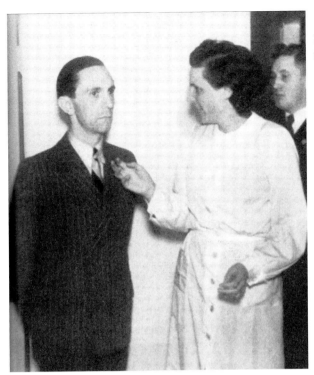

28. Joseph Goebbels visits the cutting room, 1937.

29. Leni Riefenstahl congratulates Hitler on his birthday in 1938. In the background: Hitler's adjutant, Albert Bormann

30. At the height of her career, at the Paris premiere of *Olympia*, 1938

31. Leni Riefenstahl during the massacre of Jewish civilians in Końskie, September 12, 1939

32. Gypsy prisoners are recruited as extras on *Tiefland*.

33. Shooting *Tiefland*, 1940

34. Otto Gritschneder, defense attorney for Leni Riefenstahl in the *Revue* trial, 1949

35. BELOW: Appearing before the Berlin tribunal, 1952

36. Image from the past: Leni Riefenstahl at the Mussolini Forum in Rome, 1950

# 12

## FLIGHT INTO

## THE PUTATIVELY APOLITICAL

### *TIEFLAND*, THE NEVER-ENDING PROJECT

IN 1940, FOLLOWING THE COLLAPSE of the "Penthesilea" project, Leni Riefenstahl turned to the uncompleted *Tiefland* project of 1934 and filmed it, with major interruptions, from the fall of 1940 to the fall of 1944. The filming was hampered by countless obstacles, delays, and accidents, as well as Riefenstahl's illnesses, and truly seemed to be an endless project until its completion and premiere in 1954.

The story line for *Tiefland* can be traced back to a romantic Spanish folk play based on an opera of the same name by Eugen D' Albert, a piano virtuoso and pupil of Franz Liszt. The play, which was very popular in Berlin in the twenties, was also based on a forgotten 1896 drama, *Terra baixa*, by Àngel Guimerà. Riefenstahl called on both in making the film, but she wanted to concentrate on the dramatic source, as she planned *Tiefland* not as a musical but a melodrama.[1]

What inspired her about the story above all was the mythical, over-the-top juxtaposition of the lowlands, or *"tiefland,"* and the mountain heights, which had played an important role in her directorial debut, *Das blaue Licht*. Riefenstahl had made thorough preparations for *Tiefland* as early as 1934, before she began work on *Triumph des Willens*. At the time, she had wanted to make the film together with Terra, the film production company. She would have been credited as coproducer and was already assured of having broad artistic say. Heinrich George and Sepp Rist were to play the male leads and Giuseppe Becce was to compose the music, as he had for *Das blaue Licht*. Hans Schneeberger would serve as cinematographer.

In the early summer of 1934, Riefenstahl traveled to Spain to begin filming. But as Terra had not delivered the necessary funding and film stock, shooting was delayed. As opposed to her situation with *Das blaue Licht*, Riefenstahl did not have total control over the project, and she reacted by suffering a physical breakdown on the day before filming finally was to begin. Terra canceled the film, and it was six years before Riefenstahl could work on *Tiefland* once again.

In *Memoiren*, it is striking how restrained Riefenstahl is in her depiction of the film's beginnings, particularly in light of the fact that she embellishes all of her other projects to the point of myth, including those that were never realized. Also striking is how she came across the material for the film and what fascinated her about it: *Tiefland* was offered to her, she maintained, and she merely accepted the offer.[2]

This understatement may be tied to the little-known fact that Hitler, in addition to the works of Richard Wagner, especially prized *Tiefland*, the opera. Hitler heard Eugen D' Albert's work for the first time in February 1908, when it was performed in Vienna one year after its successful world premiere in Berlin. He was still raving about the performance decades later, which was a production of Alfred Roller, whom he held in high esteem. Brigitte Hamann, the biographer of the young Hitler, confirms: "Already as 'Führer of the pan-German Reich,' H. demonstrated his love for *Tiefland*. At any rate, he requested that the opera be performed on October 27, 1938, on the occasion of his official visit to the Vienna State Opera. This came as a surprise to conductor Hans Knappertsbusch as well as to the members of the philharmonic, as they had counted on a Wagner request and not this ancient Roller production from 1908."[3]

*Tiefland*'s total division between the "good, unspoiled" mountains and the "evil, decadent" lowlands, which are in battle with each other, exactly suited Hitler's simplistic ideas. As Hamann writes, quite early on he formed "a very distinct worldview, according to which he clearly preferred bipolar theories: the doctrine of the master race versus the slave race; the strong versus the weak; blondes versus those with dark hair; all accompanied by a clear division between good and evil."[4] *Tiefland* had all of this.

Clearly Riefenstahl had already decided to film Albert's opera in 1934, and thus it seems possible that the project was based on a direct

suggestion by or even at the express wish of the Führer, which the director wisely later wished to conceal. Even if the suggestion had come from
Hitler, this doesn't mean that Riefenstahl didn't also have a very personal
interest in *Tiefland*, for this project had a substantive as well as a creative
connection to *Das blaue Licht*: what she had accomplished with the earlier
film using limited means, she now wanted to accomplish fully—the perfect mountain film, the crown jewel of the genre.

As was the case with *Das blaue Licht*, the director of *Tiefland* was primarily concerned with the film's painterly effect. And the women who
stand at the center of both films, both played by Riefenstahl, are conspicuously similar. In *Tiefland* it is a persecuted beauty who—like Junta in
*Das blaue Licht*—is delivered up in a strangely passive way to the events
occurring around her.

In the postwar period, Riefenstahl masked her choice of the *Tiefland*
project as an "escape from the war."[5] After her return from Poland, according to Riefenstahl, Goebbels apparently presented her with several
offers to make propaganda films in support of the war effort, all of which
she rejected. It is at least doubtful whether these offers in fact existed.
*Tiefland* was, of course, an escape; she could retreat from the real violence
of the war to the world of the mountains, until the point when she finally
moved to Tirol, in the fall of 1943.

Riefenstahl herself later described her return to the *Tiefland* project: "I
had actually given up on *Tiefland*. Having once not completed it, I no
longer wished to make it at all. Later, I had no connection to the subject.
If I made it during the war nevertheless, it was as an emergency stopgap,
because I had no desire to make the other films, propaganda and the
like."[6] And with *Tiefland*, Riefenstahl could indeed escape the war and
further offers of propaganda films to a great extent. But she could not,
nor did she wish to, sever her ties to the regime.


ON ORDERS FROM AND AT THE WISH OF THE FÜHRER

A 1942 activity report of Riefenstahl Film, Inc., includes the statement:
"Feature film *Tiefland*, to be created on orders from the Führer and with
the support of the Reich Ministry for Enlightenment and Propaganda."[7]

As the regime spared no expense in the making of *Tiefland*, this is also a case in which there can scarcely be any serious talk of "artistic freedom," as Riefenstahl and her apologists later presented it.[8] This project was not a withdrawal into private life, as Riefenstahl claimed after the fact. As before, she was given advantages that no other filmmaker could have hoped for.

Yet something had changed. There was no question that once the war began she no longer enjoyed a privileged access to Hitler, which she had exploited for her own purposes in the early years of the dictatorship. There were extremely few personal meetings with the Führer in these years, as Hitler was occupied almost exclusively with conducting the war.

Like all other major figures of the Third Reich, at the end of 1939 Riefenstahl had to accustom herself to taking everything she once had talked to the Führer about to Martin Bormann, Hitler's secretary. Though this at first appeared to be a loss of prestige, she soon adjusted to the new situation and developed a good relationship with Bormann. After Rudolf Hess flew to Scotland in May 1941—in all probability to explore how willing Great Britain was to wage peace, only to land in a British jail—Bormann became leader of the Party Chancellory and, after 1943, "secretary to the Führer." He was one of Hitler's most loyal and submissive subjects. Once the war began, he did not leave Hitler's side, and within a very short time had made himself indispensable. He was the éminence grise of the regime, plotting and stirring up trouble, and rising to become one of the Nazi government's most influential men. This was because he decided who would have direct access to Hitler and who would not, which problems would be presented to the dictator and which he would not even be informed of. According to Henry Picker, Bormann was "equipped with a near seamless knowledge of things and people on the political stage of the pan-German Reich, well informed on each and every significant meeting Hitler held (with the exception of those with the Wehrmacht, SS, and police), every visit, planning session, ambition, every opinion that Hitler held in terms of ideas, people, institutions, and organizations."[9]

Riefenstahl, too, was referred to Bormann during the filming of *Tiefland* whenever Hitler's approval was required or she needed his support in terms of some problem or additional funds. Because Martin Bormann was well aware of Hitler's high opinion of the director, he was always willing to help her. Riefenstahl's film partner Bernhard Minetti confirmed this: "She dealt only with Hitler's secretary, Bormann, that is, she had direct access to him. She used this advantage very cleverly; if there was something she couldn't get, she threatened to go to his superior."[10]

So even in the midst of the war Riefenstahl was able make a film financed by the regime without having to answer to anyone or even produce results. If anyone tried to stand in her way, she would bring up her "orders from the Führer." As Fritz Hippler, then head of the Reich Film Department, corroborates, it came to the point where "Leni has been filming for years and no one has seen any of it, and Goebbels hasn't been allowed to interfere."[11] Goebbels deliberately stayed out of it, knowing that he would not be able to exercise influence over Riefenstahl's film project in any case. On March 30, 1940, he noted in his diary: "Leni Riefenstahl is having difficulties with her new film, *Tiefland*. But I don't want to get too involved in the matter." On December 16, 1942, his final diary entry concerning Riefenstahl reads: "Leni Riefenstahl reports to me on her *Tiefland* film. It has developed into a true rat's nest of entanglements. All told, over five million have already been poured into this film and it still won't be finished for another year. Frau Riefenstahl has been made very ill by the work and the burden of responsibility, and I suggest straightaway that she go away for some rest before she takes on more work. I'm glad to have nothing to do with this disagreeable affair and therefore to have no responsibility to answer for."

After 1945, the question continually arose concerning who had financed *Tiefland*. It had been Hitler himself who had funded it, and in doing so he had created the unique situation of investing party and Reich money in a feature film that in no way contributed to the war effort. And there are two instances of Hitler's direct intervention in the financing of the film. Sections of *Tiefland*—the takes to be used for the prologue—were to be filmed in the Italian Dolomites. After Riefenstahl received 350,000 lire (roughly 50,000 reichsmarks) in the early spring of 1940 and an additional 450,000 lire the next year, her third request for funds, in the summer of 1942, was turned down by the Ministry of Economics. At this she went over Bormann's head to Hitler, who decided that "if at all possible, the funds requested by Riefenstahl-Film GmbH should be made available."[12] So Riefenstahl once again received the sum she requested, 350,000 lire.

A similar situation occurred in the summer of 1943, when Riefenstahl wanted to film in Spain and additional funds, 240,000 pesetas, were denied her (320,000 had already been approved).[13] Minister of Economics Walther Funk (not, as Riefenstahl stated, Joseph Goebbels), who administered the scarce currency reserves, rejected the request, citing the foreign currency situation in the Reich and the consequences of the war economy, thus introducing yet another power struggle with the director. Soon enough, however, he was forced to capitulate to her influence. Riefenstahl again turned to Bormann, who in turn spoke to the Führer. Hitler pointed to the fact that Riefenstahl's film would bring in considerable sums once it was finished, and therefore the director should receive the foreign funds she requested.[14]

Financially speaking, Riefenstahl's film assumed a dimension comparable only to such large-scale prestige productions as Ufa's jubilee film *Münchhausen* (1943) and Veit Harlan's epic *Kolberg* (1945), examples of what German film was capable of achieving in a time of "total war." That Tobis announced *Tiefland* as "the most expensive talking picture" of the time speaks to the fact that in the end, Riefenstahl's project devoured greater sums of money than the other two productions. At an estimated production cost of 7,000,000 reichsmarks,[15] *Tiefland*, which in the end cost roughly 8,500,000 reichsmarks, was one of the most expensive films of the Third Reich after *Kolberg*.

In view of the regime's financing of the film, Riefenstahl's complaint decades later that there had been "no mention of compensation"[16] when in the winter of 1940–41 costly *Tiefland* sets were destroyed at the order of the Ministry of Propaganda appears as cynical as her lament over the alleged shortage of funding for the project.

The fact that Riefenstahl's studio dates were canceled, several expensive sets torn down, and actors and camera crew reassigned was the result of Riefenstahl's own scheduling problems and not a conscious act of "sabotage" on the part of the Ministry of Propaganda. The studios, actors, and cameramen that Riefenstahl laid claim to far beyond the agreed-upon time schedule were urgently needed elsewhere. Her *Tiefland* project could not always be considered a priority, as other studios' productions would have suffered or even been canceled.[17]

## FLIGHTS OF FANCY

*Tiefland* is an allegorical tale of the struggle between the highlands and the lowlands, manifested in the rivalry between the power-hungry Marquis Don Sebastian (played by Bernhard Minetti) and the poor shepherd, Pedro (Franz Eichberger), both vying for Martha (Leni Riefenstahl), the gypsy dancer. The omnipotent marquis, who controls the area, is unscrupulous and merciless in his domination of his village, Roccabruna, and its population. He diverts the area's only water source to his own pastures, leaving the villagers and their livestock without water.

Then Martha, a beautiful and exotic gypsy, arrives in the oppressed village, and her inventive and spirited dances soon enthrall the men of Roccabruna. Martha becomes the lover of Don Sebastian and tries to convince him to make water available to the villagers again. But Don Sebastian refuses, and following a vehement disagreement during which he strikes Martha, she flees to the mountains—and into the arms of Pedro. The shepherd nurses the distraught dancer back to health, accepting it as a sign that the woman he has fallen in love with, a stranger to him until then, has come to him in the mountains.

In the end, the battle over the beautiful gypsy leads to a duel in the course of which Don Sebastian, who had demanded Martha's return, is strangled by Pedro. This not only ends the competition for Martha's affection but frees the peasants of Roccabruna from the "slave driver" and unscrupulous tyrant, the hated marquis. At the end of the film, true love triumphs over egotistical greed. To the sounds of Albert's music, Martha and Pedro ascend to the pure and innocent world of the mountains, leaving behind them the avariciousness and cupidity of the lowlands.

Riefenstahl wrote the script for *Tiefland* during the first half of 1940, together with Harald Reinl, whom she had met in 1931 during the filming of *Der weisse Rausch* (*The White Frenzy*). Like her directorial debut, *Tiefland* was a consciously unreal, artificial film set in a highly stylized landscape inspired by the paintings of Goya and El Greco. Whereas she had planned the "Penthesilea" project as a color film, she could envision *Tiefland* only in high-contrast black and white. And it would not have been a Riefenstahl project without her ego-driven goals: "At that time, I wanted to try to shoot in black and white in such a subtle way that the film would hold its own beside color film, as black-and-white cinematic art."[18] By exploiting the full range of technical possibilities with this project, the director hoped to prove that black-and-white film could achieve effects that color film could not.

When she began preparations for the film, she assumed that it would be shot entirely on location in Spain, as she had originally planned in 1934. But when Mussolini's troops marched into France in early summer of 1940, filming in Spain became impossible and the shoot was moved from the Pyrenees to the Karwendel mountains. As a consequence, a Spanish ambience had to be created in deepest Bavaria, and a good number of scenes planned for filming on location in Spain were transferred to the film studio, calling for extravagant and expensive sets that quickly inflated the cost of the project.

In addition to Bernhard Minetti, Franz Eichberger, Maria Koppenhöfer, and Aribert Wäscher in the main roles, Riefenstahl once again engaged the farmers of Sarntal, who ten years before had worked as extras and lay actors on *Das blaue Licht*. When they arrived for the shoot, Riefenstahl was horrified to find that they had shaved especially for the occasion, and the director had to have her makeup crew create fake beards for them.

Following the extensive preparations, filming began on August 1, 1940, in Mittenwald at the foot of the Karwendel mountains, where the Spanish village of Roccabruna, with its castle and mill, had been re-created. After a hiatus of eight years, Leni Riefenstahl once again was standing before the camera. Filming was to continue until the fall of 1944—alternating between summers in Tirol or the Dolomites and winters in the film studio in Babelsberg, and finally in the Barrandov Studio in Prague. While millions of soldiers were dying on the battlefields of the most devastating war of the twentieth century, and cities and villages were being bombed, Riefenstahl spared no expense in perfecting her imaginary world. Among other expenses, she had the entire set of the Roccabruna village torn down and rebuilt, solely because she wasn't pleased by it.

At another point, while filming in the Dolomites—which had the appropriate mountain backdrop but not the mountain lake she required—the director had an artificial lake, complete with cement bottom, dug on the spot and placed grass and shrubs along the banks to make it look real. She located a water source with the help of a dowser and engaged fifty Italian workers to form a bucket brigade to fill the artificial lake with water. (Unconfirmed rumors circulated that forced laborers carried the water on their backs.) Once this was completed, a herd of sheep, which the script had grazing on the bank, had to be located and placed at various points dictated by the cameras. Riefenstahl had salt strewn on the banks so that the sheep would position themselves correctly. But the animals became so thirsty from the salt that soon they had all but drunk the lake dry, and it had to be refilled three times in the same laborious fashion.

The filming of *Tiefland* also dragged on due to the continual delays caused by the director's illnesses, in addition to unforeseen problems and accidents. Though half of the film had been completed by 1941, and 90 percent by spring of 1942, from that point on it took more than two years, at enormous cost, until the final clapboard sounded. At one point in 1942, when Riefenstahl experienced a serious collapse and was suffering from depression, filming was canceled indefinitely. Many of her crew had committed to other film projects and no one seemed to believe any longer that *Tiefland* would be completed. And yet Leni Riefenstahl rallied once more and continued her work. After a nine-month hiatus, in the summer of 1943 she headed with her team to Spain, where scenes were to be filmed featuring six hundred bulls, scenes that could be shot only on location. After that, due to Riefenstahl's recurring ailments, the project again stalled for almost a year. In Prague's Barrandov Studios, the largest film studio in Europe, the director had a huge, highly stylized mountain landscape created for one single thirty-second final take. At its end, four years after shooting commenced, the last clapboard fell in the fall of 1944.

## A LONG AFTERMATH: GYPSIES FOR RIEFENSTAHL

After 1945, bitter disputes surrounded the casting of *Tiefland*. The crux of the disagreement was the fact that Riefenstahl had engaged Sinti and Roma internees as extras. Originally, when shooting was planned for Spain, the extras—in keeping with Riefenstahl's preference for "authentic

types"—were to be Spaniards. When these plans collapsed, it was proposed that the Spanish extras be transported to Mittenwald, which
proved unrealistic due to the war. But as the director insisted that the
extras' faces have "Spanish coloring," someone came up with the idea of
using interned Gypsies, an uncomfortable "detail" at the periphery of the
filming, which Riefenstahl later tirelessly tried to conceal. The director
reacted to no criticism more vehemently than to this sore point in her
biography.

Before 1945, only those within German film circles knew the origin
of *Tiefland*'s extras. The public first heard about it in the postwar period
and reacted with indignation. On May 1, 1949, the illustrated magazine *Revue* covered the scandal for the first time. An article by Erika
Schmachtenberger, which struck like a bomb and which Riefenstahl
deemed "hair-raising,"[19] stated that the director had gone to a concentration camp and personally chosen Gypsies whom she then forced to
become "film slaves." Despite, or perhaps precisely because of, the public
outcry, Riefenstahl refused to be intimidated; she knew what this kind of
serious reproach could mean in her pending denazification hearing. She
labeled the accusations a "defamation of character" and initiated proceedings against Helmut Kindler, the publisher of *Revue*. That she conducted
this as a "Poor Law" case[20] while appearing in court dressed in the latest
elegant fashions drew the spite of journalists, who followed the trial with
great interest.

The eleven-hour hearing that took place on November 23, 1949, at
the Municipal Court of Munich created headlines across the country. The
press reported "heated arguments"[21] and "razor-sharp verbal duels."[22]
Photos show Riefenstahl, whom the counsel for the defense would not
allow to complete even one sentence, gesticulating wildly on the witness
stand. She repeatedly leaped up out of her chair in anger to rebut the
accusations against her, for example, when a woman forced to play a
Gypsy in *Tiefland* claimed to have been better off in the concentration
camp than on the set of Riefenstahl's film.[23] The reporter from the *Süddeutsche Zeitung* noted, "She knows when an outburst is due, she knows
when to matter-of-factly pull out her thick horn-rimmed glasses and read
something from the files with a soft 'triumph of the will.'"[24]

When she reported to the court her determination to finish the film
and premiere it at movie theaters, the lawyer for *Revue* countered, "Do

you really believe that there are people who will want to see a film when they know that some of your extras were gassed at Auschwitz?"[25] But even this did not cause Riefenstahl to doubt her actions. She distanced herself totally from the accusation that she was in any way culpable: "I didn't have anyone gassed; that is outrageous."[26]

The majority of the public in the courtroom was on Riefenstahl's side, and her statements were often met with gales of laughter and even applause. Many of the court reporters were reminded of a kind of "festival atmosphere." This positive reaction had much to do, of course, with the fact that postwar German society still manifested a great aversion to the Sinti and Roma.

As her entire crew, including Harald Reinl, Walter Traut, and Bernhard Minetti, testified on her behalf, she was victorious in the end. Not all of the statements made in *Revue* could be proved, particularly the claim that it had been Riefenstahl who had personally selected the Gypsies in the concentration camp. Helmut Kindler, publisher of *Revue*, was fined 600 marks for printing libelous statements.

But this was not the last trial that Riefenstahl was to stand in the matter of the *Tiefland* extras. In the 1980s, she brought suit in the same matter against the filmmaker Nina Gladitz, who reiterated the accusations against Riefenstahl and researched the matter so extensively that the case was completely reintroduced. The lawsuit—the last sensational trial in Riefenstahl's life—again made headlines. For her documentary *Zeit des Schweigens und der Dunkelheit* (*Time of Silence and Darkness*), which Westdeutscher Rundfunk (WDR) screened for the first and only time in September 1982, Gladitz had located witnesses who had been *Tiefland* extras and had survived the war. Her star witness was Josef Reinhardt, who had been thirteen years old at the time. She accompanied him to the former site of the Maxglan internment camp, near Salzburg, but they also went to Mittenwald, where the sets for *Tiefland* were constructed. The film documents a difficult search for clues: people who once had lived in close proximity to the "Gypsy camp" supposedly knew nothing of it, and the owner of a barn in which the extras were locked up hadn't any opinion at all on the use of internees in the film.

Two central assertions in the documentary were specific attacks on Riefenstahl. First, several witnesses agreed that Riefenstahl was personally at the camp and chose the extras herself. The second assertion was made by Josef Reinhardt, who stated that as a thirteen-year-old he had explained to Leni Riefenstahl, as instructed by his father, that the Gypsies of Auschwitz were going to be killed. She had promised to support and protect his family—a promise she had not kept.

It was this last statement in particular, supported only by Reinhardt's word, that Riefenstahl reacted to vehemently: "Though I promised myself no longer to bring charges against such accusations, I feel so distressed by the film of a certain Frau Gladitz, which was broadcast on WDR, that I could not let these new allegations stand. I had to bring suit. The lies have gone beyond the limits of what can be endured."[27]

In an initial proceeding in 1983, Riefenstahl was granted a temporary order prohibiting further screenings of the documentary. Gladitz appealed the decision, and there followed a lawsuit that went on for years, conducted by the regional court in Freiburg. Because Nina Gladitz had far better arguments and proof than the publisher of *Revue* had once presented, her film was finally released, with one major injunction that concerned making a cut. She was allowed to continue to assert that Riefenstahl personally had selected Gypsies at the camp and that they were forced laborers and received no compensation for their work—to Riefenstahl an "incomprehensible decision."[28] But a scene in the film that suggested that Riefenstahl already knew about Auschwitz and the fate of the Gypsies in 1941, the year, that is, in which the mass murders began, had to be cut from the film. Gladitz refused to make this cut, and *Zeit des Schweigens und der Dunkelheit* disappeared into the archives. The film that Riefenstahl deemed "aggressive" and "deceitful," a "slanderous botchwork," has never since been shown in public.[29]

What really did happen, once one gets past the lawsuits and statements made by Riefenstahl? To counter the accusations, the director maintained after 1945 that Maxglan had not been an internment camp at all. During the *Revue* trial, she even tried to present Maxglan as a "public welfare" or "relief" camp or as a "receiving camp for wandering Gypsies," thus denying the truth. Riefenstahl succeeded in this with the help of a statement by Anton Böhmer, former head of Salzburg's criminal investigation division. Not until the trials of the 1980s did it surface that Böhmer had in fact been an SS Sturmbannführer and had signed the list of Gypsy extras used in *Tiefland*.[30]

While it is true that Maxglan was not in fact a concentration camp run by the SS but a "Gypsy assembly camp" formally under the command of the police, it nevertheless was a forced labor camp similar to a concentration camp, fortified by a barbed-wire fence and two guard towers. Its occupants, who at the order of Himmler systematically had been interned since 1938 as a "non-European foreign race," received substandard lodging, were treated badly, and were put into forced labor. They lived in constant fear that they would be sent to concentration or death camps. Two hundred thousand of the three hundred thousand Sinti and Roma who were living in Germany at the time were murdered at Auschwitz. Consequently, the Maxglan camp was nothing less than a "preliminary stage of annihilation."[31]

In the court case of 1949, Riefenstahl covered herself in two respects: not only did she try to downplay the significance of Maxglan, she also claimed never to have been there. It had not been she but her former assistant director Harald Reinl and her production manager Hugo Lehner who had selected the extras from the 250 Sinti and Roma internees. "I couldn't be there myself. I was still in the Dolomites, scouting visuals."[32] Josef Reinhardt and members of his family uniformly and explicitly countered this in Gladnitz's documentary, stating that it had been Riefenstahl who had come to the camp in the company of two men and selected them personally. Another witness, Rosa Winter, seventeen years old at the time, confirmed that she, too, had been personally chosen by Riefenstahl: "We were all at the assembly camp. And then she arrived with the police and selected people. And I was among them and others as well, mostly young people, which is what she needed."[33]

The director's well-known perfectionism, which dictated that she control even the smallest detail, suggests that Riefenstahl would have gone to Maxglan personally rather than leave the selection of extras to someone else, though in the end it is her word against the others'. And even had it not been Riefenstahl but members of her crew who had chosen the extras, even if she had not seen with her own eyes how people were interned there, it would not change the fact that she unscrupulously used victims of Nazi racial policies for her own purposes.

The first of the sixty-eight Gypsy adults and children assigned to her were brought under guard to the film set in Mittenwald on October 4,

1940. During the shooting of the film, they were under constant surveillance by two Salzburg policemen and at night were locked into a barn, not merely "provided with lodging," as Riefenstahl so nicely put it.[34] But her statement that she personally had a good, almost friendly, relationship with her extras does appear to be correct: "The Gypsies, adults as well as children, were our favorites."[35] Almost all of the surviving extras stated that they were better treated on Riefenstahl's set than in the camp and that the director personally treated them in an extraordinarily friendly manner. They were neither harassed nor humiliated as at the camp.

Despite the fact that the child extras addressed Riefenstahl as "Aunt Leni" and that the extras viewed the film work as an improvement over life at the camp, their work on the feature film remained forced labor. The Gypsies themselves were not given the choice of performing in *Tiefland*. And during the shoot they remained internees, who were sent back to the camp as soon as Riefenstahl no longer needed them.

According to statements made by survivors, they were never paid for their work on the film. Whether their wages really were paid to the camp officials, as Riefenstahl claimed, or whether the extras were placed at her disposal free of charge can no longer be verified. Even if a meager fee had been paid, Leni Riefenstahl, in taking advantage of the forced labor of internees, would still have directly benefited from National Socialist racial policies.

Riefenstahl, who had employed the services of the extras from Maxglan in the fall of 1940, called them back for further filming the following year. In 1942, as she was shooting scenes at the Babelsberg Studio, she was given access to Sinti and Roma from the Marzahn camp, which the Nazis had erected during the Olympic Games.[36] In March 1943, just like the Sinti and Roma from Maxglan one month later, they were deported to Auschwitz-Birkenau, where many of them were killed.[37] Riefenstahl presents things quite differently: "We saw almost all of them again after the war. They said that working with us had been the most wonderful time of their lives. No one forced them to say this."[38]

We can only speculate about whether the director expended any thought on the fate of the people she had used in her film for their "Mediterranean coloring," or whether she didn't care what happened to the Sinti and Roma once she no longer needed them—just as the question of whether she knew, or even had an inkling, of the mass murders occurring in the concentration camps must remain open. Whatever the case, she doesn't seem to have suffered any moral conflicts concerning her actions, or exhibited any compassion. Even in retrospect she seemed to have no feelings of guilt. She allegedly said to the film publicist Curt Riess, who in the postwar period briefly served as ghostwriter on her memoirs, "If the Führer felt they belonged there, then they belonged there."[39]

That she never seriously revised this opinion is evidenced by her behavior during the related trials after the war. She argued about details but never expressed regret or apologized. She refused to discuss the subject and stubbornly persisted in her version of the story, which long since has been refuted.

## CULTURAL FILM PRODUCER

Even though the facts surrounding the production of *Tiefland* prove otherwise, after the war this feature film was continually used as evidence of Riefenstahl's apolitical wartime stance. Parallel to the film, however, she continued to be entrusted with official and highly political documentary film projects for the regime, though as producer, not director. In the first half of the forties, Riefenstahl accepted lucrative contracts for her own company, Riefenstahl-Film, founded in 1939, in her capacity as the regime's chief documentary filmmaker and propagandist, the "filmmaker of the movement." These contracts brought her wealth and—had they been realized—would have enhanced her reputation. Her direct patron was Albert Speer, her indirect patron once again Adolf Hitler, who took care of the financing of the plans, most likely from his "cultural fund."

Hitler's cultural fund was administered by Martin Bormann and was fed, among others, by royalties from *Mein Kampf*, by the high sums he earned from the Reich Postal Ministry in accordance with the "personality law" in exchange for allowing his image to be used on postage stamps,[40] by bequests he received, and by resources from the Adolf Hitler Endowment of the German Economy, established by Gustav Krupp von Bohlen und Halbach.[41] All of this meant that Hitler had access to inexhaustible funds (estimated at close to 100,000,000 marks annually), for which he was accountable to no one.[42] He used the funds for projects dear to his heart or that he considered personal, such as the acquisition of paintings for the "Führer Museum" that he was planning for Linz, the extensive renovations at Obersalzberg, and gifts presented to Eva Braun or deserving party members. In addition, Hitler's confidante Winifred Wagner received several hundred thousand reichsmarks annually as an advance for the Bayreuth Festival.[43]

The "cultural film," developed by Ufa in the twenties, represented a hybrid of documentary and feature film. According to the film scholar Peter Longerich, until the collapse of the Third Reich, this genre was considered "an excellent means of propaganda, due to the authoritarian and instructive character traditionally attributed to it in Germany."[44] The films were of a scientific nature, especially biological and medical, but some were also devoted to innovations in technology and industry and some were cultural-historical works or films on various landscapes and customs. As of 1934, this type of cultural film was an obligatory part of any screening.

Already by March 9, 1939, Riefenstahl had suggested to Goebbels that her film company produce "national political education films" for the Ministry of Propaganda. These could not be realized, however, due to the war.[45] Presumably, Riefenstahl viewed this work—which her firm and not she herself would make—to be a logical continuation of the instructional sports films she had brought to movie theaters after *Olympia*.

Beginning in 1940, Riefenstahl landed prestigious commissions as a producer of cultural films. In December 1942, she could report to the Berlin Chamber of Industry and Commerce commissions equaling almost 8,000,000 reichsmarks for *Tiefland*, for "the production of archival and documentary material for the Office of the General Inspection of Buildings and for the Reich Ministry for Arms and Munitions," and for the "production of documentary footage for Reich Minister Speer." For each contract she received an all-inclusive fee of 10 percent of the total budget.[46] By the end of 1942, she had a staff of forty employees handling these assignments, among them many former members of her documentary film productions. In addition to a planned but unrealized film on the Todt Organization, which, among other projects, was responsible for the construction of Germany's autobahns, one project warranted her special attention: a major documentary on Hitler's plans for rebuilding Berlin, which was to be called "The Führer Builds His Capital" and would inform Germans for the first time of the dictator's plans.

According to statements by Riefenstahl, the film project originated with Albert Speer, who suggested it to her in August 1939, shortly before war broke out. Presumably, however, the commission came directly from Hitler, for he placed at her disposal a budget of 700,000 reichsmarks for the film.[47] As this project was devoted to Hitler's megalomaniacal plans for the world capital, "Germania," the film was especially close to his heart. Shooting proceeded from 1940 to February 1943, when it was canceled due to the war.

Because Riefenstahl was busy filming *Tiefland*, she put her former mentor Arnold Fanck in charge of directing the film. Though Fanck apparently worked autonomously on the project for the most part, he nevertheless was under Riefenstahl's supervision. As her employee, he earned 4,000 reichsmarks a month, which allowed him to move into a new villa on Berlin's Wannsee. Not only was he now financially dependent on his former pupil, he was almost forced to bend to her artistic demands. For it was she, after all, who had set the new standard for documentary films in the Third Reich. In Riefenstahl's employ, and using film material already shot for the failed Berlin project, he realized two short films exploring the work of Hitler's two favorite sculptors: *Josef Thorak, Werkstatt und Werk* (*Josef Thorak, Studio and Work*) (1943) and *Arno Breker* (1944). Arnold Fanck filmed their heroic statues just as Riefenstahl once had filmed ancient Greek statues for *Olympia*. Though he apparently had no objections to the work at the time, he later viewed it with bitterness, and, apparently out of bruised vanity, distanced himself from Riefenstahl after the end of the Third Reich, having nothing good to say about her.[48]

## PRIVATE HAPPINESS AND UNHAPPINESS

Riefenstahl repeatedly suffered long bouts of illness for almost the entire time it took to produce *Tiefland*. She experienced a physical breakdown in the winter of 1940: "The strain was too much for me. The chronic pain reappeared that I had been subject to ever since making the mountain films. Up until then it could always be treated, but this time nothing helped. It was too much for my nerves. I was taken to the hospital."[49] Gallbladder problems she had experienced for many years worsened to the point that she was hospitalized several times during 1940. And in the period that followed, work on her films was continually interrupted or delayed because of visits to hospitals, sanatariums, and homeopaths, without any improvement in her condition. Nevertheless, her will to continue working remained unbroken: "I didn't under any circumstances want to cancel the film. I kept working with the help of artificial means—camphor shots, intravenous injections, Novalgin, and all sorts of other medications to shore me up."[50] She even continued work on part of the film from a stretcher, during which all the scenes in which she appeared had to be postponed. In the spring of 1941, she again met with Hitler, whom she had not seen for months. He had heard of her illness and paid her a visit: "He was encouraging and offered to send me to his physician, Dr. Morell."[51] Presumably during this visit, in which he spoke confidently of Germany's certain victory, he invited her to come to Obersalzberg after the war in order to write screenplays together: "At first I thought he was joking, but then I realized he was serious."[52] It was a film project on the history of the Catholic Church that seemed to interest him most. The collaboration between the two was never to be, but Riefenstahl later accepted Hitler's generous offer to send her to his personal physician.[53]

It was not only illnesses but also the expanding air war that increasingly were taking Riefenstahl away from filming and forcing her to face bitter reality. Returning to her villa in Dahlem after filming in the mountains in 1941 and 1942, she experienced the bombing of Berlin close-up. On March 1, 1943, she witnessed one of the heaviest attacks on the city, which seemed to her like "the end of the world": "Doors blew off their frames, all of the windows shattered. I thought my eardrums would burst, the detonations were so loud . . . The next morning we counted almost two hundred firebombs on my property, and from the branches of a tree near the balcony of my house hung the body of a British pilot, torn to pieces."[54]

With the help of Albert Speer, she relocated to Kitzbühel, Austria, and it was here in November 1943 that she moved into the Seebichl house at the base of the Wilder Kaiser mountain. It was roomy enough to accommodate members of her crew, and in addition she was able to add editing and screening rooms and a studio for sound editing. Again with Speer's help she transferred the major part of her film material to Seebichl, to protect it from the bombing. After the annexation of Austria, the far safer area of Tirol had become a favorite and more affordable vacation spot for Germans, and once the war began it turned into a hermetically sealed world to which film celebrities of the Third Reich could flee the horrors of war.[55] Leni Riefenstahl could continue to work on her film project here as if the war didn't exist.

But in one respect her life was similar to that of millions of other women of her era: she constantly worried about the life of the man she loved. In the fall of 1940, in the first year of filming *Tiefland*, she met Peter Jacob, a mountain infantryman on leave from the front in Kitzbühel, who had stepped in as Bernhard Minetti's double in the film. According to Riefenstahl, Jacob "conquered" her against her will: "I tried everything to get out of this man's path. Just to escape repeating what I had gone through eleven years earlier, when Hans Schneeberger left me. I had sworn to myself that I wouldn't do that."[56] But the officer wouldn't give up, and she finally accepted him: "Never before had I felt such passion, never before had I been so loved. The experience went so deep that it changed my life. It was the beginning of a great love."[57]

But Peter Jacob's furlough ended and he had to leave. The constant waiting for his return and her concern for his well-being became a crucial part of Riefenstahl's life and often superimposed itself on the problems she was having with *Tiefland*. The relationship between the two functioned beautifully as long as they were separated by distance. Riefenstahl received letters from him daily, often several times a day. But in December 1940, a few months after they met, when Jacob spent the Christmas holidays in Kitzbühel with his celebrated girlfriend, their first serious problems emerged, "which became unbearable." After this, all of their meetings seemed to run hot and cold, and Riefenstahl sometimes perceived them as moments of happiness and sometimes as torture: "Peter's feelings were as explosive as a volcano, which both drew me to him and at the same time frightened me."[58] Despite these early warnings and problems, she was convinced of her love for him and of the genuineness of his feelings—as soon, that is, as he returned to the front and again wrote passionate letters to her that were "like medicine."

At first the letters arrived from the Greek front, but soon they were arriving from the Eastern front, where Jacob, who in the interim had been awarded the Knight's Cross for his services in the France campaign, was assigned in the summer of 1941. Shortly before he was sent east he brought up marriage for the first time, a thought that Leni Riefenstahl at first was not particularly pleased by, having up until that point remained independent and unattached. The longer the war progressed, the more difficult it became to maintain their constant contact, and sometimes there would be no news from Jacob for weeks. After the couple spent a few weeks together in December 1941 and January 1942, the relationship suffered a crisis. When Jacob didn't contact her for days after his departure, Riefenstahl became worried and tried to locate him. When she discovered that the ship that was to take him to the arctic front had not yet sailed and that he had spent the previous week with another woman at Berlin's Hotel Eden, Riefenstahl suffered a breakdown. She fell into a deep depression, refused to eat, and spent several weeks in bed, totally impassive. Her doctor urged her to separate from Jacob. Nevertheless, during Peter Jacob's next leave from the front, the couple became engaged. But it was their separations that dominated the turbulent relationship, times in which Riefenstahl tried to distract herself in work: "And then the inevitable day arrived when we, like hundreds of thousands of others on every day during this period, said good-bye again. For an indeterminate amount of time and uncertain of ever seeing one another again."[59]

Despite his notorious infidelity, Riefenstahl accepted Jacob's proposal of marriage, and after two nerve-racking years of engagement the two were married. The woman who her whole life had insisted on her freedom and independence decided, at forty-two years of age, to take a risk she was soon to regret. She took the name Riefenstahl-Jacob following the wedding, which took place in Kitzbühel on March 21, 1944, and was announced by the press at the beginning of April. It was a typical wartime wedding, celebrated with a small circle of friends. Peter Jacob was granted special leave, and Riefenstahl's parents, who rarely saw their daughter after work on *Tiefland* had begun, traveled to Berlin, though they were less than happy about the marriage.[60] On April 30, only a few weeks after the ceremony (and, according to an earlier statement, on the day of the wedding itself), Riefenstahl met with Adolf Hitler for the last time.[61] He apparently had received word of Riefenstahl's marriage from members of his circle and invited her and her husband to nearby Obersalzberg. As she had not seen him for three years, she was shocked to find Hitler, who already was showing strong signs of Parkinson's disease, looking many years older, tired, listless, and sunken into himself. The man who held the fate of Germany in his hands was a human wreck.[62] At the advice of his doctors, Hitler had left his "headquarters" in East Prussia for Obersalzberg on March 16, fleeing the disastrous news of the military's collapse. In his old, familiar surroundings he was trying to free himself from his dark mood and to slow his loss of strength, which had already led to major signs of physical decline.[63]

At this final meeting, Hitler delivered a one-hour monologue, during which he didn't speak to Peter Jacob even once, nor did he ask Riefenstahl how she was. Instead, in a monotone, he fantasized about the "pan-German Reich." His one-time admirer experienced a Führer that Albert Speer had come to know all too well during this period: a ruined man with "constant mood swings that ranged from depression to aggression, from self-pity to grandiose ideas on future projects."[64] In contrast to their earlier meetings at which he was friendly and attentive, this last encounter seemed unreal to her and led to a spontaneous cooling of her former enthusiasm.[65] Three months later, on July 20, 1944, at the Wolf's Lair, Hitler's headquarters in East Prussia, Count Claus Schenk von Stauffenberg attempted to assassinate Hitler, which Hitler escaped with only a slight wound.

July 20 was a dark day for Leni Riefenstahl in three respects. In mid-July, her father, who had long suffered from heart disease, died at the age of sixty-five. His funeral took place on July 20 in Berlin, where the putsch against Hitler was crushed behind the scenes. Due to the volatile situation, Albert Speer was unable to attend the funeral.[66] And Riefenstahl herself would have been avidly following the radio reports to find out whether the Führer had survived the assassination attempt. A few days after July 20, Riefenstahl found out that her beloved younger brother, Heinz, thirty-eight years old, had been killed at the Eastern front that very same day: "This misfortune happened at the very hour that the bomb exploded at the Führer's headquarters and that I was standing at my father's grave."[67]

Having allowed her relationship with her family to lapse to a great extent during the filming of *Tiefland* and her turbulent liaison with Peter Jacob, Riefenstahl greatly deepened her contact with her mother at this point. Following her husband's death, Bertha Riefenstahl at first remained in her home in Zernsdorf, east of Berlin. Then in February 1945, with Albert Speer's help, she left the Reich capital, where heavy fighting was taking place, and moved in with her daughter in Kitzbühel. She would continue to live with her daughter until her death, twenty years after the war ended.

## THE LAST MONTHS OF THE WAR

The Third Reich had long since been defeated by the time Goebbels's propaganda machine, ever optimistic, announced: "We will keep marching, even if everything falls apart. For today Germany is ours, and tomorrow the world." Riefenstahl was in Tirol when the war ended, where she was again working feverishly on *Tiefland*, though there were barely any movie theaters left in the country in which the film could have been shown. Even in the last months of the regime, when it long had been clear that Germany would lose the war, Riefenstahl was totally uncompromising in her demands, almost all of which were met immediately.

As the war situation continued to worsen in the fall and winter of 1944, Riefenstahl attempted to recruit a whole series of former crew members and friends to come to Kitzbühel to help finish *Tiefland*, in order to spare them being drafted into the war. So, for example, she was able to save her former cameraman and lover, Hans Schneeberger, who by that time was over fifty years old, from being called up for service in the home guard known as the Volkssturm. But she was not successful in February 1945, when she attempted to get Arnold Fanck and his wife to Kitzbühel under the pretense that she needed him to finish the film.

When filming was completed in the late fall of 1944, Leni Riefenstahl had more than one hundred thousand meters of exposed film, which she then began to edit. But the interruptions continued. When she received news that her husband was wounded and in a hospital in Merano, she traveled to the war zone to visit him. Back in Kitzbühel, working with her female cutters, she completed work on *Tiefland* at the time the regime was collapsing and the Third Reich capitulating. Preparations had been made for recording the score, performed by the Vienna Philharmonic, but the necessary postproduction synchronization, for which Riefenstahl required the presence of Bernhard Minetti and Maria Koppenhöfer in April 1945, could not be completed. Riefenstahl acknowledged in her memoirs that only later did she comprehend how surreal the situation was at the time: "It is quite unclear to me today why we absolutely had to complete *Tiefland* when everything was collapsing around us. It was senseless, barely comprehensible. Perhaps it was my Prussian sense of duty, but I wasn't alone in this, everyone else was doing the same."[68]

After Riefenstahl had been interrogated by American and French soldiers following the end of the war, she was expelled from Austria by the French military government, and all of the negatives for *Tiefland* were confiscated and taken to Paris by officers of the Section Cinéma. It would take eight years and a battle of nerves before the negatives were returned to her. Completing the film that had been nearly finished in 1945 became her idée fixe, not least because she had great hopes that *Tiefland* would prove to be her major comeback as a filmmaker. News that her property would be returned to her alternated with reports that all of the confiscated *Tiefland* negatives would be destroyed. With the support of highly placed French politicians and Henri Langlois, head of the Cinémathèque Française in Paris, she succeeded at the end of 1952 in getting the film rolls transferred from Paris to Vienna, as "German property in Austria."

The Austrian government assigned two trustees to the film, whom she had to deal with from that time forward. In Vienna, in the summer of 1953, with money from the sale of her villa in Berlin, she established Junta Film, together with her former collaborator, Guzzi Lantschner, in order to complete *Tiefland*. She concluded distribution deals with Allianz Film in Germany and with International Film in Austria, which brought her the funds necessary to lease cutting rooms. Only after she could prove that Plessner Film in Kufstein was a cooperative partner was she permitted to receive the fifty-two crates of film from Paris and have them sent to Munich. In sorting through the material, she determined that the rough edit of the film, completed before the war ended, had been disassembled in Paris, rendering the sound unusable. On top of this, four rolls of the original negative were missing. Despite extensive investigations, the irreplaceable material could not be located. So there was nothing left for her to do but to completely reedit and resynchronize the film.

Twenty years after Riefenstahl first planned the project, ten years after the last clapboard had sounded, the film finally completed its long odyssey and was premiered. The seventh film of Leni Riefenstahl made the *Guinness Book of World Records* as the film with the longest production time.[69] It premiered in Stuttgart on February 12, 1954, the only film of her career not to receive its world premiere at the Ufa-Palast am Zoo in Berlin.

The reviews of *Tiefland* attempted to be objective, dipping occasionally into the polemical, and for the most part avoided attacking Riefenstahl for her role in the Third Reich. The film was considered an anachronism, a relic from a vanished world. As a film of the forties and the last mountain film in cinema history, its stylized artifice did not suit the postwar period.

In contrast to *Das blaue Licht*, made under modest conditions, the unlimited possibilities that Riefenstahl was granted in making *Tiefland* were her undoing. One of the most expensive films of the Third Reich was panned as a melodrama "pregnant with meaning." The *Stuttgarter Zeitung* called the film "a textbook case of masterly and refined boredom, the images moving at the pace of a footsore snail."[70] Even before the film opened, the director herself must have realized that despite all the tricks that makeup, soft focus, and lighting could achieve, she could not pass in the role of a very young and seductive Gypsy, playing opposite Franz Eichenberger, twenty years younger: "When I saw myself on the screen, I was embarrassed. There was no doubt about it, I was miscast. How could I have made such a mistake?"[71] It was the end of Riefenstahl's acting career. *Tiefland*, the film that she had begun with great hope, became a monument to her failure.[72]

Once the film had earned back its production costs, she withdrew *Tiefland* from distribution: "I felt that the subject and style were long outdated."[73] Most German movie theater owners, at any rate, didn't dare schedule screenings of the film, not wanting to damage their own reputation by showing the new film by Hitler's favorite filmmaker. So *Tiefland* disappeared for decades into the private archives of the director, and only in the 1990s was it made available to the public again, in videotape format.

The attempt to send *Tiefland* to the Cannes Film Festival as the German entry for 1954 failed from the very beginning. The suggestion came from Jean Cocteau, president of the Cannes jury that year. An admirer of Leni Riefenstahl, whom he once had called the "genius of film," Cocteau had personally created the French subtitles for the movie. The German federal government rejected this request, however, as it wasn't prepared to promote the "filmmaker of the Führer" on an international stage. In addition, *Tiefland* in no way represented the films that were being made in the young Federal Republic of Germany. Leni Riefenstahl did not understand that a potential scandal had been avoided with this. She saw the rejection not as the logical consequence of her past involvement with the Nazi dictatorship but as a bitter personal affront: "I could expect nothing of the German government."[74]

On the subject of Leni Riefenstahl, *Tiefland* was not given any special notice for a long time—with the exception of the discussion surrounding the use of the Gypsy extras. Only at the beginning of the nineties did the film reemerge, with the largely unconvincing attempt to attribute to it a subversive significance. In connecting the plot of the film to the person and autobiography of the director, it was assumed that with her film, Riefenstahl had wished to contribute to the demise of the Nazi regime and call for the overthrow of Hitler. Don Sebastian, the "wolfish" autocrat played by Bernhard Minetti, was said to have been an incarnation of Hitler; Riefenstahl had reflected her own story in the dancer Martha, her involvement in a brutal dictatorship, and her pact with evil that at the end of the film was terminated with the murder of the tyrant. In 1990, the filmmaker Helma Sanders-Brahms was the first to thus interpret *Tiefland*: "The film not only tells the story of a Gypsy who becomes the lover of a tyrant and learns to hate the tyrant and wish for his death—it also tells the story, fairly openly, of Leni Riefenstahl, who served the usurper and became aware that she had given her talent, her art to the wrong person."[75] So the mask of melodrama was used to disguise a call to resistance.

There is no evidence or point of reference to support this audacious theory, and it should not be taken seriously. The film that the Nazi regime spent millions on and for which Riefenstahl enjoyed countless privileges cannot, even from a distance of several decades, be refashioned as an act of resistance critical of the regime. There is no credible evidence in Riefenstahl's biography that she inwardly distanced herself from Hitler before the Third Reich collapsed, or that she took a critical view of his regime. And most likely the director would have used the film in her own defense after 1945 had she intended the slightest criticism of the regime. But the project was initiated in 1934, a time when it cannot seriously be assumed that she would have wished for "tyrannicide."

In August 2002, a few weeks before her one hundredth birthday, the story of the *Tiefland* extras once again attracted attention worldwide. After Riefenstahl blatantly asserted in an interview in April of that year that she "had seen all of the Gypsies who had worked on *Tiefland* again, after the end of the war,"[76] the association Rom, Inc., of Cologne, which fostered cooperation between Roma and non-Roma, threatened to bring charges against her.[77] The star witness for Rom was seventy-six-year-old surviving extra Zaezilia Reinhardt, who was shocked by the disrespect Riefenstahl exhibited toward the memory of her many family members who had been murdered. In order to quell this highly unpleasant subject before her birthday celebrations, and at the advice of her attorneys, Riefenstahl declared on August 14, 2002, that she would never again assert that she had seen all of the Gypsy extras again after 1945.[78] Independently of this, the public prosecutor's office in Frankfurt instituted preliminary proceedings against Riefenstahl. The charges: denial of the Holocaust, sedition, and defamation of the memory of the dead. Within one month the charges were dropped and further prosecution abandoned. The prosecutor's office gave Riefenstahl's advanced age and the public's lack of interest in the prosecution of the case as the reason for its dismissal.

But as a result of the renewed discussion, two previously unknown accounts surfaced that demonstrated as no others before just how deeply Riefenstahl had been involved in the Nazi regime. During the filming of *Tiefland*, extra Anna Blach had been assigned to stand in for Riefenstahl in a horseback scene that had proved too dangerous for Riefenstahl herself. Riefenstahl was so satisfied with her work that she granted Anna

Blach a wish: after speaking with her mother, who also had been forced into service as a *Tiefland* extra, Anna Blach requested that her six siblings be released from concentration camps—her two sisters from the women's camp, Ravensbrück, and her four brothers from Dachau and Buchenwald. Alluding to the fact that it was difficult for her to communicate with Hitler in wartime, Riefenstahl promised Blach that at least one of her siblings would be freed. And indeed, at Riefenstahl's personal intervention, one of her brothers was released a few weeks later. But he was arrested again and, along with his siblings and parents, transported to Auschwitz, where he died. Anna Blach was also taken to the Gypsy section of the Auschwitz-Birkenau concentration camp following the conclusion of her work on *Tiefland* and was the sole member of her family to survive the Holocaust.

A further case, involving surviving *Tiefland* extra Rosa Winter, who at seventeen was chosen by Riefenstahl to work on the film, demonstrates that Riefenstahl not only had the power to have people released from concentration camps but could also arrange to have them sent there. When Rosa Winter discovered that her mother was to be sent from the "collection camp" of Maxglan to a distant concentration camp, she ran away from the *Tiefland* set, fearing she would never see her mother again. She was captured and sent to a prison in Salzburg. A short time later, Riefenstahl paid a personal visit to her cell, obviously expecting Rosa Winter to beg her forgiveness. But when the young Gypsy proved far too proud for that, Riefenstahl snarled at her, "You'll go to a concentration camp!" Shortly thereafter, Rosa Winter was sent to Ravensbrück. She, too, was the sole surviving member of her family, and today is able to bear witness to Riefenstahl's true degree of power during the Third Reich. Based on her own experience, Winter considers it impossible that Riefenstahl was unaware of what was going on in the camps, as the director incessantly asserted after 1945.[79]

Riefenstahl's disregard for human life during the shooting of *Tiefland* is astonishing. Apparently without any moral scruples, she exploited those persecuted by the Nazis' racial laws to her own advantage. The only thing that mattered to her was her film. Once filming was completed and her Gypsy extras were no longer of any use to her, she became totally uninterested in their fate. Nor was she interested in the fact that after

1945 the names of most of the *Tiefland* extras could be found on the lists of those who perished at Auschwitz. Until her death, Riefenstahl continued to insist that she had been a totally apolitical artist, but these two cases effectively prove that during this period she quite personally held power over the life and death of others.

# 13

## NOT IMMUNE AFTER ALL?

### RIEFENSTAHL AND ANTI-SEMITISM

AFTER THE WAR, Riefenstahl claimed that she had not taken Hitler's racist views, his ideas on the "superiority of the Aryan race," which were the core of *Mein Kampf*, seriously, adding that she had rejected them personally. "I totally rejected his racist ideas, that's why I could never have joined the NSDAP, whose socialist views I agreed with . . . Many people at the time believed that his racial doctrine was only a theory, nothing more than election propaganda."[1] She continued to maintain this into advanced old age. *Die Macht der Bilder* (1993), a documentary film on her life and career, ends with Riefenstahl's statement, "People always expected me to express guilt . . . Not one anti-Semitic word has ever crossed my lips, nor have I ever committed one to paper. I was never anti-Semitic, that's why I didn't join the party. So what have I got to be guilty about?"

However, following Hitler's seizure of power, the Nuremberg "racial laws" of 1935, and the Końskie massacre at the latest, even Riefenstahl must have grasped that the Nazis' persecution of the Jews served not merely as election propaganda but indeed was intended seriously.

At any rate, when Riefenstahl's persistent claims are weighed against statements made by her contemporaries, a different picture emerges. Not of someone who in the least supported the Nazi anti-Semitism that ended in genocide, but of a woman who, given her personal bias against Jews, hoped to profit from their exclusion from the German cultural industry.

Though Riefenstahl was faced with critical court proceedings throughout the last decades of her life, this central point, an indication of how truly political her career was during the Third Reich, was never systematically investigated. To do so would have been to posit several obvious questions: Could she have risen to the position of propagandist and film ambassador of a racist, anti-Semitic regime without at least accepting the racial biases of the Nazis? Did she simply ignore Hitler's fanatical, bigoted tirades against the Jews because she didn't want to acknowledge them; did she accept them without contradiction; or might she even have supported them to some degree?

Whatever the case, she turned to Hitler at a time when she was making openly anti-Semitic statements, as she was deeply offended by the bad reviews of *Das blaue Licht* in—according to her—the Jewish press. In 1976, Harry Sokal gave an account of Riefenstahl's May 1932 reaction: "A bad loser all of her life, she used the occasion of the negative reviews of her film to become a fervent anti-Semite overnight. Her long years of friendly relations with a huge number of Jewish people were forgotten."[2] Riefenstahl, in turn, declared Sokal's words to be "false to the core."[3]

Yet Sokal's account is confirmed by a number of other statements by her contemporaries, the most prominent being the highly respected film critic Rudolf Arnheim, now living in Ann Arbor, Michigan. Arnheim first met Riefenstahl two months before Hitler seized power and confirms that she made anti-Semitic comments in conversation with him. Before he emigrated, Arnheim was one of the major film theoreticians of the twentieth century and a leading cultural and media critic. He was one of the Weimar Republic's leading film critics, writing for Carl von Ossietzky's *Weltbühne*, among other publications.[4]

On November 3, 1932, as part of the regular Southwest German Radio Frankfurt broadcast "The Person in Front of the Lens," Arnheim conducted a twenty-five-minute conversation with Leni Riefenstahl, of which neither transcript nor audio recording survives.[5] Arnheim spoke for the first time about their encounter in 1999: "I became acquainted with Leni Riefenstahl during a series of interviews I conducted with German actresses and directors, and one day it was Leni Riefenstahl I interviewed. This was before the time of the Nazis . . . During our conversation she said to me, 'Do you know, as long as Jews are film critics, I'll never have a success. But you'll see, when Hitler takes the wheel everything will change.' That was perhaps five or six months before Hitler 'took the wheel.' It was a friendly talk, in no way acrimonious."[6]

At ninety-eight years of age, Arnheim remembered the encounter clearly but didn't see anything special in Riefenstahl's anti-Semitism, commenting that she was driven by the same racial prejudice that marked the majority of the German middle class of the time.[7] Yet Arnheim's recollection confirms that two months before Hitler came to power, Riefenstahl expressed exactly the anti-Semitism that she later, with good reason, tried to sweep under the rug.

Directly after the seizure of power, Riefenstahl discovered the consequences that this political development held for those who opposed the new regime or for those whom the National Socialists were displeased with for "reasons of race." In addition to her friend and patron Harry Sokal, many of her formerly large circle were forced to leave Germany due to their heritage or politics—because they could not or did not wish to live in a country ruled by Hitler. Béla Balázs, screenwriter and codirector of *Das blaue Licht*, left the country, and as a Jew and Communist was forced to remain in exile in Russia. Max Reinhardt, who once had hired her to dance at the Deutsches Theater, emigrated to America. Director G. W. Pabst, whom she had called a friend and whose direction of *Die weisse Hölle vom Piz Palü* elicited from her the best acting of her career, went to Hollywood in 1933.[8] And Erich Maria Remarque, her friend in the 1920s who had reputedly written sections of his novel *All Quiet on the Western Front* in her apartment,[9] was forced to leave Germany as well.

The Jewish director Josef von Sternberg, with whom Riefenstahl was associated at the beginning of the thirties, was no longer allowed to make films in Germany after Hitler came to power, and his masterpiece, *The Blue Angel*, was banned. Manfred George, a friend of Riefenstahl who was an editor at the Berlin paper *Tempo*, also emigrated to America, where he published the emigrant newspaper *Aufbau*.

In her memoirs, Riefenstahl depicts her reaction to her friends' departures. In the spring of 1933, returning to Germany from filming in Switzerland, she found her circle of friends significantly reduced. "My mail included a letter from Prague from my friend Manfred George, in which he wrote that, like many of his Jewish acquaintances, he had had to emigrate, because he could no longer work in Germany . . . I wept as I held the letter in my hands. I heard from more and more friends and acquaintances that they had left Germany . . . What kind of terrible things must have happened! I couldn't understand any of it. What was I to do?"[10]

Riefenstahl did nothing, other than selfishly trade her Jewish friends and patrons for new ones who held an NSDAP party book. In February 1937, she enthusiastically told a reporter from the *Detroit News*: "To me, Hitler is the greatest man who ever lived. He truly is without fault, so simple and at the same time possessed of masculine strength. He asks nothing, nothing for himself. He's really wonderful, he's smart. He just radiates. All the great men of Germany—Frederick the Great, Nietzsche, Bismarck—had faults. Nor are those who stand with Hitler without fault. Only he is pure."[11]

## "HERE YOU HAVE FOUND YOUR HEAVEN"
### RIEFENSTAHL AND JULIUS STREICHER

The clearest evidence that Riefenstahl was not as critical in the face of Nazi racial hatred as she later claimed is her consequent silence concerning her friendship with Julius Streicher, one of the Nazi era's most virulent anti-Semites. Streicher was gauleiter of Franconia, and he also published the anti-Semitic weekly newspaper *Der Stürmer*, whose message above all else was: "The Jews are our misfortune." Nevertheless, a friendship developed between Streicher and Riefenstahl—whom many party members avoided due to his unending anti-Semitic tirades and perceived as detestable—that was to last for the entire period of the Third Reich. Riefenstahl met Streicher in September 1933 at the latest, while filming her first Nuremberg party rally. Streicher, the "leader of Franconia," was one of those responsible for seeing to it that the rally was seamlessly organized.

When Riefenstahl met Streicher for the first time, she purportedly "got goose bumps" and asked him, "How can you publish a paper as terrible as your *Stürmer*?"[12] And yet she obviously had no problem meeting professionally and socially with a man of his reputation, who, according to witnesses, could not utter three sentences without mentioning the "international Jewish conspiracy." She personally invited him to Berlin for the world premiere of *Sieg des Glaubens*[13] and instructed him, as already mentioned, to represent her in the case of "the claims made against me by the Jew Béla Balázs."[14]

One year later, at the 1934 Nuremberg rally, the two met again. Streicher not only generously provided Riefenstahl with a magnificent house for her film crew, he also took care of all necessary support services, for which she expressly thanked him in her book *Hinter den Kulissen des Reichsparteitagfilms* (Behind the Scenes of the Reich Party Rally Film).[15] The newspapers reported that Riefenstahl did not leave Nuremberg until meeting Streicher for an "informal tea," where they had a relaxed chat.[16] When *Triumph des Willens* finally premiered, the director once again did not neglect to write to "dear Herr Streicher" and warmly invite him to Berlin: "You must be present on this day, otherwise it would make me sad. I'm still working day and night—but the film will be wonderful and I'm beginning to feel happy inside, because I think the film will be finished in just a few days. I enclose a copy of my book, which the Führer wrote so wonderfully about. In friendship, Yours, Leni Riefenstahl."[17]

In September 1935, as Riefenstahl was filming the short Wehrmacht film *Tag der Freiheit!* in Nuremberg, she again met with Streicher, who immediately called on her once Riefenstahl had moved with her team into their "film home." Hans Ertl, one of her cameramen, later recalled, "One of the first to visit us there, as master of the house in some sense, was Gauleiter Julius Streicher."[18]

By 1937, Riefenstahl and Streicher were addressing each other in the familiar *du* form. A letter from the gauleiter to the director, bequeathed to the Federal Archive in Berlin and which Riefenstahl later called a "forged document,"[19] provides a revealing look at the character of the relationship between the politician and the film diva:

Nuremberg, July 27, 1937

Dear Leni,

I must repeat it to you in writing as well: The hours we spent at your house were an experience for us all. With its creation you once again have confirmed what we all know inside: hallowed is the space set foot in by a good person! Those who wish to know you most profoundly must pass through the rooms of your house, and whoever has done so and taken leave of them without it having made an impression on his soul is without feeling and will never understand you or be able to interpret what you have created in all its greatness.

You, too, shall always be lonely, shall always remain, must remain, lonely. That is your fate as well. But it is also your fate to be surrounded by the unpretentiousness and naturalness of these simple people, and this fate is your good fortune.

Remain misunderstood by those who cannot understand, let them make jokes, let them make fun! Laugh and go your way, the way of a great calling. Here you have found your heaven and in it you will be eternal.

Yours,

Julius Streicher[20]

This letter, which Streicher wrote following his first visit to Riefenstahl's newly completed villa in Dahlem, was highly embarrassing to the director after 1945. For Streicher's letter contradicts statements she made during her first interrogation by the German Intelligence Service of the U.S. Army: "I had no contact with any other party functionaries [other than Hitler and Goebbels]; I saw them only occasionally at official events. I never received an invitation from a party functionary, and if I had I would have rejected it."[21] Julius Streicher's letter proves the opposite.

Riefenstahl even maintained contact with Streicher long after he had fallen out of favor with Hitler. Once it became apparent that he was involved in a corruption scandal and was proved that he had not transferred profits from the Aryanization of Jewish property to the Reich as ordered, a party court stripped him of his offices in February 1940 and banished him to his estate, Pleikershof bei Fürth.

In her memoirs, Riefenstahl records only one meeting with Streicher, during which she allegedly was critical of him.[22] In truth, as we have seen, she was friends with him from the beginning to the end of the Nazi regime. And as even Leni Riefenstahl could not maintain after 1945 that Streicher's anti-Semitism had escaped her, she simply kept silent on her personal contact with him.

## KNEW NOTHING?

Despite her contact with Hitler and Streicher, Riefenstahl claimed she knew next to nothing about the persecution of the Jews. The truth was otherwise. As early as the 1933 party rally, at which she was filming *Sieg des Glaubens*, Hitler's closing speech ended in a tirade against the Nazis' enemies at home and abroad, with the Jews topping the list. Even though Riefenstahl didn't include this speech in her film, she must have been confronted with it over and over again in the weeks that followed. As Claudia Lenssen established, "From today's point of view, it seems unbelievable that she didn't perceive the racism in the public speeches, for she had that material on her editing table for weeks."[23]

Additionally, a closer look at Riefenstahl's films reveals that she knew exactly what was going on. In *Triumph des Willens* she not only quoted Streicher's anti-Semitic message that "A people that does not respect the purity of its race will be destroyed," she also inserted shots of Streicher nodding in agreement as Hitler, in his closing speech, spoke of "the German nation's best racial quality."

According to her own statements, it was only later that she perceived what Jews in Germany had suffered: "On the one hand, I am grateful that [Hitler] protected me from my enemies, such as Goebbels and others, and that he regarded me so highly as an artist. But it angered and shamed me when I returned from the Dolomites in the fall of 1942 and saw in Munich, for the first time, how Jewish people were forced to wear the yellow star."[24]

But she had known much earlier what was going on in Germany and knew, above all, how the world was reacting to it. As opposed to the millions of Germans who were indoctrinated by the state press, Riefenstahl, on her visit to America in November 1938, had experienced directly how the Nazis' racial policies were received abroad. Her sole reaction was to deny what was going on in Germany.

There is no evidence that, due to her proximity to the regime, Riefenstahl knew more than others did about the mass annihilation of the Jews. But it is obvious that, like most Germans, she knew enough to be sure that it was better not to know even more. Without doubt, she was neither that naïve nor that devoted to her art alone. The various rumors that circulated about the crimes committed in the camps and the fate of the deported Jews would have been unavoidable.

Even though there is no record of what she thought about these things, it is known that she at least opposed Nazi policies on euthanasia, though this did not cause her to distance herself from the regime. The zoologist Bernhard Grzimek, who met Riefenstahl during the filming of *Tiefland*, reported in his memoirs that in the summer of 1942 he spoke with her in the Dolomites about the Nazis' program of euthanasia and about the forced sterilization of the sick and disabled, which Riefenstahl roundly rejected.[25]

Despite her closeness to the National Socialist regime, Riefenstahl held a largely individual opinion on the much-discussed "Jewish question." Like many high-ranking party functionaries she, too, acted according to the catchphrase "I will decide who is a Jew." As soon as the Jewish critics who once had so disparaged her directorial debut had been driven from Germany, and her career was secure and her fame no longer threatened, Riefenstahl seems to have had no further fear of contact. She stated that she continued to go to her Jewish doctors well into the thirties, until they emigrated, and shopped in Jewish stores, though this was highly disapproved of at the time. This earned her the criticism of Nazis faithful to the party line, but her privileged status prevented them from doing anything against her.

There were a few cases in the 1940s when Riefenstahl used her influence to help those who were being persecuted and save them from the worst. While filming in Kitzbühel, she was called on one day by a friend of Evelyn Künneke (not, as Riefenstahl later stated in her memoirs, by the cabaret performer herself),[26] whose father, Eduard Künneke, a famous composer and operetta director, had been expelled from the Reich Film Chamber for reasons of race. Künneke's wife, a well-known opera singer, was labeled a "half-Jew" according to the Nuremberg Racial Laws. Despite the pressure exerted on him, the composer resolutely refused to agree to a divorce and found himself forbidden to work and stripped of his means of support. Riefenstahl stepped in at Evelyn Künneke's request and wrote to Goebbels, who immediately set up a meeting.[27] A few days later the professional ban against Künneke was lifted—due to Riefenstahl's intervention alone, as Evelyn Künneke later confirmed.[28]

There were similar cases in which Riefenstahl used her position to help those who were in danger. The film historian Lotte Eisner, who emigrated in 1933 and considered herself a strong critic of the director, noted in her memoirs that Riefenstahl protected the Jewish wife of the production designer Robert Herlth from being arrested by the Gestapo. Herlth, responsible for creating the sets used in the prologue to *Olympia*, turned to Riefenstahl, who immediately saw to it that his wife remained unharmed, as Herlth related to Lotte Eisner after 1945.[29]

Riefenstahl also arranged for the Jewish wife of her onetime friend and press chief, Ernst Jaeger, who had emigrated to the United States, to be released from a concentration camp, as Jaeger reported after the war.[30] In the winter of 1944–45, Riefenstahl's former colleague Heinz von Jaworsky turned to her for help. He had been expelled from the Reich Film Chamber and humiliated by being drafted as a basic soldier when it was discovered that his grandmother was of Jewish heritage. But this time Riefenstahl's interventions failed and she could do nothing more than advise him to remain calm and not call attention to himself. Jaworsky survived the war.

That Riefenstahl cooperated with the regime and made films for the Führer while simultaneously coming to the aid of individuals who were being persecuted is part and parcel of the contradictions of her life, the dimensions of which are difficult to reconstruct in retrospect.

There is no question that it is to Leni Riefenstahl's credit that she used her influence in individual cases in a positive way and was able to help. She never talked about her motivations for this or mentioned her interventions in her own defense. But this is surprising only at first glance. Had she called more attention to her successful intercessions, it would have been an admission that she was well aware of the horrors of the concentration camps and the deportations and that her influence was far greater than she later wished to admit. Neither fact suited the image of the artist who lived only for her work and who knew nothing of the dark side of the regime that she served.

After 1945, motivated by self-protection, she labored to create the image of a woman who from the beginning was immune to the Nazis' racial madness. In truth, her oft-repeated litany "Never in my life was I an anti-Semite"[31] was totally calculated, a fact that Jewish emigrants then returning to Germany recognized immediately. Because Riefenstahl, despite the pose, never showed any regret, her former friends distanced themselves from her. In 1950, for example, when she again met her former patron Harry Sokal after he had returned to Germany to found a new film production company, she expressed no regret about what he had gone through and saw no reason to offer an apology. Sokal was not inclined to engage in a discussion with her: "When I returned to Germany in 1950 and met her in Munich, I quickly got the impression that she was still sad about having lost the Führer and the Thousand-Year Reich. I left without saying another word to her."[32]

Like many of those who once went along with the Nazis' racial policies, profited from them, agreed with them, or at the very least tolerated them, Riefenstahl after the war was constantly driven by the fear that she would encounter hostility and criticism based on her behavior. "I was never a Nazi, but the Germans from the concentration camps will be in power. I think there is much they will misunderstand."[33]

This fear of being "misunderstood," which in reality was the fear that her role in the Third Reich would be understood correctly, marked her thinking into advanced old age, not least because international Jewish organizations were relentlessly protesting against her and serving as a reminder of just which regime it was that she had served. When in 1994 she was invited to the Jerusalem Film Festival, where Ray Müller's film biography on her had won an award, she refused to attend, informing the festival's management that she would not be understood in Israel.[34]

Only when she was very old did Riefenstahl admit that "Hitler's terrible anti-Semitism was his downfall. He was like a lovely apple that, due to his hatred of the Jews, was rotten within."[35]

# The New Beginning

# 14

## COLLAPSE AND NEW BEGINNING, 1945

### COURT CASES AND SHATTERED HOPES

THE END OF THE WAR and the victory of the Allied Forces meant a major turning point for Leni Riefenstahl. Hitler's "Thousand-Year Reich," which she had glorified in her films, lay in ruins. The men she had conspicuously accompanied for years and developed special relationships with were dead or exposed as criminals whose politics had cost millions of people their lives. Suddenly, her life up until that point was totally called into question, and again and again she was confronted with questions about her past in the Third Reich. But as she was unprepared to take responsibility or express any guilt concerning what had occurred, all efforts she made toward her own rehabilitation failed.

The first postwar years were particularly difficult for Riefenstahl, because she once had been so open about her sympathy for the Führer and his regime that this could not be denied. Not only her films but also the photos capturing her in the relaxed and affable company of those in power had burned themselves deeply in the public memory. Unlike the majority of Germans, she could not merely disappear or lean back and talk of "the Nazis," because both inside Germany and abroad she was much too strongly identified with Hitler's regime and its criminal acts, which were in the process of being exposed.

At exactly what point Riefenstahl realized she had joined a dangerous game and how far-reaching the consequences might be is open to debate. Her former colleague Heinz von Jaworsky got the impression from her, in the winter of 1944–45, a few months before the war ended, that although Riefenstahl was convinced the war had been lost,[1] she remained loyal to the Führer nevertheless. But she did say that he was surrounded by criminals.[2]

Her depiction of the last months of the war is noticeably indifferent in her memoirs as well. On the one hand, she declared that she was totally preoccupied with completing *Tiefland* and worried about the fate of her husband. On the other, she continually made observations that reveal moments of concern and reflection, showing that she did indeed think about the scale of what had happened and also about the possible consequences to her personal life. "It seemed to me as if we were all on a ship that was slowly sinking in the tides."[3]

In Tirol, she wept when she heard that Adolf Hitler had "fallen in the battle for the Reich capital," as Hitler's suicide in the "Führer bunker" was disguised at the time: "I cannot describe what I felt at this moment. I was overcome by a frenzy of emotions—I threw myself onto my bed and cried all night."[4] Albert Speer, whose relationship to Hitler so noticeably paralleled that of Riefenstahl, reacted similarly. When he heard of Hitler's suicide, he broke down in tears next to a photo of the Führer. "My nerves were shot. As I propped up his picture I began to sob. That was the end of my relationship to Hitler, only then was the spell broken and his magic destroyed."[5]

Just like Speer, Riefenstahl reacted to Hitler's death and the demise of the Third Reich primarily in relation to her own life. At this moment she was much more interested in what would become of her career than in the fall of the National Socialist regime or the question of what responsibility she bore.

She was now forced to face a totally new experience, that of being suddenly abandoned by an entire population that had once held her in high esteem, admired, and even envied her, and that now turned to her in resentment and anger. All at once she was indicted for her artistry and her moral stance, and confronted with the necessity of having to justify her actions in the Third Reich.

If attention was paid to her, it was paid in a polemical fashion. One example was a newspaper article from the late forties titled "The Unavoidable One," which gives an impression of Riefenstahl in the first years after the fall of Hitler's regime:

Everyone was sleeping; only one woman kept waking up. And that was Leni Riefenstahl. This alone is evidence of the strength and energy every German woman must envy. Personally, I consider her show of stamina at the many celebrations held in the Reich Chancellory as a kind of athletic performance, impressive enough to be considered for a medal at the Olympic Games. Leni Riefenstahl's attorney wishes the same as I, that the truth will be spoken about Leni Riefenstahl's relationship to Hitler. For example, that Leni Riefenstahl was a frequent guest at Hitler's parties and receptions. If she attended them unwillingly, then she is a better actress than previously thought. For she always seemed truly thrilled to be among Hitler's closest circle. There was the film premiere, for instance, after which Hitler presented her with a bouquet of flowers. She was so moved by this that she fell to the floor in a faint; or at least fell to the floor. (Esteemed attorney: I say "moved," but perhaps she fainted because she found Hitler's presence intolerable . . .) At any rate, there are indications that Frau Riefenstahl did not exactly reject Hitler. The interior decorator who designed her apartment is prepared to testify—under oath—that she instructed him to place a comfortable armchair in her bedroom. "So that the Führer will be comfortable if he'd like to watch me as I fall asleep!" Frau Riefenstahl explained.

Let there be no misunderstanding: there is not the slightest reason to assume that Hitler wanted to do anything in Leni Riefenstahl's bedroom other than watch her fall asleep. And even that we have heard only from Frau Riefenstahl's own lips. Far be it from us to call her a liar. Rumors about a more intimate relationship doubtlessly are based on conjecture. There are many witnesses to the fact that Hitler never wanted anything from Frau Riefenstahl. Indeed, a whole group of people with whom Hitler was close would even be prepared to swear that he was a little afraid of her, and that he found her personally rather unlikable. Whereas she, on the other hand, left no stone unturned in staying as close to him as she could, pleading with his housekeeper and others to let her know when he had a free moment. But we've spent far too much time talking about Frau Riefenstahl.[6]

In the postwar period, Leni Riefenstahl tried in vain to present herself as a victim. And subjectively, there is no doubt that she perceived herself as such. She was incapable of comprehending that the animosity and pointed questions that were directed at her were a logical consequence of her devotion to Hitler and the National Socialists. As she increasingly came to believe in her own self-justifying statements and myths, she truly felt she was being unjustly persecuted, and the period following 1945 was a hell to her. Only in 1997 did she admit being able to comprehend the rejection she had encountered after 1945: "Actually, I saw my fate as justified, for I thought to myself: You deserved it, you believed in Hitler, and now you must suffer."[7]

## "WITHOUT RIGHTS AND ROBBED OF MY FREEDOM"

By April 1945, Leni Riefenstahl had already been arrested in Kitzbühel by American soldiers. Her earlier attempts to go into hiding—in Mayrhofen or at an inn in remote Tuxer Joch, for example—had failed, as no one wanted to risk harboring the Führer's director and confidante. On the day after the fighting ended in Tirol, a sergeant of the Sixty-fourth Division who was unfamiliar with the name Riefenstahl appeared at her home, where she lived with her colleagues and her mother, and requisitioned the spacious house for use by GIs. The director and her coworkers were then quartered at nearby Hörlahof, which previously had belonged to Hitler's foreign minister, Joachim von Ribbentrop.

A short time later, the screenwriter Budd Schulberg visited Riefenstahl, and one result of this visit was "Nazi Pin-Up Girl," a much-discussed article published in *The Saturday Evening Post*. He was in search of the original negatives of Riefenstahl's *Sieg des Glaubens* and *Tag der Freiheit!*, which he wanted to use as evidence against the war criminals being tried in Nuremberg. By this point, however, the films were no longer in Riefenstahl's possession, and since then have been considered lost. An official of the Party Chancellory of the NSDAP allegedly came to get them shortly before the end of the war. At their meeting, Riefenstahl explained to Schulberg that her films were not propaganda films but documentaries. She had been able to make these films, she stated, because

Hitler had been a great patron of artists and was himself a profoundly artistic individual.[8]

Obviously, by this time Riefenstahl had decided how she was going to depict her role in the Third Reich to the outside world, in order to remain as safe as possible. She did not deviate from this line at her first hearing, when questioned by officers of the U.S. Seventh Army. For this hearing she was taken from Kitzbühel to Dachau, where the Americans had set up an internment camp for prominent prisoners. Interned at the camp with Riefenstahl were Hermann Göring and two Hitler adjutants, Julius Schaub and Wilhelm Brückner. In addition there were those who had served the Führer as secretaries and housekeepers, and his personal photographer, Heinrich Hoffmann.

At Dachau, Riefenstahl was confronted not only with questions about her work during the Third Reich and her connections with the Nazi leadership but also with the truth about the concentration and death camps. When she no longer could close her eyes to the crimes of the regime she so willingly had served, she reacted with outbursts of screaming and sobbing, and the hearings repeatedly had to be postponed.

But as horrible as the truth was to her, she was not at this time prepared to accept that Hitler was responsible for what had happened. She believed that his corrupt subordinates, Goebbels, Bormann, and Himmler, were to blame for the Nazi terror and the genocide of millions of innocent people. They were the ones truly responsible, not the man whom she had admired and viewed as her idol.[9] Even decades later she called her confrontation with the truth about the genocide carried out by the Nazis during the interrogation at Dachau the worst event of her life. She had never been able to get the pictures she was shown there out of her head, she said.[10]

And yet the period during which she was questioned doesn't appear to have been totally negative. Despite the somewhat serious physical and psychological burdens, Riefenstahl was treated in a friendly manner on the whole. The atmosphere was even relaxed enough for the camp commander to invite her to tea several times, a fact confirmed by Christa Schroeder, Hitler's secretary, also interned at Dachau: "Saturdays the commander held small parties, to which Leni Riefenstahl, Annemarie Schauermann, Countess Czerniceck, Fräulein Müller, and Magdalene Wanderer were invited. They'd return only early the next morning."[11]

The confidential final report issued by the German Intelligence Service on May 30, 1945, reveals that directly after the war Riefenstahl had already come up with explanations for major parts of her story, which indicates that even before the demise of the Third Reich she had given very careful thought to which defense strategy would be most beneficial to her.

Every answer she gave to officers Hans Wallenberg and Ernst Langendorf during the days-long interrogation was calculated for damage control. Consequently, she consistently spoke of only one single party film she had made, the shooting of which was hindered and boycotted by leading Nazis. During the first interrogation she already was portraying Goebbels as her archenemy and denying all personal relationships or friendships with highly placed Nazi functionaries. And she claimed to have met with Hitler only on official occasions. She also stressed that she was a star before the Nazis came along and that she did not owe her career to their protection. Thus she owed gratitude to no one. In addition, she swore that she had received no financial backing from the regime. She had never been interested in money or fame; her only concern had always been artistic perfection: "I was my own boss, no one could tell me what I had to do. If I had received the impression that my artistic freedom would be restricted, I would have left the country."[12] That she attained this position only through Hitler's protection is something she did not mention to the U.S. officers.

Long after this version of events had been refuted by documents produced later, she continued to stick to her story. Even in old age she said, "My highest commandment is the truth. I do not lie. From the beginning. Earlier, I did this unconsciously. Later, I thought to myself: Why? It's greatly uncomfortable to lie. How quickly one contradicts oneself then."[13]

The German Intelligence Service's final report arrives at a judgment that is only partially correct:

One may believe her statements or not. Nevertheless, she gives the impression of honesty, and the fear that she expresses in terms of the regime and its Führer appears equally as honest. It is possible that she really didn't know what was going on around her.

That was her sin of omission, which appears all the worse because she, more than any other, had the opportunity to recognize the truth. She's a product of the moral corruption characteristic of that regime. But it would be wrong to view her as an ambitious woman who associated herself with the triumphs of the NSDAP for reasons of fame and prosperity. She certainly was not a fanatic National Socialist who sold her soul to the regime. Her admiration for Hitler closed her eyes to what the regime meant for Germany. His protection safeguarded her artistic activities, as opposed to those of so many others. In addition, he also protected her from the political climbers, allowing her to create a dream world in which she could live with "her art." Only occasionally did the reality behind this dream burst onto the scene. Given her lack of a moral stance, which occasionally showed strength and character, one might consider her behavior irrelevant. One fact remains, however. This moral stance apparently did not derive from opportunistic motives, but from the desire to continue dreaming her dream, to devote her life entirely to art. If what she said is true, she never comprehended, and does not comprehend even today, that in dedicating her life to art, she gave expression to a brutal regime and contributed to its glorification.[14]

Despite the skepticism the interrogating officers felt toward Leni Riefenstahl, she was released from Dachau on June 3, 1945, without further formalities and with a declaration stating that she was "exonerated." With this, she held in her possession a document certifying that after initial questioning there were no charges against her. She had nothing more to fear from the American occupying power. The fact that at these first interrogations she had extricated herself by retreating to her status as an apolitical and apparently irreproachable artist allowed her to hope that she now could continue with her career.

Much relieved to have gotten off so lightly, she returned to Kitzbühel, where she continued editing *Tiefland* at her home. During this period completing the film seemed to be the only thing that truly interested her, an impression also held by the American officers.[15]

One month after Riefenstahl was released from the American internment camp, the province of North Tirol, of which Kitzbühel was part, was placed under French occupation. With this, the certificates issued by the American occupation officials were rendered worthless, resulting in a number of interrogations and prison terms. This time, Riefenstahl was interned for a longer period, at the Innsbruck Women's Prison, among others, and at times placed under house arrest in Kitzbühel.

This back-and-forth between arrests and release had much to do with the fact that Riefenstahl was caught in the power struggle between the nationalistic French military government and the more Communist-oriented police force, the Sûreté. The two groups disagreed on how the prominent filmmaker was to be treated. In retrospect, the constant interrogations by the French military government appeared to her as a period of pure "arbitrariness," "chicanery," and "spiritual torture."[16]

During this period, the German public heard next to nothing of the fate of Leni Riefenstahl, which soon led to rumors about her whereabouts. Albert Speer, together with many of his ministry colleagues, was interned at the Kransberg Castle outside Bad Nauheim in September 1945 and questioned about the technical aspects of the war. He reported that the speculation had nothing to do with reality, as the internees without exception were treated well and civilly. "There were stories circulating that we were mistreated, were given nothing to eat. Rumor had it that Leni Riefenstahl was languishing in a dungeon."[17]

Bertha Riefenstahl, the director's mother, arranged for her daughter to be released and allowed to return to Kitzbühel in the interim periods, where she took care of her.

Behind the scenes, meanwhile, Riefenstahl's fate was being debated. Her transfer from the Austrian to the German occupation zone, which also was controlled by the French, was planned for the beginning of August 1945, though initially it was prevented. But in April 1946, when the Communist daily L'Humanité published a photomontage that showed her in the arms of French military commander Antoine Bethouart, whom Riefenstahl claimed never to have met personally, she was immediately expelled from the Austrian zone and sent to the German occupation zone of the French army.

The French military government, to which she continued to be subject, ordered her taken to Königsfeld bei Villingen, to a settlement of

Moravians who had willingly collaborated with the Nazis during the Third Reich and who therefore were under close guard by the French army. She was assigned a two-room apartment at Friedrichstrasse 24 and once a week had to appear before the French police. Despite the peaceful atmosphere of the small Black Forest community, she felt "without rights and robbed of my freedom."[18] As the French army had seized her villa in Kitzbühel, her assets, and also her private bank account and that of her production company (for a total of 330,000 marks),[19] as well as all of the film material for *Tiefland*, she lived with her mother and husband on a bare subsistence. It would take her years to have her confiscated property returned to her, including her villa in Dahlem.

Until 1948, Riefenstahl lived in Königsfeld in extremely reduced circumstances, always attempting to get back her personal property, the *Tiefland* material in particular, so that she could finish the film and earn money from it. Due to the stress of this period, all the infirmities that had plagued her during the filming of *Tiefland* returned, including her deep depression.

The first postwar Olympic Games took place in 1948, at which she was to be presented with the Olympic Diploma that had been awarded to her shortly before the outbreak of the war. But she did not receive permission to travel, and the diploma was mailed to her instead. Holding it in her hands she must have felt, among other emotions, scorned. Living in poor conditions in the Black Forest, fighting to have her property returned to her, the award was a reminder of her past triumphal march through Europe. As she wrote to her former cameraman Richard Angst, "I have accepted the fact that everything that I created is lost, once and for all. I have nothing and am living . . . in great poverty—I have no hope that I will be able to work again in the future. And almost all of my friends have abandoned me—it is truly a bitter end to a life."[20]

## SCENES FROM A MARRIAGE

The relationship between Leni Riefenstahl and Peter Jacob, which from the beginning had oscillated between moments of great happiness and total disillusionment, did not survive the early years after the war. From their first meeting, their love affair, not atypical for the war years, was subject to major interruptions. And apparently it was precisely these periods of long separation that kept their love alive for so long. Whereas their brief times together were always marked by conflict and tension, after which Riefenstahl repeatedly considered separating from Jacob, the letters that her fiancé and future husband wrote to her from the front always persuaded her that the relationship could be saved. As the war was coming to an end, however, it became clear that the marriage long since had failed.

Despite the fact that Jacob cheated on her again and again, she couldn't bring herself to divorce him. And in the period after the war, when countless people had turned away from her and she had no one other than her mother and a few former associates who remained loyal to her, she couldn't imagine life without him. Added to this was the fact that at this point she had no money of her own and depended on the wages her husband earned at a wine shop in Villingen to buy food for her mother and herself. So there was nothing left for her but to continue living in extremely cramped circumstances with a husband she loved more than all else but who continually humiliated and disappointed her: "He did many things that caused me much suffering. Our fondness for one another was increasingly turning into a love-hate relationship, but circumstances were such that we couldn't attempt even a separation."[21]

For a long time she vacillated between her great love for Jacob, a love she hadn't felt for any man since Hans Schneeberger in the twenties, and the knowledge that he would never be faithful to her. Unable to come to a decision, she fell into a deep depression. But the situation became more and more intolerable, and she separated from her husband in the early summer of 1947. Shortly thereafter she suffered a nervous breakdown and was taken to a psychiatric clinic in Freiburg for treatment. When she was released in August and returned to Villingen, Peter Jacob informed her that their divorce had been finalized in the interim. Leni Riefenstahl retained the name Helene Jacob on her passport.

Although she knew that the relationship, problematic from the start, did not have a future, it took her a long time to completely separate from Jacob, even after the divorce. She remained friends with him until 1952, always aware that the relationship was not good for her. Jacob supported her during this period in every way possible. He gave her the money he earned, stood at her side through the denazification proceedings, and testified on her behalf in court cases, including the one involving the *Tiefland* extras.

But their attempt to start over again with each other failed. The pain caused by his betrayals and the declarations of love that alternated with humiliating rejections were harder to bear than the animosity she encountered from others. She took it as a personal defeat that ten years after the failure of her relationship with Schneeberger, her second serious attempt at a long-term relationship had ended. It took her almost ten years after the separation from Peter Jacob to get over the painful experience.[22] In retrospect, true to her proclivity for melodrama and myth, she described not only her career but also her private life from childhood on as one single struggle. Just as, in her own mind, she was the perpetually misunderstood artist who created her art only at great personal sacrifice, virtually "out of pain," so was any success in her private life the product of great struggle and adversity. "My entire life consisted of opposition. My own rule for myself was never to give up. How else could I have survived this life."[23]

She portrayed her love life as a struggle for affection and recognition, which in the end no man could truly give her. Here, too, there is a huge chasm between self-perception and reality, for with the exception of her painful relationships with Froitzheim, Schneeberger, and Jacob, Riefenstahl was the one who chose the men she had affairs with throughout her life. And if one believes the statements of her contemporaries, these affairs conformed exactly to Riefenstahl's requirements: she sought out the men, bestowed favors upon them, and then decided when the relationship was over. But Riefenstahl herself never commented on the many brief liaisons she had with camera crew and others who worked with Arnold Fanck.

By 1933, she was functioning in a man's world as an ambitious career woman and solo performer. The rumors that circulated about her love life and her casual sexual relationships—Walter Frentz, one of her closest collaborators, called her a "man-eating plant,"[24] and Heinz von Jaworsky, who had known Riefenstahl since 1930, said that she was a "nymphomaniac"[25]— made it difficult for Riefenstahl to form a serious relationship.

The course of her life corresponded almost exactly with the resolution she had made as a young woman in the face of her parents' disastrous marriage: never to subjugate herself to a man and always to go her own independent way. Paradoxically, Froitzheim, Schneeberger, and Jacob, men who could and did stand up to her and who didn't automatically obey her, were those with whom she became involved in intense and obsessive relationships. The woman who was otherwise so self-confident and power conscious, who revealed no weaknesses when it came to her career, who always maintained her financial independence, lost control in these relationships. She became emotionally dependent in a way that even she described as subjection,[26] and so she unconsciously repeated the pattern set by her parents, which she had been determined to avoid.

She was far ahead of her time in the way she saw her role in life. This doomed her desire for an equal partnership and seemed to be the reason that she plunged almost masochistically into needy relationships that were difficult for her to extricate herself from. Her admission that "I feel like a woman and think like a man"[27] and "I am one hundred percent a man and one hundred percent a woman,"[28] confirm that ultimately she desired something that was unattainable.

The fact that she entered into a long-term relationship and finally even a marriage with Jacob was due to her situation at the time. At the beginning of the forties, for the first time since she originally appeared in public as a dancer, she encountered the extremely bitter experience of being dissatisfied with her work. *Tiefland* was connected with so many setbacks and disappointments that she not only reacted with psychosomatic illnesses but also, breaking her own vow to herself, escaped into a relationship that went much further than her other affairs.

But in the end, even Peter Jacob had problems with the way she repeatedly and unconditionally threw herself into her career. "I was too tied up with my work. The men simply felt that I put it ahead of everything."[29] For her entire life Riefenstahl was so strongly and uncompromisingly fixated on her career that she always ended up choosing her profession above all else. It was more important to her than any relationship.

Leni Riefenstahl never desired a family and children, at least she never expressed this desire publicly. When asked by journalists if she had ever wanted to have children, she always brusquely replied that she saw her films as her children. Following the painful divorce from Peter Jacob, it would take Riefenstahl almost twenty years, until she was in her mid-sixties, before she entered into a new relationship, one that would become the longest of her life.

### EXONERATED?

Just like millions of other Germans in the period following the war, Leni Riefenstahl had to submit to a denazification proceeding. But in the end, the "denazification" of Germany was an illusion. The desire of the Allies to reeducate Germans and make them accountable for their involvement in the Third Reich was soon replaced by the emerging realpolitik. Even those who had been deeply involved in the National Socialist regime were allowed to participate in rebuilding the country, in the economic and political spheres as well as in the educational and judicial systems. The denazification proceedings did not prevent formerly zealous Nazis from going underground or from being cleared of wrongdoing through false statements and *Persilscheine*, certificates that absolved them of unlawful activity.

The denazification tribunals were of particular significance to Leni Riefenstahl because their decisions would determine whether or not she would be permitted to continue to work or have her property and the *Tiefland* materials returned to her by the French authorities. The director quickly realized that it was important for her to portray herself in the proceedings as an apolitical artist and to play down or, better yet, deny the privileges that she had enjoyed in the Third Reich. Her only chance was to keep her true involvement from being made public.

From 1948 to 1952, a total of four tribunals investigated the extent to which Riefenstahl had supported and profited from the Nazi regime. Three times she was judged "not to be in violation of the law" and once to be a "follower." This was because many of the documents available today, which could have been used to refute Riefenstahl's statements, were not available at the time. On top of this, her testimony was supported under oath by former colleagues who had made their careers in

Riefenstahl's shadow during the Third Reich and who now appeared as witnesses for the defense out of loyalty to her. As none of the judgments prevented her from working, Riefenstahl could live with them.

Others who also had been involved with the Nazis were not as lucky. Emmy Göring, for example, was judged to be a "major offender," and Hitler's friend Winifred Wagner was an "offender." Those in these categories or that of the "lesser offender" had to deal with far-reaching consequences, such as being prohibited from working or having their assets seized or being required to perform reparation labor. Being sentenced to a work camp for a period of ten years was the most extreme measure of compensation in the denazification process. Riefenstahl's colleague Heinrich Hoffmann, who in his role as Hitler's photographer was considered an accomplice of the dictator, in addition to being involved in the National Socialist theft of art, was sentenced to four years in prison and prohibited from working for five years. Despite the general danger of being elevated to a higher category of involvement, Riefenstahl appears from the beginning to have reckoned on receiving a milder sentence, which turned out to be correct.

But at the beginning this looked quite different. Before each hearing the press repeatedly and consciously worked against Riefenstahl receiving such a mild sentence by pointing to her involvement in the Third Reich and revealing background information on her career in Nazi Germany unknown until then. Riefenstahl cleared the first denazification tribunal without great difficulty, however, and without having to defend herself against concrete attacks by the press. Referring to the fact that the director had never been a member of the NSDAP or any of the party's organizations, the tribunal, after hours of agitated discussion, delivered the mildest sentence possible and on November 5, 1948, declared that Leni Riefenstahl was "not in violation of the law" and not to be placed into any of the denazification categories.[30] The German press reacted to the judgment with anger. Increasingly it became clear that it was above all the "little" people who were most adversely affected by the denazification proceedings, whereas those who had truly profited from the regime—such as Riefenstahl—got off easily.

In addition to the press, the French military government protested against the lenient judgment of the Villingen tribunal and appealed the court's decision, so Riefenstahl had to go through another denazification proceeding. Six months later, on July 6, 1949, this second court convened before the Tribunal of the Baden State Commissioner's Office for Political Expurgation, in Freiburg.

A few weeks before this second hearing, in order to prevent another mild verdict, the illustrated magazine *Revue*, which in the early postwar years had quickly become Riefenstahl's chief adversary, published the first accusations that in *Tiefland*, Riefenstahl had used "film slaves" chosen from concentration camps and forced to work for her. Not only did this cause a major public reaction, it also created difficulties for her in court. She had to respond to every rumor circulating about her and was not permitted to engage a lawyer.

Yet once again Riefenstahl knew how to appear so convincing that her anecdotes and protestations were believed. She simply dismissed the incriminating telegrams she once had sent to Hitler as forgeries. The accusations of the *Tiefland* extras she declared to be unfounded. The verdict, once again, was "not in violation."[31]

But Riefenstahl's denazification process remained incomplete. The press published new documents that proved that the truth prior to 1945 was not what Riefenstahl would have had the tribunal members believe. The French authorities were not willing to accept that the Freiburg tribunal had come to the same conclusion as the Villingen tribunal, despite its more exhaustive examination of her role in the Third Reich, and again objected to the judgment, necessitating yet another tribunal. But this time Riefenstahl was not questioned. On December 16, 1949, the Baden State Commissioner's Office for Political Expurgation, in Freiburg, conducted the third denazification proceeding in the case of Leni Riefenstahl. Sensitive to the objections raised by the French military government, the judges came to the conclusion that although she had not been a party member, Riefenstahl had made propaganda films for Hitler and therefore had been active in the Nazi regime, thus incriminating herself. The second Freiburg tribunal therefore ruled that Riefenstahl, in absentia, was a "follower."[32]

Though "follower" was not in keeping with the way she portrayed herself, an image she increasingly believed in, she reacted to the third judgment with practical optimism. In her memoirs she responds with the simple comment, "That was preferable to me as well."[33]

Following the successful conclusion of the proceedings, in early 1950 she was finally allowed to leave the French occupation zone and move to Munich with her mother. As the decision of the denazification authorities in the French zone had no validity in Berlin, her villa in Dahlem remained under seizure; even after years of investigation, it was still unclear how she had financed the house in 1936. The rumors that Hitler had presented her with the villa as recompense for *Triumph des Willens* refused to go away.[34] To arrange for the release of the confiscated house, which had been badly damaged by firebombs, Riefenstahl saw no recourse but to appear in Berlin before a fourth and final tribunal. The Berlin tribunal took place on April 21, 1952, and upheld the judgments of the first two denazification proceedings in Villingen and Freiburg, absolving Riefenstahl of complicity.

As with the Freiburg tribunal three years earlier, the press attempted to hinder the anticipated mild verdict through new reports of scandal. A short time before the hearing began, *Revue* again published accusations that Riefenstahl was deeply incriminated and again questioned her image as an allegedly apolitical artist. For the first time, it published the photos of Leni Riefenstahl the war reporter, who had been an eyewitness to the massacre in Końskie. But those who had worked with her unanimously confirmed her defense statements, and she was able to convince the judges otherwise. At this point in time, proof supporting the story published by *Revue* was lacking. At the end of the eight-hour proceedings, the judges of the Berlin tribunal came to the conclusion that Riefenstahl had successfully refuted all of the accusations brought against her. Once again she was found to be "not in violation of the law."

Riefenstahl could now take possession of her property in Berlin. She sold the Dahlem villa in 1953 and invested the proceeds in finishing *Tiefland*, living in the interim in Munich, in relatively modest circumstances. Together with her mother, she occupied a four-and-a-half-room apartment on the sixth floor of a new building at Tengstrasse 20, in Schwabing. In order to afford the rent, Riefenstahl at first had to sublet several of the rooms. Munich quickly became her new hometown: "Freed from the proceedings, from prisons and slander, I recuperated day by day."[35]

The start of a new life, which, after her successful denazification process, she surely imagined would be simpler, was not to be so easy.

Again and again the shadow of the past caught up with her, and new and sometimes slanderous rumors emerged about her role in the Third Reich. Thus unable to establish herself in German postwar society, she comforted herself with the "fan letters" that reached her from abroad, where her films were being shown at many universities. In Germany, a public showing of her work was unthinkable.

## SEDUCED OR SEDUCTRESS?

Like many Germans of her generation, Leni Riefenstahl had a difficult time coming to terms with her past after 1945. She no longer wished to recall the enthusiasm with which she had glorified National Socialism during the Third Reich. She repeated like a mantra that she had been pushed, almost forced, to make her films, that she had been unable to refuse Hitler's orders and massively hindered in her work by Goebbels and other party functionaries.

Those who were familiar with the pictures that showed a laughing Leni Riefenstahl at Hitler's side and who had seen in movie theaters how the director had elevated Adolf Hitler to the role of charismatic Führer were not prepared to believe her empty assertions. In Riefenstahl they did not see someone who had been seduced, as she tried to present herself, but rather they saw a seductress.

Because the majority of Germans, who in one way or another were involved in the power structure of the Third Reich, were not willing to face their own uncomfortable and shameful past, they sought out personalities who would become stand-ins for the responsibility the German *Volk* shared in what had transpired. Questions that one avoided oneself were directed at those well-known public figures of the Third Reich who had survived, as it was generally believed that, given their proximity to power, these people must have known more. Rainer Rother describes the phenomenon this way: "What 'we could not have known' must have been known by others who were more powerful, more influential, or more famous."[36]

As much as Riefenstahl declared otherwise, she was seen as a political artist, a careerist who had become involved in a dangerous power game and who, after the war ended, was justifiably met with hostility and marginalization. Even if the many court cases and denazification tribunals were decided in Riefenstahl's favor, the collective memory of the German people blamed her for her earlier actions and her public image.

Riefenstahl's inability to distance herself from the role she played in the Third Reich determined the debate about her and her work during the postwar years. She turned a deaf ear to all criticism and deflected every rebuke. This reflected her personality, on the one hand, as she had never been able to view her own actions in an objective, self-critical way. On the other hand, this doubtless also had to do with the fact that Riefenstahl was unwilling to accept criticism, in terms of her enthusiastic involvement with Hitler, from other Germans, the majority of whom had supported Hitler and profited from the Nazi regime. She justifiably found it hypocritical that the same Germans who once also had believed in Hitler were now attacking her, and that committed Nazis, or at least those who had sympathized with the regime, were now claiming to be democrats overnight.

Unlike Albert Speer, who dealt with the same issue in a way that he as well as others could live with, Leni Riefenstahl was unable to face the attacks in a similarly confident manner and admit responsibility—as Speer did—and instead concealed the true degree of her own involvement. But she was no intellectual skilled in strategy. Rather, she stuck to the stories she had concocted, long after they had been disproved.

In contrast to the many filmmakers who reestablished themselves relatively quickly after 1945 and were able to continue their careers almost uninterrupted, Riefenstahl remained an outcast—permanently. Even if her having been made a "collective scapegoat" had more to do with the state of postwar German society than with the role she had played in the Third Reich, one cannot take seriously the view that Riefenstahl had been "stoned with words."[37] Despite such claims, the questions about her connection to the Nazi regime were justified, no matter what motivated them. Until the end of her life she never showed any willingness to honestly confront her past, and so there could never be a reconciliation between Riefenstahl and the German people.

The psychoanalyst Margarete Mitscherlich came to this conclusion:

Many things fell apart, but not Leni Riefenstahl. Up until today she wears an invisible armor, apparently without an Achilles heel.

Anyone who tries to confront the most gifted propagandist of the master race with the fact that she perhaps had done her part to contribute to the mass hysteria of "holy Germany," and in doing so shared responsibility for the mass suffering that this unholy Reich brought about, merely provokes rage in her, but never the grief and memory work that could lead her to self-knowledge and atonement . . . Though she had much in common with them, Riefenstahl is not a typical representative of typical German repression and denial. She is much more a superdenier, obsessed with a masculine madness, someone who possesses an above average ability not to remember what she doesn't want to remember.[38]

## LAWSUITS CONCERNING RIGHTS AND HONOR

Nothing marked Riefenstahl's postwar life more than the countless lawsuits she filed to defend herself against rumors, to fight for the rights to her films, and, above all, to have her version of her life story accepted as the accurate one. Riefenstahl claimed to have won more than fifty lawsuits. Though she admitted that "even dealing with judicial issues made me ill,"[39] charge followed upon charge. The first suits she conducted in 1948 as "legal aid" cases were based on the experience of her tribunal proceedings. At all costs she wanted to invalidate certain statements the press had made in its attempt to weaken her position before the denazification authorities.

The cases that drew the most attention were the lawsuits brought against the publishers of *Revue*, which she conducted, as she declared at the time, "to protect her honor and defend herself against major professional and financial damages."[40] In addition to these concrete cases, there were repeated attacks by scandalmongering journalists, some of whom attempted to destroy her reputation by insinuating that she had enjoyed intimate relations with Hitler or other Nazi functionaries, rumors to which Riefenstahl was particularly sensitive.

All of the lawsuits that Riefenstahl instigated during the period after the war intended to use civil law to prevent journalists, authors, and filmmakers from creating works that she saw as a defamatory. At first she introduced the suits primarily because the negative headlines threatened to influence the decisions of the tribunals. But later it became increasingly important to her to create a certain image of herself. After that, Riefenstahl reacted with a lawsuit whenever voices were raised that seriously questioned her version of things.

Soon it was no longer merely a matter of using the lawsuits to adjust and control her image with the public, but also to secure the commercial rights to her films from the Third Reich, *Triumph des Willens* and *Olympia*, in order to be able to continue to profit from works she had made at Hitler's instruction and with funds from the NSDAP or the German Reich. One spectacular case was against the Swedish company Minerva-Film. In 1960, Minerva produced the documentary *Mein Kampf*, by the German filmmaker Erwin Leiser, who had used roughly three hundred forty meters (less than fifteen minutes) of material from Riefenstahl's *Triumph des Willens*. Minerva had purchased a copy of the propaganda film and the rights to it from the State Film Archives of the German Democratic Republic. Riefenstahl, infuriated that the material had been used without her approval and financial participation, found this to be a "serious copyright infringement" and "intellectual theft."[41] Minerva rejected Riefenstahl's claim to a share of the profits and did not recognize her rights to *Triumph des Willens*. Unimpressed, the director lay claim to all German and international rights to the film and, according to newspaper reports, demanded that Minerva grant her 100,000 deutsche marks[42] from the earnings of *Mein Kampf*. The Swedish film company argued that Riefenstahl had never owned the rights to *Triumph des Willens*, as she had produced the film for the NSDAP and therefore the rights lay with the party and, after 1945, with the party's legal successors.[43] Counter to Riefenstahl's claim that she collected 80,000 marks, neither Minerva nor Erwin Leiser paid the director anything. But Riefenstahl intimidated the German and Austrian distributors of the film to the point that they paid her 40,000 marks.[44]

The suit against Minerva was brought by Friedrich A. Mainz, the former director of Tobis.[45] At the beginning of 1950, Mainz had written a check to Riefenstahl for 10,000 marks—which enabled her to rent her apartment in Schwabing—so that Riefenstahl, at the advice of her attorneys, would make him her chief creditor and transfer to him the rights to screen the film.[46]

The fact that after 1945 the leading Nazi propagandist continued to want to profit from her notorious propaganda film was met with irate criticism. On December 11, 1960, the *Berliner Morgenpost* published the disparaging remark, "So Leni Riefenstahl saw the film *Mein Kampf*. She did not go home in silence and shame. She was reminded of the glorious hours she spent at the crank of the brownshirts' camera—raking it in. Filthy lucre." The lawsuit concerning the issue of who held the commercial rights to Riefenstahl's films lasted for close to ten years, until January 10, 1969, when the German Federal High Court, after careful examination of documents obtained from the Federal Archive in Coblenz and the German Institute for Film Studies in Wiesbaden, ruled in the third instance that the NSDAP, not Leni Riefenstahl, was the holder of the rights to *Triumph des Willens*, and therefore the Federal Republic of Germany was to administer these rights. The statutory declarations submitted to prove the opposite were rejected by the court as not credible.[47]

Leni Riefenstahl considered the court's decision in favor of the Swedish production company to be unjust, a politically motivated "misjudgment," and explained her disagreement with Erwin Leiser as follows: "Leiser was horrible. He was a Jew and full of hate and maybe he thought the same things about me that the others thought."[48] Even many years later she spoke of Erwin Leiser as her "intimate enemy."[49]

Though the German Federal High Court had deprived her of the right to share in the earnings of *Triumph des Willens*, Riefenstahl found a way behind the scenes to do just that. On January 16, 1964, five years before the court's decision, she signed an agreement with Transit-Film Distribution, which, at the authorization of the Federal Republic of Germany, administered the film legacy of the Third Reich, with the Federal Republic functioning as sole partner. The agreement, which the two parties agreed to keep secret, guaranteed that for every screening of *Olympia*, the rights to which still were not clear at the time, Leni Riefenstahl would receive 70 percent of the take, and Transit would receive 30 percent. In addition, every public screening of the film required her approval, so she had control over where and under what conditions her film could be shown.[50]

Five years later, after the German High Court had rendered its judgment concerning *Triumph des Willens*, this agreement was upheld, and five

years after that, in 1974, Riefenstahl was granted the same rights regarding *Triumph des Willens* that she was awarded for *Olympia*. This despite the
fact that the Federal Film Archive, following a lengthy investigation,
had come to the conclusion that the films Riefenstahl had made between
1933 and 1945 had not been produced by her, but by the NSDAP or the
Reich.[51] The agreements were valid for thirty years, after which the commercial rights were to revert to Transit alone. When the *Olympia* agreement expired in 1994, it was secretly extended so that Riefenstahl could
continue to profit from both films until her death. Though the two films
were declared to be property of the state, the German Federal Government and the Federal Ministry of the Interior relinquished their claim as
the films' sole owner, to Riefenstahl's advantage.

The film scholar Rainer Rother surmised that the reason for the pro-
visions of these secret behind-the-scenes agreements, which resolved the
contentious copyright issues in Riefenstahl's favor, was political expedi-
ency. By granting Riefenstahl the rights to her films, undeservedly and
against the finding of the Federal High Court, it was assured that at least
until the director's death responsibility for the controversial films could
be avoided. Until she died, Riefenstahl collected 70 percent of the proceeds of every screening.[52]

The secret agreement, honored for decades and counter to the ruling
of the German High Court, should have created a scandal, and yet it was
barely publicly acknowledged. It was impossible to get information on
this delicate legal issue from either of the participating parties. Today the
Film Archive of the Federal Archive matter-of-factly refers those who
wish to screen Riefenstahl's films from the period of the Third Reich
either to Leni-Riefenstahl Film[53] or to Transit-Film.[54] The latter, in turn,
explains that "for reasons of stipulated confidentiality, no information"
can be provided[55] and—in an irony of history—refers all questions of
commercial use to Leni Riefenstahl Productions.


### FAILED FILM PROJECTS


The certificate of nonobjection issued to Leni Riefenstahl by the Berlin
Tribunal in 1952 wasn't of much use to her in postwar Germany. She

could no longer work as a director, but, contrary to Riefenstahl's repeated intimations, it cannot be said that there was a "ban on her work."

Though at first she had assumed that she could simply pick up her directing career without any great problem, she soon realized how hard it was to find financiers and partners who were prepared to work with her. And often the offers she did receive were later retracted, once the press published new sensational reports on the alleged "Führer's paramour" or when it became clear that Riefenstahl's work method soon would break the budget.

So for Leni Riefenstahl, the fifties and sixties were a time of countless failed or unrealized projects. Between 1953 and 1963, a total of thirteen feature and documentary film projects were not completed. Only two of them reached any sort of concrete phase, but they, too, failed. From Riefenstahl's point of view, this was due to the press's "slander campaigns" and "unjustified criticism," and to attacks by her "enemies," who were responsible in the end for the demise of each of her failed projects. Although after the tribunal and denazification proceedings she was officially allowed to work again, Riefenstahl maintained that constant "aspersions" made this impossible: "I had . . . written and prepared a great number of film scripts. And each time they were destroyed at the last minute by these reports in the press."[56]

In addition to her negative image, her overweening ambition, her perfectionism, and her unpredictable work habits scared away many producers, something the director didn't want to see or at least didn't want to admit. At any rate, there was never the concerted "boycott" that Riefenstahl always insisted there had been. The failure of her plans had its own history.

Her initial film projects after the war were developed in Italy. As German animosity toward her showed no sign of subsiding, she gladly accepted the invitation of the Italian film producer Alfredo Panone[57] to come to Rome in 1950. Certainly she hoped Italians would accept her more than her fellow Germans. In the summer of 1950, her hair now dyed a titian red, she arrived in Rome. Having escaped the impoverished circumstances under which she had been living in Germany, Riefenstahl appeared visibly happier and freer in Italy. No one talked to her about the past; everyone greeted her in a friendly and sympathetic manner: "Blue skies, balmy weather, and smiling people allowed me to forget the gray-ness I had left behind in Germany . . . After a long creative drought I was full of ideas."[58]

The Italian press reported on her new projects positively and in detail. Whereas in Germany almost no one wanted to associate with her, Italian celebrities enjoyed being photographed with her and gave her the feeling for the first time since the war that resuming her career was possible. She met Countess Edda Ciano, Mussolini's daughter, and Roberto Rossellini, the star director of the neorealist movement, who was particularly enthu-siastic about *Das blaue Licht.* The actors Vittorio De Sica, Gina Lollo-brigida, Anna Magnani, and Jean Marais; the writer Tennessee Williams; and the musician Carl Orff introduced themselves as well.

But she had less luck than she'd hoped for with the film projects she developed while in Italy. Neither "Der Tänzer von Florenz" (The Dancer of Florence), an homage to Harald Kreutzberg, whom Riefenstahl had admired as a young dancer, nor the large-scale semidocumentary moun-tain film "Ewige Gipfel" (Eternal Heights), in which the first-ever climbs up four famous summits, from Mont Blanc to Mount Everest, would be re-created, attracted any attention. After these attempts, Riefenstahl wrote a treatment for the ski film "Die roten Teufel" (The Red Devils), in which Alfred Panone's production firm, Capitol Pictures, exhibited great interest.

"Die roten Teufel" represented, to a certain extent, Riefenstahl's re-turn to her "Penthesilea" project in a more modern form, in a way she felt would be commercially successful in postwar movie theaters. The ancient battle of the sexes now took the form of a light and entertaining ski com-edy, à la Arnold Fanck.[59] The original idea for the film had come to her in 1930, when she was filming the ski sequences for *Stürme über dem Mont Blanc,* but from the beginning she had conceived of it only as a color film, which didn't exist at the time. "I was fascinated by the impression color would make against a white background—I imagined a symphony of color, rhythm, and music—an Olympic dream in snow."[60]

Though Capitol Pictures took out major ads announcing the film in the Italian papers in October 1950—"*I Diavoli Rossi—diretto da Leni Riefenstahl*"—the film, which was to have starred Vittorio De Sica and the young Brigitte Bardot, never materialized. Even Riefenstahl's attempt to finance the project herself, the cost of which was said to have reached the extraordinary sum of 2,000,000 deutsche marks, failed when she was unable to find a financial partner. Riefenstahl returned to Germany deeply disappointed, her hopes of being able to work abroad shattered.

Despite the bitter setback, she did not give up on drafting new projects and developing treatments for films, none of which were ever realized. She expected great things of one project in particular, a collaboration with Jean Cocteau, which undoubtedly would have improved her post-war reputation. She and Cocteau, whom she had met in Kitzbühel shortly after the war, planned to make a film called "Friedrich and Voltaire," about the friendship between the king of Prussia and the French philosopher. Despite corresponding on it for years, they never completed the script. When Cocteau died in 1963, the plan was shelved once and for all.

All of the new projects and treatments that Riefenstahl developed as of the mid-1950s circled around a subject that was to become the total focus of her attention from that time forward: Africa. Fascinated by Ernest Hemingway's novel *The Green Hills of Africa*, she developed an intense interest in the "black continent." She planned projects to be filmed there in part in an effort to get to know Africa itself. The first and most important of these projects was the film "Die schwarze Fracht" (Black Cargo), about the modern slave trade between Africa and the countries of the southern Arabian Peninsula. Riefenstahl had come across a newspaper article in which a missionary spoke of up to fifty thousand abductions a year. She decided to make this the subject of a feature film in which she would play the starring role, but which otherwise would be cast with African lay actors. She planned to shoot the entire film on location in East Africa, with only a small crew.

After plans failed for a collaboration with Gloria-Film, run by Ilse Kubaschewski, Riefenstahl decided to finance the film herself and flew to Sudan and Kenya to scout locations. During this trip she was seriously injured in an automobile accident and was in a coma for several days. Suffering from head injuries and broken ribs, she was forced to spend a number of weeks in the European Hospital in the Kenyan capital of Nairobi. But this life-threatening experience did nothing to dampen her fascination for Africa. Enraptured by the steppe landscape and the people of East Africa, she returned to Germany brimming with enthusiasm and more convinced than ever that "Die schwarze Fracht" must be made at any price. "The visual images I had inside me took control and wouldn't let go."[61]

Her subsequent attempt to produce the film through her own newly founded production firm, Stern-Film,[62] was, however, doomed to failure from the beginning. There were so many problems and delays that the budget was exhausted before Riefenstahl shot even one meter of film. In addition, her cameraman, Heinz Hölscher, has stated that despite months of preparing for "Die schwarze Fracht," a concrete shooting schedule was never developed. Riefenstahl was unable to create limits for herself. In the end, it was "she alone, her own self" who was the cause of her failure.[63]

# 15

## RIEFENSTAHL DISCOVERS
## A NEW WORLD

THOUGH THIS FIRST FILM PROJECT in Africa was never realized, Leni Riefenstahl turned to the continent she had found fascinating from the very first moment: "The world I had lived in until then was made up of the mountains, the ice of Greenland, the lakes of Mark Brandenburg, the metropolis of Berlin. Here—I felt it right away—a new life began . . . Africa embraced me—forever."[1]

While Riefenstahl was away on her lengthy travels, there was less and less talk of her in Germany, something she could only have welcomed at that point. If there was a negative report on her in the press, she either didn't hear of it at all or got word of it only much later. Liberated at least temporarily from her past, Riefenstahl visibly blossomed. During her long stays in Africa, she left behind the hostility in her homeland that she found so unjust. Instead, she submerged herself in a pleasantly different world, one in which she found two things that no one who knew about her or her past extended to her—trust and protection.

Riefenstahl's flight from the problems of the present were, to a certain extent, symptomatic of the sixties, as the biographer Claudia Lenssen noted: "In the Africa passages [of her memoirs], Leni Riefenstahl relates the hippie dream of that epoch: she sets off to escape the complications in her life, to find a promised land and to begin again."[2] While it is true that Riefenstahl believed that her first trip to Africa was a primal experience, she wasn't there in an attempt to find herself. She wanted to get away from herself and her uncomfortable past. Africa became a world in which she was not ill treated and could gather new strength.

As with every change in Riefenstahl's life—at least in her portrayal—
her involvement with the Nuba, a tribe living in the south of Sudan and
generally without contact with the outside world, was the result of an
"awakening." In 1956, when in Nairobi to film the failed "Schwarze
Fracht," she came upon an old issue of the German illustrated magazine
*Stern*, which featured a photo by George Rodger showing a muscular
Nuba wrestler covered in white ashes and carried on the shoulders of a
friend. This image mesmerized her: "This picture changed my life."[3]

## THE FIRST SUDAN EXPEDITION TO THE NUBA

Finding her way to the Nuba was more difficult than Riefenstahl had
imagined. But she never gave up, despite the effort and exertion it cost
her. Neither the German travel bureaus nor the Sudanese minister of
tourism nor other officials in the Sudanese capital of Khartoum could help
her locate the Nuba, who lived to a great extent untouched by civilization
in Kordofan, a province in the south of the country: "Perhaps the Nuba I
was looking for no longer existed, perhaps I was chasing a phantom."[4]

It took six years after the Rodger photograph had first brought the
Nuba to her attention for Riefenstahl to go in search of them. In 1962,
"leaving everything behind,"[5] the sixty-year-old Riefenstahl joined an
expedition of the German Nansen Society, which started out from Khartoum to travel to southern Sudan. Riefenstahl had been allowed to take
part in the expedition on the condition that she make a short double-8 film
on the work of the society under the title "African Diary" (which was never
completed). Nevertheless, she succeeded in steering the expedition from
the planned route. Despite growing tensions and disputes between her and
the other members of the group, it was agreed that the expedition would
make a six-hundred-mile detour so that she would be able to reach the
Nuba Mountains, a district that could be entered only with the special permission of the Sudanese government, permission that she had obtained.

After days of traveling over dusty trails, after repeated interruptions
and organizational difficulties, the group finally made its way to the
Nuba Mountains, difficult as they were to access. The photo by George
Rodger in hand, Riefenstahl directed the expedition into ever more

remote and impassable areas, until finally, near the settlement of Tadoro, she encountered the first intricately adorned Nuba, who had just gathered for their ritual tribal wrestling matches.

So in November 1962 she finally had reached the destination of her dreams, with the Masakin-Qisar-Nuba, one of roughly one hundred Nuba tribes. They seemed to her "like beings from another star": "It was all so fantastic and unreal, I felt like I was on another planet."[6] Even before she tried to make contact with them, she pulled out her camera: "I was in a daze and didn't know what to photograph first. Everything was so foreign, so strange, and so unbelievably fascinating . . . I soon found myself in their midst, their hands stretched out toward me. Faces smiled at me and I soon felt that I was among good people."[7]

And all of her hopes truly were fulfilled. For many years the Nuba were her new life, and in the end also a respectable source of income. When Leni Riefenstahl traveled to Sudan she filled her bags with a whole series of Leica and Leicaflex cameras, light meters, and enormous quantities of Agfa color film. Those familiar with her lifelong, goal-oriented behavior will find it hard to believe that it was sheer curiosity, based only on the photograph by George Rodger, that caused her to seek out the Nuba.

Once she had arrived in the Nuba Mountains, she was so enthralled by this totally exotic world that she wanted to discover more about the life of the tribe, which seemed so harmonious, and also to develop personal connections with its members. She decided to use the next weeks to study the customs and rituals of the Nuba at length. It quickly became clear to her that this would be possible only if she spoke their language. As she was never without a notebook and a tape recorder, she was able to accomplish this within a short period of time.

The Nuba overcame their initial shyness before the white woman prepared to live among them as they covered great distances. "They felt the understanding I had for them and became more trusting. They touched my arms, the light color of which astonished them. And they also shyly touched my blond hair, saying 'jorri' [pretty]. They accompanied me wherever I went."[8]

Riefenstahl's first visit to the Nuba lasted seven weeks, during which her relationship to them became close. She left the Nuba Mountains with a serious promise to return. Following further expeditions in other regions of the Sahel in the weeks that followed, she returned to Munich after ten months in Africa. During this period she had exposed more than two hundred rolls of film. Even though, to her great annoyance, some of them were ruined, she was proud of what she had done—"my first work as a photographer."[9]

Following her first visit to the Nuba, she returned every other year to Sudan, which soon became her second homeland, in order to visit the tribe. Even though a few months after her first visit the unrest that had been brewing since Sudan declared independence in 1956 again erupted, leading to a bloody civil war, she continued to journey to the Nuba Mountains, as the remote area was unaffected by the political upheaval at the conflict's beginning. She usually stayed for six to seven months during the dry season, living amid the Nuba in their village community. Her second stay, for which she brought film equipment, was interrupted by a personal tragedy. News reached her from Munich that her eighty-four-year-old mother, with whom she still lived on Tengstrasse, had died, on January 14, 1965.

In 1966–67, after her first book of photographs of the Nuba had appeared, she traveled for a third time to Sudan, this time without taking film equipment along but glad to be in the company of her friends again. She felt so comfortable in the Nuba Mountains that during this period she planned to have a simple round house built according to the local style and to live among the Nuba forever. She had even chosen the place in the Nuba Mountains where she wished to be buried. Her love of Sudan did not go unnoticed by the government in Kordofan—not least because of her photographs, which soon aroused interest around the world. In 1973, President Jaafar al-Numeiri conferred Sudanese citizenship upon her, in recognition of the contributions she had made to the country.[10] And in 1977 she was honored with the country's highest order.[11]

## IN PURSUIT OF THE IMAGE

Even though Leni Riefenstahl claimed that she had not traveled to the Nuba in order to take pictures, it was the pictures she brought back with her and that were published in illustrated magazines and books that signaled her much-talked-about and controversial comeback and established her new career as a photographer. After various German magazines initially refused to publish the pictures, not least due to the Riefenstahl name, the first Nuba photographs appeared in *African Kingdom*, published by Time-Life, and it caused a sensation in the United States.

Now even German publishers got wind of the opportunity to make a profit, and in 1966 *Stern* magazine, under the title "Leni Riefenstahl Photographs the Nuba—What the White Man Has Never Before Seen," published an extended series of photographs of Riefenstahl's first visit to the Nuba. Publication in many European and American magazines followed, as well as invitations to give slide presentations in Germany and America. With these earnings Riefenstahl financed further photography expeditions to Sudan. But a few years would pass before List Verlag in Munich published her first volume of photos, *Die Nuba. Menschen wie von einem anderen Stern* (*The Nuba: People From Another Star*).[12] Her subsequent trips to Sudan were undertaken almost solely in search of new and more spectacular images.

Riefenstahl's second book of photographs, *Die Nuba von Kau* (*The Nuba of Kau*), appeared in 1976 and was devoted to another Nuba tribe, which the seventy-two-year-old photographer had discovered in an even more remote region of the Nuba Mountains. A year earlier, when *Stern* magazine and Britain's *Sunday Times Magazine* had published several of these new pictures, it appeared that the second volume of photographs would be even more successful than the first. All of the major international pictorials, from a Time-Life publication to *The Sun*, *L'Europeo*, and *Paris-Match*, published the images, which were celebrated by critics as a unique hymn to the beauty of the human form. Not only abroad but also in her homeland Riefenstahl now received the recognition she no longer seriously expected. In 1975 a series of photographs published in *Stern* won Riefenstahl the Gold Medal of the Art Directors Club of Germany, for "best photographic achievement of the year."

The two Nuba books—followed in 1982, on the occasion of Riefenstahl's eightieth birthday, by *Mein Afrika*, photographs from diverse regions of East Africa—tell the story of the "noble savage," who, untouched by Western civilization, lives in total harmony with nature. Over the years, it took more and more effort for Riefenstahl to deliver those images she imagined of an "untouched" life in Africa that so captivated the world. The two Nuba volumes exhibit clear and revealing differences, which have much to say about Riefenstahl's understanding of Africa.

The first volume of photographs, taken between 1962 and 1969, shows a stronger documentary, almost ethnological, interest than the second, which was more concerned with presenting beautiful pictures that would sell well around the world. The photographs from her first visits are evidence of Riefenstahl's genuine interest in the living conditions of "her" Nuba, whom she not only viewed as the objects of her artistic work but in whose lives she was seriously involved. Her astonishment and curiosity as well as her intense closeness to her subjects can be felt in the photographs. The images are dedicated to harvesttime, to the traditional round houses, tools, cattle trading, and nutrition, but also to homemade musical instruments, dances, ceremonies, and rituals, which Riefenstahl writes about in detail.

The pictures of the first volume already reveal the mark of a strongly selective eye. Even by the time of her first visit, the Nuba were no longer living as totally untouched as Riefenstahl attempted to suggest. The neighboring village had an approved school, something the reader is informed of but not shown. Nor does she mention the conflicts between the Nuba farmers and the nomadic tribes that passed through their territory. The fact that a civil war, in which more than 1.5 million Sudanese lost their lives, was raging from 1955 to 1972, the period during which most of the photographs were taken, did not prevent Riefenstahl from producing images of a safe and peaceful world. Here, too, she turned her lens solely on the beautiful objects she was interested in and closed her eyes to the cruel reality that surrounded her—true to the motto that ruled her life: "Reality doesn't interest me."[13]

## A FILM ON THE NUBA

Almost inevitably, Riefenstahl wanted to make a documentary film on the Nuba once the first photos of the tribe were published. Based on the sensation her photographs caused, she could once again hope to find financial backers for such a project and so begin her comeback as a director. In 1964, two years after she had discovered "her" Nuba, she returned to the Nuba Mountains fully outfitted with film equipment and shot scenes from the Nuba's everyday life and festivals. This enterprise was funded by Odyssey Productions, an American firm that placed 60,000 deutsche marks at the director's disposal. In exchange, Odyssey was to receive the world rights to the film, with Riefenstahl sharing in the profits. The film that Riefenstahl was to bring back from her expedition would be used to attract further funders and coproducers, who in turn would finance the completion of the film.

But to Riefenstahl's horror, the film processor in Munich ruined almost all of the film she had delivered, giving it a green tint that rendered it unusable. She was therefore unable to deliver to her American financiers any convincing footage by the deadline. At this point they canceled the contract, and yet another film project dear to her heart failed: "Inside, I felt a world collapse . . . I now had completely lost my last chance to build an existence for myself again."[14]

Even after Odyssey dropped the project, Riefenstahl could not let go of the idea of a Nuba film, and she tried to find other sources of funding to keep the project alive. Through contracts and book royalties, she collected enough money by 1968–69 to make her fourth expedition to Sudan. Although she shot film of this expedition and others that followed, her Nuba film was never completed.

Today, that material is located in Riefenstahl's private archive. During the expeditions of 1964–65, 1968–69, and 1974–75, roughly three thousand meters of film were exposed, creating a unique document that shows the vanished life of the two Nuba tribes to which Riefenstahl already had dedicated two volumes of photographs. To this day only a portion of this material has been shown. In 1976, the director allowed the BBC to broadcast excerpts from the films. In 1993, *Die Macht der Bilder*, the documentary that Ray Müller created on Riefenstahl's life, offered a few shots from the uncompleted Nuba film. And during the Riefenstahl retrospective at the Film Museum in Potsdam in 1998–99, the public was shown a few select scenes.

But Leni Riefenstahl had already discussed how the Nuba were to appear and from what points of view she wished to depict them in an interview conducted in 1972.[15]

## FINAL VISIT

In February 2000, twenty-three years after her last visit to Sudan, Riefenstahl returned one last time to the place where she once had felt happy
and free from burden. She wanted to see if her Nuba friends had survived
the decades-long turmoil of the Sudanese civil war, in which thousands
had died. Among her entourage was filmmaker Ray Müller, under contract for Odeon Film of Munich, who was making a one-hour documentary of the trip under the title *Leni Riefenstahl. Ein Traum von Afrika* (*Leni
Riefenstahl: A Dream of Africa*).[16]

The enterprise, in addition to the strain it put on an aged Riefenstahl,
was in no way without its dangers, because Sudan—particularly the southern part of the country, which was heavily laced with land mines—was still
fighting a civil war. Right before Riefenstahl's arrival, fighting again
broke out in the Nuba Mountains and, as no one could guarantee her
safety, she was advised to wait until the situation eased. Her attempts to
negotiate behind the scenes with both the government and the rebels
failed. In the end the group set off without receiving the approval of the
Sudanese government.

Despite the tension and the strain of the trip, as well as the disappointment over the fact that virtually nothing survived of the former
landscape, Riefenstahl conducted herself completely professionally as
soon as she noticed that the cameras of Ray Müller's team were on her.
After returning from the trip, Müller recorded his impressions: "The
more film we shoot, the longer she stands before the camera, and
the more she blossoms . . . Leni Riefenstahl is incredibly professional at
every moment . . . No protest, no raised voice. Leni Riefenstahl will do
anything to get a good picture." As soon as she noticed the camera running, she precisely staged the image she wished to present: "She keeps
people engaged, plays Leni Riefenstahl, and hypnotizes a group of Sudanese with her photographs. Then she beams in triumph."[17]

The group, which also included a Sudanese government spokesman,
flew from Khartoum to Kadugli. While there, a significant occurrence
took place, documented by Ray Müller:

Suddenly I hear a scream. Leni, who had been talking to a black
man in djellaba and white turban, clambered up the loading ramp

of the Toyota, sobbing. What was wrong? It took a moment until she could speak, then, white as chalk, she explained what had happened. The man was a Nuba. When she had lived here before, he had been a small boy, but he could well remember two of her best friends. Now they were dead. Leni Riefenstahl is shattered by this news. Seconds later her face fills with anger. "You didn't film these important scenes!" And we hadn't. First, because we weren't permitted to film in military areas, and second, because no one could have anticipated what the man would tell her . . . I am fascinated. Upset one minute, in the next this woman is already thinking about the dramatic effect of her pain. The line between life and film is for Leni Riefenstahl a fluid one. What had just occurred was a key scene, she was correct in that. Leni retreats, pouting.[18]

From Kadugli the group continued on its way to the Nuba Mountains, arriving on February 29, 2000. The ninety-seven-year-old Riefenstahl was totally exhausted by the effort of the trip and the heat of the steppes, which reached 104 degrees. But as the cars reached the Nuba Mountains, she blossomed. News of her arrival had spread like wildfire, and she was greeted by a large and celebratory crowd. She soon was surrounded by a number of elderly Nuba who knew her from before. Despite the chaotic and demanding scenes that followed, Riefenstahl appeared overjoyed and repeatedly allowed herself to be embraced. Carrying copies of photographs she had taken years earlier, she attempted to locate her friends from the past and find out what had become of them.

In the midst of this emotional moment for all concerned, the reality of the civil war intruded. The sound of shots and mortar fire brought an immediate end to the visit. The ancient helicopter that was to return the group to Khartoum, a Russian model that wasn't even equipped with seat belts, crashed shortly after takeoff, in the interior of the country near El Obeid. The pilot had discovered engine damage at an altitude of 150 feet and attempted, unsuccessfully, to land. The helicopter fell from an altitude of 15 feet and rolled over several times. Most of the passengers, including Riefenstahl, were knocked unconscious. Only four of the ten passengers were otherwise injured, none of them fatally. Riefenstahl finally was forced to recognize that what remained of "her" Africa and "her" Nuba was only a dream that no longer had anything to do with reality. The only thing that endured was the memory of the happiest period of her life: "Perhaps what Leni experienced with the Nuba, for the first time, was more than admiration. Perhaps it was here that she learned what love is."[19]

FASCINATING FASCISM?

Riefenstahl's amazing and initially smooth comeback, this time as a photographer, was not to remain unchallenged. Her appreciation of the beautiful, strong, and healthy body, the heroic, erotically alluring prototype of the "noble savage" that she transfigured in her Nuba photographs into the emblem of archaic physical perfection, again brought Riefenstahl criticism in the 1970s. What set off this change in the perception of Riefenstahl was a two-part article, which has become legendary, by the essayist and filmmaker Susan Sontag, first published in the *New York Review of Books* in 1975 under the title "Fascinating Fascism." In the article, Sontag used the Nuba photographs as the occasion to submit Riefenstahl's aesthetics to a critical test, and this set off major discussions worldwide. She considered the Nuba volumes to be the final stage of Riefenstahl's rehabilitation, which had begun in the United States in the seventies, much earlier than in Europe, after influential artists and performers such as Mick Jagger, David Bowie, and Andy Warhol increasingly expressed solidarity with Riefenstahl and her allegedly timeless longing for beauty.

Susan Sontag represented the view that the photographs of the Nuba were part of a specific and highly problematic aesthetic and political continuity and, following Riefenstahl's mountain films and the propaganda films of the Third Reich, formed the "third section of her triptych of fascist visuals."[20] Riefenstahl's depictions of the Nuba called to mind Nazi ideology, as they corresponded to concepts of the fascist aesthetic. In her work before, during, and after the Third Reich there was as little room for human imperfection as there was in the racial constructs of the "Aryan master race," and so there are no old, ill, or disabled Nuba to be found in her published photographs. Just as she once had staged pictures of taut, muscular Olympic athletes, she now idolized the physical perfection and flawless bodies of the Nuba. In both cases she was interested exclusively in propagating what was beautiful and robust and vital.

While Sontag in no way disputed the beauty and the power of the Nuba photographs, she did interpret the worldwide interest aroused by the books as a phenomenon that should not be permitted to go unchallenged. The success of Riefenstahl's photos, according to Sontag, did not exactly "augur well for the keenness of current abilities to detect the fascist longings in our midst."[21]

Before Sontag presented these objections, the Nuba photos had indeed been viewed in a broadly decontextualized manner. People were interested in the spectacular images without in any way finding it suspicious that their creator was the leading propagandist of the Third Reich. For that reason, Sontag's criticism was perceived as that much stronger, and it split her readers into two camps: those who suddenly saw the pictures as problematic, and those who were unable to discern anything negative about them just because they were taken by Leni Riefenstahl.

Riefenstahl reacted to Sontag's attack with a total lack of understanding. She could not or did not want to distinguish what the Nuba pictures had to do with her earlier work for Hitler. Instead of confronting the criticism, she alluded to her personal understanding of beauty, which had remained unchanged her whole life and at no point had anything to do with political conditions or concepts. She had always, she said, been inspired by what was "beautiful, strong, and healthy." She was unable to see the parallels to the Nazis' cult of the body: "That's just the way they look. Before I went to Africa I was unaware of that. One could, of course, photograph the Nuba in a way that does not acknowledge their beauty. But I'm unable to do that."[22]

Riefenstahl's angry reaction to Sontag's analysis of her photographs of the Nuba did nothing to stop the photographs suddenly being seen in a completely different light. Even though Sontag's comments, published in Germany in the weekly *Die Zeit*, were not met with unanimous approval—on the contrary, they were harshly criticized, for example, in feminist circles[23]—they became decisive in framing the debate on Riefenstahl over the last three decades. Sontag's argument revived the discussion about Riefenstahl's role in the Third Reich, which the success of the Nuba volumes had, for a time, pushed into the background.

Sontag's theses led to a merging of questions about Riefenstahl's aesthetic—which could and should be asked independently—with moral questions about Riefenstahl's career in the Third Reich and her consequent refusal after 1945 to take any responsibility for her actions. The moral discomfort that people continued to feel with the propagandist of the Third Reich found expression in the criticism of her aesthetic form and therefore avoided the real questions.

## UNEDUCABLE PROPAGANDIST OR BRILLIANT ARTIST?

Sontag's influential essay established the image of an uneducable and "eternal fascist," which became a constant topic in the discussion surrounding Riefenstahl. By not only criticizing her involvement in Hitler's regime but also viewing the works she created after the war as a continuation of her work for the Third Reich, in addition to branding her style and her concept of beauty as generally "fascist," people gave Riefenstahl no chance to redefine herself or to distance herself from her past. Whether Riefenstahl in fact comprehended all of this is another story.

To attack Riefenstahl as an uneducable ultrareactionary was accepted for a long time as good form: "It's a given among leftist intellectuals that Leni Riefenstahl is not to receive absolution . . . Any effort toward a composed and unbiased treatment of the question is, for German authors, doomed from the beginning, for very simple and very complex reasons. The inclination to distance oneself from her, in order not to be suspected of fascist leanings oneself, is very strong."[24] Those who wanted to contest Riefenstahl's own myth and the interpretations intended to exonerate her as an apolitical artist often overshot their mark, registering the propagandistic significance of the films that Riefenstahl made for the Third Reich too highly.

The criticism that Hilmar Hoffmann made of Riefenstahl—that it was only through her films that Germany could unite internally, and that they made Hitler's rise to total power possible[25]—is as false as the claim made by Guido Knopp that *Triumph des Willens* laid the cornerstone for the "Führer cult."[26] Historians such as the British Hitler biographer Ian Kershaw long ago proved that the German population's opinion shift in favor of the Nazis had already taken place to a large extent in the spring and summer of 1933, not after Riefenstahl's first party rally film was screened in December of that year. And the cornerstone of the cult surrounding the Führer was laid considerably earlier. By the twenties, Adolf Hitler had established a cult around his own personality and with his seizure of power ascended to the throne of collective messiah figure for millions of Germans.[27] By the time *Triumph des Willens* arrived in movie theaters in March of 1935, the Hitler cult had long been in existence. Even though there is no question that her films had a powerful effect and contributed to the Germans' support of Hitler, they did not play the central and unique role in the early years of the dictatorship assigned to them in retrospect.

Although for the last decades of her life there were bitter battles over the person of Riefenstahl, there is one point on which practically everyone agrees—her extraordinary talent, her status as a brilliant film artist. The Polish film historian Jerzy Toeplitz, for example, speaks of her "indisputable talent,"[28] and even the American Amos Vogel, who includes her films in the canon of the most subversive works in film history and who sees *Triumph des Willens* as a "deeply dangerous masterwork," admits that Riefenstahl is "without doubt one of the greatest directors."[29]

Such statements have always been grist for the mill to those who have fought for Riefenstahl's exoneration. They argue that if Riefenstahl's genius is uncontested by even her fiercest critics, then with the passing of time the political condemnation of her activities in the Third Reich should be dropped, or at least toned down. Riefenstahl's irrefutable place in film history is used as an argument for forgiving the artist, for no longer burdening her with questions about her past, for viewing her films as works of art and not as documents of her political and moral entanglements.

In this way, Leni Riefenstahl became known as "one of the most talented women of this century," who was "marked from the beginning because of three films she made in the thirties."[30] And because Riefenstahl's own statements that her films had been dedicated to art and never to National Socialism were continually used in support of this argument, they gained in significance. The rebirth of Leni Riefenstahl's reputation as an apolitical artist whose works are purely aesthetic is increasingly touted.

As a result of such reasoning, Riefenstahl apologist Charles Ford makes the claim that "film genius is too rare to be rejected. It is totally irrelevant whether we love the person or not. We should allow cinematographic talent to flourish."[31]

Neither the image of the ultrareactionary nor that of the brilliant artist, however, has anything to do with Riefenstahl herself. The case of Leni Riefenstahl defies facile judgments and rash reproach. She was a great artist and a willing propagandist for the Nazi regime. She was politically naïve and yet created a furor with political subjects in a highly political time. She was never a member of the NSDAP but one of Hitler's most fervent admirers. The public discussion concerning her was never as complex or contradictory as Leni Riefenstahl herself.

Looking at Riefenstahl's complete oeuvre, which many find fascinating, one recognizes definite and recurring tendencies that characterize her work before, during, and after the Nazi era: her fascination with the beautiful and the strong, her mythologizing of nature, a concentration on purely positive messages, and an avoidance of the negative. Viewed through her lens, Riefenstahl's subjects take on a new artistic and strongly stylized significance. However, her fanaticism regarding beauty, her quest for beautiful, stylized images, and her aesthetic of the human body, all of which are palpable in her work, belong to a long tradition that developed independently of fascism and that fascism absorbed for a time.

There was no artistic realm, whether of the fine arts, architecture, music, or literature, in which the Nazis succeeded in establishing their own independent "expression of art for a new era." In all of these spheres they took existing tendencies and tried, usually unsuccessfully, to employ them for their own ends. It was no different with film: the majority of the films created under the swastika were mediocre features lacking any relevance to film history. Riefenstahl's documentaries are the only works from this chapter of German filmmaking that attained international fame and that are still talked about today. Yet they did not develop any definitive fascist stylistic or visual criteria or set any norms. While it is true that Leni Riefenstahl was the leading figure of National Socialist film, she had no direct imitators within the Third Reich and remains a singular phenomenon in the history of cinema.

A close investigation of Riefenstahl's life offers evidence that the manner in which Riefenstahl developed her career in the Third Reich, the extent of the privileges she enjoyed, the demands she made, and the uncompromising way she treated those who got in her way are morally questionable. But if this moral judgment is due to the fact *that* she glorified the criminal regime of the Nazis and not *how* she did so, and originates in a blanket denunciation of the aestheticism of Riefenstahl's visual style, then this misses the point: it is not the heroic images of the beautiful and strong Nuba that are questionable. What is questionable is that Leni Riefenstahl, as former propagandist of a system that criminally pursued the exclusion of those who did not meet the ideal of the "healthy body," created these images without recognizing the parallels. This does not speak for the sensitivity of the artist, but it cannot be used as the basis for accusing her of fascism in the work she created after the war.

To label Riefenstahl's oeuvre as a "triptych of fascist images" does not do justice to the historical context of her artistic expression. Her aesthetic is open to attack because Riefenstahl never distanced herself from the films she created during the Third Reich, which then became the key documents of fascism's self-representation. In the end, it was this refusal that brought her entire work into disrepute.

# 16

## THE TEMPORARILY FINAL CAREER

### ICONS OF AGE

In the 1990s, a third and new point of view was added to the two traditionally accepted ways of viewing Leni Riefenstahl. As of her ninetieth birthday in 1992, Riefenstahl was increasingly seen as an icon of vitality, as an "astounding example of lifelong activity and attractiveness,"[1] as an active, self-confident, and contentious woman who had weathered the heights and depths of an entire century and was all the more fascinating because of it.

This viewpoint probably was created by Riefenstahl herself. Following the success of her Nuba photographs, Riefenstahl once again conquered an entirely new territory for herself. At a point when others long since had retired, she didn't consider stopping and continued with her international comeback. At seventy-plus years of age, she earned her certification as a scuba diver and began photographing and then filming underwater.

And so, in the 1970s and '80s, she created remarkable photographs of sea flora and fauna. Her two books of undersea photography enjoyed the success of the Nuba volumes and were celebrated worldwide. Photography had brought triumph back into Leni Riefenstahl's life. Therefore, it was only logical that she continue along this path into advanced old age and, after the publication of the photography books, go on to make a film on coral reefs, the colors and forms of which fascinated her.

Just as the Nuba Mountains of Sudan had offered her shelter in the sixties, in the seventies it was the underwater world that became her new "paradise." Photos of Riefenstahl in neoprene wet suit and diving mask soon were a part of the public's understanding of her. The photographer admitted having been fascinated by the sea her whole life, though she came to diving very late: "I love the sea almost as much as the mountains; I loved it before I had any idea that I would ever get to know the underwater world."[2] When the aged Riefenstahl experienced life underwater for the first time, it was a revelation to her. Diving became her elixir, not least because the underwater weightlessness allowed her to forget the complaints of age.

Just as she had once fled to Africa to escape the problems confronting her in Germany, she now dove, quite literally, out of reality into the depths of the sea, where criticism and hostility could not reach her. She would remain in this environment for weeks, sometimes for months at a time, "spared of the media and journalists."[3]

Once again, of course, it was a key experience that introduced her to this new world. In 1972, on a recuperative vacation in Malindi, Kenya, on the Indian Ocean, the seventy-year-old snorkeled in the sea for the first time and saw a coral reef with countless fish, shimmering in all imaginable colors: "I was watching a big green fish nibbling at the coral, when suddenly I was interrupted by whistles and calls. Everyone was already in the boat; I was the only one still in the water, alone. It seemed inconceivable that an entire hour had gone by. I had lost all track of time."[4] She was gripped by the thought that she could experience for herself what she had seen up until then only in the films of Hans Hass and Jacques Cousteau. The underwater world "has occupied me constantly ever since. It calls to me like a fata morgana."[5]

One year later, in 1973, she returned to Kenya, this time equipped with snorkel, mask, and fins. But she needed a diving certificate for further explorations. As no diving school was going to accept a seventy-one-year-old woman as a student, she claimed that she was twenty years younger—the first time in her life that she resorted to such a lie—listing her birth date as 1922 instead of 1902 on the application: "Despite taking twenty years off my life, I was still the oldest participant by far. They accepted me with a shrug of the shoulders and probably thought, 'She'll never make it!'"[6] Only after she had passed the test did she tell her diving instructors her true age.

It is no surprise that for Riefenstahl diving was not to remain a hobby. She soon wished to capture the fascinating underwater world on film, to treat it as an artistic experience: "At first I was fascinated by the fish in all their variety and splendid colors, then it was the coral and the tiny sea denizens I wanted to take pictures of."[7]

In 1974 she set off on her first dedicated diving trip, to the Red Sea, and, inspired by Douglas Faulkner's book *This Living Reef*, began taking simple underwater shots. She was fascinated by the flora and fauna, more colorful here than in the Indian Ocean. Despite the fact that the water was teeming with sharks, she made numerous dives to the coral reefs, which she found especially captivating. She still treated underwater photography purely as a hobby, but making it a profession was only a matter of time: "I was much too interested in diving to be able to concentrate on photographing. I sensed how difficult it would be to capture an image exactly as I saw it with my own eyes."[8]

Six months later, when visiting the Caribbean island of Roatán off the coast of Honduras, where there still existed a few untouched undersea areas to explore, she came equipped with a new professional camera in order to be able to perfect her images. But she didn't get around to taking any photographs. A hurricane destroyed large sections of the island and killed eight to ten thousand people, precluding further dives.

Only in 1975, when she dove off the coast of Grand Cayman Island in the Caribbean, where she came into contact with marine biologists and underwater photographers, could she begin to explore underwater photography in a professional manner: "I took pictures during each dive. And I noticed that in using only one lens—I had only a 35-mm with me—I couldn't photograph everything I wanted to. I needed a wide-angle and a macro lens . . . I tried to expand my knowledge of underwater photography by reading the literature. I kept a record of each shot, in order to learn from my mistakes."[9]

Underwater photography became a new aesthetic challenge for the seventy-three-year-old. Of course, Riefenstahl wasn't satisfied until her exposures met her own high standards and could stand up to pictures taken by leading underwater photographers. As always, she was less interested in creating photographic documents than in capturing the beauty of the underwater world, composing images, playing with the colors and shapes of the sea, heightening them artistically to create compositions that finally satisfied her. She was inspired by the coral reefs' symphony of color, and on each dive, now using a reflex camera, her priority was to capture spectacular images. From then on, she never dove without looking through the lens of a camera. Her hobby was now a profession. In becoming more skilled technically, and through the use of underwater lights, she was soon able to take more and more complex and accomplished photographs. The only thing that bothered her was that she couldn't control the "staging" of the pictures: "Fish accompany me— but when I want to photograph them, they won't stand still."[10]

When the first underwater photographs by Riefenstahl appeared, they met with enormous success. Just as her pictures of the Nuba had provoked enthusiasm, this work also received excellent reviews, and for the most part this time without critical or malicious undertones. The technical perfection of the work was praised as well as the fascinating effect of the images. And, in truth, almost every one of the published photographs was a minor work of art, particularly those depicting her favorite motifs— shells and sponges and, above all, blooming coral. Her coral reefs resemble abstract, unreal landscapes, rendered in captivatingly glowing colors.

With a twelve-year interval, Riefenstahl published two volumes of underwater photographs. The first, *Korallengärten* (*Coral Gardens*) appeared in 1978 in Germany, the United States, England, France, Italy, and Spain. In 1990, seventeen years after qualifying for her diving certificate, and following further dives in various parts of the world, she published *Wunder unter Wasser* (*Underwater Wonders*). The book was the result of more than one thousand dives and was created in close collaboration with her colleague Horst Kettner, who accompanied her on each of her trips.

Riefenstahl had biologists and ocean researchers write the captions for both books. Reviews drew particular attention to the painterly aspect of the works, which were partly realistic but also partly abstract. In fact, what particularly fascinated Leni Riefenstahl was the possibility—using the correct technical skills and way of seeing—of being able to compose pictures underwater: "In my heart of hearts I'm always a painter, too. That's why as a photographer I always try . . . to dissolve the realism of a photograph in the painterly."[11] It was a totally new experience for Riefenstahl to have the underwater pictures, in contrast to those of the

Nuba, accepted without judgment, to have the beauty of the images praised without being accused at the same time of a fascist aesthetic or having them interpreted as an example of ultraconservatism. But this, of course, had to do in part with the subject of her photographs.

Riefenstahl didn't trust this peaceful interlude, remarking with resigned irony, "After it has been said that my films promoted a fascist aesthetic, that I photographed the Nuba like the SS, they are sure to find brown fish in my underwater books as well."[12] Even though some feature writers endeavored to see the pictures as "Triumph of the Fishes,"[13] there were no serious attacks on the books in this respect.

In her almost thirty years of experience as a deep-sea diver, the increasing pollution of the world's oceans did not escape her notice any more than did the dramatic reduction in the wealth of underwater species. She watched in shock as the species-rich coral reefs, which she had observed only years before, suddenly neared extinction: "What happened? Within just a few years . . . the reef fishes were destroyed. I made this painful discovery when I returned to the same reefs in the Red Sea following a three-year absence. I no longer recognized the life on the reefs."[14]

Based on this experience, Riefenstahl not only joined Greenpeace, the environmental protection organization, but also used the forewords of her books and her interviews to oppose those who hunted with harpoons as well as unthinking sports divers whose sole aim was to kill as many fish as possible and so contribute to the dramatic decimation of the fish population.[15]

### LATE HAPPINESS

The royalties from the sales of the Nuba and underwater photography books soon enabled Leni Riefenstahl to build her own house, after having lived for thirty years in the four-room apartment on Munich's Tengstrasse. In 1978, she bought a piece of land right outside Pöcking, not far from the Starnberger See. She was fascinated by the property because of a huge ancient oak under which she wanted her home to be built, and she timed its completion for her seventy-sixth birthday. The house was a modern and tasteful villa, protected by beech trees and a thick hedge but without fences or high walls, a detail Riefenstahl liked to point out.[16]

Huge façades of glass connect the interior of the house to the luxurious garden.

Located in the house's basement is the meticulously administered private archive, a cutting room, a darkroom, and an office in which she oversaw her huge photography archive. Her home, the place where Riefenstahl was often interviewed, became a true retreat in the final years of her life.

In 1997, twenty years after it was built, she expanded the house in time for her ninety-fifth birthday. To accommodate a digital-editing system, which she planned to use for her future films, she added a new wing, which included a basement office and a large reception area on the ground floor, solely dedicated to Riefenstahl's lifework. The room holds enlargements of images taken from her photography books and a library containing the first editions of her books in all languages.

Riefenstahl shared the villa in Pöcking with Horst Kettner, forty years younger than she, whom she met on her 1968–69 expedition to Sudan. She was looking at the time for a driver and cameraman, someone who could assist her on the Nuba film project: "I wanted someone who was stable and healthy and who, furthermore, enjoyed the work. In addition, he should not only be a good driver, but also able to repair cars. And as I couldn't afford a cameraman on top of this, it would be necessary that he understand something of film technique. That was my best-case scenario."[17] Kettner, who was twenty-five at the time, proved to be that "best-case scenario."

Horst Kettner grew up in Czechoslovakia as the child of German parents, and when Riefenstahl first met him he spoke only broken German. He made an extremely positive impression on her from the beginning: "I greeted a somewhat shy young man, very tall, slim, and good looking. From the first moment on, his face inspired trust."[18] Having had only negative experiences with her earlier expedition assistants, she found that Kettner fulfilled all of her expectations: "Horst more than proved his worth. Industrious, calm, and empathetic, he was an ideal comrade. No work was too great for him or too challenging, and he was skilled in solving all kinds of technical problems."[19] Immediately following this first expedition, they went on vacation together, first to Rhodes, then to Capri.

Kettner soon moved into Riefenstahl's apartment on Tengstrasse, and in 1978 into the house in Pöcking. He placed his life in the service of Riefenstahl, endured the highs and lows with her, and, with his "somewhat devil-may-care sympathy,"[20] as one journalist put it, passionately defended Riefenstahl's legend. The press repeatedly speculated on the nature of Riefenstahl and Kettner's relationship. Though she had never been with any other man for such a long time, Riefenstahl consistently refused to talk to journalists about the relationship, wishing to protect their privacy: "One should retain a little bit of intimacy for oneself."[21] The filmmaker Ray Müller, who knew the director for more than a decade and who was often in contact with her and Horst Kettner when they were filming, sums it up: "He is her creation, her right arm. Leni does nothing without him, can't do anything without him . . . a real-life 'Harold and Maude.' The secret of their relationship is work together, travel together."[22]

Four years after she moved into her house on Starnberger See, Leni Riefenstahl began writing her long-anticipated autobiography. She had first announced she was writing her memoirs in 1951. But more than three decades went by before she actually began work on them. Publishers in Germany and abroad had repeatedly offered her high advances for the book, but for a long time she couldn't bring herself to face this difficult task.

Finally, at the beginning of the 1980s, she signed a contract with Albrecht Knaus Verlag. Two factors contributed overwhelmingly to getting the project to a concrete stage: the anticipated high royalties, which would allow her to continue to travel and realize her projects, and her wish, after all the hostilities, to write a book that would finally tell the "truth" about her.

In writing her memoirs, Riefenstahl consulted her archive, newly organized for this purpose, and quoted from newspaper articles, letters, and trial documents that supported her version of the story. Bringing long-accepted facts into line with her own anecdotes and correcting major parts of her life story such that her assertions appeared logical was an extensive and demanding undertaking. The work on the book cost Riefenstahl a great deal of energy, and in retrospect she did not remember these years fondly: "It was a terrible time."[23]

The finished product was more than nine hundred pages long. Reviewers were hard on the author and criticized the garrulously deceptive book as the "dumb prattle of a toady"[24] and the "triumph of repression."[25] The Riefenstahl critic Erwin Leiser made it his business to expose some of her most obvious falsehoods, such as those concerning the financing of the films she made during the Third Reich, and to challenge Riefenstahl's version with documents proving the opposite. He called the memoirs an arche-type of the "art of repression."[26]

Positive responses were few. Only friends of Riefenstahl, such as Will Tremper, who considered himself the midwife of the memoirs, argued in the author's defense: "Whatever it was that Leni Riefenstahl did to 'deserve' to be the only German woman to be denounced throughout the years, I always found the hounding of her, even before I got to know her personally, cruelly hypocritical."[27]

The older she became, the more pronounced was the phenomenon of Riefenstahl's "promotion to the status of a cultural monument," as Susan Sontag described it in 1974.[28] The critical disputes surrounding her receded further and further into the background, replaced by an enthusi-astic, or at least respectful, tribute to Riefenstahl's ceaseless vitality. The fascination with her long and colorful life became more prominent, and for many, her advanced age and her ongoing activity alone were worthy of praise.

Representative of this new view of Riefenstahl is the exceedingly naïve description of the director by Angelika Taschen in the foreword to the pictorial volume she published, *Leni Riefenstahl—Fünf Leben* (*Leni Riefenstahl—Five Lives*). Speaking of their collaboration, Taschen wrote: "At work, she forgets her severe back pains and crawls around the floor on all fours like a young girl, rearranging the pictures . . . I am deeply impressed by her vitality and grace. Her eyes, shining with curiosity and enthusiasm, her girlish charm, and her almost shy smile make me totally forget that this woman is ninety-seven years old."[29]

This new respect for Riefenstahl meant that the critical issues sur-rounding the director were addressed less and less. Whether the debate on Riefenstahl's guilt had gone on long enough or was a final capitulation to her consistent refusal to face her own past remains an open question. But increasingly Riefenstahl was granted what she herself considered to be a "fair interview," a sign of a "turn to reason." In discussing a tele-vision interview with the director in 1999, one critic expressly connected this development to Riefenstahl's advanced age: "Riefenstahl has never seemed so free and relaxed on German television. Which one cannot begrudge her at almost one hundred years of age."[30]

The contradictions of her life continued to recede into the back-ground, while the legend and myth of Leni Riefenstahl became more significant than what actually occurred: "In the new evaluation of Riefenstahl, the attitude of not wanting to know exactly what happened plays a noticeable role," writes Rainer Rother.[31]

She was treated with unusual consideration in the year of her one hundreth birthday. Her lies about her life were rarely met with indignation. Instead, she was provided with even more platforms from which to repeat stories that had been refuted years before. She was nearing a general absolution.

The consequences of those latest developments are clear: what Riefenstahl had said about her life in the preceding decades was increasingly accepted as truth. As one scarcely expected insight from her late in life, Riefenstahl's remarks were accepted without reflection. Beyond the two pictures of her that emerged in the postwar period—that of the uneducable ultraconservative and of the brilliant but in the end apolitical artist— a new facet of the Riefenstahl myth emerged: while still alive, the artist entered the realm of legend customarily reserved for those who have died. She became the icon of her own aged vitality. This image of Riefenstahl resonates with the public much more than the contentious interpretations of past decades ever could have. Whereas the dispute concerning her role in the Third Reich kept people from seeing Riefenstahl in a positive light for decades, tribute now was paid to Leni Riefenstahl the "cultural monument," something that earlier never was granted to Hitler's propagandist and the woman who lied about her past.

The "normalization debate" of the 1980s and '90s, being waged again, was of great help to the artist in this. The intensified demand for a "final reckoning" with an awkward "past that will not fade" benefited the elderly Leni Riefenstahl. There can be no final reckoning for either the Germans or for Riefenstahl, demonstrated in part by discussions such as the *Historikerstreit* (historians' dispute) of the 1980s and the Goldhagen controversy, as well as the debate on the Wehrmacht exhibit of the 1990s. Hitler's regime left behind such a legacy of destruction that this period of German history continues to be a German trauma to the present day.[32]

# Conclusion

# THE RIEFENSTAHL RENAISSANCE

THOUGH LENI RIEFENSTAHL'S FILMS were long considered taboo, or at the very least treated as historical documents of National Socialism, in the past few decades they have been freed from the political context in which they were created and recognized as aesthetic statements of a high order that can stand on their own.

In addition to Riefenstahl's works, the artist herself attracted interest and became an object of fascination to many. The woman considered infamous for being Hitler's filmmaker increasingly became a media star, a cult figure initially courted for the sake of breaking taboo. In showing Riefenstahl's films and pictures again in public and acknowledging to a lesser extent what was politically problematic about them while emphasizing their artistic significance, they could become objects of aesthetic reflection. Famous photographers and ad campaigns quoted her photographs, as directors did her films and musicians used certain of her aesthetic elements in their stage shows. Riefenstahl's films and photographs were transformed from political provocations to works referenced without reflection, and thus they were incorporated into the visual memory of the twentieth century.

In the beginning, this turn toward Riefenstahl had to do, above all, with curiosity and a certain pent-up demand. While there had been a great deal of discussion about the artist, her notorious films, and her guilt or innocence, very few people had actually seen her work from the Third Reich. For this reason, and in part because it was still verboten to be interested in Riefenstahl and to view her films without prejudice, the renewed interest in her ushered in a phase of enduring fame that began before she died. As summarized by Rother, "There is no other famous artist from the period of the Nazi regime who has exhibited the kind of lasting influence as has Leni Riefenstahl."[1]

## AMERICA'S REDISCOVERY OF RIEFENSTAHL

This new, "less constricted" picture of Leni Riefenstahl began circulating in the United States much earlier than in Europe, a process closely watched in Germany.[2] Constantly confronted with her past in the Old World, in America the director experienced what she had always so fervently desired—recognition as an artist. In separating her work and her aesthetic from the context in which they were created, her images could be used for a multitude of purposes: in music videos and ads and for postcards and posters.

Despite the furor unleashed by Susan Sontag's mid-seventies essay "Fascinating Fascism," in the United States Riefenstahl became a symbolic figure in the period that followed, a figure no longer viewed only negatively but admired for her extraordinary creative potential. But the Riefenstahl renaissance did not proceed entirely smoothly in the United States. Since the 1970s, Jewish organizations in particular have vehemently opposed the uncritical consideration of Riefenstahl's works, which they consider a downplaying of National Socialism. Despite protests, the Museum of Modern Art in New York presented the first retrospective of films by and with Leni Riefenstahl in 1966, which met with great interest and fueled continued debate.

Attempts by American feminists to stylize Riefenstahl as an early champion of women's emancipation failed. Some were prepared to overlook her Nazi past, as for many decades Riefenstahl was the sole major female filmmaker, but this unwise attempt at inclusion provoked sharp criticism. The director, as she herself admitted in interviews, could not be held up as a serious illustration of feminist goals.[3] While it was true that she had fought for a place in what had been a strictly male domain, she had never been concerned with the situation of women in general but only with her own career.

In 1974, as guest of honor at the first Feminist Film Festival in Telluride, Colorado, where she was celebrated as a model for women in the film industry, her untimely "inclusion in the tiny ancestors' gallery of women filmmakers"[4] ignited protests worldwide.[5] And it was the German women's movement that most vehemently opposed American feminism's Riefenstahl revival.[6] Despite the protests, the festival management decided to screen all of Riefenstahl's films. In the end, it was argued, they were honoring Leni Riefenstahl the artist, not Leni Riefenstahl the person—as if the two could be separated. When Paul Kohner, the coproducer of *SOS Eisberg*, urged prominent guests from the film industry to refuse to participate in the award ceremony held at the Sheridan Opera House, he was met with naïve reactions. Journalists quoted Gloria Swanson, one of the major Hollywood stars of the twenties, as saying, "Why should I refuse to take part? Is Leni Riefenstahl waving a Nazi flag? Hitler is dead, isn't he?"[7] Riefenstahl was overwhelmed by the support she received. She remarked to a journalist: "It's like before the war. They like me."[8]

This event set the cornerstone of Riefenstahl's rediscovery in America. But she must have been aware that despite this acceptance there would always be protests against her. She canceled the photo sessions that were to follow the award ceremony, as she didn't want to be filmed against the backdrop of the demonstrators' anti-Nazi and anti-Riefenstahl banners. She willingly accepted the honor but carefully edited out any awkward acknowledgment of the protests.

In the period that followed, it was primarily celebrities who showed support for Riefenstahl: the pop artist Andy Warhol invited her to his Factory, the German showmen Siegfried and Roy were photographed by and with her in Las Vegas, Steven Spielberg repeatedly stated that he would like to meet her, Francis Ford Coppola called himself one of her admirers, and the star photographer Helmut Newton took her portrait and paid homage to her aesthetic style in many of his own pictures.[9]

But it was pop stars above all who took Leni Riefenstahl as their aesthetic model. Years before Madonna planned to play Riefenstahl in a TV miniseries she was developing, Mick Jagger of the Rolling Stones acknowledged Riefenstahl, admitting that he was an admirer of her films and that he had seen *Triumph des Willens* dozens of times. He not only appeared with her in a photo spread in the *Sunday Times*, shot by his wife of the time, Bianca Jagger, he also repeatedly used the aesthetic style of her party rally films, which he considered to be entertainment, as the basis for his stage shows. David Bowie expressed himself in a similar fashion, calling Hitler history's first "rock star" and "media artist" and acting as if there had been only a "decorative" side of German fascism. "He wasn't a politician, he was a media artist. How he worked his audience! The girls got hot and sweaty, and the guys wished they were the ones up there. The world will never see anything like it again. He turned the whole country into his stage show."[10] It was in this atmosphere that Riefenstahl rose from persona non grata to superstar, to the ur-mother of an anarchic pop ideal.[11]

As a result of the renaissance the artist experienced in American pop discourse, her pictures also were reevaluated and quoted in new films. George Lucas, who once called Riefenstahl the "most modern filmmaker," freely acknowledged that he borrowed from *Triumph des Willens* for several scenes in his *Star Wars* films. In fact, the closing sequence of the first movie is clearly reminiscent of Riefenstahl: the film's heroes stride to martial music across a *via triumphalis* of granite slabs, past block formations of uniformed masses, to mount a stone tribunal and be received in the end by an ovation from the crowd. Riefenstahl herself felt honored by this: "When such a great director does that, it is certainly a compliment. I know that Lucas and Spielberg and whatever all their names are value me greatly. I don't encounter the prejudices in America that I do in Germany."[12]

But American films that quoted Riefenstahl didn't get off entirely uncritically, as shown by the 1994 Disney film *The Lion King*, by Rob Minkoff. In the opening sequence, in which the "king of the lions" is filmed from below as he sits alone on his throne on a platform set high above the masses and receives their ovation, the perception of similarities to *Triumph des Willens* was unavoidable, leading the press repeatedly to mention "angles cribbed from Riefenstahl."[13]

Despite critical reminders, the Riefenstahl renaissance in America advanced to the point that her images were used in films, photography books, music videos, and ads without adverse reaction. The costumed marching soldiers of Michael Jackson's music video "HIStory," for example, find their choreographic predecessors in *Triumph des Willens*. And Annie Leibovitz, longtime companion of the Riefenstahl critic Susan

Sontag, quoted the director unreservedly when invited by the Committee for the Olympic Games to photograph the 1996 Summer Games in Atlanta, Georgia. Many of the black-and-white photographs of athletes in her *Olympic Portraits* look like stills from Riefenstahl's *Olympia* film of 1936.[14]

Soon Riefenstahl the person became an object of interest in America. She exultantly acknowledged how positively her memoirs were received in the United States, whereas in Germany the book was met with malice.[15] Soon after its appearance, the book climbed to fifth place on the *New York Times* bestseller list, and a fourth printing was issued only three weeks after publication. Even the feared critic John Simon praised the book.[16]

But the essentially less biased reception that Riefenstahl enjoyed in the United States should not disguise the fact that there have always been critics who found this development problematic. There were protests in 1997, for example, when it was reported that Riefenstahl was to receive a life-achievement award from a little-known Hollywood group, the Society for Cinephiles, at a film festival in Los Angeles, California. As demonstrations were anticipated, Riefenstahl's participation in the event was kept secret, and the ninety-five-year-old director accepted the prize before the audience to applause and a few boos.[17] The award unleashed a storm of indignation from a number of Jewish organizations, which saw the honor as part of a worldwide campaign to rehabilitate Riefenstahl and the entire Nazi era. At the same time, honoring Riefenstahl was said to be an insult to all of those who were victims of the Holocaust. Rabbi Yitzchok Adlerstein, director of the Jewish Studies Institute at Yeshiva of Los Angeles, justified his objections with the comment, "Honoring Leni Riefenstahl is just as wrong as giving Adolf Hitler a prize for interior design, should it ever turn out that he was a good housepainter."[18]

Two years later, on March 3, 1998, Riefenstahl was among the guests of honor at the seventy-fifth anniversary celebration for *Time* magazine, held at New York City's Radio City Music Hall. Referred to in the U.S. press as the "party of the decade," it was attended by such luminaries as Bill Clinton, Mikhail Gorbachev, Norman Mailer, Elie Wiesel, Bill Gates, and many Hollywood stars, all of whom had been featured on a *Time* magazine cover at some point during the preceding seventy-five years. Riefenstahl had graced the cover in the summer of 1936, during the Olympic Games in Berlin. Other than the model Claudia Schiffer, she was the only German guest at the event and was apprehensive about how the other guests would receive her. But this time she had worried for nothing: "I was terribly afraid of what would happen when my picture appeared on the huge screen. But I received a standing ovation."[19] A short time later, *Time* chose her as the sole woman among its list of the one hundred most important artists of the twentieth century. This marked the apex of the American Riefenstahl renaissance, which lasted for three decades.

## ON THE DIFFICULTY OF MAKING A FILM
## ON LENI RIEFENSTAHL

In 1992, Omega Film of Munich, in cooperation with several European television networks, commissioned a three-hour documentary project on the occasion of Riefenstahl's ninetieth birthday. The film, the much-praised *Die Macht der Bilder* (released in English as *The Wonderful, Horrible Life of Leni Riefenstahl*), was broadcast on television one year later, after which it was also screened in movie theaters in many countries and received a number of awards. But in the beginning, finding a director for the film proved more difficult than Omega Film had imagined. Fifteen of the directors who were asked, among them such well-respected names as Hans-Christoph Blumenberg, turned down the offer. Other directors who showed interest were rejected by Riefenstahl. Finally, a director for the million-mark project was found—the then all but unknown Ray Müller. He stated from the beginning that his film was to be neither glorification nor tribunal. His idea was to present a fair assessment of Riefenstahl's life and work, an idea that proved impossible, however, as he had to depend on her collaboration.

The shoot proved extremely problematic, with constant tensions and conflicts. As usual, Riefenstahl would hear no criticism, and several temper tantrums, caught on video and included in the film, demonstrate the thin ice that Müller had been treading on. At the same time, this footage demonstrated why a direct confrontation with uncomfortable truths was avoided in the end. Müller joked with journalists that the film should be called "Duel with a Legend" or "Leni's Last Picture Show": "She always expected us to make an homage—and I always said, 'If we make an homage, it won't be broadcast.' Until the very end, this was something she didn't understand."[20]

When it came to artistic issues, Riefenstahl, as usual, answered Müller's questions willingly and not without pride, whereas it was impossible to ask critical questions concerning the relationship between art and politics. Müller's *Die Macht der Bilder*, therefore, is yet another example of a failed dialogue with the artist. Georg Seesslen's estimation is particularly apt: "An object of observation by the name of Leni Riefenstahl puts up resistance to being interviewed, sometimes violently, sometimes through obstruction. She tries to use the film to her own advantage, then tries to destroy it when she is threatened with the loss of control of it. The filmmaker tries perseverance, affability, and assuming the role of an attentive son or pupil. That is to say, he wants to get Leni Riefenstahl to talk by any means, but her armor is not to be penetrated."[21]

In the end, the film comes to no definite verdict, closing with Riefenstahl's question, "What am I guilty of, then?" With great skill, Riefenstahl succeeded in turning the film into her own instrument of defense.

After filming was completed, however, she was still not satisfied. So the international success that *Die Macht der Bilder* enjoyed came as a surprise to her.[22] Riefenstahl's relationship to this film, even in retrospect, was ambivalent. She expressed the opinion that had Ray Müller "asked fewer critical questions," she would have been able to talk more about many interesting aspects of her artistic work. "The film contains several falsehoods and misunderstandings—and I could have said more of importance had there been fewer provocative questions. But the director had no contact with me at all and came loaded down with prejudices. Parts of his work are good nevertheless. At any rate, I suffered a lot during the filming."[23]

*Die Macht der Bilder* was screened in movie theaters in the United States, Japan, and many European countries, where it ran for weeks. Everywhere it was shown, attendance was high. At the end of 1993, the picture received the Emmy for Best International Film. By the time it garnered the Special Award of Film Critics of Japan, it had won eight international prizes. Though it went home empty-handed from German film festivals and awards ceremonies, *Time* chose it as one of the ten best documentary films of the twentieth century.[24]

*Die Macht der Bilder* was not the last film planned on Leni Riefenstahl's life. Ten years after Ray Müller's film, two further projects were in the planning or preparation stage. Producers in both America and Germany speculated that Leni Riefenstahl would continue to be a subject of interest and would draw audiences numbering in the millions. "The plan to make a film of Riefenstahl's life alone is evidence of a change in her public image. A persona non grata has become popular, not despite but because of the sobriquet 'Nazi filmmaker.'"[25] After decades of social exile, in the last ten years of her life Riefenstahl became a figure in the world of the arts. So it comes as no surprise that the film industry as well is interested in the subject of Leni Riefenstahl.

After the appearance of *Memoiren*, a number of prominent stars and directors showed an interest in the theme: Madonna, Jodie Foster, and Sharon Stone have been discussed for the role of Riefenstahl. The first concrete negotiations were initiated by Madonna in the first half of the nineties, when she was planning a TV miniseries on Riefenstahl's life in which she would star. But Riefenstahl was afraid that Madonna would make a sensational biopic and refused to sell her the rights.[26] After the collapse of these negotiations, Jodie Foster fought for years—initially behind the scenes—for the rights to Riefenstahl's memoirs.[27] Only in 1999 did she have a press spokesperson announce that she was planning a film on Riefenstahl's life and would play the director herself.

Following a period of correspondence, the two women met, once in New York and also at Riefenstahl's villa on the Starnberger See. At this point, Jodie Foster assumed that she would be able to come to an agreement with Riefenstahl. She told the press that she considered Riefenstahl one of the "best filmmakers of all time" and praised her "phenomenal talent," which had to be acknowledged "whether one appreciates her or not . . . The life of this woman, who is equally hated and admired, is truly worthy of filming. The film on Leni Riefenstahl will be great. I admire this woman."[28]

But things were to turn out otherwise. Despite exhaustive preliminary talks with Foster, for whom Riefenstahl had great respect as a director, at the end of November 1999 she decided against the project, choosing instead a German producer, Odeon Film of Munich, as she felt her personal rights were better protected in Germany than in the United States. "As no one can safeguard their personal rights in the American film industry, can't even protest against untruths, I couldn't sell her the rights. They could have made up lies about me having an affair with Hitler or being a crazy Nazi whore, which has happened often enough. I can't allow them to spread lies about me."[29]

Jodie Foster has never made a public statement about the reasons why negotiations with Riefenstahl failed; she has said only that the project didn't fall through because of money. As by this point she had invested hundreds of thousands of dollars in the feature film project, she decided to go ahead with it anyway. One day after Odeon Film announced their project, Foster announced through a publicist that she was going to make an unauthorized film on Riefenstahl.

Odeon announced in November 1999 that, in collaboration with the producer Thomas Schühly, a former assistant to Peter Zadek at the Schauspielhaus in Bochum, it would film Riefenstahl's memoirs as an "adventure film with an international cast." Schühly, a successful producer of films by Rainer Werner Fassbinder as well as such box-office successes as *The Name of the Rose* (1986) and *Der Totmacher* (*Deathmaker*) (1995), had met Riefenstahl for the first time that year. The heart of his film was to be Riefenstahl's adventures with the Nuba, with her career during the Third Reich represented only in flashback. There is no reason to expect a critical approach to Riefenstahl's life from him, for the very reason that he was personally chosen by the director. In 2003, both film projects—Jodie Foster's as well as Thomas Schühly's—fell through.

## THE FINAL COMEBACK

Decades after she had brought *Tiefland* to movie theaters in 1954 and considered her directing career long over, Riefenstahl decided to make a new film, one about the underwater world.

Just as she had desired to make a film about the Nuba following the success of her African photographs, so she now developed the idea, in tandem with her new passion for diving and underwater photography, to bring the undersea world to the movie screen. In 1975, two years after they had passed their diving tests together, Riefenstahl and Horst Kettner experimented for the first time with a borrowed underwater film camera. From that time on they took their own film equipment along with them on all of their expeditions.

In the 1990s, Riefenstahl announced that she would create a film from the footage she had shot over the previous two decades. But the film was long in coming, as other projects or illnesses caused repeated delays. Even after the final scenes had been completed, Riefenstahl seldom worked on the film, which she began editing in 1997, without interruption. In order to generate interest in the project, however, she allowed excerpts from the film to be shown onboard during flights of a German airline, and several completed scenes were included in a Riefenstahl retrospective held in Potsdam in 1998–99.

Riefenstahl edited the film in her basement studio in Pöcking. In order to work with the newest technology, the 16-mm film that had been shot in the early years of the project was digitized and mixed with video footage in a computerized editing facility. More than forty years after Riefenstahl edited her last film, *Tiefland*, she again learned to use the latest technological developments.

Several months after her ninety-ninth birthday, editing on the film was completed. The only thing lacking was the music. As her former composer Herbert Windt was no longer alive, at the end of 2001 she contacted American composer Giorgio Moroder, who had created scores for the films *Flashdance* (1983) and *Top Gun* (1986) and was especially well-known for his 1984 rescoring of the silent film classic *Metropolis*.

In January 2002, Riefenstahl's announcement in the newspaper *Die Welt* that she would present her new film on the occasion of her one hundreth birthday seven months later made headlines around the world. What no one seriously had considered possible was within reach. Forty-eight years after the premiere of her last feature film and seventy years after making her directorial debut with *Das blaue Licht*, the director was screening a new work, thus establishing the longest directorial career in film history. Like all of her films, *Impressionen unter Wasser* (*Underwater Impressions*) (2002) was edited not as a documentary but according to her own artistic point of view, even though the forty-five-minute work contains footage of aquatic wildlife never before photographed or filmed.[30]

Riefenstahl decided against using any commentary, and her magnificent color images are accompanied only by the music of Giorgio Moroder, which, before the premiere, the composer called "slightly sumptuous, dramatic, somber."[31] For Riefenstahl, the film represented a long-anticipated chance to demonstrate once more and for the last time her aesthetic skills and abilities as a filmmaker. With *Impressionen unter Wasser*, Riefenstahl created a cinematic monument to herself as a director and to the last great passion of her life.

## FROM RENAISSANCE TO REHABILITATION

The increasing historical distance from the Third Reich, the discussion of the "line" that finally was to be drawn between the present and her problematic past, as well as a respect for her advanced age all led to an increasingly unbiased acceptance of Riefenstahl.

Toward the end of her life, there were no longer protests against her public appearances, for example, her surprise appearance as guest of honor at the 2000 German Film Prize awards. Curiosity and interest replaced indignation and anger. The fascination with the woman who had lived for a century and who was still planning new film projects and departing on a diving expedition to the Maldives was evidenced everywhere.

The most amazing thing about the final stage of her life was that people who had long opposed Riefenstahl suddenly joined in this fascination, so much so that it seemed that in her centennial year, Riefenstahl's past would be draped in the mantle of forgetfulness.

In January 2002, *Die Welt* published an interview with the director by Hilmar Hoffmann, former president of the Goethe-Institut. Hoffmann for decades had been extremely disapproving of Riefenstahl and her work, and following the death of Erwin Leiser was considered Riefenstahl's sharpest critic. Now, however, her onetime opponent spoke glowingly of her, invoking the "film-historical brilliance" of her works and avoiding critical questions. The entire tone of the talk was aimed at reconciliation, a fact the editorial commentary that introduced the interview did not neglect to mention: "In the intervening years, the frontline positions have been respectfully resolved—and now the president of the

Goethe-Institut and the ninety-nine-year-old filmmaker could meet for a relaxed conversation."[32]

It was also part of the Riefenstahl renaissance that the director began to overcome her fear of contact. The discussions of the postwar period presented the artist either as intractable reactionary or apolitical film genius, which served to block access to her and lead to highly emotional debates. These debates almost always ended in her total damnation, in order that the second party not be considered politically suspect. The demonizing of Riefenstahl and the emotional dimension of the debate had for decades steered every discussion of the director into a dead end. It is significant that one result of this "new openness" was the destruction of this old pattern.

The danger of this most recent development, however, is that Riefenstahl's own version of her life story, which underwent a multitude of revisions, is gaining in significance and in public acceptance. The few attempts to oppose this development have been submerged in the flood of new enthusiasm for Riefenstahl and her art.

If Riefenstahl was a social outcast for decades, due to her refusal to confront her past and the responsibility she bore for her actions, by the end of her life she had attained a middle ground where she did not have to modify her version of her past. Before, no one had believed what she said, but in the end questions on her life and her career were frequently avoided—whether out of resignation in the face of her inability to deal with them or purely and simply out of respect for her advanced age and impressive vitality.

So the path was paved from the Riefenstahl renaissance to her rehabilitation. Interestingly, this development does not seem ideologically motivated, as was definitely the case in decades past with the efforts made by her apologists.[33] Rather, the basic motive appears to be a widespread attitude of not wanting to know more, increasingly evidenced even among journalists and Riefenstahl's former critics. Riefenstahl's rehabilitation, therefore, was not due to the long-standing demand for her to admit moral responsibility, but was a result of a questionable comprehension of history, which desires to attain "normality" at any price.

It is precisely this watering down of the discussion on Leni Riefenstahl that makes urgent a more exact examination of and a new and thorough confrontation with her life, her work, and her career. A knowledge of the stations of her life and of her public perception and reception, the attempt to reconstruct the motivations for her actions and acknowledge the contradictions of her biography—all are necessary to prevent people from capitulating uncritically and without reflection to the "power of the images," and from granting the fascinating figure of Leni Riefenstahl more significance than the historical and biographical facts.

# NOTES

PREFACE: APPROACHING A MYTH

1. In a correspondence from her secretary, Riefenstahl informed me that she would fully support my book if it was a "true and good book." Note from Gisela Jahn, Leni Riefenstahl Productions, February 22, 2000.
2. To date, no one has been given access to Riefenstahl's meticulously maintained private archives. But the archives do not promise to reveal anything essentially new. Knowing how completely Riefenstahl tried to control her public image herself, one can assume that her archives hold nothing that would contradict the image of her life that she so carefully constructed.
3. Note from Gisela Jahn, Leni Riefenstahl Productions, of February 22, 2000: "You can see in *Memoiren* exactly what is true, and what is not."
4. Leni Riefenstahl, quoted by Frank Deford, "The Ghost of Berlin," *Sports Illustrated*, August 4, 1986.
5. See David B. Hinton, *The Films of Leni Riefenstahl*, 2nd ed. (New York, 1991).
6. See, for example, Glenn B. Infield, *Leni Riefenstahl: The Fallen Film Goddess* (New York, 1976) and Rainer Rother, *Leni Riefenstahl. Die Verführung des Talents* (2000).


1. BERLIN IN THE TIME OF THE KAISER

1. Leni Riefenstahl, *Memoiren* (Munich, 1987), 15.
2. Ibid., 30.
3. Ibid., 20.
4. At Riefenstahl's first solo dance performance in 1923 her only concern was how her father would react. What she had failed to achieve throughout her childhood and youth—the recognition of her father—she succeeded in attaining with her triumph as a dancer: "Had he forgiven me? On this evening I celebrated my first great victory. My father not only had forgiven me, he was deeply moved." Ibid., 62.
5. Ibid., 30.
6. Ibid.
7. Ibid., 15.

8. Ibid., 20.
9. Ibid.
10. Ibid., 15.
11. Ibid.
12. Ibid., 29.
13. Ibid., 24.
14. Ibid., 16.
15. Ibid., 26ff.

## 2. FIRST CAREER STEPS

1. The program is reprinted in *Memoiren*, 38. See also holdings under "Leni Riefenstahl" in the German Dance Archives, Cologne.
2. Riefenstahl, *Memoiren*, 42.
3. Ibid., 56.
4. Claudia Lenssen, "Leben und Werk," in *Leni Riefenstahl* (Filmmuseum Potsdam, 1999), 25.
5. Riefenstahl, *Memoiren*, 82.
6. Ibid., 50.
7. Infield, *Leni Riefenstahl*, 163.
8. Riefenstahl, *Memoiren*, 58.
9. Ibid.
10. Ibid.
11. Ibid., 59.
12. Ibid.
13. Bella Fromm, *Als Hitler mir die Hand küsste* (Reinbek, 1994), 149.
14. Riefenstahl, *Memoiren*, 30.
15. In 1933, looking back at her beginnings as a solo dance performer, Riefenstahl confessed that she really had harbored much higher hopes for her first appearance than she later admitted. "After the evening in Berlin it hit me like a wave, a wave of success, of unexpected, incomprehensible, unbelievable success. The unknown dance student had become recognized overnight. Reality left ambitious dreams far behind." Leni Riefenstahl, *Kampf in Schnee und Eis* (Leipzig, 1933), 9.
16. Riefenstahl, *Memoiren*, 61.
17. Rother, *Leni Riefenstahl*, 21.
18. Ibid., 24.
19. In this context, Riefenstahl falsely quoted in *Memoiren* a newspaper review that did not cover the debut evening but rather a dance performance that Riefenstahl gave in Munich somewhat later.
20. *Münchener Zeitung*, October 26, 1923.
21. *Die Zeit*, October 30, 1923.
22. Riefenstahl, *Memoiren*, 64.
23. Ibid.
24. Contrary to her own statements, Riefenstahl was not the first soloist to whom Max Reinhardt had made such an offer. Niddy Impekoven, for example, had appeared in a solo performance in October 1919.
25. Jutta Klamt's best-known choreographies had titles such as "The Pilgrim," "Lament on the Death of a Hero," "Idol Worship," and "A Hymn for Mass."

26. Riefenstahl, *Memoiren*, 64.
27. Ibid., 69.

3. STAR OF MOUNTAIN FILMS

1. Riefenstahl, *Memoiren*, 51.
2. Director Arnold Fanck had not been able to find a distributor for this film (as was also the case with his earlier works). He rented the movie theater on Nollendorfplatz and had the film screened there. After seventy-two days of sold-out screenings, the Deutsch-Amerikanische Film-Union became its distributor.
3. Riefenstahl, *Memoiren*, 70.
4. Riefenstahl, *Kampf in Schnee und Eis*, 10ff.
5. Jan-Christopher Horak, "Dr. Arnold Fanck: Traüme vom Wolkenmeer und einer guten Stube," in *Berge, Licht und Traum. Dr. Arnold Fanck und der deutsche Bergfilm* (Munich, 1997), 20.
6. Arnold Fanck, *Der Kampf mit dem Berge* (Berlin, 1931), 9.
7. Arnold Fanck, letter to the editor, *Dresdner Neuesten Nachrichten*, 1930, cited in Horak, *Berge, Licht und Traum*, 146.
8. The very first intertitle of *Der heilige Berg* (1926) reminds moviegoers of the authenticity of the images: "The celebrated athletes who appear in the film *Der heilige Berg* request the public not to consider their achievements mere tricks of photography, which they would not agree to."
9. See Jürgen Trimborn, *Der deutsche Heimatfilm der fünfziger Jahre* (Cologne, 1998), 60–67.
10. Harry Sokal (real name Henry R. Sokal), who followed Riefenstahl to Berlin in 1923, stated in 1945 that not only did he attend many showings of *Der Berg des Schicksals* with Riefenstahl, but he also accompanied her to the Dolomites and introduced her to Luis Trenker. (See also statements made by Harry Sokal in Ilona Brennicke and Joe Hembus, *Klassiker des deutschen Stummfilms 1910–1930* [Munich, 1983], 190). Luis Trenker confirms in his memoir, *Alles gut gegangen*, that indeed it was Harry Sokal who introduced Riefenstahl to him at the Karersee Hotel. In her 1933 book *Kampf in Schnee und Eis*, she makes no mention of anyone accompanying her, whereas in her 1987 book *Memoiren* she erroneously says it was her brother, Heinz, who went with her on this first trip to the Alps. She also stated to Curt Riess that she had traveled to the Alps with her brother. See Curt Riess, *Das gab's nur einmal. Die grosse Zeit des deutschen Films* (Hamburg, 1956), 246.
11. Riefenstahl, *Kampf in Schnee und Eis*, 11.
12. Ibid., 12.
13. Luis Trenker, *Alles gut gegangen* (Hamburg, 1965), 209.
14. Ibid.
15. Horak, "Dr. Arnold Fanck," 39. I express my gratitude to Jan-Christopher Horak for meeting with me on this subject on January 15, 2002. See also Arnold Fanck, *Er führte Regie mit Gletschern, Stürmen und Lawinen. Ein Filmpionier erzählt* (Munich, 1973), 160; and Riefenstahl, *Memoiren*, 79ff.
16. The fact that he was involved with *Der heilige Berg* from the beginning was confirmed by Sokal to Glenn Infield. See Infield, *Leni Riefenstahl*, 163. Fanck's company was close to ruin, as a result of his perfectionism, which caused his production costs to soar.
17. In both *Kampf in Schnee und Eis* (9ff) and *Memoiren* (69ff), Riefenstahl depicts the obsessiveness that drove her to mountain films.

18. That Riefenstahl used Sokal to achieve her personal goals is demonstrated by the fact that four years later, during the filming of *Die weisse Hölle vom Piz Palü*, Sokal, at Riefenstahl's request but against the wishes of Arnold Fanck, named G. W. Pabst, who would feature Riefenstahl in the best light, codirector.

19. Riefenstahl, *Memoiren*, 82.

20. In the Dolomites, Riefenstahl and Schneeberger practiced climbing barefoot, which she would be required to do in her next role for Arnold Fanck. But the project, "Die schwarze Katze," a film set in the Alps in the post–World War I era, was never realized.

21. Riefenstahl, *Memoiren*, 98.

22. Ibid., 117.

23. Ibid., 110.

24. Anna Maria Sigmund, *Die Frauen der Nazis* (Vienna, 1998), 103.

25. See Béla Balázs, "Der Fall Dr. Fanck," in *Revisited. Der Fall Dr. Fanck. Die Entdeckung der Natur im Deutschen Bergfilm*, ed. Frank Ammann, Ben Gabel, and Jürgen Keipereni (Frankfurt am Main, 1992), 4–7.

26. The personnel connections between the mountain films of the twenties and the films of the Third Reich are not limited solely to Riefenstahl and Trenker. Many cameramen who were discovered and trained by Fanck and who made a lasting mark on the mountain film genre were hired by Leni Riefenstahl after 1933 for her film projects in the Third Reich. Among them were Sepp Allgeier, Walter Frentz, and Guzzi Lantschner. The connection was obvious: Fanck's technicians pioneered outdoor cinematography and therefore possessed the necessary skills required for the major documentary film projects of the thirties.

27. Thomas Brandlmeier, "Sinngezeichen und Gedankenbilder. Vier Abschnitte zu Arnold Fanck," in Horak, *Berge, Lichte und Traum*, 77.

28. *Der Montag Morgen*, December 20, 1926.

29. *Weltbühne*, April 8, 1927.

30. Siegfried Kracauer, *Von Caligari zu Hitler. Eine psychologische Geschichte des deutschen Films* (Frankfurt am Main, 1984), 120.

31. Ibid., 271.

32. See Horak, *Berge, Lichte und Traum*; Christian Rapp, *Höhenrausch. Der deutsche Bergfilm* (Vienna, 1997).

## 4. EMBARKING ON A NEW CAREER

1. Riefenstahl, *Kampf in Schnee und Eis*, 18.

2. Ibid., 24.

3. In his memoirs, Trenker acknowledges that "Dr. Arnold Fanck was my master. I'm above all indebted to him for giving me the opportunity to see the potential of images in nature, as well as for the fundamental concepts of setting up and ending a scene . . . From the beginning I felt great respect for and gratitude to this pioneer of German outdoor films." *Alles gut gegangen*, 201.

4. Herman Weigel, "Interview mit Leni Riefenstahl," *Filmkritik* 16, no. 188 (August 1972): 395.

5. Riefenstahl, *Memoiren*, 137ff.

6. Ibid., 396.

7. See Rapp, *Höhenrausch*, 144.

8. Riefenstahl, *Kampf in Schnee und Eis*, 40.

9. Ibid., 47.

10. Weigel, "Interview mit Leni Riefenstahl," 396.

11. The exception was the failed 1927 project "Wintermärchen." After the project was relegated to the files, he never returned to this sort of fairy-tale material, something that Riefenstahl considered a shortcoming.

12. Rother, *Leni Riefenstahl*, 36.

13. Lenssen, "Leben und Werk," 47.

14. See "Filmarbeit wie noch nie . . . Ein Gespräch mit Leni Riefenstahl," *Mein Film* 328 (1932): 4.

15. Riefenstahl, *Memoiren*, 137ff. This version had already been recorded one year after the film premiered. See Riefenstahl, *Kampf in Schnee und Eis*, 67.

16. In all, Schneeberger worked on more than 120 films and in 1954 received the Bundesfilmpreis (Federal Film Prize) for his work.

17. Riefenstahl, *Memoiren*, 139.

18. Riefenstahl, *Kampf in Schnee und Eis*, 70.

19. Ibid., 73.

20. Lenssen, "Leben und Werk," 49.

21. See Joseph Zsuffa, *Béla Balázs: The Man and the Artist* (Berkeley, 1987), 219.

22. Giuseppe Becce, composer and president of the Association of Berlin Film Music Directors, already had written music for the Luis Trenker films *Berge in Flammen* and *Der Feuerteufel*. He was also responsible for the music for the sound version of *Die weisse Hölle vom Piz Palü*. In addition, Becce composed the music for the silent film *Wege zu Kraft und Schönheit*.

23. Film program supplement to the *Illustrieren Film-Kurier* 14, no. 1748 (1932): 5.

24. Ibid.

25. Quoted in Riefenstahl, *Memoiren*, 150.

26. Hermann Sinsheimer, *Berliner Tageblatt*, morning edition, March 26, 1932.

27. Horak, "Dr. Arnold Fanck," 26.

28. See Peter Reichel, "Bildende Kunst und Architektur," in Wolfgang Benz, Hermann Graml, and Hermann Weiss, eds., *Enzyklopädie des Nationalsozialismus* (Munich, 1997), 154.

29. Werner Jochmann, ed., *Adolf Hitler, Monologe im Führerhauptquartier 1941–1944. Die Aufzeichnungen Heinrich Himes* (Hamburg, 1980), 406.

30. Paul Ickes, quoted in Riefenstahl: *Kampf in Schnee und Eis*, 5ff.

31. For the international response to the film, see Audrey Salked, *A Portrait of Leni Riefenstahl* (London, 1996), 78.

32. *Film-Kurier*, February 19, 1935, 1.

33. *Illustrierter Filmkurier* 1932, no. 1748, and 1938, no. 2797.

34. On June 8, 1935, Goebbels prohibited the screening of films that were made before Hitler seized power and on which Jews had worked. When possible, the scenes with Jewish actors were excised so that the films could be distributed in the Third Reich. Ulrich Liebe refers to the fact that the 1935 sound version of Arnold Fanck's 1929 film *Die weisse Hölle vom Piz Palü* was missing all scenes featuring the Jewish actor Kurt Gerron. See Ulrich Liebe, *Verehrt, verfolgt, vergessen. Schauspieler als Naziopfer* (Weinheim, 1992), 52. Gerron was taken to the Theresienstadt concentration camp in 1944 and was killed at Auschwitz in the fall of 1945.

35. Riefenstahl, *Memoiren*, 140.

36. When the film returned to theaters after the war, the prologue and epilogue of the original version were missing. Only when the original was restored in 2001 was the original framework reinstated.

37. Lenssen, "Leben und Werk," 49.

38. Riefenstahl, *Memoiren*, 139.

39. The letter in which Balázs demanded the money has not survived, only Riefenstahl's reaction to it. See Riefenstahl file, Berlin Document Center, Bundesarchiv Berlin, letter of Leni Riefenstahl of December 11, 1933.

40. Letter from Leni Riefenstahl to Béla Balázs, February 21, 1932, in the posthumous papers of Béla Balázs, Akademie der Wissenschaften Budapest, no. 5021/320.

41. When he visited Berlin in January 1933, he had already requested payment of his outstanding fee, but apparently Riefenstahl put him off until later. See Zsuffa, *Béla Balázs*, 229.

42. Riefenstahl file, Berlin Document Center, Bundesarchiv Berlin, letter of Leni Riefenstahl of December 11, 1933.

43. Riefenstahl only indirectly commented on this incriminating document, which was first published in Infield's *Leni Riefenstahl*. In her memoirs, she maintained that in his book, Infield had made use of "forged letters and documents" (851).

44. Riefenstahl stated that from the time of postproduction, Sokal had taken over all money and organizational matters (*Memoiren*, 149). This is entirely credible. As Balázs at this point had already left for Moscow and therefore had not necessarily been informed of this agreement, it is not improbable that Balázs later, from exile in Moscow, mistakenly sent his demand for money to Riefenstahl instead of to Sokal. It was against this demand that Riefenstahl went to Streicher for help.

## 5. "I WAS INFECTED"

1. Harry Sokal, "Über Nacht Antisemit geworden?" *Der Spiegel*, November 8, 1976. Riefenstahl wrote a letter to *Der Spiegel* after Sokal's article was published, maintaining that Sokal's statements were "false to the core" and that she had never been an anti-Semite. See Leni Riefenstahl, "Nie Antisemitin gewesen," letter to the editor, *Der Spiegel*, November 15, 1976.

2. This had already been posited three years earlier, in 1935. See Oskar Kalbus, *Vom Werden deutscher Filmkunst* (Altona, 1935), 2: 66.

3. Tobis press file, 1938, theater collection of the University of Cologne.

4. Riefenstahl, *Memoiren*, 152.

5. Ibid., 157.

6. Ibid.

7. In her memoirs, Riefenstahl mentions that she heard the speech at the end of February 1932. During this period Hitler spoke only once at the Sports Palace, on February 27.

8. See Max Domarius, ed., *Hitler. Reden und Proklamatioinen 1932–1945* (Munich, 1962), 141.

9. Riefenstahl, *Memoiren*, 152.

10. Ibid.

11. According to Harry Sokal, Riefenstahl read *Mein Kampf* before she began shooting *Das blaue Licht*, that is, in the summer of 1931, a good year before she claimed to have read it. See Sokal, "Über Nacht Antisemitin geworden?" That she closely read *Mein Kampf* is confirmed by Riefenstahl herself. *Memoiren*, 182.

12. Albert Speer, *Spandauer Tagebücher* (Frankfurt am Main, 1997), 128.
13. Riefenstahl, *Memoiren*, 154ff.
14. See Ernst Sorge, *Mit Flugzeug, Faltboot und Kamera in den Eisfjorden Grönlands* (Berlin, 1933), 147.
15. Riefenstahl, *Memoiren*, 157.
16. According to Riefenstahl, Hitler's personal photographer, Heinrich Hoffmann, wanted to take pictures of her first encounter with Hitler. But Hitler forbade it, saying the photographs could do Riefenstahl damage. Ibid.
17. Otto Dietrich, *Zwölf Jahre mit Hitler* (Munich, 1955), 191. It is surprising that Riefenstahl, in a 1946 interview with Budd Schulberg, maintained that the fateful meeting with Hitler had taken place in his Berlin apartment. See Hamilton T. Burden, *Die programmierte Nation. Die Nürnberger Reichsparteitage* (Gütersloh, 1970), 136.
18. Riefenstahl, *Memoiren*, 158.
19. Sorge, *Mit Flugzeug, Faltboot und Kamera*, 147.
20. Riefenstahl, *Kampf in Schnee und Eis*, 80.
21. See Goebbels's diary entry of December 11, 1932: "Leni Riefenstahl was also there. And Frau [Emmy] Sonnemann [who later was Göring's wife]. Extraordinarily likable. Magda and L. Riefenst. flirted with Balbo." All Goebbels's diary entries are from Elke Fröhlich, ed., *Joseph Goebbels. Die Tagebücher, Sämtliche Fragmente* (Munich, 1987).
22. Riefenstahl, *Memoiren*, 183.
23. Ibid., 186.
24. Quoted in Friedelind Wagner, *Nacht über Bayreuth. Die Geschichte der Enkelin Richard Wagner* (Cologne, 1994), 119ff.
25. Evidence of Riefenstahl's close relationship to Hitler is presented by Rudolf Diels, head of the Gestapo. In the initial stage of Hitler's dictatorship, Diels tried to exercise his moderate influence on him in matters of legalizing state authority and securing the government's monopoly on power in the face of the SA, for example, by going through Riefenstahl. He asked Leni Riefenstahl to speak to Hitler about these subjects. See Rudolf Diels, *Lucifer ante portas* (Stuttgart, 1950), 22.
26. Riefenstahl, *Memoiren*, 212.
27. Ibid., 193, 194.
28. See Ernst Jaeger, "How Leni Riefenstahl Became Hitler's Girlfriend, Part 1," *Hollywood Tribune*, April 28, 1939.
29. Joseph Goebbels's diary entry of May 26, 1933, states: "Yesterday: wonderful trip to Heiligendamm. Unsuccessful picnic. Splendid sea! Boss along. Also Leni Riefenstahl."
30. A photograph from the time shows Leni Riefenstahl together with Joseph Goebbels at the filming of the Ufa Heimat film *Du sollst nicht begehren*, which premiered in October 1933 as Ufa's first true National Socialist film.
31. Riefenstahl told the columnist Bella Fromm in September 1933: "He asked me to dinner a couple of times every week." See Fromm, *Als Hitler mir die Hand küsste*, 151.
32. Riefenstahl verified this in September 1933, in a personal conversation with Bella Fromm. Ibid., 151ff.
33. Ibid., 161.
34. Quoted in Jochmann, *Adolf Hitler*, 235.
35. Quoted in Martha Schad, *"Das Auge war vor allen Dingen ungeheuer anziehend,"* Freundinnen und Verehrerinnen, in Ulrike Leutheusser, ed., *Hitler und die Frauen* (Stuttgart, 2001), 131.

36. Riefenstahl, *Memoiren*, 158.

37. Ibid., 197.

38. Manfred Koch-Hillebrecht, *Homo Hitler. Psychogramm des deutschen Diktators* (Munich, 1999), 289.

39. Lothar Machtan, *Hitlers Geheimnis. Das Doppelleben eines Diktators* (Berlin, 2001), 289.

40. Another clandestine joke also made reference to intimate relations: "Leni Riefenstahl is to be reimbursed for the films she creates for the Third Reich. It has been decided to award her a brown shirt. At the end of the award ceremony, she expresses her gratitude by holding up the shirt and saying, 'I'll always keep it up, and never forget the movement.'" In Jans-Jochen Gamm, *Der Flüsterwitz im Dritten Reich* (Munich, 1963), 99.

41. Carl Zuckmayer, *Geheimreport* (Göttingen, 2002), 93.

42. Testimony of Christa Schroeder given to CIC officer Erich Albrecht in Berchtesgaden on May 22, 1945, quoted in Christa Schroeder, *Er war mein Chef. Aus dem Nachlass der Sekretärin von Adolf Hitler* (Munich, 1985), 227.

43. Magda Goebbels (née Magda Quandt) reported her husband's opinion in this matter to Otto Wagener, who belonged to the inner circle of the NSDAP in the years preceding Hitler's seizure of power. See Wagener's papers on Magda Quandt, Institut für Zeitgeschichte, ED/60/25, 153901547.

44. Ernst Hanfstaengl, *Zwischen Weissem und Braunem Haus. Memoiren eines politischen Aussenseiters* (Munich, 1970), 286. Recalling this evening, Riefenstahl mentions Hitler, Joseph Goebbels, and Hanfstaengl as well as Heinrich Hoffmann, but not Magda Goebbels. See Riefenstahl, *Memoiren*, 181ff.

45. Rudolf Diels, head of the Gestapo, reported on this episode, which took place in 1933: "One day he summoned me to furiously show me an emigrant newspaper that featured illustrated reports in which he was represented half clothed, with his 'girlfriend' Riefenstahl holding a glass of champagne and sitting on his lap. He was beside himself, though it was obvious that it was a crude photomontage." Diels, *Lucifer ante portas*, 78ff.

46. Karl-Wilhelm Krause, *Zehn Jahre Tag und Nacht* (Hamburg, 1949), 35.

47. Riefenstahl, *Memoiren*, 159ff.

48. Ibid., 312.

49. Interview with Anni Winter, Munich, March 30, 1948, in the Musmanno Archives, Duquesne University, Pittsburgh, Pennsylvania. See also Infield, *Leni Riefenstahl*, 159.

50. Quoted in Schad, "Das Auge war von allen Dingen ungeheuer anziehend," 110.

51. Schroeder, *Er war mein Chef*, 155, 363.

52. Quoted in "Darüber schweigt Leni Riefenstahl," *Revue* 16/52, 6. A copy of the handwritten letter is included.

53. Riefenstahl, *Memoiren*, 290. During her first interrogation by the U.S. Army in May 1945, Riefenstahl also said that Hitler had never asked her private questions. See the final report of the German Intelligence Service on the interrogation of Leni Riefenstahl, May 30, 1945, Institut für Zeitgeschichte, Munich, F 135/3, Bl. 1.

54. In one of his table talks in Obersalzberg on March 13, 1944, for example, Hitler said, "Riefenstahl does it right." See Adolf Hitler, *Monologe im Führerhauptquartier 1941–1944. Die Aufzeichnungen Heinrich Heims*, ed. Werner Jochmann (Hamburg, 1980), 406.

55. Rudolf Augstein, quoted in *Der Spiegel*, August 10, 1987.

56. Speer, *Spandauer Tagebücher*, 198.

57. See Hilmar Hoffmann, "Und die Fahne führt uns in die Ewigkeit," in *Propaganda im NS-Film* (Frankfurt am Main, 1988), 147.

58. Leni Riefenstahl, quoted in Ray Müller's documentary film *Die Macht der Bilder*, Zweites Deutsches Fernsehen, 1993.

59. Gitta Sereny, *Das deutsche Trauma. Eine heilende Wunde* (Munich, 2000), 326ff.

60. Even during the war, Hitler expressed this opinion. See Henry Picker, *Hitlers Tischgespräche im Führerhauptquartier* (Munich, 1981), 129.

61. Brigitte Hamann, *Hitlers Wien. Lehrjahre eines Diktators* (Munich, 2001), 97.

62. Hitler, quoted on January 26, 1942, speaking of the architect Gerdy Troost; Winifred Wagner; Gertrud Scholtz-Klink, head of the Nazi Women's League; and Leni Riefenstahl, in *Monologe im Führerhauptquartier 1941–1944*, 235.

63. Hamann, *Hitlers Wien*, 101.

64. Albert Speer, quoted in Dan van der Vat, *Der gute Nazi. Leben und Lügen des Albert Speer* (Berlin, 1997), 399.

65. Joachim C. Fest, *Speer. Eine Biographie* (Berlin, 1999), 140.

66. "One thing is sure: Everyone who worked closely with him over a period of time was expressly submissive to him." Gitta Sereny, *Das Ringen mit der Wahrheit. Albert Speer und das deutsche Trauma* (Berlin, 1995), 168.

67. Speer, *Spandauer Tagebücher*, 17.

68. Albert Speer, *Erinnerungen* (Frankfurt am Main, 1969), 44.

69. Speer, *Spandauer Tagebücher*, 113.

## 6. THE "FÜHRER'S FILMMAKER"

1. The film historian Günther Peter Straschek arrived at this number after extensive research. See Jan-Christopher Horak, "Exilfilm," in Wolfgang Jacobsen, Anton Kaes, and Hans Helmut Prinzler, eds., *Geschichte des deutschen Films* (Stuttgart, 1993), 101; also Horak, *Fluchtpunkt Hollywood. Eine Dokumentation zur Filmemigration nach 1933* (Munich, 1986).

2. For more on the minister of propaganda's vague goals, see Felix Moeller, *Der Filmminister. Goebbels und der Film im Dritten Reich* (Berlin, 1998), 63ff, 106ff, 162ff.

3. Riefenstahl File, Berlin Document Center, Bundesarchiv Berlin, application of Leni Riefenstahl for acceptance into the Reich Film Chamber, October 2, 1933.

4. See Karsten Witte, "Film im Nationalsozialismus," in Jacobsen et al., *Geschichte des deutschen Films*, 121.

5. Joseph Goebbels, speech delivered to a group of theater directors on May 8, 1933, in Erwin Leiser, *"Deutschland erwache!" Propaganda im Film des Dritten Reiches*, rev. ed. (Reinbek, 1978), 46.

6. Quoted in Paul Werner, *Scandalchronik des deutschen Films von 1900–1945* (Frankfurt am Main, 1990), 218.

7. Ibid., 238.

8. Fest, *Speer*, 110.

9. Rudolf Herz, *Hoffmann & Hitler. Fotografie als Medium des Führer-Mythos* (Munich, 1994), 38.

10. Anna Maria Sigmund, *Die Frauen der Nazis II* (Vienna, 2000), 178ff.

11. Riefenstahl, *Memoiren*, 179.

12. Ibid., 181.

13. Ibid., 187.

14. Ibid., 181.

15. Ibid., 203.

16. The minister of propaganda and his wife had six children within a short space of time. This earned Magda Goebbels the first Honor Cross for German Mothers in 1938, a new medal for women who presented the Führer with a large number of children. At Goebbels's wish, the entire family repeatedly had to pose for the newsreel cameras as the ideal National Socialist family.

17. Wilfried von Oven, quoted in Guido Knopp, *Hitlers Frauen und Marlene* (Munich, 2001), 178.

18. Riefenstahl's version of things unconsciously supports this, as Goebbels's sexual advances date from the time of filming *Sieg des Glaubens*.

19. See Fromm, *Als Hitler mir die Hand küsste*, 247.

20. Fritz Hippler, quoted in Knopp, *Hitlers Frauen und Marlene*, 175.

21. Traudl Junge, quoted in Koch-Hillebrecht, *Homo Hitler*, 380.

22. Elizabeth Bronfen, "Zwei deutsche Stars. Leni Riefenstahl and Marlene Dietrich," in Wolfgang Jacobsen, Hans Helmut Prinzler, and Werner Sudendorf, eds., *Filmmuseum Berlin* (Berlin, 2000), 176.

23. Heinrich Fraenkel and Roger Manvell, *Goebbels. Der Verführer* (Cologne, 1960), 218. "Because [Goebbels] couldn't stand Riefenstahl, he even tried to sabotage her work on these films. But Riefenstahl succeeded in forging ahead with Hitler and securing his support against the conniving minister." See also Alice Schwarzer, "Leni Riefenstahl. Propagandistin oder Künstlerin?" *Emma*, January–February 1999, 42.

## 7. THE TRANSITION TO DOCUMENTARY FILMS

1. See Wolfgang Becker, *Film und Herrschaft. Organisationsprinzipien und Organisationsstrukturen nationalsozialistischer Filmpropaganda* (Uelzen, 1973), 21.

2. Alan Bullock, *Hitler. Eine Studie über Tyrannei* (Düsseldorf, 1989), 361.

3. Riefenstahl told Gitta Sereny that the idea for the "light domes" originated with her and was appropriated by Albert Speer. But this is unlikely; even though she had used bright spots to light the evening and night scenes of the rallies, these had no function above and beyond the filming. See Sereny, *Das Ringen mit der Wahrheit*, 160.

4. Riefenstahl, *Memoiren*, 197ff. The film on Horst Wessel was made by Franz Wenzler with the title *Hans Westmar* (1933).

5. In 1933, after she returned from Switzerland, Riefenstahl, together with Ufa, planned to make a spy film, "Mademoiselle Docteur," which, however, was rejected by the Wehrmacht ministry. In this film, Riefenstahl was to assume a starring role but not act as director.

6. Application of Leni Riefenstahl for acceptance into the Reich Film Chamber, October 2, 1933, Riefenstahl File, Berlin Document Center, Bundesarchiv Berlin.

7. Herman Weigel, "Interview mit Leni Riefenstahl," 399.

8. See "Leni Riefenstahl übernimmt künstlerische Leitung des Reichsparteitag-Films," *Licht-Bild-Bühne*, August 25, 1933.

9. When mentioning the "Hitler film" in his diaries, Goebbels never concretely says that this is a film on the September 1933 Nuremberg rally. However, as there is no record of any other project being negotiated with Riefenstahl in the summer of 1933, it can be assumed that the "Hitler film" was the first party rally film.

10. Arnold Raether was responsible for the party films *Das junge Deutschland* (1932), *Hitlerjugend in den Bergen* (1932), *Hitler über Deutschland* (1932), and *Deutschland erwacht*

(1933), which were considered significant only within the NSDAP and rarely shown outside the party.

11. Arnold Raether, quoted in Joself Wulf, *Theater und Film im Dritten Reich. Eine Dokumentation* (Frankfurt am Main, 1989), 366.

12. *Film-Kurier*, September 4, 1933.

13. Letter from Lange to Allwörden, August 28, 1933, Riefenstahl File, Berlin Document Center, Bundesarchiv Berlin.

14. Letter to Carl Auen from the NSBO Reich Film Group, September 6, 1933, ibid. In her statement of membership in the organization of Reich Film Professionals, Riefenstahl thus could sign the passage that read, "I specifically confirm that I am of Aryan heritage. Neither I nor my parents are of Jewish or any other foreign racial heritage." See membership declaration of Leni Riefenstahl for admittance to the Reich Film Professionals, October 2, 1933, ibid.

15. See, for example, "Der Absturz der Bergsteigerin," *Baseler Nationalzeitung*, June 26, 1937; and Padraic King, "The Woman Behind Hitler," *Detroit News*, February 21, 1937.

16. Interview, "Wie war das wirklich mit Adolf Hitler?" *Bunte* 8 (2000): 59ff. She made a similar statement during her first interrogation by the German Intelligence Service of the U.S. Army, June 30, 1945.

17. Speer, *Erinnerungen*, 74.

18. Riefenstahl attempted to suggest that she herself had financed the film, which was commissioned by the party. According to her, in order even to begin work on the film she had to borrow money from her father. See Riefenstahl, *Memoiren*, 207.

19. "Der deutsche Kamera-Stil," *Der deutsche Film. Zeitschrift für Filmkunst und Filmwirtschaft*, Sonderausgabe (1940–41): 26. See also *Film-Kurier*, January 25, 1936, 1.

20. *Rheinisch-Westfälische Filmzeitung*, March 30, 1935.

21. Cf., "Schule Riefenstahl. Der absolute Film," *Film-Kurier*, January 25, 1936.

22. Rother, *Leni Riefenstahl*, 107.

23. "Gibt es einen deutschen Kamerastil?" *Der deutsche Film* 3, no. 7 (1939), 176ff.

24. Stephan Dolezel and Martin Loiperdinger, "Adolf Hitler in Parteitagsfilm und Wochenschau," in Martin Loiperdinger, Rudolf Herz, and Ulrich Polhman, eds., *Führerbilder. Hitler, Mussolini, Roosevelt, Stalin in Fotografie und Film* (Munich, 1995), 85.

25. Waldear Lydor, "Sepp Allgeier erzählt vom Reichsparteitag-Film," *Film-Kurier*, November 25, 1933, 3.

26. In an interview with *Film-Kurier* on November 25, 1933, she explained her principle of editing: "The main difficulty was to give a fluidity to events that were always repeating themselves, to enhance them, to find transitions. In a word, to give the film a rhythmical movement."

27. In reality, the party rally of 1933, as opposed to Riefenstahl's film, took the following course: on August 31, the party leadership met and the official greeting took place in the Nuremberg Town Hall, followed by the opening ceremonies in the Congress Hall. On September 1, the SA and SS staged their parade with its ritual honoring of the dead and the dedication of the "blood flag." On September 2, there were parades by the various party formations on the parade grounds and in the streets of Nuremberg, followed by fireworks that evening. The rally ended on September 3 with a closing ceremony.

28. See Peter Hagen, "Der Sieg des Glaubens. Die Weltaufführung des Films vom Reichsparteitag," *Der Angriff*, December 2, 1933.

29. *Völkischer Beobachter*, December 1, 1933.

30. Joseph Goebbels, *Film-Kurier*, December 2, 1933.
31. See, for example, "Botschafterin des deutschen Films. Bericht über Leni Riefenstahls Vorträge in England," *Film-Kurier*, May 2, 1934.
32. See Martin Loiperdinger and David Culbert, "Leni Riefenstahl, the SA, and the Nazi Party Rally Films, Nuremberg 1933–1934," *Historical Journal of Film, Radio and Television* 8, no. 1 (1988).
33. Leni Riefenstahl, quoted in Müller, *Die Macht der Bilder*.
34. Riefenstahl, *Memoiren*, 212.
35. Charles Ford, *Leni Riefenstahl. Schauspielerin, Regisseurin und Fotografin* (Munich, 1982), 60.
36. Burden, *Die programmierte Nation*, 137.
37. Martin Loiperdinger, "'Sieg des Glaubens.' Ein gelungenes Experiment nationalsozialistischer Filmpropaganda," *Zeitschrift für Pädagogik*, special issue 31 (1993): 39, 47.

## 8. RIEFENSTAHL SHAPES THE FACE OF THE THIRD REICH

1. Riefenstahl quoted in Müller, *Die Macht der Bilder*.
2. Riefenstahl, *Memoiren*, 208.
3. Curt Riess concludes that Hitler had already decided to make a second party rally film in 1934, even before shooting for *Sieg des Glaubens* began: "Leni, he [Hitler] ordered, was to travel to Nuremberg at least to take a look at things and shoot some footage, so that the party rally film for the next year would go more smoothly." Riess, *Das gab's nur einmal*, 468.
4. The distribution agreement with Ufa, dated August 28, 1934, mentions a letter dated April 19, 1934, in which Hitler commissioned Riefenstahl to make the film. See Bundesarchiv Berlin, R109/1029b, Record no. 1021.
5. *Völkischer Beobachter*, March 29, 1935.
6. Herbert Seehofer, quoted in *Licht-Bild-Bühne*, October 23, 1934.
7. Leiser, *"Deutschland, erwache!,"* 30. And in fact, by order of the party leadership, which continued until 1938, no other film was made of a party rally. Only the newsreels showed them.
8. Leni Riefenstahl, *Hinter den Kulissen des Reichsparteitagfilms* (Munich, 1935), 11.
9. Fromm, *Als Hitler mir die Hand küsste*, 206.
10. William Shirer, *Aufstieg und Fall des Dritten Reiches* (Bindlach, 1990), 227.
11. Riefenstahl, *Hinter den Kulissen des Reichsparteitagfilms*, 11.
12. *Völkischer Beobachter*, September 1, 1934.
13. Bundesarchiv Berlin, R 109 I/1029b, Bl. 28.
14. Ibid., Record no. 1021.
15. See Lenssen, "Leben und Werk," 59. Walter Traut, Riefenstahl's close colleague, confirmed in a letter to the Reich Film Group of November 5, 1943, that Riefenstahl was making a film for the NSDAP at the order of the führer; see Letter of Walter Brau, November 4, 1934, Traut File, Berlin Document Center, Bundesarchiv Berlin.
16. All film scholars who have seriously addressed this issue as well as the judges of the German Federal High Court in 1969 have come to the conclusion that *Triumph des Willens*, just as *Sieg des Glaubens* and the short film *Tag der Freiheit!*, was produced and funded by the NSDAP. See also Martin Loiperdinger, *Rituale der Mobilmachung. Der Parteitagsfilm "Triumph des Willens," von Leni Riefenstahl* (Opladen, 1987), 45. This is confirmed by the fact that the censor's card for the 16-mm version of *Triumph des Willens* names the NSDAP as producer.

17. Letter from Leni Riefenstahl to Karl Auen, August 17, 1934, Riefenstahl File, Berlin Document Center, Bundesarchiv Berlin.

18. Letter from Leni Riefenstahl to Karl Auen, August 29, 1934, ibid.

19. Rother, *Leni Riefenstahl*, 216.

20. Emil Schünemann wrote in a letter to the editor of *Die Welt*: "I additionally would like to note that what I said at the time to Leni Riefenstahl's secretary was that it was beneath my dignity to make that sort of propaganda film. As trouble was brewing for me after that, at the suggestion of Herr Alberti, who was then the head of the cultural department and Herr Auen's superior, I changed my story and said that it was beneath my dignity to work under Leni Riefenstahl. I then went to England for a few months. Riefenstahl had received a villa in Dahlem as a gift from her Führer. She also was boasting that she could go in and out of her Führer's office without ever having to make an appointment. She could have handed me over to the Gestapo at any point, had Herr Alberti not covered for me." *Die Welt*, January 25, 1949.

21. The film historian Siegfried Kracauer was the first to posit this oft-repeated claim. Kracauer's theories were very influential in the discussion of Riefenstahl's work. See Kracauer, *Von Caligari zu Hitler*, 352ff.

22. Riefenstahl, *Memoiren*, 224.

23. Riefenstahl, *Hinter den Kulissen des Reichsparteitagfilms*, 18.

24. *Film-Kurier*, February 1, 1935.

25. Knopp, *Hitlers Frauen und Marlene*, 177.

26. *Rheinisch-Westfälische Filmzeitung*, September 29, 1934.

27. Weigel, "Interview mit Leni Riefenstahl," 402. This incorrect title was also used by Claudia Lenssen; see "Leben und Werk," 63.

28. *Film-Kurier*, February 1, 1935.

29. Quoted in Loiperdinger, *Rituale der Mobilmachung*, 45.

30. Riefenstahl quoted by Michel Delahaye, "Leni et le loup. Entretien avec Leni Riefenstahl," *Cahiers du Cinéma* 170 (September 1965).

31. Riefenstahl, *Hinter den Kulissen des Reichsparteitagfilms*, 28. In an interview shortly before the film premiered, Riefenstahl stated that *Triumph des Willens* was constructed "like a symphony." In choosing this term she referred directly to the editing technique used in Walter Ruttmann's compilation film *Berlin. Die Sinfonie der Grossstadt.*

32. See *Film-Kurier*, December 7, 1934, on a visit by Hitler, and December 18, 1934, on a visit by Rudolf Hess.

33. The censor's record of the original version of *Triumph des Willens*, officially evaluated on March 26, 1935, has not been located.

34. Leni Riefenstahl, speech delivered at the Lessing-Hochschule. See also *Film-Kurier*, April 4, 1935, 3.

35. Headline in *Reichsfilmblatt*, February 23, 1935, 3.

36. This motif goes back to the tradition of Hitler's so-called Germany flights, in which he visited fifty cities in July 1932 during an election campaign marathon. Hitler was the first person in the history of politics to use the airplane as a campaign tool. In using this, *Triumph des Willens* conveys that Hitler's party was the first to exploit modern technology to its utmost for its own purposes. The slogan of the time "Hitler over Germany" connoted modernity and speed.

37. Leni Riefenstahl, "Wie der Film vom Reichsparteitag entsteht—Eine Unterredung mit Leni Riefenstahl," *Magdeburger Tageszeitung*, January 13, 1935.

38. Leni Riefenstahl, "Über Wesen und Gestaltung des dokumentarischen Films," in *Der deutsche Film. Zeitschrift für Filmkunst und Filmwirtschaft* (Berlin, 1941), 19.

39. Speer, *Erinnerungen*, 75.

40. Klaus Kreimeier, *Die Ufa-Story. Geschichte eines Filmkonzerns* (Munich, 1992), 297.

41. See David B. Hinton, *The Films of Leni Riefenstahl*, 2d ed. (New York, 1991), 46. Riefenstahl declared Speer's version of the story to be the product of confusion: Speer had witnessed the lighting tests in the Congress Hall in September 1934, which she made together with Rudolf Hess. Speer then had mistakenly connected this with the reshoot.

42. *Film-Kurier*, March 30, 1935, 1.

43. Ibid., 2.

44. Ewald Demandowsky, "Der Reichsparteitagsfilm—Ein einmaliges Ereignis in einmaliger Gestaltung," *Völkischer Beobachter*, March 30, 1935.

45. *Film-Kurier*, September 25, 1934, 1.

46. At the same World's Fair, Albert Speer, to his and Hitler's surprise, received the Grand Prize for his model of the construction of the grounds of the Nuremberg party rally.

47. *Film-Kurier*, March 3, 1935, 1; March 20, 1935, 2.

48. Weigel, "Interview mit Leni Riefenstahl," 400.

49. Riefenstahl File, Berlin Document Center, Bundesarchiv Berlin.

50. Membership application of July 24, 1935, ibid.

51. Rother, *Leni Riefenstahl*, 22.

52. Adolf Hitler, foreword to Riefenstahl, *Hinter den Kulissen des Reichsparteitagfilms*, prepublished in *Film-Kurier*, March 18, 1935, 1.

53. Riefenstahl, *Hinter den Kulissen des Reichsparteitagfilms*, 7. Riefenstahl's argument that she published the book in order to name all of the colleagues she could not mention in the film's credits is also a purely self-protective statement. Every film of the period was accompanied by an illustrated program that contained the names of all members of the crew. Any moviegoer could purchase one.

54. It has been repeatedly and erroneously reported that Buñuel at the time tried in vain to make an antifascist film from Riefenstahl's film but failed in the end due to the strength of Riefenstahl's images. A look at Buñuel's memoirs clearly contradicts this version. See Luis Buñuel, *Mein letzter Seufzer*, 5th ed. (Berlin, 1999).

55. Ibid., 250.

56. Goebbels saw the film in 1942 at the Biennale in Venice and disparaged it as "the worst, the most devious thing that the Jews could have come up with." See Fritz Hippler, *Die Verstrickung* (Düsseldorf, 1981), 247.

57. Unlike *Triumph des Willens*, the NSDAP was named as the official producer of *Tag der Freiheit!* After the war, Riefenstahl (in *Film Culture* [Spring 1973]:103) criticized Ufa for the fact that the opening credits gave the false impression that the party, and not her company, had produced the film. This statement is no more believable than those made concerning *Sieg des Glaubens* and *Triumph des Willens*. Also doubtful is the possibility that the film was shown in movie theaters without the opening credits having received Riefenstahl's blessing.

58. In the previous party rally films, Riefenstahl had rejected scenes that she found lacking in quality. Hitler's traditional speech on culture is missing from *Triumph des Willens* for this reason, and in *Sieg des Glaubens* even his closing speech, which was considered the high point of each rally, is absent.

59. Riefenstahl, *Memoiren*, 227.

60. Ibid.

61. Ibid., 229.

62. The party rally took place at the beginning of September 1934. The Wehrmacht had sworn allegiance to Hitler only the month before, at which time the decision was made that the Wehrmacht would participate for the first time in an NSDAP party rally.

63. Sigmund, *Die Frauen der Nazis*, 109.

64. Riefenstahl, *Memoiren*, 245.

65. "Wie der neue Wehrmachtsfilm entstand. Leni Riefenstahl erzählt," *FilmWelt*. The exact date of publication is unknown, but presumably it was published before or around the time of the *Tag der Freiheit!* premiere, in December 1935 or January 1936. My sincere thanks to Lars Kluge, Berlin, for information on this article.

66. After the premiere at the Reich Chancellory, a gala party was held on December 30, 1935, at the Ufa-Palast am Zoo in Berlin. On February 26, 1936, Riefenstahl participated in the Italian premiere of the film and afterward met with Mussolini. The film opened in German cinemas in January 1936, distributed by Ufa, and was shown together with the spy film *Der höchste Befehl* by Gerhard Lamprecht.

67. Gerhard Schoenberner, "Ideologie und Propaganda im NS-Film," in Uli Jung, ed., *Der deutsche Film. Aspekte seiner Geschichte von den Anfängen bis zur Gegenwart* (Trier, 1993), 101.

## 9. PERFECT BODIES

1. "Never again did I want to make a documentary film, I had sworn that to myself." Riefenstahl, *Memoiren*, 126.

2. Luis Trenker confirmed this in 1967 in a conversation with the historian Werner Maser. Werner Maser, *Adolf Hitler. Legende, Mythos, Wirklichkeit*. 12th ed. (Munich 1971), 323, 581. See also Trenker, *Alles gut gegangen*, 324ff.

3. Knopp, *Hitlers Frauen und Marlene*, 183.

4. Picker, *Hitlers Tischgespräche im Führerhauptquartier*, 305.

5. Saul Friedländer, *Das Dritte Reich und die Juden* (Munich, 1998), 198.

6. Victor Klemperer, *Tagebücher 1935–1936*, 2nd ed., ed. Walter Nowojski (Berlin, 1999), 111, 75.

7. Bundesarchiv-Filmarchiv Berlin, Film File 1679.

8. *Film-Kurier*, April 27, 1936, spoke of a mission "assigned Leni Riefenstahl by the guardian of film, Reich Minister Dr. Goebbels." *Film-Kurier*, May 13, 1936, confirmed that "the commission to make the Olympics film, which is an honor in itself, was awarded to her by Dr. Goebbels." And Henry McLemore wrote in a 1938 article in the *Hollywood Citizen News*, which went unchallenged, that *Olympia* had come into being at "Hitler's behest."

9. Riefenstahl, *Memoiren*, 236ff.

10. Bundesarchiv Berlin, R2/4788, Bl. 216f. The entire contract is reproduced in Leiser, *"Deutschland erwache!"* 127ff.

11. In May 1936, a contract was signed with Willy Zielke concerning the prologue. The cost of the prologue suggested by Zielke was set at 60,000 reichsmarks. Zielke agreed to produce two edited sound versions: his "interpretation based on the existing script" and another "according to the interpretation of Frl. Riefenstahl." He was paid a flat fee of

10,000 reichsmarks for his work. See Contract, Estate of Willy Zielke, Filmmuseum Potsdam.

12. Willy Zielke, "Kurze Beschreibung meiner Freiheitsberaubung im Dritten Reich," Estate of Willy Zielke, Filmmuseum Potsdam, 5.

13. Hans Ertl, *Meine wilden dreissiger Jahre* (Berlin, 1982), 243.

14. Zielke wasn't, as Riefenstahl represented it, only at the institution in München-Haar (where she visited him in February 1937 and had him picked up in 1944). He was first in a hospital on the right bank of the Isar, and then in Schwabing Hospital. After that he went to München-Haar, and finally to Neufriedenheim Hospital and the sanitarium and asylum in München-Egelfing. See Zielke, "Kurze Beschreibung meiner Freiheitsberaubung im Dritten Reich," 8, 17.

15. Letter written by Ilse Zielke, May 18, 1988, Estate of Willy Zielke, Filmmuseum Potsdam.

16. Riefenstahl, *Memoiren*, 282.

17. Zielke, "Kurze Beschreibung meiner Freiheitsberaubung in Dritten Reich," 10.

18. Leni Riefenstahl, *Schönheit im Olympischen Kampf* (Berlin, 1937), endpaper.

19. Zielke, "Kurze Beschreibung meiner Freiheitsberaubung im Dritten Reich," 14.

20. See also Rother, *Leni Riefenstahl*, 188ff.

21. This was confirmed by the former Reich film director Fritz Hippler: "She greatly hindered my newsreel men. But what could we do? Riefenstahl's troops were just stronger than mine." Quoted in Knopp, *Hitlers Frauen und Marlene*, 184. See also Hippler, *Die Verstrickung*, 155ff.

22. Riess, *Das gab's nur einmal*, 560.

23. Knopp, *Hitlers Frauen und Marlene*, 179, 185.

24. Fromm, *Als Hitler mir die Hand küsste*, 249ff.

25. Leni Riefenstahl, quoted in Müller, *Die Macht der Bilder*.

26. Report on the cash audit of Olympia-Film GmbH, carried out October 3–8, Bundesarchiv Berlin, R55/503, Bl. 1–15. Reichsministerium für Volksaufklärung und Propaganda, Vorprüfstelle.

27. See "Der Absturz einer Bergsteigerin," *Baseler Nationalzeitung*, June 26, 1937. At the same time, an article titled "Der gefallene Engel des Dritten Reiches" appeared in the *Schweizer Weltwoche*.

28. Riefenstahl, *Memoiren*, 286.

29. Lenssen, "Leben und Werk," 63.

30. Arnold Fanck, "Was soll mit der Verfilmung der Olympiade erreicht werden?" Estate of Arnold Fanck, Filmmuseum Munich.

31. Riefenstahl, *Memoiren*, 304.

32. Sigmund, *Die Frauen der Nazis*, 111.

33. It is unclear whether Riefenstahl was in the Tirol coincidentally, as she maintained, or purposefully—perhaps even in Hitler's entourage.

34. "Premiere of the *Olympia* Film on the Day Before Adolf Hitler's Birthday," *Film-Kurier*, March 31, 1938.

35. Speer, *Erinnerungen*, 123.

36. Leni Riefenstahl, quoted in *Film-Kurier*, April 9, 1938.

37. Riefenstahl, *Memoiren*, 261.

38. *Marianne*, Paris, July 6, 1938.

39. *Helsingin Sanomat*, Helsinki, August 6, 1938.

40. *Observer*, London, March 1938.
41. *Intransigeant*, Paris, July 3, 1938.
42. Notation of March 16, 1939, Bundesarchiv Berlin, R 55/1328, Bl. 6.
43. Riefenstahl, *Memoiren*, 313ff.
44. Michael E. Birdwell, *Das andere Hollywood der dreissiger Jahre* (Vienna, 2000), 58.
45. While still in Germany, Riefenstahl had turned to Paul Kohner for help in offering the distribution rights to *Olympia* to Metro-Goldwyn-Mayer. See letter from Leni Riefenstahl to Paul Kohner, September 16, 1936, Kohner Collection, Stiftung Deutsche Kinemathek, Berlin.
46. Whereas in *Memoiren*, Riefenstahl erroneously stated that she was confronted with this hostility upon arrival in America, she confirmed in a 1972 interview that a reception had been planned for her in New York and that the boycott took place only when she arrived in Hollywood. See Weigel, "Interview mit Leni Riefenstahl," 405.
47. *Berlingske Tidende*, Copenhagen, March 1938.
48. *Aftenposten*, Oslo, March 1938.
49. *Stockholms Tidningen*, Stockholm, March 1938.
50. In Hilmar Hoffmann's extensive discussion of *Olympia*, the positive American reviews of 1938–39, for example, are not mentioned. Hilmar Hoffmann, *Mythos Olympia. Autonomie und Unterwerfung von Sport und Kultur* (Berlin, 1993), 153ff.

## 10. PRIVILEGES OF A STATE ARTIST

1. A plan of Riefenstahl's property and villa is published in Hans Josef Zechlin, *Landhäuser* (Berlin, 1939).
2. See letter from Emil Schünemann, *Die Welt*, January 25, 1949.
3. Undated newspaper article, circa 1938, publication unknown, Riefenstahl File, Theater Collection of the University of Cologne.
4. Riefenstahl, *Memoiren*, 310.
5. See letter by Julius Streicher, July 27, 1937, Riefenstahl File, Berlin Document Center, Bundesarchiv Berlin.
6. On April 1, 1933, Alfred Riefenstahl became member 1670383 of the NSDAP. Bundesarchiv 3200/S0019, Documents of the NSDAP Municipal Chancellory.
7. Bundesarchiv Berlin, R/31609, Bl. 33–35.
8. Ibid., R3/1609.
9. I am grateful to Herbert Wilczek, who then lived at Prager Strasse 7, for this information.
10. Heinrich von Kleist wrote *Penthesilea* in 1808, and it quickly became the literary scandal of its era. For a long time afterward no one dared adapt the play for the stage. Its first production took place only in 1876, at the Hofbühne in Berlin, and was not especially well received.
11. Riefenstahl, *Memoiren*, 223. She also confirmed this in 1997: "After *Triumph* in 1934, I had Hitler's word that I could freely determine my own work until the end of my life! That was the price!" *Zeit-Magazin*, August 29, 1997, 12.
12. Leni Riefenstahl's inscription to Adolf Hitler in the deluxe edition of Kleist's *Penthesilea*, quoted in *Bunte* magazine, March 13, 2003. The volume was sold at auction in Munich in May 2003. The auction house did not reveal how the book had found its way from Hitler's library to private ownership. The Library of Congress in Washington is in pos-

session of other titles that Riefenstahl inscribed to Hitler. See Timothy W. Ryback, "Hitler's Forgotten Library," *The Atlantic*, May 2003.

13. Quoted by Herman Weigel from Leni Riefenstahl's 1939 manuscript "Why I am Filming Penthesilea" in Weigel, "Randmerkungen zum Thema," *Filmkritik* 16, no. 188 (August 1972): 430. If and when Riefenstahl's article was published is unknown.

14. Riefenstahl, *Memoiren*, 216.

15. In view of the extensive private archive of Leni Riefenstahl, which appears to have survived the war virtually intact, it is strange that the screenplay of "Penthesilea" was lost. Only her extensive and detailed notes, costume sketches, and character descriptions survive. It is conceivable that the "Penthesilea" project never evolved beyond this, that a script was never written or completed. See *Filmkritik* 16, no. 188 (August 1972): 416ff.

16. Riefenstahl, *Memoiren*, 339.

17. Weigel, "Interview mit Leni Riefenstahl," 407.

18. See Rother, *Leni Riefenstahl*, 110ff.

19. Bundesarchiv Berlin, R 4606/2693, Bl. 46, 47.

20. Ibid., Bl. 46.

21. Ibid., Bl. 37.

## 11. A SECRET FILM PROJECT

1. See Rother, *Leni Riefenstahl*, 119ff., 140–45.

2. Riefenstahl had been involved with Hermann Storr since she met him at the end of 1937 during the sound editing of *Olympia*. In the summer of 1938, the couple went on holiday to Italy, where he accompanied her to the biennale, at which she was honored for the film.

3. Riefenstahl, *Memoiren*, 345, 349.

4. Ibid., 342ff.

5. Ibid., 344.

6. Speer's statements unquestionably confirm that the screening took place in Obersalzberg. See Speer, *Erinnerungen*, 176.

7. Ian Kershaw, *Hitler 1936–1945*, 2nd ed. (Stuttgart, 2000), 291.

8. The ceremony that took place in Moscow was captured on film by Riefenstahl's colleague Walter Frentz for the Wochenschau newsreels.

9. Riefenstahl, *Memoiren*, 345.

10. Ibid., 349.

11. Ibid.

12. In her memoirs, Riefenstahl mistakenly dates her departure for the front September 8 (*Memoiren*, 350). But a document delivered to the Military Archives of the German Federal Archives (Bundesarchiv-Militärarchiv, W 01-6/377, Bl. 1) establishes that the "Riefenstahl Special Film Unit" set out from Berlin at 7:00 a.m. on September 10. In *Memoiren*, Riefenstahl stated that she arrived at general headquarters in Lubliniec "already around noon," and traveled on to Końskie that same day. *Memoiren*, 350.

13. Erich von Manstein, *Verlorene Siege* (Frankfurt am Main, 1966), 43.

14. Ibid.

15. Riefenstahl, *Memoiren*, 350.

16. Riefenstahl erroneously dates the event as September 9, 1939; *Memoiren*, 350.

17. See Helmut Krausnick, *Hitlers Einsatztruppen. Die Truppen des Weltanschauungskrieges 1938–1942* (Frankfurt am Main, 1993), 48; Szymon Datner, *55 dni Wehrmachtu w Polsce. Zbrodnie dokonane na polskiej ludnosci cywilnej w okresie* (Warsaw, 1967), 221–52; Eugeniusz C. Król, "Leni Riefenstahl. Zycie i twórczość. Przyczynek do dyskusji o miejscu i roli artysty w państwie totalitarnym," in *Acta Universitatis Wratislaviensis* 2214 (Warsaw, 2001), 374ff. I am grateful to Dr. Umbrie of the Military-Historical Research Office in Potsdam, letter of March 22, 2000.

18. Riefenstahl, *Memoiren*, 351.

19. See Knopp, *Hitlers Frauen und Marlene*, 197ff. I am grateful to Dr. Eugeniusz C. Król, University of Warsaw, for information in this matter. The photographs were found in Częstochowa after the war. Judging from the stamp they bore, it can be assumed they came from the photography lab at Klosterstrasse 11, where negatives were developed and prints made. They were included in the collections of the Jewish Historical Institute in Warsaw and today are located in the Archive of the Institute of National Remembrance.

20. Kershaw, *Hitler 1936–1945*, 341.

21. Riefenstahl, *Memoiren*, 351.

22. Manstein, *Verlorene Siege*, 44.

23. Riefenstahl, *Memoiren*, 908.

24. Ibid., 352.

25. Hitler had left Berlin on September 3. He always calculated that France would join the war, and when it did he wished to be able to move his headquarters as quickly as possible to the west, by means of his "special train."

26. Military Archives of the German Federal Archives, RW 4/261, Bl. 136.

27. Riefenstahl, *Memoiren*, 353.

28. Ibid., 354.

29. See Rother, *Leni Riefenstahl*, 120.

30. Military Archives of the German Federal Archives, W 01-6/377, Bl. 1.

31. Ibid.

32. Ibid.

33. Ibid.

34. Ibid., Bl. 2.

35. See the stamp of date of receipt—September 13, 1939—on the quoted document. Ibid., Bl. 1.

36. Ibid., RW 4/261, Bl. 136.

37. Herz, *Hoffmann & Hitler*, 303.

38. *Film-Kurier*, September 11, 1935.

39. Riefenstahl, *Memoiren*, 367.

40. Military Archives of the German Federal Archives, RW 4/261, Bl. 136.

41. Only one document, dated October 18, 1939, that mentions the possibility of a propaganda film to be made in occupied Poland addresses the footage shot by the Special Film Troop Riefenstahl. The report concerns a meeting held three days before with Dr. Fischer, head of the Reich propaganda office in Lodz. One topic considered was opening Polish movie theaters again at the earliest possible date, in order for propaganda films to have an effect on the population. Toward this end, for example, screenings of German reconstruction projects in Poland that already had been produced by the propaganda companies

were to be increased. Commander in Chief Ost elaborated: "Footage taken by Riefenstahl could also be used." Ibid., Bl. 380.

42. Hippler had directed all other films that appeared under his name, such as *Der Westwall* (1939) and the inflammatory, anti-Semitic *Der ewige Jude* (1940). See Hippler, *Die Verstrickung*, 182ff.

43. Ibid., 200ff.

44. Weigel, "Interview mit Leni Riefenstahl," 407.

45. Ulrich Gregor and Enno Patalas, *Geschichte des Films, Vol. 2 (1940–1960)* (Reinbek, 1976), 308.

46. See Rother, *Leni Riefenstahl*, 142; Salked, *Portrait of Leni Riefenstahl*, 207; Lenssen, "Leben und Werk," 78.

47. Riefenstahl, *Memoiren*, 351.

48. Military Archives of the German Federal Archives, RW 4/261, Bl. 136.

49. Rother, *Leni Riefenstahl*, 142.

50. Riefenstahl, *Memoiren*, 350.

51. Riefenstahl File, Berlin Document Center, Bundesarchiv Berlin.

52. See "Darüber schweigt Leni Riefenstahl," *Revue*, April 19, 1952, 6ff. At this point in time, the date of the massacre was given as September 5. Only in the 1990s was the date corrected to September 12. Preceding this, the newspaper *Die Tat* pointed out on December 3, 1949, that Riefenstahl had been an eyewitness to the execution of Jews during the war. Following the positive decision of the tribunal, proceedings were never taken against *Revue*.

53. Riefenstahl, *Memoiren*, 508.

54. *Der Tagesspiegel*, April 22, 1952: "Witnesses confirmed her depiction of events, according to which she happened to be present when a number of Poles were forced to dig a grave with their bare hands for four German soldiers who apparently had been brutally murdered. She had protested to Reichenau, the army commander in charge, against the mistreatment and execution of the gravediggers and quit her activities as front reporter the day after this event."

55. Compare the commentary on the court's opinion, ibid.


## 12. FLIGHT INTO THE PUTATIVELY APOLITICAL

1. Director Adolf Edgar Lico had already used the material for his 1922 film starring Lil Dagover, Michael Bohnen, and Ilka Grüning.

2. Riefenstahl maintained that Terra offered her *Tiefland* in spring 1934 (*Memoiren*, 216). But this cannot be correct, as Ufa had already planned a *Tiefland* project with Riefenstahl, which was never realized. It can be assumed that Terra then took on the filming of *Tiefland* because Riefenstahl herself initiated the project and suggested a collaboration.

3. Hamann, *Hitlers Wien*, 92.

4. Ibid., 334.

5. Weigel, "Interview mit Leni Riefenstahl," 407.

6. Ibid., 402ff.

7. Bundesarchiv Berlin, R55/69, Bl. 29, Correspondence from Riefenstahl-Film to the Berlin Chamber of Industry and Commerce, December 2, 1942.

8. See, for example, Ford, *Leni Riefenstahl*, 117.

9. Picker, *Hitlers Tischgespräche im Führerhauptquartier*, 33.

10. Bernhard Minetti, *Erinnerungen eines Schauspielers* (Stuttgart, 1986), 151.

11. Veit Harlan, *Im Schatten meiner Filme* (Gütersloh, 1966), 158.

12. Bundesarchiv Berlin, R 43/II 810b, Bl. 81.

13. Ibid., Bl. 91.

14. Ibid., Bl. 81–93.

15. Because of covert financing by the NSDAP and the Reich, the exact amount of the production costs cannot be ascertained. Riefenstahl stated in postwar proceedings that *Tiefland* had cost 4.3 million reichsmarks, which is too low an amount by far. By December 16, 1942, Joseph Goebbels had noted in his diary that "over five million have already been poured into this film." The two years that followed, in which Riefenstahl continued to work on *Tiefland*, saw added not only the costly filming in Spain and in the Prague studios, but also excessive postproduction costs, for which, due to Riefenstahl's subsequent demands, yet further excessive sums were made available.

16. Riefenstahl, *Memoiren*, 365.

17. Riefenstahl File, Berlin Document Center, Bundesarchiv Berlin, R 109 I/1034b, Bl. 43.

18. Weigel, "Interview mit Leni Riefenstahl," 407.

19. Riefenstahl, *Memoiren*, 468.

20. "Poor Law" exempted less prosperous parties to a legal case from all or part of the legal fees incurred at trial.

21. *Hamburger Abendblatt*, November 25, 1949.

22. *Sozialdemokrat*, November 29, 1949.

23. Quoted in *Revue* 44 (December 11, 1949).

24. *Süddeutsche Zeitung*, November 26, 1949.

25. Ibid.

26. Leni Riefenstahl, quoted in *Quick*, December 11, 1949.

27. Riefenstahl, *Memoiren*, 472.

28. Ibid., 476.

29. I am grateful to Klaus Liebe and Vera Romboy for the opportunity to view the film at Westdeutscher Rundfunk in Cologne.

30. This document and others by Böhmer in this context are included in Documentionsarchiv des österreichischen Widerstands, ed., *Widerstand und Verfolgung in Salzburg 1933–1945. Eine Dokumentation* (Vienna, n.d.), 511ff.

31. Sybil Milton, "Vorstufe der Vernichtung. Zigeunerlager nach 1933," *Vierteljahreshefte für Zeitgeschichte* 1 (January 1995): 115–30.

32. Riefenstahl, *Memoiren*, 361.

33. Quoted in Knopp, *Hitlers Frauen und Marlene*, 195. See also Rosa Winter, *Soviel wie eine Asche*, in Karin Berger, ed., *Ich geb Dir einen Mantel, dass Du ihn noch in Freiheit tragen kannst. Widerstehen im KZ. Österreichische Frauen erzählen* (Vienna, 1987), 78.

34. Riefenstahl, *Memoiren*, 471.

35. Ibid., 361.

36. See Ulrich Enzensberger, "Lieber noch zwei Jahre Auschwitz als noch einmal von den Russen befreit werden," *Tageszeitung*, March 9, 1985.

37. Josef Reinhardt, in agreement with other witnesses, stated in Gladnitz's film that many of his relatives, who also were forced to work for Riefenstahl as extras, died at Auschwitz. Reinhardt speculates that up until the time of their deaths in the gas chambers, these rel-

atives hoped that Leni Riefenstahl would come to save them. See Nina Gladitz, *Zeit des Schweigens und der Dunkelheit*, Westdeutscher Rundfunk, 1982. The majority of the twenty-three thousand Sinti and Roma, who at the end of 1942 were living in the "Gypsy camp" constructed in Auschwitz-Birkenau, died of starvation, in epidemics, as a result of medical experimentation, or in the gas chambers.

38. Riefenstahl, *Memoiren*, 361ff. Leni Riefenstahl made a similar statement to the author, on May 24, 1997, in Pöcking.
39. Leni Riefenstahl to Curt Riess, quoted by Erwin Leiser, *Weltwoche*, March 26, 1987.
40. Wulf C. Schwarzwäller, *Hitlers Geld. Vom armen Kunstmaler zum millionenschweren Führer* (Vienna, 1998), 179ff.
41. The Adolf Hitler Endowment of the German Economy was a fund financed by German businessmen who profited from association with the National Socialist party, and also by funds "contributed" by Jewish businessmen.
42. Schwarzwäller, *Hitlers Geld*, 195.
43. Ibid., 199ff.
44. Peter Longerich, "Nationalsozialistische Propaganda," in Karl-Dietrich Bracher, Manfred Funke, and Hans-Adolf Jacobsen, eds., *Deutschland 1933–1945. Neue Studien zur nationalsozialistischen Herrschaft*, 2nd rev. ed. (Bonn, 1993), 307.
45. Letter from Leni Riefenstahl to the Propaganda Ministry, March 9, 1939, Riefenstahl File, Berlin Document Center, Bundesarchiv Berlin.
46. Letter from Riefenstahl-Film GmbH to the Chamber of Industry and Commerce, December 2, 1942, ibid., R55/69, Bl. 29f.
47. Letter from the general inspector of buildings for the Reich capital to the Reich minister and chief of the Reich Chancellory, May 11, 1940, ibid., R43II/389, Bl. 13.
48. Arnold Fanck, *Er kämpfte mit Gletschern, Stürmen und Lawinen* (Munich, 1933).
49. Riefenstahl, *Memoiren*, 365.
50. Ibid., 366.
51. Ibid., 367.
52. Ibid.
53. National Archives, Washington, DC, File 746-748, R 45, publication on microfilm, T-253. See also Infield, *Leni Riefenstahl*, 191.
54. Riefenstahl, *Memoiren*, 389ff.
55. It was precisely in the last weeks and months of the war that the elite of the film world gathered in Tirol. Erich Kästner, an illegal member of an Ufa film team in Mayrhofen (he was a pacifist and thus forbidden to work), noted in his diary: "Marika Rökk is out walking her baby in its carriage. Leni Riefenstahl has arrived from Kitzbühel." See Erich Kästner, *Notabene 45. Ein Tagebuch von Erich Kästner* (Zürich, 1961), 130.
56. Riefenstahl, *Memoiren*, 363.
57. Ibid., 364.
58. Ibid., 365, 366.
59. Ibid., 370.
60. Ibid., 394.
61. At her first interrogation by the German Intelligence Service of the U.S. Army, Riefenstahl gave the date of her last meeting with Hitler as March 21, 1944. See the Concluding Report of the German Intelligence Service on the Interrogation of Leni Riefenstahl of May 30, 1945, Munich: Institut für Zeitgeschichte, F 135/3, Bl. 1.

62. A short time later, on June 6, 1944, Joseph Goebbels noted in his diary: "From a distance he looks sorely tested, a stooped man whose shoulders seem ready to collapse under the burden of responsibility."

63. "Loss of strength, deformity of the spine, trembling of left arm and leg, as well as constant stomach and intestinal pain forced him, beginning on March 16, 1944, to spend four months (with interludes in Berlin) relaxing at Berghof." Picker, *Hitlers Tischgespräche im Führerhauptquartier*, 244.

64. Speer, *Spandauer Tagebücher*, 328.

65. Riefenstahl, *Memoiren*, 397.

66. Sereny, *Das Ringen mit der Wahrheit*, 514.

67. Riefenstahl, *Memoiren*, 398.

68. Ibid., 402.

69. Patrick Robertson, *Das neue Guiness Buch Film* (Frankfurt am Main, 1993), 122.

70. *Stuttgarter Zeitung*, February 13, 1954.

71. Riefenstahl, *Memoiren*, 525.

72. In his memoirs, Bernhard Minetti spoke of the reasons for this failure, which Riefenstahl was loath to admit during her lifetime: "She demanded of herself . . . something she was unsuited for: to act, without being an actress." *Erinnerungen eines Schauspielers*, 150.

73. Riefenstahl, *Memoiren*, 525.

74. Riefenstahl, *Memoiren*, 527.

75. Helma Sanders-Brahms, "Tyrannenmord," in Hans Helmut Prinzler, ed., *Das Jahr 1945* (Berlin, 1990), 173. Five years later, Sanders-Brahms's thesis was taken up by Robert von Dassanowsky, and again at the end of the nineties by Thea Dorn.

76. Leni Riefenstahl, *Frankfurter Rundschau*, April 27, 2002.

77. I am grateful to Kurt Holl, Association Rom, Inc., Cologne, for making the charges available to me.

78. Declaration to cease and desist by Leni Riefenstahl, August 14, 2002. See also Susan Tegel, "Leni Riefenstahl's 'Gypsy Question,'" in *Historical Journal of Film, Radio and Television* 23 no. 1 (2003): 3.

79. In regard to the cases of Rosa Winter and Anna Blach, see the documentary film *Riefenstahlremix* by Tina Leisch (Austria, 2003). I am grateful to Tina Leisch for her advice and information.

## 13. NOT IMMUNE AFTER ALL?

1. Riefenstahl, *Memoiren*, 153.

2. Sokal, "Über Nacht Antisemit geworden?"

3. Leni Riefenstahl, "Nie Antisemitin gewesen," letter to the editor, *Der Spiegel*, November 15, 1976.

4. After Arnheim had been awarded six honorary doctorates from various American colleges, in 1993 he received an honorary doctorate from the Carl von Ossietzky University in Oldenburg. Arnheim, once a comrade of Ossietzky, was honored for his contributions to the psychology, history, and philosophy of art; film and broadcasting theory; and cultural and media criticism. In 1978 he also was the recipient of the German Film Prize, for his "many years' service and outstanding work in German film."

5. Rudolf Arnheim, *Kritiken und Aufsätze zum Film* (Frankfurt am Main, 1979), 326.

6. Arnheim was interviewed by the journalist Tita Gaehme on October 8, 1999. Portions of the interview were included in the radio feature "I Always Trusted Reality—On Rudolf Arnheim," broadcast by German Radio on January 21, 2000. I am grateful to Tita Gaehme for this information and for permission to use the text.

7. I am most grateful to Rudolf Arnheim for information received on February 11, 2002.

8. G. W. Pabst was not comfortable with Hollywood's studio system and following a lengthy interlude in France returned to Germany in 1939, where he continued to make films.

9. Riefenstahl, *Memoiren*, 100ff.

10. Ibid., 194.

11. King, "The Woman Behind Hitler." Riefenstahl repeatedly spoke to foreign journalists of her sympathy for Hitler. See, for example, an interview she gave in London to Pembroke Stephens, "Hitler—By a Woman. His Film Star Friend Flies Here," *Daily Express*, April 26, 1934.

12. Riefenstahl, *Memoiren*, 208.

13. This is verified by the invitation that Riefenstahl extended to Streicher the following year to attend the premiere of *Triumph des Willens*: "My dear Herr Streicher, I most warmly request that you accept this invitation to the premiere of *Triumph des Willens* on March 28 at the Ufa-Palast in Berlin, as you did last spring." Quoted from a facsimile of the letter in Fred Hahn, *Lieber Stürmer, Leserbriefe an das NS-Kampfblatt 1924–1945* (Stuttgart, 1958), 51.

14. Letter of Leni Riefenstahl, December 11, 1933, Riefenstahl File, Berlin Document Center, Bundesarchiv Berlin.

15. Riefenstahl, *Hinter den Kulissen des Reichsparteitagfilms*, 17.

16. See *Fränkische Tageszeitung*, September 13, 1934.

17. Quoted in Hahn, *Lieber Stürmer*, 51.

18. Ertl, *Meine wilden dreissiger Jahre*, 200ff.

19. Riefenstahl, *Memoiren*, 612.

20. Letter from Julius Streicher, July 27, 1939, Riefenstahl File, Berlin Document Center, Bundesarchiv Berlin.

21. American Intelligence Report on Leni Riefenstahl, May 30, 1945, p. 3, Institut für Zeitgeschichte, Munich.

22. Riefenstahl, *Memoiren*, 209ff.

23. Lenssen, "Leben und Werk," 67.

24. Riefenstahl, *Memoiren*, 395.

25. Bernhard Grzimek, *Auf den Mensch gekommen. Erfahrungen mit Leuten* (Gütersloh, 1974), 131.

26. Conversation with Evelyn Künneke, March 28, 2000.

27. Riefenstahl, *Memoiren*, 233ff.

28. Conversation with Evelyn Künneke.

29. Lotte Eisner, *Ich hatte einst ein schönes Vaterland. Memoiren* (Heidelberg, 1984), 159ff.

30. See Ernst Jaeger's statement in *Aktuelle Filmnachrichten der Allianz Film GmbH* 2 (January 20, 1954): 6ff.

31. Leni Riefenstahl interview, "Wie war das wirklich mit Adolf Hitler?" *Bunte* 8 (2000): 60.

32. Sokal, quoted in Infield, *Leni Riefenstahl*, 234.

33. Quoted in Budd Schulberg, "Nazi Pin-Up Girl," *Saturday Evening Post*, March 30, 1946.

34. *Kölner Stadt-Anzeiger*, June 30, 1994.

35. Riefenstahl, "Wie war das wirklich mit Adolf Hitler?" 56.

14. COLLAPSE AND NEW BEGINNING, 1945

1. Riefenstahl was not as uninformed about the war as she later represented herself to be. Though by then she rarely met privately with Hitler, she would have been better informed than most Germans. After all, throughout the war she had remained in contact with her former colleague Walter Frentz, whom Hitler had assigned as a film reporter to the "Führer's headquarters" in East Prussia. From Frentz she heard "quite a bit." Riefenstahl, *Memoiren*, 405.

2. Henry Jaworsky (Heinz von Jaworsky), interview in *Film Culture*, Spring 1973, 150.

3. Riefenstahl, *Memoiren*, 400.

4. Ibid., 408.

5. Speer, *Erinnerungen*, 491.

6. "Die Unvermeidliche" (date and place of publication unknown), Theater Collection of the University of Cologne, Personal File Leni Riefenstahl.

7. Leni Riefenstahl, in an interview in *Zeit-Magazin* 36 (October 29, 1997): 12.

8. Schulberg, "Nazi Pin-Up Girl," 39ff.

9. See Final Report of the German Intelligence Service on the testimony of Leni Riefenstahl, May 30, 1945, Institut für Zeitgeschichte München, F135/3.

10. Riefenstahl, *Memoiren*, 415ff.

11. Schroeder, *Er war mein Chef*, 405.

12. Final Report of the German Intelligence Service on the testimony of Leni Riefenstahl, Bl. 1.

13. Interview mit Leni Riefenstahl, *Bunte* 8 (2000): 56.

14. Final Report of the German Intelligence Service on the testimony of Leni Riefenstahl, Bl. 4.

15. Irving Rosenbaum, quoted in Guido Knopp's TV documentary *Hitlers Frauen und Marlene* (Leni Riefenstahl episiode), Zweites Deutsches Fernsehen, 2001.

16. Riefenstahl, *Memoiren*, 432.

17. Speer, *Erinnerungen*, 507.

18. Riefenstahl, *Memoiren*, 440.

19. Ibid. Riefenstahl stated that, in addition to the 300,000 reichsmarks in her company account, her private account with 30,000 reichsmarks and the accounts of her mother (4,000 reichsmarks) and her husband, Peter Jacob (2,000 reichsmarks), were seized.

20. Letter from Leni Riefenstahl, October 3, 1946, Estate of Richard Angst, Stiftung Deutsche Kinemathek, 4.3-85/03-2.

21. Riefenstahl, *Memoiren*, 436.

22. Ibid., 559ff.

23. Ibid., 590.

24. Deford, "Ghost of Berlin," 56.

25. Jaworsky, interview in *Film Culture*, 135.

26. About her relationship with Froitzheim, Riefenstahl said, "I thought of running away despite my dependence" (*Memoiren*, 59). In terms of Peter Jacob, she describes similar feelings: "I wanted to separate from this man for reasons of my own self-preservation, but his words acted on me like a poison" (ibid., 389). His letters "had an almost magic effect on me" (ibid., 365). "I was a prisoner of my own emotions" (ibid., 386).

27. Richard Corliss, "Riefenstahl's Last Triumph," *Time*, October 10, 1993.

28. Schwarzer, "Leni Riefenstahl," 42.

29. Ibid., 43.

30. Riefenstahl File, Berlin Document Center, Bundesarchiv Berlin; Spruchkammer Villingen: Begründung der Eingruppierung Leni Riefenstahls in der Sitzung vom 5.11.1948.

31. Riefenstahl File, Berlin Document Center, Bundesarchiv Berlin; Spruchkammer Freiburg: Begründung der Eingruppierung Leni Riefenstahls in der Sitzung vom 6.7.1949.

32. Riefenstahl File, Berlin Document Center, Bundesarchiv Berlin; Badisches Staatskommissariat für politische Säuberung. Spruchkammer Freiburg: Entscheidung im politischen Säuberungsverfahren gegen Leni Riefenstahl-Jacob vom 16.12.1949. The cost of the proceedings, 28,000 deutsche marks, had to be paid by Riefenstahl.

33. Riefenstahl, *Memoiren*, 464.

34. This rumor was reported, for instance, by Emil Schünemann, who in 1934 had refused to work as a cameraman under Riefenstahl's direction, in an interview after the war. See *Die Welt*, January 25, 1949.

35. Riefenstahl, *Memoiren*, 467.

36. Rother, *Leni Riefenstahl*, 15.

37. Bronfen, "Zwei deutsche Stars," 172.

38. Margarete Mitscherlich, *Über die Mühsal der Emanzipation* (Frankfurt am Main, 1994), 161.

39. Riefenstahl, *Memoiren*, 848.

40. Riefenstahl quoted in *Der Spiegel*, no. 40, 1949.

41. Riefenstahl, *Memoiren*, 605. In 1954, Riefenstahl had for the first time claimed the rights to *Triumph des Willens* when she demanded her share of the profits from *Bis Fünf vor Zwölf*, a film that included clips from her party rally film. She claimed that she did receive payment and that she donated it to charity.

42. *Berliner Zeitung*, December 9, 1960; *Welt der Arbeit*, January 27, 1961. See also Rother, *Leni Riefenstahl*, 162.

43. See Leiser, *"Deutschland, erwache!"* 125.

44. Erwin Leiser, quoted in *Neue Zürcher Zeitung*, January 19, 1978.

45. After the war, Mainz reestablished himself as a film producer, with successful films such as *Canaris* (1954) and *Des Teufels General* (1954).

46. Cf. Riefenstahl, *Memoiren*, 607.

47. German Federal High Court Decision, January 10, 1969, Az IZR. 48/67, 13ff.

48. Leni Riefenstahl, interview in *Film Culture*, Spring 1973.

49. Leni Riefenstahl, in conversation with the author in Pöcking, May 24, 1997.

50. Bundesarchiv Berlin, R 109 I/2163, agreement of January 16, 1964.

51. Ibid., letter of April 1, 1968. Cf. Rother, *Leni Riefenstahl*, 171.

52. Rother, *Leni Riefenstahl*, 165.

53. Letter to the author from the Film Archive of the Federal Archives, February 22, 2000.

54. Letter to the author from the Film Archive of the Federal Archives, March 7, 2000.

55. Letter to the author from Mark Grünthal, Transit-Film GmbH, March 15, 2000.

56. Riefenstahl interview with *Welt am Sonntag*, December 24, 2000, 29.

57. Panone had worked in the Italian embassy in Berlin before the war, where Riefenstahl had met him. Afterward he owned the production company Capitol Pictures and offered support to the artist he admired.

58. Riefenstahl, *Memoiren*, 489.

59. See "Lenis Rote Teufel. Ein Gespräch mit Frau Riefenstahl," *Cahiers du Cinéma* 170 (September 1965).

60. Riefenstahl, *Memoiren*, 519.

61. Ibid., 549.

62. Riefenstahl founded the company together with her former colleague Walter Traut, who in the intervening years had made such films as *08/15* (1955) and *Der Arzt von Stalingrad* (1958).

63. Heinz Hölscher, quoted in Knopp's documentary *Hitlers Frauen und Marlene*, Leni Riefenstahl episode.

## 15. RIEFENSTAHL DISCOVERS A NEW WORLD

1. Riefenstahl, *Memoiren*, 550.

2. Lenssen, "Leben und Werk," 94.

3. Leni Riefenstahl, in conversation with the author in Pöcking, May 24, 1997.

4. Leni Riefenstahl, *Die Nuba. Menschen wie von einem anderen Stern* (Munich, 1973), 9.

5. Riefenstahl, *Memoiren*, 627.

6. Ibid., 656.

7. Riefenstahl, *Die Nuba*, 9.

8. Riefenstahl, *Memoiren*, 637.

9. Ibid., 675.

10. Ibid., 810.

11. Ibid., 871. Riefenstahl did not state which medal she received.

12. The subtitle is said to have been suggested by Albert Speer, with whom Riefenstahl collaborated in the editing and shortening of the text. Riefenstahl, *Memoiren*, 779ff.

13. Riefenstahl, interview in *Der Spiegel*, August 18, 1997, 202.

14. Riefenstahl, *Memoiren*, 707.

15. Weigel, "Interview mit Leni Riefenstahl," 410.

16. The fifty-eight-minute film combines footage taken in 2000 with formerly unpublished Nuba photographs from Riefenstahl's archive. The first broadcast was planned for 2002, but no date was set at the time of the publication of this book. It was released on DVD in 2003. I am indebted to Fritjof Hohagen, Odeon Film, Munich, for this information of February 19, 2002.

17. Ray Müller, "Der Besuch der alten Dame," 66, 68.

18. Ibid., 68.

19. Ibid.

20. Susan Sontag, "Fazinierender Fascismus," in *Im Zeichen des Saturn* (Frankfurt am Main, 1983), 108.

21. Ibid., 117.

22. Riefenstahl interview in *Der Spiegel*, August 18, 1997, 205.

23. See the conversation between Adrienne Rich and Susan Sontag, *Frauen und Film* 14 (December 1977): 6–35.

24. Bärbel Dalichow and Claudia Lenssen, "Focus Leni Riefenstahl," in *Leni Riefenstahl*, ed. Filmmuseum Potsdam (Berlin, 1999), 7.

25. Hilmar Hoffmann, in a discussion broadcast by the TV station ARTE that followed the first showing of the documentary film *Die Macht der Bilder*, in 1993.

26. Knopp, *Hitlers Frauen und Marlene*, 11.

27. Ian Kershaw, *Der Hitler-Mythos. Führerkult und Volksmeinung* (Stuttgart, 1999).

28. Jerzy Toeplitz, "Der Film im Zeichen des Hakenkreuzes," in *Geschichte des Films*, Vol. 3 (1934–1939) (Berlin, 1992), 270.
29. Amos Vogel, *Film als subversive Kunst. Kino wider die Tabus—von Eisenstein bis Kubrick* (St. Andrä-Wörden, 1997), 176.
30. Antje Olivier and Sevgi Braun, *Anpassung oder Verbot. Künstlerinnen und die 30er Jahre* (Düsseldorf, 1998), 263.
31. Ford, *Leni Riefenstahl*, 132.

## 16. THE TEMPORARILY FINAL CAREER

1. Dalichow and Lenssen, "Focus Leni Riefenstahl," 7.
2. Riefenstahl, *Memoiren*, 737.
3. Leni Riefenstahl in a letter to the author, September 15, 1997, Maui, Hawaii.
4. Leni Riefenstahl, *Korallengärten* (Munich, 1978), 7ff.
5. Riefenstahl, *Memoiren*, 796.
6. Riefenstahl, *Korallengärten*, 8.
7. Riefenstahl, *Memoiren*, 797.
8. Riefenstahl, *Korallengärten*, 10.
9. Ibid., 14.
10. Riefenstahl, *Memoiren*, 858.
11. Leni Riefenstahl, quoted in *Unterwasserfotografie* 2 (1998): 64.
12. Leni Riefenstahl, quoted in *Die Welt*, September 20, 1982.
13. Mariam Lau, "Triumph der Fische," *Süddeutsche Zeitung*, December 4, 1998, 15.
14. Riefenstahl, *Korallengärten*, 15.
15. For example, in her first book of underwater photography she issued an appeal against underwater harpooning. Riefenstahl, *Korallengärten*, 16.
16. Leni Riefenstahl, in conversation with the author, Pöcking, May 24, 1997.
17. Riefenstahl, *Memoiren*, 740.
18. Ibid., 742.
19. Ibid., 753.
20. Joachim Hauschild, "Eine Frau mit Vergangenheit," *Stern-TV-Magazin*, March 24, 1994, 7.
21. Leni Riefenstahl, quoted in "Wie war das wirklich mit Adolf Hitler?" *Bunte* 8 (2000): 58.
22. Müller, "Der Besuch der alten Dame," 66.
23. Riefenstahl, *Memoiren*, 909.
24. Fritz Raddatz, "Hitler lobte Helenes Apfelstrudel," *Die Zeit*, October 9, 1987.
25. Margarete Mitscherlich, *Stern*, October 8, 1987.
26. Erwin Leiser, "Die Kunst des Verdrängens," *Israelitisches Wochenblatt für die Schweiz*, June 19, 1987.
27. Will Tremper, "Wie die Memoiren entstanden," *Bunte*, June 4, 1987.
28. Sontag, "Fazinierender Fascismus," 106.
29. Angelika Taschen, foreword to Taschen, ed., *Leni Riefenstahl—Fünf Leben* (Cologne, 2000), 17ff.
30. Timo Fehrensen, "Eindrucksvolles Gespräch," *Frankfurter Rundschau*, March 13, 1999.
31. Rainer Rother, "Leni Riefenstahl. Renaissance einer Legende," *Der Tagesspiegel*, August 22, 2000.
32. See Ian Kershaw, "Trauma der Deutschen," *Spiegel Special* 1 (2001): 6–13.

CONCLUSION: THE RIEFENSTAHL RENAISSANCE

1. Rother, *Leni Riefenstahl*, 10.
2. See Hans Egon Holthusen, "Riefenstahl in Amerika," *Merkur* 29, no. 325 (1975).
3. See Riefenstahl in conversation with Alice Schwarzer, "Leni Riefenstahl. Propagandistin oder Künstlerin?" *Emma*, January–February 1999.
4. Lenssen, "Leben und Werk," 114.
5. R. Andrews, "Hitler's Favorite Filmmaker Honored at Colorado Film Festival," *New York Times*, September 15, 1974.
6. *Frauen und Film* 14 (December 1977).
7. Infield, *Leni Riefenstahl*, 9.
8. Ibid., 11.
9. Helmut Newton was an admirer of Riefenstahl and her visual sense, and her aesthetic informed many of his photographs. He expressed his appreciation of the artist, "even if her Nazi subjects were shits." Quoted in Knopp, *Hitlers Frauen und Marlene*, 151.
10. Quoted in Leiser, *"Deutschland, erwache!"*, 9.
11. See Georg Seesslen, "Blut und Glamour," in *Leni Riefenstahl*, Filmmuseum Potsdam, 192–213.
12. Leni Riefenstahl, in an interview with Andreas Hutzler, *Stern*, December 2, 1999, 284.
13. The German weekly *Die Zeit*, which titled its review "Triumph des Willens," as well as the *Frankfurter Allgemeine Zeitung* attacked the film in December 1994, linking it to Riefenstahl's aesthetic. It was not only that individual scenes were reminiscent of *Triumph des Willens*, it was also the manner in which the Lion King's rule was based in a myth of natural law. In addition, the film was charged with racist overtones. Nor did critics ignore the score of German film composer Hans Zimmer, in which were heard clearly Wagnerian tones. See also Daniel Kothenschulte, "Triumph des Wildnis," *Stadtrevue Köln* 1 (1995): 112ff.
14. Annie Leibovitz, *Olympic Portraits* (Boston, 1996).
15. Leni Riefenstahl in conversation with the author, Pöcking, May 24, 1997.
16. *New York Times Book Review*, September 26, 1993.
17. Letter from the festival organizer Kevin John Charbeneau to Leni Riefenstahl, September 10, 1997. I am grateful to Leni Riefenstahl Productions for access to this document.
18. Quoted in *Die Welt*, September 4, 1997.
19. Riefenstahl, "Wie war das wirklich mit Adolf Hitler?" *Bunte*, 59.
20. Ray Müller, *Frankfurter Rundschau*, March 26, 1994.
21. Georg Seesslen, *Tanz mit Adolf Hitler. Faschismus in der populären Kultur* (Berlin, 1994), 89.
22. Leni Riefenstahl, in conversation with the author, Pöcking, May 24, 1997.
23. Leni Riefenstahl, letter to the author, October 25, 1993.
24. In addition, *Die Macht der Bilder* won the 1993 Special Jury Prize in Graz, the 1993 Silver Hugo Award in Chicago, the 1993 National Film Board Prize in Montreal, the 1994 Golden Gate Award in San Francisco, the 1994 Silver Enzian in Trento, and the 1994 Golden Space Needle Award in Seattle.
25. Rother, *Leni Riefenstahl*, 13.
26. Leni Riefenstahl, in conversation with the author, Pöcking, May 24, 1997.
27. Foster first wrote to Riefenstahl in 1997. (Leni Riefenstahl, in conversation with the author, Pöcking, May 24, 1997.) Foster had already thoroughly investigated Riefenstahl's films as part of her film studies while a student at Yale University.

28. Announcement of the Deutsche Presse Agentur news service, January 18, 2000.
29. Riefenstahl, "Wie war das wirklich mit Adolf Hitler?" 59.
30. Leni Riefenstahl in conversation with the author, Pöcking, May 24, 1997.
31. Giorgio Moroder, quoted in *Der Spiegel*, January 22, 2002, 151.
32. Hilmar Hoffmann, "Zum 100 mein neuer Film. Interview mit Leni Riefenstahl," *Die Welt*, January 18, 2002.
33. Charles Ford, for instance, traces the questions justifiably asked of Riefenstahl after 1945, which he considers examples of malicious "persecution" and "chicanery," back to a leftist "Marxist-Leninist" conspiracy that consciously hindered the continued work of one "of the best women filmmakers in the world." Ford, *Leni Riefenstahl*, 10ff.

# SELECT BIBLIOGRAPHY

Adam, Peter. *Kunst im Dritten Reich*. Hamburg, 1992.

Albrecht, Gerd, ed. *Der Film im Dritten Reich*. Karlsruhe, 1979.

———. *Nationalsozialistische Filmpolitik: Eine soziologische Untersuchung über die Spielfilme des Dritten Reiches*. Stuttgart, 1969.

Alkemeyer, Thomas. *Körper, Kult und Politik: Von der "Muskelreligion" Pierre de Coubertins zur Inszenierung von Macht in den Olympischen Spielen von 1936*. Frankfurt: Campus, 1996.

Allgeier, Sepp. *Die Jagd nach dem Bild: Achtzehnjahre als Kameramann in Arktis und Hochgebirge*. Stuttgart, 1931.

Amann, Frank, Ben Gabel, and Jürgen Keiper, eds. "Revisited. Der Fall Dr. Fanck. Die Entdeckung der Natur im deutschen Bergfilm." *Film und Kritik 1* (1992).

"American Intelligence Report on Leni Riefenstahl. May 30th, 1945." *Film Culture 77* (1992).

Arnheim, Rudolf. *Film as Art*. Berkeley: University of California Press, 2006.

———. *Film Essays and Criticism*. Madison: University of Wisconsin Press, 1997.

Bach, Steven. *Marlene Dietrich: Life and Legend*. Cambridge: Da Capo Press, 2000.

Backes, Klaus. *Hitler und die bildenden Künste: Kulturverständnis und Kunstpolitik im Dritten Reich*. Cologne: Dumont, 1988.

Balázs, Béla. "Revisited. Der Fall Dr. Fanck. Die Entdeckung der Natur im deutschen Bergfilm." *Film und Kritik 1* (1992).

Barkhausen, Hans. *Filmpropaganda für Deutschland im Ersten und Zweiten Weltkrieg*. Hildesheim: Olms Presse, 1982.

———. "Die NSDAP als Filmproduzentin." In Moltmann and Reimers, *Zeitgeschichte im Film- und Tondokument*.

Barsam, Richard Meran. *Filmguide to Triumph of the Will*. Bloomington: Indiana University Press, 1975.

Bataille, Georges. *Die psychologische Struktur des Faschismus. Die Souveränität*. Berlin: Matthes & Seitz, 1997.

Becker, Wolfgang. *Film und Herrschaft: Organisationsprinzipien und Organisationsstrukturen nationalsozialistischer Filmpropaganda*. Uelzen, 1973.

Behrenbeck, Sabine. *Der Kult um die toten Helden: Nationalsozialistische Mythen, Riten und Symbole 1923 bis 1945*. Vierow: SH-Verlag, 1996.

Below, Nicolaus von. *At Hitler's Side: The Memoirs of Hitler's Luftwaffe Adjutant 1937–1945.* London: Greenhill Books, 2004.

Bennecke, Heinrich. *Hitler und die SA.* München: Olzog, 1962.

Benz, Ute, ed. *Frauen im Nationalsozialismus. Dokumente und Zeugnisse.* Munich: C. H. Beck, 1993.

Benz, Wolfgang. *A Concise History of the Third Reich.* Berkeley, University of California Press, 2006.

Berg-Pan, Renata. *Leni Riefenstahl.* Boston: Twayne Pub, 1980.

Berson, Arnold. "The Truth about Leni Riefenstahl." *Films and Filming 7 (1965).*

Beyer, Friedemann. *Die Ufa-Stars im Dritten Reich: Frauen für Deutschland.* Munich: Heyne, 1991.

Birdwell, Michael E. *Celluloid Soldiers: Warner Bros.'s Campaign Against Nazism.* New York: New York University Press, 2001.

Boberach, Heinz, ed. *Meldungen aus dem Reich 1938–1945: Die geheimen Lageberichte des Sicherheitsdienstes der SS.* Herrsching: Pawlak, 1984.

Bock, Hans-Michael, ed. *Cinegraph. Lexikon zum deutschsprachigen Film.* Munich: Edition Text und Kritik, 1984.

Bock, Hans-Michael, and Michael Töteberg, eds. *Das Ufa-Buch.* Frankfurt, 1992.

Bohlen, Friedrich. *Die XI. Olympischen Spiele Berlin 1936: Instrument der innen und aussenpolitischen Propaganda und Systemsicherung des faschistischen Regimes.* Cologne: Pahl-Rugenstein, 1979.

Borghese, Alessandra. "Un Introduction con Leni Riefenstahl." *Leni Riefenstahl. Il Ritmo di un Sguardo.* Milan, 1996.

Bracher, Karl-Dietrich. *The German Dictatorship: The Origins, Structure and Effects of National Socialism.* Orlando: Holt, Rinehart & Winston, 1972.

Bracher, Karl-Dietrich, Manfred Funke, and Hans-Adolf Jacobsen, eds. *Deutschland 1933–1945. Neue Studien zur nationalsozialistischen Herrschaft.* 2nd ed. Bonn, 1993.

Bramsted, Ernest K. *Goebbels und die nationalsozialistische Propaganda 1925–1945.* Frankfurt: S. Fischer, 1971.

Brandlmeier, Thomas. "Sinngezeichen und Gedankenbilder. Vier Abschnitte zu Arnold Fanck." In Jan-Christopher Horak, ed., *Berge, Licht und Traum.*

Brandt, Hans-Jürgen. *NS: Filmtheorie und dokumentarische Praxis: Hippler, Noldan, Junghans.* Tübingen: Niemeyer, 1987.

Brecker, Arno. *Im Strahlungsfeld der Ereignisse.* Preussisch Oldendorf, 1972.

Brenner, Hildegard. *Die Kunstpolitik des Nationalsozialismus.* Reinbeck: Rowohlt, 1963.

Brock, Bazon, and Achim Preis, eds. *Kunst auf Befehl? Dreiunddreißig bis Fünfundvierzig.* Munich: Klinkhardt u. B., 1990.

Bronfen, Elisabeth. "Zwei deutsche Stars: Leni Riefenstahl und Marlene Dietrich." In Jacobsen, *Filmmuseum Berlin.*

Broszat, Martin. *Der Nationalsozialismus: Weltanschauung, Programm und Wirklichkeit.* Stuttgart, 1960.

Bruns, Jana. *Between Black and White. The Apotheosis of Jesse Owens in "Olympia."* Stanford, 1997. (unpublished manuscript)

Bulgakowa, Oksana. "Riefenstein: Demontage eines Klischees." *Leni Riefenstahl.* Berlin: Filmmuseum Potsdam, 1999.

Bullock, Alan. *Hitler: A Study in Tyranny.* London: Harper Perennial, 1991.

Buñuel, Luis. *My Last Sigh.* Minneapolis: University of Minnesota Press, 2003.

Burden, Hamilton T. *Die programmierte Nation: Die Nürnberger Reichsparteitage.* Gütersloh: Bertelsmann, 1970.

Canetti, Elias. *Crowds and Power.* New York: Farrar, Straus and Giroux, 1984.

Centro Culturale di Milano and Alessandra Borghese, eds. *Leni Riefenstahl. Il Ritmo di un Sguardo* (catalog for the Italian exhibition). Milan, 1996.

Chaplin, Charles. *Charles Chaplin: My Autobiography.* New York: Simon and Schuster, 1964.

Cocteau, Jean. "Four Letters by Jean Cocteau to Leni Riefenstahl." *Film Culture 56/57* (1973).

Cook, Pam, and Philip Dodd, eds. *Women on Film: A Sight and Sound Reader.* London: Temple University Press, 1993.

Cooper, Graham. *Leni Riefenstahl and Olympia.* Lanham: Scarecrow Press, 2001.

Courtade, Francis, and Pierre Cadars. *Geschichte des Films im Dritten Reich.* Munich: Hanser, 1982.

Culbert, David. "Leni Riefenstahl and the Diary of Joseph Goebbels." *Historical Journal of Film, Radio and Television* 1 (1993).

Culbert, David, and Martin Loiperdinger. "Leni Riefenstahl's 'Tag der Freiheit': The 1935 Nazi Party Rally Film." *Historical Journal of Film, Radio and Television* 1 (1992).

Dalichow, Bärbel, and Claudia Lenssen. "Focus Leni Riefenstahl" *Leni Riefenstahl.* Berlin: Filmmuseum Potsdam, 1999.

Delahaye, Michel. "Leni et le loup. Entretien avec Leni Riefenstahl." *Cahiers du Cinéma* 170 (1965).

Diekmann, Irene, and Joachim H. Teichler, eds. *Körper, Kultur, Ideologie: Sport und Zeitgeist im 19. und 20. Jahrhundert.* Bodenheim, 1997.

Diels, Rudolf. *Lucifer ante portas.* Stuttgart, 1950.

Dietrich, Marlene. *Marlene.* New York: Grove Press, 1989.

Dietrich, Otto. *Hitler.* Chicago: H. Regnery, 1955.

Doelzel, Stephan, and Martin Loiperdinger. "Adolf Hitler in Parteitagsfilm und Wochenschau." In Loiperdinger et al., *Führerbilder.*

Domarus, Max. *Hitler: Speeches and Proclamations, 1932–1945: The Chronicle of a Dictatorship.* Wauconda: Bolchazy-Carducci Publishers, 2004.

Donner, Wolf. *Propaganda und Film im Dritten Reich.* Berlin, 1995.

Dorn, Thea. *Marleni: Preussische Diven blond wie Stahl.* Frankfurt: Verlag der Autoren, 2000.

Downing, Taylor. *Olympia.* London: BFI Publishing, 1993.

Drewniak, Boguslaw. *Der deutsche Film 1938–1945.* Düsseldorf, 1987.

Eisner, Lotte. *Die dämonische Leinwand.* Frankfurt: Fischer, 1980.

———. *Ich hatte einst ein schönes Vaterland: Memoiren.* Heidelberg: Wunderhorn, 1984.

Elsaesser, Thomas. "Leni Riefenstahl: The Body Beautiful, Art Cinema and Fascist Aesthetics." In Pam Cook and Philip Dodd, eds., *Women on Film.*

Ertl, Hans. *Bergvagabunden.* Munich: Nymphenburger Verlagsbuchhandlung, 1952.

———. *Der Kampf mit dem Berge.* Berlin: 1931.

———. *Meine wilden dreissiger Jahre: Bergsteiger, Filmpionier, Weltenbummler.* Berlin: Herbig, 1982.

Fanck, Arnold. *Er führte Regie mit Gletschern, Stürmen und Lawinen. Ein Filmpionier erzählt.* Munich: Nymphenburger Verlagsbuchhandlung, 1973.

Faris, James C. "Leni Riefenstahl and the Nuba Peoples of Kordofan Province, Sudan." *Historical Journal of Film, Radio and Television* 1 (1993).

Faulstich, Werner, and Helmut Korte, eds. *Fischer Filmgeschichte, Volume 2 (1925–1944).* Frankfurt: Fischer, 1991.

Fest, Joachim C. *The Face of the Third Reich: Portraits of the Nazi Leadership.* New York: Pantheon, 1970.

———. *Hitler.* Orlando: Harcourt, 1974.

———. *Speer: The Final Verdict.* Orlando: Harcourt, 2001.

Filmmuseum Potsdam (Museum of Film, Pottsdam), ed. *Leni Riefenstahl* (catalog for the German exhibition). Including articles by Oksana Bulgakowa, Bärbel Dalichow, Claudia Lenssen, Felix Moeller, Georg Seeslen, and Ines Walk. Berlin, 1999.

Fischer, Helmar Harald. "Was gestrichen ist, kann nicht durchfallen": Trauerarbeit, Vergangenheitsbewältigung oder sentimentalische Glorifizierung? Wie sich Schauspieler an ihre Arbeit im Dritten Reich erinnern." *Theater heute* 9 (1989)

Fischer, Lothar. *Tanz zwischen Rausch und Bindung. Anita Berber 1918–1928 in Berlin.* Berlin: 1984.

Ford, Charles. *Leni Riefenstahl. Schauspielerin, Regisseurin und Fotografin.* Munich: Heyne, 1982.

Fraenkel, Heinrich, and Roger Manvell. *Goebbels. Der Verführer.* Munich: Heyne, 1989.

Freund, Gisele. *Photography and Society.* Boston: David R. Godine Pub, 1979.

Friedländer, Saul. *Nazi Germany and the Jews: Volume 1: The Years of Persecution 1933–1939.* New York: Harper Perennial, 1998.

Fromm, Bella. *Als Hitler mir die Hand küsste.* Reinbek: Rowohlt Verlag, 1993.


Gamm, Hans-Jochen. *Der Flüsterwitz im Dritten Reich.* Munich: List Verlag, 1963.

Giesler, Hermann. *Ein anderer Hitler. Bericht seines Architekten. Erlebnisse, Gespräche, Reflexionen.* Assenhausen: Leitfaden Verlag, 1977.

Giordano, Ralph. *Die zweite Schuld oder Von der Last ein Deutscher zu sein.* Hamburg: Rasch und Röhring Verlag, 1987.

Goebbels, Joseph. *Kampf um Berlin.* Munich: 1934.

———. *Die Tagebücher. Sämtliche Fragmente.* Elke Fröhlich, ed. Munich: 1987.

———. *Vom Kaiserhof zur Reichskanzlei.* Munich: 1934.

Goergen, Jeanpaul. *Walter Ruttmann. Ein Portrait.* In *Walter Ruttmann. Eine Dokumentation,* edited by Jeanpaul Georgen. Berlin: 1989.

Göring, Emmy. *An der Seite meines Mannes. Begebenheiten und Bekenntnisse.* Göttingen: Schütz Verlag, 1967.

Gorter, Wolfgang: *Wir vom Bergfilm.* Munich: Bergverlag, 1951.

Grzimek, Bernhard: *Auf den Mensch gekommen. Erfahrungen mit Leuten.* Gütersloh: Bertelsmann Verlag, 1974.


Haffner, Sebastian. *Geschichte eines Deutschen. Erinnerungen 1914–1933.* Berlin, 2000.

———. *The Meaning of Hitler.* New York: Macmillan, 1979.

———. *Von Bismarck zu Hitler. Ein Rückblick.* Munich, 1989.

Haman, Brigitte. *Hitler's Vienna: A Dictator's Apprenticeship.* New York. Oxford University Press, 1999.

Hamburger Institut für Sozialforschung, ed. *Vernichtungskrieg. Verbrechen der Wehrmacht 1941 bis 1944* (catalog for the German exhibition). Hamburg, 1996.

Hamburg Institut for Social Research. *The German Army and Genocide Crimes against War Prisoners, Jews, and Other Civilians 1939–1944.* New York, 1999.

Hanfstaengl, Ernst. *Zwischen Weissem und Braunem Haus. Memoiren eines politischen Aussenseiters.* Munich, 1970.

Hanisch, Michael. *Auf den Spuren der Filmgeschichte. Berliner Schauplätze.* Berlin, 1991.

Harlan, Veit. *Im Schatten meiner Filme. Selbstbiographie.* Gütersloh, 1966.

Hart-Davis, Duff. *Hitler's Olympics: The 1936 Games.* London, 1988.

Heer, Friedrich. *Der Glaube des Adolf Hitler. Anatomie einer politischen Religiosität.* Munich, 1968.

Heer, Hannes, and Klaus Naumann, eds. *War of Extermination. The German Military in World War II, 1941–1944.* Berghahn Books, 2000.

Heinzlmeier, Adolf. *Nachkriegsfilm und Nazifilm. Anmerkungen zu einem deutschen Thema.* Frankfurt am Main, 1988.

Herz, Rudolf. *Hoffmann & Hitler. Fotographie als Medium des Führer-Mythos.* Munich, 1994.

Hickethier, Knut, ed. *Film in der Geschichte.* Berlin, 1997.

Hildenbrand, Fred. *Tageblätter. Vol. 1 (1923/24).* Berlin, 1925.

Hinton, David B. *The Films of Leni Riefenstahl.* 2nd edition. New York, London, 1991.

Hinz, Berthold, Hans-Ernst Mittig, and Wolfgang Schäche, eds. *Die Dekoration der Gewalt. Kunst und Medien im Faschismus.* Giessen, 1979.

———. *NS-Kunst: 50 Jahre danach. Neue Beiträge.* Marburg: Jonas Verlag, 1989.

Hippler, Fritz. *Betrachtungen zum Filmschaffen.* Berlin, 1942.

———. *Die Verstrickung. Einstellungen und Rückblenden.* Düsseldorf, 1981.

Hitchens, Gordon. "Interview with a Legend." In *Film Comment.* 3 Jg., 1 (1965).

———. "Leni Riefenstahl interviewed by G. Hitchens." In *Film Culture*, Nr. 56–57/1973.

Hitler, Adolf. *Mein Kampf.* Mariner Books, 1998.

———. *Monologe im Führerhauptquartier 1941–1944.* Notes by Heinrich Heims. Werner Jochmann, ed. Hamburg, 1980.

———. *Reden, Schriften Anordnungen. Februar 1925 bis Januar 1933.* Vol. IV. Christian Hartmann, ed. Munich, 1997.

Hofer, Walter. *Der Nationalsozialismus. Dokumente 1933–1945.* Frankfurt am Main, 1988.

Hoffmann, Heinrich. *Hitler, wie ich ihn sah.* Munich, Berlin, 1974.

Hoffmann, Hilmar. *100 Jahre Film von Lumière bis Spielberg. 1894–1994.* Düsseldorf, 1995.

———. *Es ist noch nicht zu Ende. Sollen Nazikunst und Nazifilme wieder öffentlich gezeigt werden?* Frankfurt am Main, 1988.

———. "Menetekel der Vergangenheit für die Gegenwart. Nachbetrachtungen zu Leni Riefenstahls Olympiafilm." In *Sport und Film. Bewegte Körper—Bewegte Bilder.* Berlin, 1993.

———. *Mythos Olympia. Autonomie und Unterwerfung von Sport und Kultur.* Berlin, 1993.

———. *"Und die Fahne führt uns in die Ewigkeit." Propaganda in NS-Film.* Frankfurt am Main, 1988.

Horak, Jan-Christopher. "Dr. Arnold Fanck; Traüme von Wolkenmeer und einer guten Stube." In Jan-Christopher Horak ed., *Berge, Licht und Traum.*

———. "Exilfilm 1933–1945. In der Fremde." In Jacobsen et al., *Geschichte des deutschen Films.*

Horak, Jan-Christopher, ed. *Berge, Licht und Traum. Dr. Arnold Fanck und der deutsche Bergfilm.* Munich, 1997.

————. *Fluchtpunkt Hollywood. Eine Dokumentation zur Filmemigration nach 1933.* Münster, 1986.

Hull, David Stewart. *Film in the Third Reich: A Study of the German Cinema 1933–1945.* Los Angeles, 1969.

Infield, Glenn B. *Leni Riefenstahl: The Fallen Film Goddess: The Intimate and Shocking Story of Adolf Hitler and Leni Riefenstahl.* New York, 1976.

Ishioka, Eiko, ed. *Leni Riefenstahl: Life* (catalog for the Japanese exhibition). Tokyo, 1992.

Iten, Oswald. *Schwarzer Sudan.* Kreuzlingen, 1978.

Jacobsen, Wolfgang, Anton Kaes, and Hans Helmut Prinzler, eds. *Geschichte des deutschen Films.* Stuttgart, Weimar, 1993.

Jochmann, Werner, ed. *Adolf Hitler. Monologe im Führerhauptquartier 1941–1944.* Die Aufzeichnungen Heinrich Heims. Hamburg, 1980.

Jung, Ulli, ed. *Der deutsche Film. Aspekte seiner Geschichte von den Anfängen bis zur Gegenwart.* Trier: WVT Wissenschaftlicher Verlag, 1993.

Junge, Traudl. *Until the Final Hour: Hitler's Last Secretary.* Arcade Publishing, 2004.

Kaes, Anton. "Film in der Weimarer Rebublik. Motor der Moderne." In Jacobsen et al., *Geschichte des deutschen Films.*

Karina, Lillian, and Marion Kant. *Tanz unterm Hakenkreuz. Eine Dokumentation.* 2nd ed. Berlin, 1996.

Kasberger, Erich. *Heldinnen waren wir keine. Frauenalltag in der NS-Zeit.* Munich: Piper, 2001.

Keiper, Jürgen. "Alpträume in Weiß." In Amann et al., *Revisited.*

Kershaw, Ian. *Hitler. 1889–1936.* New York: Norton, 2000.

————. *Hitler: 1936–1945: Nemesis.* New York: Norton, 2001.

————. *The "Hitler Myth": Image and Reality in the Third Reich.* New York: Oxford University Press, 1987.

————. *Hitler: Profiles in Power.* New York: Longman Publishing Group, 1991.

————. "Trauma der Deutschen." *Spiegel Special* 1 (2001).

Klabunde, Anja. *Magda Goebbels.* Time Warner Trade Publishing UK, 2002.

Klemperer, Victor. *Tagebücher 1933–1945.* Edited by Walter Nowojski. 2nd ed. Berlin: Aufbau, 1999.

Klinksiek, Dorothee. *Die Frau im NS-Staat.* Stuttgart: Deutsche Verlags-Anstalt, 1982.

Knopp, Guido. *Hitler's Frauen und Marlene.*

Koch-Hildebrecht, Manfred. *Homo Hitler. Psychogramm des deutschen Diktators.* Munich: btb, 1999.

Koebner, Thomas. "Der unversehrbare Körper." In Hickethier, *Film in der Geschichte.*

König, Stefan. "Der Mythos vom heiligen Berg. Kleine genealogische Abhandlung in Sachen deutscher Bergfilmtradition." In Horak, *Berge, Licht und Traum.*

Körner, Thorsten. *Ein guter Freund. Heinz Rühmann. Biographie.* Berlin: Aufbau Verlag, 2001.

Kracauer, Siegfried. *Von Caligari zu Hitler. Eine psychologische Geschichte des deutschen Films.* Frankfurt am Main, 1984.

Krause, Karl-Wilhelm. *Zehn Jahre Tag und Nacht.* Hamburg: Laatzen, 1949.

Kreimeier, Klaus. "Dokumentarfilm 1892–1992. Ein doppeltes Dilemma." In Jacobsen, *Geschichte des deutschen Films.*

————, ed. *Fanck–Trenker–Riefenstahl. Der deutsche Bergfilm und seine Folgen.* Berlin, 1972.

————. *Die Ufa-Story. Geschichte eines Filmkonzerns.* Munich, Vienna, 1992.

Krockow, Christian. *Die Deutschen in ihrem Jahrhundert. 1890–1990.* Reinbek: Rowohlt, 1990.

Krol, Eugeniusz C. "Leni Riefenstahl. Zycie i tworczosc. Przyczynek do dyskusji o miejscu i roli artysty w panstwie totaltarnym." In *Acta Universitatis Wratislaviensis, Nr. 2214. Worclaw 2001.*

Krüger, Arnd. *Die Olympischen Spiele 1936 und die Weltmeinung. Ihre außenpolitische Bedeutung unter besonderer Berücksichtigung der USA.* Berlin, Munich, Frankfurt am Main, 1972.

Kurbjuweit, Dirk. "Wie sexy dürfen Nazis sein?" *Spiegel Reporter* 2 (2000).


Lang, Jochen. *Adolf Hitler. Gesichter eines Diktators.* Hamburg, 1968.

Leibovitz, Annie. *Olympic Portraits.* Boston: Little Brown and Company, 1996.

Leiser, Erwin. *"Deutschland erwache!" Propaganda im Film des Dritten Reiches* (new ed.). Rowohlt: Reinbek, 1978.

*Leni Riefenstahl. Heft 188 der Filmkritik.* Volume 16. August 1972.

*Leni Riefenstahl. Riitta Raatikainen* (catalog for the Finnish exhibition). Kuopio, 1996.

Lenssen, Claudia. "Die fünf Karrieren der Leni Riefenstahl. In *epd Film* 1 (1996)

————. "Leben und Werk." In Filmmuseum Pottsdam, *Leni Riefenstahl.*

Leutheusser, Ulrike, ed. *Hitler und die Frauen.* Stuttgart, Munich: Deutsche Verlags-Anstalt, 2001.

Ley, Michael, and Julius H. Schoeps, eds. *Der Nationalsozialismus als politische Religion.* Bodenheim: Philo Verlagsgesellschaft, 1997.

Liebe, Ulrich. *Verehrt, verfolgt, vergessen. Schauspieler als Naziopfer.* Weinheim, Berlin: Beltz Verlag, 1992.

Löffler, Sigrid. "Was habe ich gewußt? Künstler im Dritten Reich: Fragen nach der verdrängten Vergangenheit." *Theater heute* 1 (1986).

Loiperdinger, Martin. "Halb Dokument, halb Fälschung. Zur Inszenierung der Eröffnungsfeier in Leni Riefenstahls Olympia-Film Fest der Völker." *Medium* 18, Volume 3 (1988).

————. *Rituale der Mobilmachung. Der Parteitagsfilm "Triumph des Willens" von Leni Riefenstahl.* Opladen, 1987.

————. "Sieg des Glaubens." Ein gelungenes Experiment nationalsozialistischer Filmpropaganda." *Zeitschrift für Pädagogik*, Beiheft 31/1993.

Loiperdinger, Martin, Rudolf Herz, and Ulrich Pohlmann, eds. *Führerbilder. Hitler, Mussolini, Roosevelt, Stalin in Fotografie und Film.* Munich: Piper, 1962.

Longerich, Peter. "Nationalsozialistische Propaganda." In Bracher et al., *Deutschland 1933–1945.*


Machtan, Lothar. *The Hidden Hitler.* New York: Basic, 2001.

Maier, Charles S. *Die Gegenwart der Vergangenheit. Geschichte und die nationale Identität der Deutschen.* Frankfurt am Main, New York, 1992.

Manstein, Erich von. *Lost Victories: The War Memoirs of Hitler's Most Brilliant General.* New York: Ballantine, 2004.

Maser, Werner. *Hitler: Legend, Myth & Reality.* Harper & Row, 1973.

Messerschmidt, Manfred. "Die Wehrmacht im NS-Staat." In Bracher et al., *Deutschland 1933–1945.*

Meyer, Fritjjof, and Klaus Wiegrefe. "Die Schlacht der Frauen." *Der Spiegel* 47 (2000).

Michalcik, Peter. *Gustaf Gründgens. Der Schauspieler und die Macht.* Berlin: List, 1999.

Mierendorff, Marta, and Walter Wicclair, eds. *Im Rampenlicht der dunklen Jahre. Aufsätze zum Theater im Dritten Reich, Exil und Nachkrieg*. Berlin, 1989.

Minetti, Bernhard. *Erinnerungen eines Schauspielers*. Edited by Günther Rühle. Stuttgart: Deutsche Verlags-Anstalt, 1986.

Mitscherlich, Alexander, and Margarete Mitscherich. *Die Unfähigkeit zu trauern. Grundlagen kollektiven Verhaltens*. Munich: Piper, 1979.

Mitscherlich, Margarete. "Triumph der Verdrängung. Über die Filmregisseurin Leni Riefenstahl und die Memoiren der glühenden Hitler-Verehrerin." *Stern* 49 (1987).

————. *Der Filmminister. Goebbels und der Film im Dritten Reich*. Berlin: Henschel, 1998.

Moltmann, Günter, and Friedrich Reimers, eds. *Zeitgeschichte im Film- und Tondokument*. Göttingen: Musterschmidt, 1970.

Müller, Hedwig, and Patricia Stöckemann. *". . . jeder Mensch ist ein Tänzer." Ausdruckstanz in Deutschland zwischen 1900 und 1945* (catalog). Gießen, 1993.

Müller, Ray. "Der Besuch der alten Dame." *Stern* 14 (2000).

Musser, Charles. "Der Dokumentarfilm." In Nowell-Smith, *Geschichte des internationalen Films*.

Noack, Frank. *Veit Harlan. "Der Regisseur des Teufels."* Munich: Belleville, 2000.

Nowell-Smith, Geoffrey, ed. *Geschichte des internationalen Films*. Stuttgart, Weimar, 1998.

Nowotny, Peter. *Leni Riefenstahls Triumph des Willens. Zur Kritik dokumentarischer Filmarbeit im NS-Faschismus*. Dortmund, 1981.

Oberzaucher-Schüller, Gunhild, ed. *Ausdruckstanz. Eine mitteleuropäische Bewegung der ersten Hälfte des 20. Jahrhunderts*. Wilhelmshaven, 1992.

Ogan, Bergan, and Wolfgang W. Weiß, eds. *Faszination und Gewalt. Zur politischen Ästhetik des Nationalsozialismus*. Nürnberg, 1992.

Olivier, Antje, and Sevgi Braun. *Anpassung oder Verbot. Künstlerinnen und die 30er Jahre*. Düsseldorf: Droste, 1998.

Panse, Barbara. "Diese Künstler sind wie Kinder." Der Reichspropagandaminister und seine besten Helfer." *Theater heute* 9 (1989).

Picker, Henry. *Hitlers Tischgespräche im Führerhauptquartier*. Frankfurt am Main, Berlin: Propyläen, 1993.

Pilgrim, Volker Elis. *"Du kannst mich ruhig Frau Hitler nennen." Frauen als Schmuck und Tarnung der NS-Herrschaft*. Reinbek: Rowohlt, 1994.

Prinzler, Hans Helmut, ed. *Das Jahr 1945*. Berlin, 1990.

Quaresima, Leonardo. "Kino als rituelle Erfahrung. 'Triumph des Willen' im Ufa-Palast." In Bock and Töteberg, *Das Ufa-Buch*.

Rabenalt, Arthur Maria. "Der Ausdruckstanz und das Theater der zwanziger Jahre." In Oberzaucher-Schüller, *Ausdruckstanz*.

————. *Joseph Goebbels und der "Großdeutsche Film."* Munich, Berlin: Herbig, 1985.

Rapp, Christian. *Höhenrausch. Der deutsche Bergfilm*. Vienna: Sonderzahl-Verlags-Gesellschaft, 1997.

Reich, Wilhelm. *Die Massenpsychologie des Faschismus*. Cologne: Kiepenheuer & Witsch, 1986.

Reichel, Peter. *Der schöne Schein des Dritten Reiches. Faszination und Gewalt des Faschismus*. Munich, Vienna: Fischer, 1991.

Riefenstahl, Leni. "Freiheit des Künstlers." *Film Kurier* 96 (1935).

———. *Hinter den Kulissen des Reichsparteitagfilms.* Munich, 1935.

———. *Kampf in Schnee und Eis.* Leipzig, 1933.

———. *Korallengärten.* Munich, 1978.

———. *The Last of the Nuba.* New York: St. Martin's Press, 1995.

———. *Leni Riefenstahl: A Memoir.* New York: Picador, 1992.

———. *Mein Afrika.* Munich, 1978.

———. *Die Nuba von Kau.* Munich: List, 1976.

———. *Olympia.* New York: St. Martin's Press, 1994.

———. *Schönheit im Olympischen Kampf.* Berlin, 1938.

———. "Über Wesen und Gestaltung des dokumentarischen Films." In *Der Deutsche Film. Zeitschrift für Filmkunst und Filmwirtschaft.* Special edition 41 (1940).

———. *Wunder unter Wasser.* Munich: Herbig, 1990.

Riess, Curt. *Das gibt's nur einmal. Die große Zeit des deutschen Films.* Hamburg: Nannen, 1956.

———. *Das gibt's nur einmal. Die große Zeit des deutschen Films nach 1945.* Hamburg: Nannen, 1958.

Rosen, C. *Das ABC des Nationalsozialismus.* Berlin, 1933.

Rosenberger, Alfred. *Der Mythos des 20. Jahrhunderts. Eine Wertung der seelisch-geistigen Gestaltungskämpfe unserer Zeit.* Munich, 1939.

Rother, Rainer. *Leni Riefenstahl: The Seduction of Genius (Propaganda Studies in Modern Political Communication).* Continuum International Publishing Group, 2002.

Rower, Jörn. "Wie viele Leben haben Sie geführt, Frau Riefenstahl." *Die Zeit Magazin* 36 (1997).

Rürup, Reinhard, ed. *1936. Die Olympischen Spiele und der Nationalsozialismus.* Berlin: Argon, 1996.

Salked, Audrey. *A Portrait of Leni Riefenstahl.* London, 1996.

Sanders-Brahms, Helma. "Tiefland." In Prinzler, *Das Jahr 1945.*

Sarris, Richard. "Notes on the Fascination of Fascism." *The Village Voice* (30.1.1978).

Schaake, Erich. *Hitlers Frauen.* Munich: Ullstein, 2000.

Schad, Martha. "'Das Auge war vor allen Dingen ungeheuer anziehend' Freundinnen und Verehrerinnen, sowie 'Die Frauen gehören heim in die Küche und Kammer.' Frauenleben unterm Hakenkreuz." In Leutheusser, *Hitler und die Frauen.*

———. *Frauen gegen Hitler. Schicksale im Nationalsozialismus.* Munich: Heyne, 2001.

Schirach, Baldur von. *Ich glaubte an Hitler.* Hamburg: Mosaik, 1967.

Schirach, Henriette. *Frauen um Hitler.* Munich, 1983.

———. *Der Preis der Herrlichkeit.* Berlin, Munich, Vienna: Herbig, 1978.

Schlüpmann, Heide. "Trugbilder weiblicher Autonomie im nationalsozialistischem Film. Leni Riefenstahls Olympia: Triumph des weiblichen Willens?" In *Sport und Film. Bewegte Körper—Bewegte Bilder.* Berlin, 1993.

Schmeer, Karlheinz. *Die Regie des öffentlichen Lebens im Dritten Reich.* Munich, 1956.

Schoenberner, Gerhard. "Ideologie und Propaganda im NS-Film." In Jung, *Der deutsche Film.*

Schramm, Percy Ernst, ed. *Das Kriegstagebuch des Oberkommandos der Wehrmacht.* Frankfurt: Bernard & Graefe, 1961.

Schreiber, Mathias, and Susanne Weingarten. "Realität interessiert mich nicht." In *Spiegel* 34 (1997).

Schroeder, Christa. *Er war mein Chef. Aus dem Nachlass der Sekretärin von Adolf Hitler.* Edited by Anton Joachimstaler. Munich, Vienna: Herbig, 1985.

Schüly, Thomas. "Die Macht der Bilder." *Welt am Sonntag* 21 (1999).

Schwarzer, Alice. "Leni Riefenstahl. Propagandistin oder Künstlerin?" *Emma*, Jan./Feb. 1999.

Seeslen, Georg. "Blut und Glamour." In Filmmuseum Potsdam, *Leni Riefenstahl*.

———. *Tanz den Adolf Hitler. Faschismus in der populären Kultur.* Berlin: Bittermann, 1994.

Seidler, Franz W., and Dieter Zeigert. *Hitler's Secret Headquarters: The Fuhrer's Wartime Bases from the Invasion of France to Berlin Bunker.* Greenhill Books, 2004.

Sereny, Gitta. *Albert Speer: His Battle with Truth.* New York: Alfred A. Knopf, 1995.

———. *The Healing Wound: Experiences and Reflections, Germany, 1938–2001.* New York: Norton, 2002.

Shirer, William Lawrence. *Rise and Fall of the Third Reich.* New York: Touchstone Books, 1981.

Sigmund, Anna Maria. *Women of the Third Reich.* NDE Publishing, 2000.

Silbermann, Alphons, and Manfred Stoffers. *Auschwitz: Nie davon gehört? Erinnern und Vergessen in Deutschland.* Berlin: Rowohlt, 2000.

Sontag, Susan. "Fascinating Fascism." In Sontag, *Under the Sign of Saturn: Essays.* New York: Picador, 2002.

Spagnoletti, Giovanni. "Gott gib uns das Brot—Er bereitet es uns und verteidigt es." Bild und Mythos Mussolinis im Film." In Loiperdinger et al., *Führerbilder.*

Speer, Albert. *Architektur. Arbeiten 1933–1942.* Berlin, 1978.

———. *Inside the Third Reich.* New York: Touchstone, 1997.

———. *Spandau: The Secret Diaries.* London: Phoenix Press, 2000.

Spieker, Markus. *Hollywood unterm Hakenkreuz. Der amerikanische Spielfilm im Dritten Reich.* Trier: WVT Wissenschaftlicher Verlag, 1999.

Sternberg, Joseph von. *Das Blau des Engels. Autobiographie.* München, Paris, London, 1991.

Stierlin, Helm. *Anziehung und Distanz. Hitler und die Frauen aus der Sicht eines Psychotherapeuten.* In Leutheusser, *Hitler und die Frauen.*

Strobel, Ricarda. "Filme gegen Hitler: Der große Diktator (1938/40)." In Faulstich and Korte, *Fischer Filmgeschichte.*

Teichler, Hans Joachim. "Sport unter der Herrschaft der Ideologie. Sport im Nationalsozialismus." In Diekmann and Teichler, *Körper.*

Thalmann, Rita R. "Zwischen Mutterkreuz und Rüstungsbetrieb: Zur Rolle der Frau im Dritten Reich." In Bracher et al., *Deutschland 1933–1945.*

Theaterwissenschaftlichen Sammlung Universität zu Köln. *Leni Riefenstahl und der deutsche Bergfilm.* Cologne, 1998.

Theweleit, Klaus. *Male Fantasies, Volume 1: Women, Floods, Bodies, History.* University of Minnesota Press, 1987.

Toeplitz, Jerzy. "Der Film des Dritten Reichs während des Krieges." In Toeplitz, *Geschichte des Films.*

———. "Der Film im Zeichen des Hakenkreuzes." In Toeplitz, *Geschichte des Films.*

———. *Geschichte des Films I-V.* Berlin: Henschel, 1992.

Töteberg, Michael. "Ich möchte hier einen Vorhang des Schweigens herunterlassen. Über die Darstellung des Dritten Reichs in Schauspielermemoiren." In Mierendorff and Wicclair, *Im Rampenlicht.*

———. "Schöne nackte Körper. Wege zur Kraft und Schönheit." In Bock and Töteberg, *Das Ufa-Buch.*

Tremper, Will. *Meine wilden Jahre.* Frankfurt am Main, Berlin: Ullstein, 1996.

Trenker, Luis. *Alles gut gegangen. Geschichten aus meinem Leben.* Hamburg: Mosaik, 1965.

Trimborn, Jürgen. *Der deutsche Heimatfilm der fünfziger Jahre. Motive, Symbole, und Handlungsmuster.* Cologne: Teiresias, 1998.

———. "Gletscher, Eis und Schnee. Die Plakate zum deutschen Bergfilm der zwanziger und dreißiger Jahre." *Plakat-Journal* 4 (1998).

———. "Der Tanz an das Meer. Ein Porträt der Tänzerin Leni Riefenstahl." *Tanzdrama* No. 48, 4 (1999).

———. "Von den heiligen Bergen und weißen Höllen. Leni Riefenstahls Kampf im Schnee und Eis." In *Leni Riefenstahl und der deutsche Bergfilm.*

Udet, Ernst. *Mein Fliegerleben.* Berlin: Ullstein, 1935.

Van der Vat, Dan. *The Good Nazi.* Great Britain: Weidenfeld & Nicolson, 1997.

Vogel, Amos. *Film als subverisve Kunst. Kino wider die Tabus—von Einstein bis Kubrik.* St. Andrä-Wördern, 1997.

Walk, Ines. "Bildproduktion und Weltmodell." In Filmmuseum Potsdam, *Leni Riefenstahl.*

Wallace, Peggy Ann. *An Historical Study of the Career of Leni Riefenstahl from 1923 to 1933.* Berkeley, 1975.

Weigel, Hermann. "Interview mit Arnold Frank." In *Filmhefte* 2 (1976).

———. "Interview mit Leni Riefenstahl sowie Randbemerkungen zum Thema." In *Filmkritik* 16 (1972).

Welch, David. *Propaganda and the German Cinema 1933–1945.* Oxford, 1983.

Werner, Paul. *Skandalchronik des deutschen Films von 1900–1945.* Frankfurt am Main: Fischer, 1990.

Wildmann, Daniel. *Begehrte Körper. Konstruktion und Inszenierung des "arischen" Männerkörpers im "Dritten Reich."* Würzburg: Königshausen & Neumann, 1998.

Wistrich, Robert S. *Who's Who in Nazi Germany.* New York: Random House Value Publishing, 1984.

Witte, Karsten. "Film im Nationalsozialismus. Blendung und Überblendung." In Jacobsen et al., *Geschichte des deutschen Films.*

———. *Lachende Erben, Toller Tag. Filmkomödie im Dritten Reich.* Berlin, 1995.

Wollenberger, H.H. *Fifty Years of German Film.* London, 1947.

Wulf, Joseph. *Theater und Film im Dritten Reich. Eine Dokumentation.* Frankfurt am Main, Berlin, 1989.

Wysocki, Gisela von. "Die Berge und die Partriarchen." In Wysocki, *Fröste der Freiheit.*

———. *Fröste der Freiheit. Aufbruchsphantasien.* 2nd edition. Frankfurt am Main, 1981.

Zechlin, Hans Josef. *Landhäuser.* Berlin, 1939.

Zglinicki, Friedrich von. *Der Weg des Films. Textband.* Hildesheim, New York, 1979.

Zoller, Albert. *Hitler privat.* Düsseldorf, 1949.

Zsuffa, Joseph. *Béla Balázs: The Man and the Artist.* Berkeley, Los Angeles, London, 1987.

# CHRONOLOGY

1902  August 22: Bertha Helene Amalie Riefenstahl (Leni) born in Berlin.

1918  Riefenstahl earns General Certificate from the Kollmorgen Lyceum. Takes dance lessons at the Grimm-Reiter School for Artistic Dance and Physical Culture.

1921  February 21: First performance as a dance student at a Grimm-Reiter School recital.

*1921–23  Instruction in ballet from Eugenia Eduardova and in expressionistic dance from Jutta Klamt (both until 1923) in Berlin and from Mary Wigman in Dresden-Hellerau (summer 1923).

1923  Summer: Meets Harry Sokal. Moves to Fasanenstrasse in Berlin. October 23 and 26: First performances as a solo dancer, Munich and Berlin. November and December: First dance tour, performing in many German cities.

1924  February–June: Second solo tour, with appearances in Germany, Austria, Switzerland, and Czechoslovakia.
      June: Knee injury during a performance in Prague ends Riefenstahl's dance career.
      In Berlin, attends a film by Arnold Fanck, *Der Berg des Schicksals*, and decides to become an actress. First contact with Luis Trenker and Fanck.

1925  Works on *Wege zu Kraft und Schönheit*.

*1925–26  Filming of *Der heilige Berg*. Affair with Luis Trenker.

1926  December 17: Premiere of *Der heilige Berg* in Berlin. Final appearance as a dancer. End of affair with Luis Trenker. Moves to Hindenburgstrasse, Berlin.

1927  Filming of *Der grosse Sprung*. Begins relationship with Hans Schneeberger.

1928  Filming of *Das Schicksal derer von Hapsburg*.

1929  Filming of *Die weisse Hölle vom Piz Palü*. Breakup with Hans Schneeberger.
      Fall: Contact with Josef von Sternberg.

1930  Filming of *Stürme über dem Montblanc*. Friendship with Ernst Udet.

1931  Filming of *Der weisse Rausch*.

*1931–32  Plans, films, and edits her directorial debut, *Das blaue Licht*.

1932  February 27: Hears Hitler speak for the first time, at the Sports Palace in Berlin.
      March 24: Premiere of *Das blaue Licht* in Berlin.
      May 22–23: Meets Adolf Hitler personally for the first time.

*1932–33  Filming of *SOS Eisberg* in Greenland and Switzerland.
      Fall 1932: Several meetings with Hitler.
      Works on first book, *Kampf in Schnee und Eis*.

1933   May 17: Goebbels speaks with Riefenstahl for the first time about a "Hitler film."
       Many meetings with Hitler and Goebbels in the period that follows.
       August 23: Hitler requests that Riefenstahl become the artistic director of the 1933
       party rally film.
       August 30–September 3: Films the NSDAP party rally in Nuremberg.
       December 1: Premiere of *Sieg des Glaubens*.
1934   April: Lecture tour in London, Oxford, and Cambridge.
       Summer: Preparatory work for the feature film *Tiefland*.
       August: Again named artistic director for film of 1935 Nuremberg party rally.
       September: Films *Triumph des Willens* in Nuremberg.
1935   March 28: Gala premiere of *Triumph des Willens*.
       May 1: State Prize of the German Reich for *Triumph des Willens*.
       September: Filming of short film *Tag der Freiheit!—Unsere Wehrmacht!* at the Nurem-
       berg party rally.
       September 9: *Triumph des Willens* takes Best Documentary Film prize at the Venice
       Biennale.
       December: Riefenstahl founds Olympia-Film, financed by the Nazi regime, as a
       dummy firm and begins preparations for filming the 1936 Olympic Games in Berlin.
       December 10: Goebbels awards Riefenstahl official commission to film Olympic Games.
       December 30: Premiere of *Tag der Freiheit!—Unsere Wehrmacht!* in Berlin.
1936   January: Meets with Mussolini in Rome.
       February: Attends Winter Olympic Games in Garmisch-Partenkirchen.
       July: Films scenes for *Olympia* in Greece.
       August: Films *Olympia* during the Summer Olympic Games in Berlin.
       September: Begins editing *Olympia*. Films prologue to *Olympia* on the Baltic Sea.
1937   July 3: Paris premiere of *Triumph des Willens*. Film is awarded the Grand Prix at the
       Paris World's Fair.
       Summer: Riefenstahl moves into her new villa on Heydenstrasse in Berlin-Dahlem.
1938   April: Riefenstahl meets briefly with Hitler after the Anschluss in Austria and issues a
       public appeal to elect Hitler.
       April 20: World premiere of *Olympia* in Berlin.
       May 1: Goebbels presents Riefenstahl with the German State Prize for *Olympia*.
       August: *Olympia* receives prize for Best Film at the Venice Biennale.
       April–October: Riefenstahl tours Europe with *Olympia*.
       November: Trip to New York and Hollywood (until January 1939). Following
       *Kristallnacht*, Riefenstahl is boycotted in the United States.
1939   June 10: International Olympic Committee awards Riefenstahl the Olympic Diploma
       in London. As the 1940 Olympic Games in Helsinki are canceled due to the war, she
       receives the award only in 1948, at the first postwar Olympics in Lausanne.
       Summer: Plans and prepares to film the unrealized feature film "Penthesilea."
       September: On a secret commission from Hitler, Riefenstahl films at the Polish front
       with a "special film troop."
       September 12: Riefenstahl witnesses a massacre of Jewish civilians by German soldiers
       in Końskie.
       October 5: With her team, Riefenstahl films the parade of German troops through
       Warsaw, which marks the end of the Polish campaign.

1940 Founds Riefenstahl-Film GmbH. Resumes filming of *Tiefland*, which was broken off in 1934 (filming continues until 1944).
Fall: Riefenstahl meets army officer Peter Jacob.

1943 Summer: Films *Tiefland* in Spain.
November: Moves to Kitzbühel in Tirol.

1944 March 21: Marries Peter Jacob.
March 30: Last meeting with Adolf Hitler, at Obersalzberg.
July: Death of Riefenstahl's father. Her brother, Heinz, dies at the Eastern front.
September: Final scenes of *Tiefland* are shot at the Barrandov Studios in Prague.

1945 May: Arrested in Kitzbühel. First interrogations by officers of the U.S. Army. Riefenstahl is incarcerated and questioned about her work in the Third Reich and her contacts with Nazi leadership.
June 3: Released from incarceration. Returns to Kitzbühel and continues editing *Tiefland*.

1946 April: The French military government expels Riefenstahl from Tirol. She moves first to Breisach am Rhein, then to Königsfeld bei Villingen.

1947 Summer: Divorces Peter Jacob. Is admitted to a psychiatric clinic.

1948 December 1: First tribunal in Villingen judges Riefenstahl "exonerated."

1949 July 6: Second tribunal, in Freiburg, also judges Riefenstahl "exonerated."
December 16: Third tribunal, in Freiburg, judges Riefenstahl a "follower" in absentia.

1950 Summer: Lengthy stay in Italy. Works on a series of new film projects, all unrealized.

1951 November 21: Premiere of the newly edited version of *Das blaue Licht*, in Rome.

1952 April 21: Fourth and final denazification process before the Berlin tribunal, again pronounced "exonerated."

1954 February 11: Premiere of *Tiefland* in Stuttgart.

1955 Summer: Lengthy stay in Spain. New film projects fail.

1956 First trip to Sudan and Kenya. Riefenstahl is seriously injured in an automobile accident.

1959 August: Riefenstahl retrospective at the Venice Biennale.

1960 Winter: Riefenstahl travels to England. Plans to make a new version of *Das blaue Licht* fail due to her involvement in the Third Reich. First legal proceedings taken against Erwin Leiser's *Mein Kampf*.

1962 Winter: Riefenstahl's first contact with the Nuba of Sudan.

1964 Winter: Second trip to the Nuba, a film and photography expedition.

1965 January 14: Death of Riefenstahl's mother, Bertha, interrupts her Africa trip.

1966 Winter: Third trip to the Nuba.

1968 Winter: Fourth trip to the Nuba. Meets Horst Kettner, from that time on her closest collaborator and companion for life.

1969 January 10: German Federal High Court rules that Leni Riefenstahl does not control the commercial rights to *Triumph des Willens*.

1970 Winter: Photo safari in East Africa.

1972 Summer: Riefenstahl photographs the Summer Olympic Games in Munich for the *Sunday Times*.
First diving expedition, in the Indian Ocean.

1973 First book of Nuba photographs published: *Die Nuba. Menschen wie von einem anderen Stern* (*The Nuba: People from Another Star*).
Winter: New expedition to Sudan, to the Nuba of Kau.

1975 Second photo expedition to the Nuba of Kau in south Sudan.

1976  Second volume of Nuba photographs, *Die Nuba von Kau*, published.
      October 30: Successful appearance on the West German Radio talk show *Je später der Abend* (*The Later the Evening*) is Riefenstahl's last live TV appearance.
1978  Moves to new villa in Pöcking on the Starnberger See.
1982  August 22: Book of photographs, *Mein Afrika* (*Leni Riefenstahl's Africa*), appears.
      Brings legal suit against filmmaker Nina Gladitz, due to serious accusations Gladitz made against Riefenstahl in her film *Zeit des Schweigens und der Dunkelheit* (*Time of Silence and Darkness*).
*1982–87  Riefenstahl works on *Memoiren*, published in August 1987.
1990  The first volume of underwater photographs appears, *Wunder unter Wasser* (*Wonders Under Water*).
1991  Winter: "Leni Riefenstahl—Life" exhibit opens in Tokyo. Lengthy visit to Japan.
1993  October 7: First screening of the documentary film *Die Macht der Bilder* (*The Wonderful, Horrible Life of Leni Riefenstahl*), by Ray Müller.
1995  October: First German retrospective of Riefenstahl's films, at the Documentary Film Festival in Leipzig.
1996  Summer: Riefenstahl exhibit in Milan, at the Palazzo della Ragione.
      November 3: Premiere of Johann Kresnik's dance theater piece, *Riefenstahl*, at the Schauspielhaus in Cologne.
1997  April: Riefenstahl exhibit in Rome, at the Palazzo delle Esposizioni, leads to heated debates in Italian press.
      August 15: Photography exhibit at Galerie Schlüter in Hamburg.
      September: In Los Angeles, Riefenstahl receives a lifetime achievement award from Cinecom, the Society for Cinephiles.
1998  March 3: As a guest of honor at Radio City Music Hall in New York, Riefenstahl takes part in the seventy-fifth anniversary of *Time* magazine.
      December 3: The exhibit "Leni Riefenstahl" opens at the Film Museum in Potsdam.
      December 6: The exhibit "Leni Riefenstahl and the German Mountain Film" opens in the Schloss Wahn, Cologne.
1999  December: The German film company Odeon-Film, in Munich, and Jodie Foster's production firm, Egg Pictures, in Los Angeles, announce feature film projects on Riefenstahl.
2000  February: Expedition to Sudan with Ray Müller's film team. Riefenstahl suffers serious injuries in a helicopter crash. From the footage taken in Sudan, Müller edits the film *Leni Riefenstahl: Ein Traum von Africa* (*Leni Riefenstahl: A Dream of Africa*).
      May 5: Riefenstahl attends the opening of the exhibit of *Olympia* photographs at the Berlin gallery Camera Work.
2001  August 22: In an interview on the occasion of her ninety-ninth birthday, Riefenstahl announces plans to make two more films and talks for the first time about plans for a Leni Riefenstahl Museum, which she will fund.
2002  March: New diving expedition to the Maldives.
      August 14: Premiere of the film *Impressionen unter Wasser* (*Impressions Underwater*), shortly before her one hundreth birthday.
      August 22: Major celebration on the occasion of Riefenstahl's one hundredth birthday, at Starnberger See.
2003  September 8: Leni Riefenstahl dies in her home in Pöcking on Starnberger See.
      September 12: Burial at the Ostfriedhof, Munich.

# ACKNOWLEDGMENTS

I could not have written this book without the generous support and advice I received from a great many people and institutions.

My gratitude, above all, goes to Leni Riefenstahl, and to her close colleagues Gisela Jahn and Horst Kettner, who over the years provided me with materials and information from Leni Riefenstahl's private archives. I thank Leni Riefenstahl for making herself available for conversations.

My most heartfelt appreciation to the staffs of the Theater Studies Collection at the Schloss Wahn and the Institute for Theater, Film and Television at the University of Cologne, in particular to Professor Dr. Elmar Buck, Dr. Joseph Garncarz, Christine Goethner, Dr. Sabine Gottgetreu, and Adam Miszta. I owe thanks to a number of archives and institutions for valuable and indispensable information: to the staffs of the German Federal Archives, especially Herr Lange; the Federal Archives—Berlin Document Centers, in particular Frau Hartisch; and the Federal Archives—Film Archive in Berlin, especially Frau Albert and Herr Schmidt. Thank you to the State Archive of Berlin, the Brandenburg State Archive in Potsdam, and Dr. Elke Fröhlich-Broszat of the Institute for Contemporary History in Munich. I also express my gratitude to the Archivo Centrale dello Stato in Rome and the Documentation Archive of the Austrian Resistance in Vienna.

Furthermore, I would like to thank the staffs and librarians of the German Film Museum in Frankfurt am Main; the German Film Institute in Frankfurt, especially Frau Brigitte Capitain; the Film Archive of Austria in Vienna; the Friedrich Wilhelm Murnau Foundation in Wiesbaden; the Berlin Brandenburg Center for Film Research, Inc., in particular Jeanpaul Goergen; the Foundation of the German Kinemathek in Berlin; and Werner Sudendorf and Gisela Pichler of the Munich Municipal Museum/Film Museum. For their support, I thank Dr. Bärbel Dalichow, Claudia Lenssen, Ines Walk, and Elke Schieber of the Film Museum, Potsdam.

For an evaluation of Leni Riefenstahl's dance career, I thank the staff of the German Dance Archive in Cologne, especially its director, Frank Manuel Peter. My gratitude also to Westdeutscher Rundfunk in Cologne, in particular to Gebhard Henke, Klaus Liebe, and Vera Romboy, as well as to André Bechtold and Maura Fracalossi of Schloss Runkelstein in Bozen.

I owe thanks to Jochen Böhler of the German Historical Institute, Warsaw; Dr. Eugeniusz C. Król of the Instytut Studiów Politycznych Polskej Akademii Nauk in Warsaw;

and Daniel Uziel of the Memorial Yad Vashem in Jerusalem for their valuable suggestions, as well as to Dr. Gerd Albrecht (Cologne), Dr. honoris causa Rudolf Arnheim (Ann Arbor), Dr. Fritz Hippler (deceased), and Evelyn Künneke (deceased).

Thank you to Colonel Friedhelm Klein and Dr. Umbreit of the Research Center for Military History in Potsdam; Commander Dr. Scheerer of the Museum of Military History of the German Federal Armed Forces in Dresden; the staff of the Federal Archive—Military Archive in Freiburg im Breisgau, especially Herr Böhm and Dr. Überscheer; military historian Dr. Ekkehart Guth, Emmedingen; and Elfriede Bergmann, Potsdam.

For discussions on Leni Riefenstahl, I wish to thank Professor Ian Kershaw of the University of Sheffield; Dr. honoris causa Joachim C. Fest; Dr. Rainer Rother of the German Film Museum in Berlin; Professor Dr. Michaela Krützen of the College of Television and Film in Munich; and Dr. Jana Bruns of the Department of History, Stanford University. For their valuable suggestions, I thank Fritjof Hohagen (Odeon Film, Inc., Munich); Professor Jan-Christopher Horak, Hollywood Entertainment Museum, Los Angeles; Dr. Hans Peter Kochenrath (deceased); Professor Hansjürgen Rosenbauer; and Herbert Wilczek (Cologne). Major assistance was provided, in addition, by Carlos Bajollo (Leichlingen), Professor Helmut Diederichs (Fachhochschule, Dortmund), Andreas Schlüter (Hamburg), Anna Zimmermann (Cologne), Lars Kluge (Berlin), and, not least, Dr. Wolfgang Müller (Berlin).

For their input I sincerely thank those students from my 1998–99 winter semester seminar, "Films of the Third Reich," and 2000 summer semester seminar, "Leni Riefenstahl." Thanks also to all those who took the time to discuss the subject with me within the framework of my 1998–99 exhibition, "Leni Riefenstahl and the German Mountain Film."

Heartfelt gratitude to my former literary agent, Dr. Uwe Heldt, of Mohrbooks Literary Agency Berlin, who generously lent his support and encouragement to this project. Thank you as well to Sabine Ibach, Sebastian Ritscher, and Barbara Brachwitz of Mohrbooks Literary Agency Zurich, and to my American agent, Alison M. Bond. My thanks to all those at Farrar, Straus and Giroux involved in the publication of this book, most especially to my editors, Ayesha Pande and Denise Oswald, for their careful, highly professional, and thorough attention to the American edition, and to publisher Jonathan Galassi for his belief in this book. Thanks to Stephanie Kramer for her help in condensing the original manuscript and to Edna McCown for her excellent translation.

My greatest gratitude goes to all those who stood by me, expressing interest in and support and understanding for my work, offering countless examples of encouragement, and never tiring of talking with me about Leni Riefenstahl. In addition to my parents, Ludwig and Erika Trimborn, I especially thank Kristiane Benedix, Barbara Bongartz, Renate Brausewetter, Sabine Herder, Miriam Jakobs, and Leslie Römermann. And, not least, I thank Robert Bales, who was supportive from the very beginning, providing inspiration and encouragement through our many stimulating and constructive discussions.

# INDEX